Damned Yankees

Chaos, Confusion, and Craziness in the Steinbrenner Era

BILL MADDEN AND MOSS KLEIN

TRIUMPH
BOOKS

Library of Congress Cataloging-in-Publication Data

Madden, Bill.
  Damned yankees : chaos, confusion, and craziness in the Steinbrenner era / Bill Madden and Moss Klein.
     p. cm.
  ISBN 978-1-60078-704-1 (pbk.)
  1. New York Yankees (Baseball team)—History. 2. Steinbrenner, George M. (George Michael), 1930-2010. 3. Baseball team owners-United States—Biography. I. Klein, Moss. II. Title.
  GV875.N4.M33 2012
  796.357'64097471—dc23
                          2011050500

This book is available in quantity at special discounts for your group or organization. For further information, contact:
  Triumph Books LLC
  542 South Dearborn Street, Suite 750
  Chicago, Illinois 60605
  (312) 939-3330
  Fax (312) 663-3557
  www.triumphbooks.com

Printed in U.S.A.
ISBN: 978-1-60078-704-1
Design by Patricia Frey

Contents

Introduction

What follows on these pages is the anatomy of a baseball team unlike any other. It is a behind-the-scenes account of the New York Yankees from 1977 to 1990, in which they went from the pinnacle of success under their bombastic, impulsive and tyrannical principal owner, George Steinbrenner, to the lowest ebb in their history.

In chronicling how Steinbrenner's frenzied operating style gradually eroded the championship teams of 1977–78 into a sorry last-place 95-loss contingent by 1990, it was also our objective to provide a unique perspective on what it was like for the reporters covering this day-to-day "circus." Graig Nettles said it all when, in describing life as a Yankee in the '70s and '80s, he related how, as a little boy, his ambition was to grow up to be a baseball player or join the circus. "With the Yankees," he said, "I got to do both."

This book had its genesis on a Yankee team charter flight from Minnesota to Newark in 1987. We were having a few cocktails in the front of the plane where the writers and broadcasters sat when Tommy John, who always preferred sitting with the writers instead of his fellow players in the back of the plane, struck up a conversation about sports writing. "You know, you guys have seen it all here," John said. "You ought to write a book about this team and how it operates like no other team. Of course, nobody would probably believe it."

In terms of how the game, as well as the manner in which it is covered, has changed, John had a point. For one thing, the beat writers today no longer travel with the team and, for the most part, stay in different hotels on the road. So their only interaction with the players is at the ballpark, on the field before games and in the clubhouse. The notion of a "Chicken" Stanley coming up to the press box before a game to tell us he was being put on the disabled list against his will—as he did that day in Anaheim in 1980—is, in retrospect, truly unbelievable. And, unlike with Steinbrenner—whose omnipresence transformed the writers into doctors-on-call, never knowing when he'd be creating a tempest while always looking to cultivate his personal real-estate, the back pages of the New York tabloids—the owners are mostly invisible.

Because we traveled with the team, stayed in the same hotels, drank in the same bars, it was a vastly different relationship between the players and the beat writers, and a lot of it had to do with Steinbrenner. As they watched helplessly as Steinbrenner fired managers and general managers and impulsively traded or released players with manic regularity, the Yankee players developed an "us versus him" mindset and were often eager to use the writers as a sounding board for their discontent. Ordinarily, this ongoing soap opera would seem to be a writer's dream—there used to be a saying among us "don't ever worry about your early story on night games, the Yankees will always provide"—but sometimes it got a little overwhelming. Like when Lou Piniella, having reached his breaking point over being platooned by Dick Howser, confided his intention to retire after a June 1980 getaway night game in Oakland. Perplexing as it may have seemed to Piniella, our priority was not having a scoop—which we knew to be temporary frustration on his part—but, rather, not missing the team charter back to Newark.

This is the story of how Steinbrenner, after spending millions on premier free agents Catfish Hunter, Reggie Jackson and Goose Gossage, to restore the Yankees to world champion status in his first years of owning the team, got carried away with his success and continually purged the organization of the managers, general managers, scouts, player development people and players who were so integral to that success. Indeed, it is the story of how Reggie, Catfish and Goose eventually begot Ed Whitson, Steve Kemp and Pascual Perez. It was a world that ceased to exist when Steinbrenner came back from his second suspension from baseball in 1993 and found that in his absence, the team had been gradually rebuilt by interim general manager Gene Michael.

Since the initial publication of this book in 1990, the Yankees went on to win four championships in five years from 1996 to 2000 and another one in 2009 after moving into a new Yankee Stadium. But those Yankees were far more corporate than chaotic, and the new stadium, with its vast clubhouse and off-limits recreation areas for the players, reflected that image. Even Steinbrenner was toned down after his return in 1993, perhaps in deference to all the improvements Michael had made to the team during his absence. Eventually, the once-blustering boss was completely silenced by the onset of Alzheimer's disease.

In addition to all the ill-conceived firings, trades and free-agent signings during Steinbrenner's heyday of lunacy—which is the essence of this book—there were all the feuds: Steinbrenner vs. Billy Martin; Steinbrenner vs. Yogi Berra; Steinbrenner vs. Dave Winfield; Steinbrenner vs. Lee MacPhail; Steinbrenner vs. Lou Piniella; and finally, the one that brought him down (albeit only temporarily), Steinbrenner vs. Fay Vincent. For the writers it was like covering a long, evolving train wreck—only in this case the victims wouldn't let us look away.

—Bill Madden and Moss Klein, January 2012

This book chronicles the Yankee saga from 1977 through 1989. Here, for quick, easy reference, are those seasons in capsule form:

1977

Record: 100–62, first (world champions)

Manager: Billy Martin

Pitching coaches: Cloyd Boyer, Art Fowler

Comings: OF Reggie Jackson (free agent), LHP Don Gullett (free agent), SS Bucky Dent (traded from White Sox), RHP Mike Torrez (traded from A's), C-1B Cliff Johnson (traded from Astros), OF Paul Blair (traded from Orioles)

Goings: OF Oscar Gamble (traded to White Sox), RHP Dock Ellis (traded to A's), RHP Doyle Alexander (free agent to Rangers), OF Carlos May (released), Elliott Maddox (traded to Orioles)

Turmoil and tumult: Jackson joins team and immediately stirs up trouble by saying "I'm the straw that stirs the drink" in a spring training interview.... Martin and Jackson clash in Fenway Park dugout.... Martin is nearly fired numerous times but goes on to win World Series, with Reggie hitting three homers in the final game.

Quote: "Man, I've been around a long time, but this team is too much. I ain't never seen nothin' like this kind of shit day after day." —Elston Howard after breaking up a dugout fight between Billy Martin and Reggie Jackson

1978

Record: 100–63, first (world champions)

Managers: Billy Martin, Bob Lemon

Pitching coaches: Art Fowler, Clyde King

Comings: RHP Goose Gossage (free agent), 1B Jim Spencer (traded from White Sox)

Goings: RHP Mike Torrez (free agent to Red Sox), LHP Ken Holtzman (traded to Cubs); President Gabe Paul (resigned)

Turmoil and tumult: Martin calls Steinbrenner a convicted liar and is fired as manager.... Steinbrenner pulls off a P. T. Barnum Old-timer's Day extravaganza by announcing Martin will return as manager in 1980.... Team comes from 14 games behind to win miracle world championship.

Quote: "One's a born liar and the other's convicted." —Billy Martin on Reggie Jackson and George Steinbrenner, respectively

1979

Record: 89–71, fourth

Managers: Bob Lemon, Billy Martin

Pitching coaches: Tom Morgan, Art Fowler

Comings: LHP Tommy John (free agent), RHP Luis Tiant (free agent), OF Bobby Murcer (traded from Cubs), OF Oscar Gamble (traded from Rangers), RHP Ron Davis (traded from Cubs in '78), OF Bobby Brown (sold from Blue Jays)

Goings: C Thurman Munson (killed in plane crash), OF Mickey Rivers (traded to Rangers), LHP Sparky Lyle (traded to Rangers), OF Paul Blair (released), RHP Dick Tidrow (traded to Cubs), DH Cliff Johnson (traded to Indians); President Al Rosen (resigned)

Turmoil and tumult: Team captain Thurman Munson is killed in the crash of his private plane.... Lemon is fired as manager and replaced by Martin ahead of schedule.... Goose Gossage sprains a thumb ligament in a shower-room scuffle with Cliff Johnson.... Team president Al Rosen resigns after numerous conflicts with Steinbrenner.

Quote: "How can a guy ever get any attention here? We got managers changing, presidents resigning, guys getting traded every week and getting in fights, and players dying." —Rookie reliever Ron Davis, who went 14–2 that year to no avail

1980

Record: 103–59, first (AL East champions)

Manager: Dick Howser

Pitching coach: Stan Williams

Comings: 1B Bob Watson (free agent), C Rick Cerone (traded from Blue Jays), LHP Tom Underwood (traded from Blue Jays), LHP Rudy May (free agent), 3B Eric Soderholm (traded from Rangers), OF Ruppert Jones (traded from Mariners)

Goings: RHP Catfish Hunter (retired), 1B Chris Chambliss (traded to Blue Jays), RHP Ed Figueroa (sold to Texas), RHP Jim Beattie (traded to Mariners), OF Roy White (Japan)

Turmoil and tumult: Steinbrenner criticizes Howser for being "outmanaged" by Earl Weaver, touching off a retaliation from Howser.... Graig Nettles misses 89 games due to hepatitis.... Yankees are swept in the AL playoffs by Royals, as Steinbrenner rips third base coach Mike Ferraro for getting Willie Randolph thrown out at the plate.... Steinbrenner fires Howser but insists Howser left on his own to accept a lucrative real estate deal in Florida.

Quote: "My advice to him would be to have a strong stomach and a long contract." —Dick Howser, talking about his successor as Yankee manager, Gene Michael

1981

Record: 59–48, first (AL champions)

Managers: Gene Michael, Bob Lemon

Pitching coaches: Stan Williams, Clyde King

Comings: OF Dave Winfield (free agent), OF Jerry Mumphrey (traded from Padres), RHP Rick Reuschel (traded from Cubs), LHP Dave Righetti (traded from Rangers in '78), 1B Dave Revering (traded from A's), P George Frazier (traded from Cardinals), C Barry Foote (traded from Cubs)

Goings: 1B Jim Spencer (traded to A's), LHP Tom Underwood (traded to A's), IF Fred "Chicken" Stanley (traded to A's), 2B Brian Doyle (traded to A's), RHP Mike Griffin (traded to Cubs), OF Ruppert Jones (traded to Padres)

Turmoil and tumult: Michael goes public on Steinbrenner, telling the Boss to stop threatening him, and is subsequently fired, with Bob Lemon taking over again.... Rick Cerone tells Steinbrenner off during Boss' postgame tirade following fourth game of AL division playoffs vs. Brewers.... Yankees lose the World Series to the Dodgers, prompting Steinbrenner to issue a public apology to New York fans.... Reggie Jackson leaves reluctantly as a free agent at the end of the season, after Steinbrenner snubs him.

Quote: "Why would you want to stay manager and be second-guessed by me when you can come up into the front office and be one of the second-guessers?" —George Steinbrenner to a disappointed Gene Michael after firing him as manager

1982
Record: 79–83, fifth

Managers: Bob Lemon, Gene Michael, Clyde King

Pitching coaches: Jeff Torborg, Jerry Walker, Stan Williams, Clyde King, Sammy Ellis

Comings: OF Ken Griffey (traded from Reds), OF Dave Collins (free agent), SS Roy Smalley (traded from Twins), C Butch Wynegar (traded from Twins), P Shane Rawley (traded from Mariners), RHP Doyle Alexander (traded from Giants), 1B John Mayberry (traded from Blue Jays), RHP Jay Howell (traded from Cubs), IF Butch Hobson (traded from Angels), DH Lee Mazzilli (traded from Rangers)

Goings: OF Reggie Jackson (free agent to Angels), SS Bucky Dent (traded to Rangers), RHP Ron Davis (traded to Twins), LHP Tommy John (traded to Angels), 1B Bob Watson (traded to Braves), OF Bobby Brown (traded to Mariners)

Turmoil and tumult: Former Olympic hurdler Harrison Dillard conducts running drills in spring training, prompting jokes that Steinbrenner has turned the Yankees into the "Bronx Burners."... Three managers, 5 pitching coaches, 3 hitting instructors, and 47 different players pass through the Yankee clubhouse.... Steinbrenner issues a statement ordering Doyle Alexander to undergo a physical, adding that he feared for the safety of the players behind the pitcher.... Goose Gossage launches into a clubhouse tirade at Steinbrenner in which he calls the Boss "the fat man."

Quote: "Which one's Espino?" —Davey Collins, after watching the myriad of players coming and going all season, bewildered when looking for backup catcher Juan Espino, who was recalled from Columbus and sent back before he ever put a uniform on

1983

Record: 91–71, third

Manager: Billy Martin

Pitching coaches: Art Fowler, Sammy Ellis, Jeff Torborg

Comings: OF Steve Kemp (free agent), DH Don Baylor (free agent), LHP Bob Shirley (free agent), OF Omar Moreno (traded from Astros), RHP John Montefusco (traded from Padres)

Goings: RHP Doyle Alexander (released), RHP Rick Reuschel (released), OF Dave Collins (traded to Blue Jays), OF Jerry Mumphrey (traded to Astros), 1B John Mayberry (released), DH Lee Mazzilli (traded to Pirates), Bobby Murcer (retired)

Turmoil and tumult: Steinbrenner fined $50,000 and suspended one week for criticizing umpires.… "Pine-tar game" results in a wild-goose chase through the city courtrooms and the American League offices.… In an international incident, Dave Winfield is arrested in Toronto for accidentally killing a sea gull with a thrown ball.… Martin is suspended twice for run-ins with umpires and comes to the brink of being fired after allowing himself to be distracted by his girlfriend in the middle of a game.… Promising shortstop Andre Robertson suffers severe neck injury in near-fatal auto accident.

Quote: "After a year like this, I have to check into a rehab center." —Public relations director Ken Nigro, upon announcing his resignation at the end of the season

1984

Record: 87–75, third

Manager: Yogi Berra

Pitching coaches: Sammy Ellis, Jeff Torborg, Mark Connor

Comings: RHP Phil Niekro (free agent), RHP Joe Cowley (minor league free agent), 3B Toby Harrah (traded from Indians), IF Tim Foli (traded from Angels), RHP Mike Armstrong (traded from Royals)

Goings: RHP Goose Gossage (free agent to Padres), 3B Graig Nettles (traded to Padres), OF Lou Piniella (retired), 1B Steve Balboni (traded to Royals), LHP Shane Rawley (traded to Phillies), SS Roy Smalley (traded to White Sox), RHP George Frazier (traded to Indians); General Manager Murray Cook (resigned)

Turmoil and tumult: Steinbrenner is enraged at General Manager Murray Cook after A's choose pitcher Tim Belcher, the Yankees' number-one amateur January draft choice, as compensation for losing a free agent.... Winfield-Mattingly batting race duel splits the team.... Berra, after being blamed by the Boss for the Yanks' early poor showing, explodes at Steinbrenner in a meeting and says, "This is your team."

Quote: "You want to know why I don't want any part of it? Because they're turning this thing into a racial thing, pitting teammate against teammate, black against white. It's gotten so they're even trying to split the clubhouse up on it." —Dave Winfield, explaining why he wouldn't pose for a picture with Don Mattingly as their batting title race went down to the final days of the '84 season

1985

Record: 97–64, second

Managers: Yogi Berra, Billy Martin

Pitching coaches: Mark Connor, Bill Monboquette

Comings: OF Rickey Henderson (traded from A's), RHP Ed Whitson (free agent), RHP Brian Fisher (traded from Braves), C Ron Hassey (traded from Cubs), RHP Joe Niekro (traded from Astros), 3B Dale Berra (traded from Pirates), RHP Rich Bordi (traded from Cubs), OF Billy Sample (traded from Rangers)

Goings: OF Steve Kemp (traded to Pirates), 3B Toby Harrah (traded to Rangers), OF Omar Moreno (released), C Rick Cerone (traded to Braves), RHP Jay Howell (traded to A's), RHP Jose Rijo (traded to A's), LHP Ray Fontenot (traded to Cubs), OF Oscar Gamble (released)

Turmoil and tumult: Berra, who Steinbrenner had promised would manage all season "win or lose," is fired after 16 games.... Martin gets involved in fights at the Cross Keys Inn bar in Baltimore on successive nights, the latter being a knockdown, drag-out affair with pitcher Ed Whitson that spills out into the parking lot and picks up again on the third floor.... Martin self-destructs, making numerous questionable managerial moves during a late-season eight-game losing streak, including sending left-handed Mike Pagliarulo up to hit right-handed.... Steinbrenner rips Winfield as being "Mr. May" during series with first-place Blue Jays in August when Yankees lose three out of four.

Quote: "I didn't say [your wife] had a pot belly, I said this woman here had a fat ass." —Billy Martin to an angry bar patron at the Cross Keys Inn in Baltimore the night before he got into a fight with pitcher Ed Whitson

1986

Record: 90–72, second

Manager: Lou Piniella

Pitching coaches: Sammy Ellis, Mark Connor

Comings: DH Mike Easler (traded from Red Sox), LHP Tommy John (free agent), OF Claudell Washington (traded from Braves), SS Wayne Tolleson (traded from White Sox), DH Ron Kittle (traded from White Sox), C Joel Skinner (traded from White Sox), RHP Tim Stoddard (traded from Padres)

Goings: DH Don Baylor (traded to Red Sox), RHP Phil Niekro (released), RHP Ed Whitson (traded to Padres), OF Ken Griffey (traded to Braves), C Ron Hassey (traded to White Sox), RHP John Montefusco (released)

Turmoil and tumult: Pitcher Britt Burns, the Yankees' most celebrated off-season acquisition, is found to be suffering from a degenerative hip problem in spring training and is sent home, never to pitch again.... Piniella goes through 43 players, including 6 shortstops and 12 different starting pitchers.... Broadcaster Howard Cosell, a longtime Steinbrenner confidant, blasts Piniella for having mismanaged "at least ten" games into Yankee losses.

Quote: "Baylor's bat will be dead by August." —George Steinbrenner's prediction about traded DH Don Baylor, which fell short of mark, as Baylor helped Red Sox to the AL pennant

1987

Record: 89–73, fourth

Manager: Lou Piniella

Pitching coach: Mark Connor

Comings: RHP Rick Rhoden (trade with Pirates), RHP Cecilio Guante (traded from Pirates), C Rick Cerone (free agent), OF Gary Ward (free agent), LHP Steve Trout (traded from Cubs), RHP Bill Gullickson (traded from Reds), RHP Charles Hudson (traded from Phillies), C Mark Salas (traded from Twins), RHP Neil Allen (traded from White Sox)

Goings: C Butch Wynegar (traded to Angels), LHP Dennis Rasmussen (traded to Reds), RHP Doug Drabek (traded to Pirates), RHP Brian Fisher (traded to Pirates), LHP Bob Shirley (released), RHP Joe Niekro (traded to Twins); General Manager Woody Woodward (resigned)

Turmoil and tumult: Steinbrenner issues rambling, profane statement blasting Piniella for not being in his room to receive a phone call. Boss also says Piniella urged that Rickey Henderson be traded.... Steve Trout comes over from Cubs and embarks on a fruitless search for the strike zone.... Piniella, who this time goes through a team record 48 players, is fired as manager and becomes general manager.

Quote: "I just won you the pennant. I got you Steve Trout." —George Steinbrenner to Lou Piniella

1988
Record: 85–76, fifth

Managers: Billy Martin, Lou Piniella

Pitching coaches: Art Fowler, Stan Williams, Clyde King

Comings: DH Jack Clark (free agent), LHP John Candelaria (free agent), RHP Richard Dotson (traded from White Sox), C Don Slaught (traded from Rangers), SS Rafael Santana (traded from Mets), DH Ken Phelps (traded from Mariners), IF Luis Aguayo (traded from Phillies), OF Jose Cruz (free agent).

Goings: C Rick Cerone (released), LHP Steve Trout (traded to Mariners), OF Dan Pasqua (traded to White Sox), OF Jay Buhner (traded to Mariners), DH Ron Kittle (released), RHP Tim Stoddard (released), DH Mike Easler (released), RHP Bill Gullickson (Japan)

Turmoil and tumult: Martin, back for the fifth time as manager, gets beaten up in a topless bar and is subsequently fired again.... Piniella, who earlier in the year resigned as general manager, becomes manager again only to be fired again at the end of the season.... Don Mattingly rips Steinbrenner for showing the players no respect.

Quote: "You come here and you play and you get no respect. They treat you like shit. They belittle your performance and make us look bad in the media. After they give you the money, it doesn't matter. They can do whatever they want. They think money is respect." —Don Mattingly, ripping Steinbrenner

1989

Record: 74–87, fifth

Managers: Dallas Green, Bucky Dent

Pitching coach: Billy Connors

Comings: 2B Steve Sax (free agent), RHP Andy Hawkins (free agent), OF Jesse Barfield (traded from Blue Jays), RHP Lance McCullers (traded from Padres), 3B Tom Brookens (traded from Tigers), OF Luis Polonia (traded from A's), RHP Eric Plunk (traded from A's), LHP Greg Cadaret (traded from A's), RHP Walt Terrell (traded from Padres), RHP Goose Gossage (free agent), DH Steve Balboni (traded from Mariners), OF Mel Hall (traded from Indians), LHP Dave LaPoint (free agent), LHP Chuck Cary (minor league free agent)

Goings: OF Rickey Henderson (traded to A's), 2B Willie Randolph (free agent), OF Claudell Washington (free agent), Jack Clark (traded to Padres), 3B Mike Pagliarulo (traded to Padres), LHP Ron Guidry (released), LHP Tommy John (released), OF Gary Ward (released), DH Ken Phelps (traded to A's), LHP John Candelaria (traded to Expos), RHP Richard Dotson (released), RHP Rick Rhoden (traded to Astros), C Joel Skinner (traded to Indians), LHP Al Leiter (traded to Blue Jays), RHP Charles Hudson (traded to Tigers); Senior Vice President Syd Thrift (resigned)

Turmoil and tumult: Rickey Henderson reports late to spring training as usual, then sets off a firestorm in the clubhouse by stating that the reason the Yankees didn't win in '88 was because of too much boozing on the team charters and after hours…. Dave Winfield is felled for the season by a serious back injury, and shortstop Rafael Santana goes down for the season with an elbow injury…. Spring training is barely a month old when former Pirate general manager Syd Thrift is brought in unexpectedly to head up the Yankee front office…. Both Ron Guidry and Tommy John are invited to spring training by Steinbrenner against new manager Dallas Green's wishes…. Green's blunt criticisms of players touches off a near mutiny…. Henderson is traded…. Despite his vow to let Thrift and Green run the team, Steinbrenner begins publicly second-guessing Green's strategies. That, in turn, prompts Green to fire back, calling Steinbrenner "Manager George."… Outfielder Luis Polonia is arrested in Milwaukee for having sex with a 15-year-old girl in his hotel room…. Steinbrenner fires Green and coaches Pat Corrales, Lee Elia, Charlie Fox, and Frank Howard and names Bucky Dent manager….

Green rips Steinbrenner for giving up on the program and chides him for bringing back his "puppet machine," which, in turn, prompts angry retorts from ex-managers Billy Martin and Lou Piniella.... Eleven days after Green is fired, Thrift resigns under duress.... As the team flounders (getting off to a 2–11 start under Dent), fan backlash over the Green firing intensifies, with daily chants of "George must go!" at Yankee Stadium.... Yankees go through a record 50 players en route to worst record since 1967.... Billy Martin killed in Christmas Day crash.

Quote: "George doesn't know a fucking thing about the game of baseball. That's the bottom line. When you've got a guy who wants total control and he doesn't know my job or the strengths and weaknesses of his ball club, you've got a big problem." —Dallas Green, after being fired by George Steinbrenner

1990

Record: 67–95, seventh

Managers: Bucky Dent, Stump Merrill

Pitching coach: Billy Connors

Comings: RHP Tim Leary (Trade from Reds), RHP Pascual Perez (Free Agent), RHP Jeff Robinson, (Trade from Pirates) C Rick Cerone (Free Agent), OF Claudell Washington (Trade from Angels), C Matt Nokes (Trade from Tigers), RHP Mike Witt (Trade from Angels)

Goings: OF Dave Winfield (Trade to Angels), OF Luis Polonia (Trade to Angels), C Don Slaught (Trade to Pirates), OF Hal Morris (Trade to Reds), RHP Lance McCullers (Trade to Tigers), RHP Clay Parker (Trade to Tigers), RHP Walt Terrell (Free Agent), RHP Goose Gossage (Free Agent), SS Rafael Santana (Released), RHP Dale Mohorcic (Released), IF Tom Brookens (Free Agent), OF Deion Sanders (Released)

Turmoil and tumult: George Steinbrenner is finally brought down as Yankee owner when Baseball Commissioner Fay Vincent, citing a $40,000 payment to known gambler Howard Spira as not being in the best interests of baseball, imposes lifetime ban on the Boss.... Flamboyant and temperamental free agent pitcher Pascual Perez arrives predictably late at spring training because of paternity suit and promptly hurts his arm in third start and misses entire season.... Dave Winfield ongoing controversy is finally resolved when he accepts trade to California.... Bucky Dent is fired after 49 games as Yankee manager and is replaced by Stump Merrill.... In Steinbrenner's final act as owner, he names his longtime "favorite son" Gene Michael as general manager, replacing Pete Peterson.… Yankees finish last for the first time since 1966 with their worst record since 1913.

Quote: "I'm really happy to get out of hell. It really was hell there. The Yankees are crazy. You never know what's going to happen. You never know who's going to play the next day. With the Yankees, they only worry about one thing, just one thing…and I don't know what that is." —Luis Polonia after being traded from the Yankees to California in April

Chapter 1

Billybrawl

At 5:45 P.M. Christmas Day, 1989, Billy Martin was killed when his late model pickup truck crashed off an icy road just outside his farm in Fenton, New York. He was sixty-one years old.

Martin was traveling with his longtime friend William Reedy, a saloon keeper from Detroit. Police reports maintained that Reedy was legally drunk behind the wheel and that Martin suffered a broken neck as he was thrown through the windshield. (In later years, Reedy and others maintained that Martin had in fact been driving.) The truck plunged some three hundred feet down an embankment and struck a concrete sluice pipe. If Martin had been wearing a seat belt, the authorities said, he probably would have walked away from the accident.

But as anybody who knew him could have testified, Billy went through life without a seatbelt. For him, the glass was never filled quite high enough, the nights never quite long enough. And if you knew him, traveled with him, spent times in saloons with him, you always had this vision of how it would end— suddenly and violently, with alcohol a major factor. You never envisioned Billy Martin living a long life and going peacefully to his Maker.

Martin's funeral, as orchestrated by George Steinbrenner, was a spectacle worthy of a great statesman, and in death Billy became everything he could have possibly ever wanted in life. After the funeral Mass before a standing-room-only crowd of nearly three thousand in St. Patrick's Cathedral, Martin was laid to rest in Gate of Heaven Cemetery in Hawthorne, New York. Buried nearby are Yankee legend Babe Ruth and Yankee Doodle Dandy, Jimmy Cagney.

Considering all he'd accomplished in a life that began inauspiciously as a street kid from a broken home in Berkeley, California, and the number of times he'd cheated death over his sixty-one years, one might think Martin died a fulfilled man.

He did not. Even though he'd managed the New York Yankees five times for Steinbrenner, he desperately wanted a sixth season at the helm and till the end was planning and talking about his comeback with friends.

Billy Martin ran the full gamut of emotions during his five terms as Yankee manager. You've seen all the pictures of Billy's stints. Pick any one. He's smiling in the beginning, fighting in the middle, and crying at the end—and all the while, he is aging. Martin changed dramatically from term to term. A few years ago *The Sporting News* ran a story on the Yankee managers during the Steinbrenner era and used pictures of Martin in each of his first four terms. The physical change from Billy I in 1976 to Billy IV, which ended in 1985, was stunning. Some might even say scary.

Between managerial stints, Martin always seemed to recover from the rigors of running a ball club, and the aging process seemed to reverse. "Billy looks tanned and rested" were words that, when spoken by Steinbrenner, could only mean curtains for whoever the incumbent Yankee manager might be. The strain and tension would leave Martin's face when he wasn't managing; the angry, haggard look softening a bit. It was as though Martin represented baseball's version of *The Picture of Dorian Gray*—but in reverse.

Without question, Martin's comings and goings epitomized the craziness of the Yankees' Steinbrenner era. Of all the hundreds of characters and personalities who've been associated with the team and interacted with the principal owner over the past two decades, none had the impact, the staying power, or the downright lunacy that Martin provided.

There was no question the strain and tension were getting to Martin in '88 when he couldn't hold his job even with the Yankees in first place. One night in early June, after Lou Piniella had resigned as general manager, Martin telephoned him. Obviously drunk, Martin repeatedly told Piniella he'd better watch out for his job, that Hawk Harrelson was politicking to become general manager. Harrelson, who was an announcer of the Yankee games for Sportschannel, was a close friend of Piniella's.

Piniella tried to tell Martin he was no longer the general manager, but Martin kept saying: "You better watch out. Harrelson is after your job." After a while Piniella gave up trying to reason with Martin and thanked him for the information.

Those who have been around the Yankees for a number of years are often asked what Billy Martin was really like. It's a question that was impossible to answer. He was many personalities, many pictures. There was the calm, jovial "in-control" Billy, and the crazed, obsessed "out-of-control" Billy. Just when he seemed like the nastiest son of a bitch ever, ready to punch some guy's lights out at the bar, he'd switch personalities and wind up picking up the guy's tab.

Above all, Billy Martin was never dull.

Moss Klein first met Martin in 1976. With one week to go in spring training at Fort Lauderdale, Klein had become the *Newark Star-Ledger* Yankee beat writer and figured he better introduce himself to Martin. For several minutes he stood outside the manager's office, trying to work up the nerve to go in and talk to Martin, who was alone at his desk. Finally he walked in and Martin looked up.

Klein had prepared a long list of questions for Martin as a defense against nervousness. After introducing himself, he asked Martin about the shortstop situation, which had been a competition between Chicken Stanley and Jim Mason that spring.

"Nobody's asked me about that for a few days," Martin said, "so they don't know I've made a decision. You're asking, so I'm telling you first. I'm going to platoon them. Stanley plays against lefties, Mason against righties. I'm sure you know it's unusual to have platoon shortstops, but that's what I'm gonna do. Write it. You'll look smart."

Then Martin leaned across the table and looked at the young reporter.

"Let's you and me have an understanding," he said. "A lot of people don't like me, and a lot of writers have burned me. I know I can be a real prick sometimes. But if you're honest with me, I'll be honest with you. Sometimes you're gonna knock me, but as long as you're fair, as long as you do your homework, I can respect that. I think we can get along pretty good."

That 1976 season was Martin's easiest. The Yankees won the American League East in a breeze and were never really challenged. Klein, who had always heard that Martin was a genius, was given an immediate demonstration—one that certainly was historic.

In the second game of the season, against the Brewers at County Stadium, the Yankees had a 9–6 lead in the ninth inning. Milwaukee loaded the bases with one out, and Don Money hit an apparent game-winning grand slam against rookie Dave Pagan. But as Money circled the bases, Martin came charging out onto the field. Pagan, who had heard all the Martin horror stories, was struck with fear and began running toward left field.

"I thought he was coming after me for giving up the homer," he said later. "If you watched me, you saw I was taking off. I didn't want him to beat me up right there on the field in front of all those fans. I just wanted to get away."

But Pagan wasn't Martin's target. First base umpire Jim McKean was. Just before Pagan had made his pitch to Money, Yankee first baseman Chris

Chambliss had called time, and McKean had stepped forward to oblige the request. Martin wanted McKean to admit that, and the umpire did. Thus, Martin had succeeded in canceling a game-winning grand slam, and the Yankees went on to win, 9–7.

The 1977 season marked the real beginning of Martin's perpetual conflicts with George Steinbrenner. The first—and one of the most volatile—came after a March 26 spring training loss to the Mets. Losing to the Mets represented the ultimate disgrace for Steinbrenner. Losing to the Mets in a game that was televised back to New York was even worse. Steinbrenner envisioned thousands of viewers, undecided as to whether to purchase Yankee or Met tickets, sitting at home, watching the game, and immediately making calls to the Mets' ticket hotline after the Yankees' loss.

Martin had no sooner gotten to his office after the game than Steinbrenner marched in and began criticizing the way the team was playing. Martin answered back. "Don't be yelling in front of the players," he said.

Steinbrenner said he'd say or do whatever he wanted. Martin shouted back again.

"Do you want to be fired right now?" Steinbrenner yelled.

"You do whatever you want, but don't yell at me in front of my players," Martin countered.

Martin then brushed past Steinbrenner and headed for the trainer's room. Steinbrenner followed. So did Gabe Paul, the team president, who had come in as the shouting match reached its midpoint and been unsuccessful in calming down the two combatants. Paul was now standing in front of Martin in the trainer's room, and when Steinbrenner started yelling again, Martin slammed his fist into a tub of ice water on the table. The ice splattered all over Paul. The players who were still in the room getting medical care from the trainers scurried out, laughing.

The scene ended with Steinbrenner storming out of the clubhouse. Later he told Paul to set up a meeting with Martin for 8:00 A.M. the next day. At the bar at the Bay Harbor Inn in Tampa that night, Martin told Klein he had had it with Steinbrenner, that he might quit the next day. It was the first of many times reporters would hear him say that. At one time or another all the managers said the same thing.

Steinbrenner and Martin had their meeting and reached a temporary peace. Later that day the Yankees lost to the Reds in 10 innings. Steinbrenner ordered another meeting. Another temporary peace. The 1977 season was a year of meetings and temporary peaces, of near firings and more meetings. It all added up to a world championship.

Winning, however, did not breed unity and tranquility between Steinbrenner and Martin—not in '77, '78, or any of the four Billy sequels.

One of the most memorable Martin blowups that 1977 season was his dugout fight with Reggie Jackson at Fenway Park on June 18. Billy always resented Reggie. He never wanted him in the first place; instead, he had wanted to sign free agent Joe Rudi, Reggie's less-publicized Oakland A's teammate.

To make matters worse, at the press conference announcing Reggie's signing with the Yankees in November of 1976, Reggie said, "I'm very happy to be coming to the Yankees to play for George Steinbrenner." Martin read that quote and never forgave Reggie for it. "He never mentioned me, and I'm the manager, right?" he said many times later.

So Martin was paranoid about Reggie, Reggie was paranoid about Martin, and both of them were paranoid about Steinbrenner. It was a lovely infernal triangle.

The dugout scene at Fenway that day was touched off when Reggie loafed on a bloop hit to right by Jim Rice in the sixth inning. After Rice hustled into second with a double, Martin immediately sent in Paul Blair to replace Reggie in right field. Reggie came into the dugout, removed his glasses, and began shouting at Martin.

"You never liked me—"

Martin took several steps toward Reggie before coaches Yogi Berra and Elston Howard stepped between them. By the time the game ended, with Boston winning, 10–4, Reggie had returned to the hotel. That night he was in a highly emotional state when he told his troubles to the writers. Martin, meanwhile, was in the hotel bar, where he said, "If a guy doesn't hustle and shows the team up, then I show the player up."

Years later, the players who had cameo roles in that famous scene remembered it with glee.

"I didn't want to go out there," said Blair, "but I had to do what Billy said. I mean, it was weird going out there like that, in the middle of an inning. As I got near Reggie, he said, 'What's going on?' I said, 'Reggie, all I know is I'm in for you.' He kind of pointed at himself, like saying, 'In for me?'"

Sparky Lyle, the reliever who replaced Mike Torrez after Rice's hit, was throwing warmups as Reggie headed in from right field to the dugout. (Lyle, it should be noted, was not a big Reggie fan.)

"I was on the mound when Blair first ran out to right," Lyle said. "I said, 'Where are you going?' He said, 'I'm going in for Reggie.' I said, 'Wow, this ought to be a good one.' Then I watched Reggie pointing at himself and shaking his head. I immediately focused on the dugout, because I knew this was gonna be one of those sights I'd want to remember."

Ron Guidry was in the dugout, sitting next to Berra.

"Yogi got hold of Billy," Guidry recalled, "and I kept kicking him [Berra], saying, 'Let him go, let them go at it.' The whole thing lasted about a minute, and one of the guys threw a towel over the dugout camera. When Ellie [Howard] sat down, he was shaking his head and saying: 'Man, I've been around a long time, but this team is too much. I ain't never seen nothin' like this kind of shit day after day.'"

Ironically, Reggie wound up saving Martin's job that weekend. The Yankees lost all three games to the Red Sox, and when the team moved on to Detroit, Steinbrenner and Gabe Paul showed up. Rumors were rampant that Martin was going to be fired, but Reggie, in a stunning show of support, requested a meeting with Steinbrenner and told him that firing Martin at this time would be bad for the team. He pointed out that it would make it look like he, Reggie, was running the team.

The following year, Paul was gone, but Martin and Steinbrenner had never needed a middleman for their fights anyway. Sure enough, on March 26, 1978, in an almost identical replay of the spring before, they got into it after the Mets game. This time the Yankees had beaten the Mets, 9–6, but committed five errors in the process. Martin stormed into the clubhouse and slammed the door of his office.

The initial guess of the reporters was that he was upset with the team's play (they had committed 29 errors in the first 16 exhibition games). Snapping and snarling at every question, Martin held a terse session with reporters, and shortly afterward coach Elston Howard came over to Moss Klein.

"They're at it again," he said, shaking his head.

Howard told Klein about the scene in the dugout in the eighth inning, when the Yankees were trailing, 6–3. Steinbrenner, who had been watching the game from his upper-level box, obviously had gotten himself worked up at the prospect of another embarrassing loss to the Mets. In the eighth inning he strode down from his box and went right into the Yankee dugout.

As Howard replayed it to Klein, "George started yelling out to nobody in particular things like, 'Let's go, we're supposed to be world champs. We can't lose to a team like the Mets.' Then, on a close play, he started yelling at the umpire. Billy was really getting pissed. Then George said something like: 'C'mon, Martin, get these guys fired up.' He said it like he was kidding, but Billy was mad as hell. He told George off, right there. He said, 'Get the hell off the bench, George, and leave the team to me, or else get rid of me and do whatever you want!'"

That time Steinbrenner relented and, in fact, stopped Martin in the parking lot after the Yankees' come-from-behind victory and engaged in a pleasant chit-chat. There weren't too many more that season. In fact, from the start the 1978 season was utter chaos, and by July, Martin, pushed to the edge of a breakdown, was fired and replaced by low-key Bob Lemon.

One of that season's more outrageous incidents occurred on a May 14 flight from Kansas City to Chicago following a 10–9 loss to the Royals. Martin was in an especially foul mood, because of the loss and because of the lackadaisical play of Mickey Rivers in center field. The flight became the most vivid example of why, in later years, the Yankees almost never flew commercial.

The problems began when the flight was delayed. That gave everybody, Martin especially, more drinking time. Once the flight got underway, Martin and his coaches were sitting in first class, with the players and writers in the coach section, mixed in with the "normal" people. Thurman Munson and Goose Gossage were in the second row of the coach section, playing country and western music on a tape deck. Before long, Munson turned the music up full blast, only to lower it and then blast it again.

A distinguished-looking businessman in a suit, seated in front of the two players, and across the aisle from Moss Klein and *Newsday's* Joe Donnelly, finally turned around and said, "Would you mind lowering that a bit?"

Munson scowled at the guy. "Mind your own business, fuckface."

The man, stunned, figured he was dealing with a lunatic and took the advice.

Martin, meanwhile, heard the music blaring and dispatched Howard to instruct the players to lower the volume. When Howard approached and relayed Martin's request, Munson responded to him as he had with the man in the row in front.

"What are you, the music coach?" he said.

Gossage, laughing, said to Munson, "You're gonna get Billy mad."

But Munson, who had had a few himself, just laughed. "Billy's so drunk he won't even remember this flight."

But this was a flight that was hard for anyone to forget.

Rivers, conducting card games in the rear of the plane, began tossing the decks around with the cards landing all over the passengers. Martin had stopped paying attention to the players and was talking animatedly—and drunkenly—to his coaches: Howard, Yogi Berra, and Dick Howser. Finally the plane landed.

But in an appropriate ending to the flight, there was ground delay because of traffic. Just what these poor unsuspecting people needed—to be stranded another 15 minutes with the Yankees.

With the plane sitting on the runway, Munson headed to the bathroom in the first-class section. On his way back he was stopped by Martin. The drunken manager started complaining about Rivers, but Munson, usually Martin's ally, wasn't interested.

"I don't care about the other guys," Munson said, which offended Martin. Now he began yelling at his semidrunk team captain.

Howser intervened, getting in the middle as Martin attempted to take a swing at Munson. The fact that Munson continued to laugh at the whole scene was getting Martin more and more enraged. Finally, to the relief of everybody, the plane began heading for the gate. But the chaos still wasn't over.

Martin told Howser to go tell Rivers that he wanted to meet with him when they got to the hotel. Howser got off the plane and waited for Rivers to reach him and relayed Martin's message.

"I don't take orders from no secretary," Rivers said. "He wants to talk to me, let him tell me."

Now Howser and Rivers began going at it, and it took Howard to step in and separate them. The next day, Rivers was benched against the White Sox and reporters spent their time pre- and postgame scurrying back and forth as he and Martin exchanged insults. As always, the situation was settled temporarily a few days later, and Martin issued an apology—both publicly and privately—to Munson, a man he admired greatly. But in subsequent years the Yankees flew almost exclusively by charter. Like the clowns, trapeze acts, and lion tamers, they traveled on their own.

Ironically, that same O'Hare Airport in Chicago marked the end of Martin's first term a couple of months later. The buildup of problems with Steinbrenner and Jackson had worn Martin to a frazzle. And on July 23, following a 3–1 getaway victory over the White Sox, Martin uttered his damning description of the two: "One's a born liar and the other's convicted."

That remark, which he encouraged reporters to use, resulted in his tearful, forced resignation the following day in Kansas City. Then, five days later, in that Old-timers' Day announcement that was bizarre even by Yankee standards, Martin was named manager for the 1980 season. Lemon, four games into his reign, was told he would manage in 1979, then become general manager in 1980.

It seemed Martin had called Steinbrenner a few hours after his resignation and apologized. They then began to talk and Martin informed the owner of the emotional strain he had felt while managing. They agreed that Martin just needed some time away from it to rest up and get back into good health.

This, of course, gave Steinbrenner the opportunity to play out the ultimate P. T. Barnum extravaganza. He had Martin smuggled into town for Old-timers'

Day, instructing aides to "keep him out of sight, quiet, and out of trouble." Then came the introductions of all the old-timers by broadcaster Frank Messer. Messer had made most of the introductions when he interrupted himself and said, "I now turn to the microphone over to [PA announcer] Bob Sheppard for two special announcements."

There were boos when Sheppard announced that Lemon would be managing the team through 1979. Upon waiting for the boos to quiet, Sheppard made the announcement that was unbelievable to everyone: "And coming back to manage the Yankees in 1980…number one, Billy Martin!"

The ovation lasted nearly eight minutes as Martin ran out onto the field and cleverly kept waving his hat to fuel the fans whenever the cheers started dying down.

In retrospect it wasn't nearly as unbelievable as so many other Steinbrenner capers that were to follow in the years to come. He also made at least one person upset, too. Joe DiMaggio, it seems, was miffed at being upstaged by all the Martin ballyhoo. And in the locker room, after a 7–3 win over the Twins, Reggie Jackson sat disconsolately in front of his locker. He had been booed loudly during the game, especially after his two strikeouts.

"I don't think I'll be back here in 1980," he said. "They'll get rid of me now. They have to, don't they?"

Naturally Martin was back ahead of schedule, replacing Lemon in June of '79. He was fired ahead of schedule, too, getting sacked for the second time after a one-punch knockdown of a marshmallow salesman in a Bloomington, Minnesota, cocktail lounge that winter.

The fights, the bar scenes—so much a part of Martin's image. Most of the time they were his fault. He'd be in a bar, refuse to ignore some loudmouth, and there would be a scene. One time during that '79 season, one of those drunken scenes occurred in the middle of Lakeshore Drive in Chicago.

Martin had been at a restaurant and was pretty well oiled when he and a companion got into a taxicab to go back to the team hotel. It seemed, though, the cabdriver was a European, who had just come on duty after playing soccer. He was still wearing his shorts, which caught Martin's eye. The two quickly became engaged in a conversation about sports, with Martin becoming increasingly abusive, making derogatory remarks about soccer players. At one point, Martin, citing the cabby's shorts, impugned the fellow's manhood.

That did it. The cabby stopped the cab in the middle of Lake Shore Drive, one of Chicago's busiest thoroughfares, and got out, challenging Martin to a fight. Martin eagerly obliged, and as the two of them began chasing each other around the cab, swinging wildly, cars were tooting their horns and swerving to avoid hitting them. At last, Martin's companion was able to corral him and shove him back into the cab. He then managed to sweet-talk the cabby into completing the journey to the hotel rather than leaving them stranded in the middle of Lake Shore Drive.

Another time that season, Martin actually wound up in the role of peacemaker in a near fight between a couple of inebriated combatants. The Yankees were in Toronto, playing the Blue Jays, who were completing their third dismal season under manager Roy Hartsfield. Martin, traveling secretary Bill "Killer" Kane, and a couple of writers all went to dinner on a Saturday night. After dinner and after a lot of drinks, the group was still sitting and talking at the table. Kane was telling a story when all of a sudden Hartsfield, drunker than all of the others, lurched over, ignoring Kane, and started talking to Martin. He left after a few minutes, and Kane resumed his story. Then Hartsfield was back again, interrupting Kane's story once more.

Kane, who had had a few drinks, too, and was known to have a hot temper, said, "Hey, you, I'm talkin' here, ya know."

Hartsfield glared at him. "I don't give a shit if you are or you aren't."

They exchanged a few more words, getting louder and louder, and Hartsfield reached out and grabbed Kane. That's when Martin intervened, moving quickly, as if he might even have some experience in such matters.

The irony of what followed was priceless. Martin got hold of Hartsfield and told the writers to "get Killer out of here." Kane was led away to get some air, and when the writers returned to get Martin, he was lecturing Hartsfield.

"You're the manager of the team in this city," Martin was saying. "You can't be going out and getting into fights in restaurants."

"But, Billy," Hartsfield said, "they're gonna fire me anyway."

"Maybe they will," said Martin, "but why make their decision easy for them?"

If only Billy Martin had listened to his own advice, maybe the myriad of similar incidents involving him would never have occurred. But Billy, being Billy, was always a bar scene waiting to happen.

Actually, Martin didn't always need a bar to get into trouble. Airports had proven to be potentially explosive places for him as well. In June of 1985 he was in bad mood after a loss to the Blue Jays in Toronto on getaway day. The airport was mobbed in Toronto because it was a Canadian holiday. When the Yankee buses arrived, traveling secretary Kane began giving out boarding passes for the Yankees' charter flight. Fearing he might miss a few of the Yankee personnel in the crowd, Kane spotted coach Jeff Torborg, a reliable sort, and gave him a stack of passes to hand out as well.

Torborg was handing out the passes when Martin and his "drinking companion" coach, Doug Holmquist, came along. Now, Martin and Torborg were not on the best of terms for a number of reasons. For one, Torborg didn't drink and therefore didn't hang out with Martin and the other coaches after games. For another, Martin resented the fact that Torborg had been given a seven-year contract by Steinbrenner after the '81 season.

Holmquist, meanwhile, was a troublemaker, a Martin crony who didn't get along with the players or the other coaches. Like Martin, he was especially troublesome when he was drinking. That was certainly the case on this day, and when Torborg had no boarding passes left for Martin, Holmquist said accusingly, "Be nice if you had saved one for the manager." Torborg tried to explain that he had simply been giving out the passes to any of the Yankees who came along, but Holmquist repeated his charge. That, in turn, seemed to convince Martin that he had been offended, and he said to Torborg, "I *am* the manager, you know."

Torborg, aware that he was dealing with two guys who had been drinking and who were trying to pick a fight, just turned and walked away. But when Martin boarded the plane, having gotten his pass from Kane, he spotted Torborg sitting a few rows back and shouted loud enough for everyone around to hear: "Thanks a lot. I got one anyway."

Although a gentleman under most circumstances, Torborg had heard and taken enough. He yelled back at Martin: "I told you what happened. I didn't do anything, Billy."

Martin immediately charged toward Torborg's seat, saying, "I know you don't like me, you never liked me."

Torborg didn't back down but instead made his point. "Billy, you're the manager," he said. "I'm one of the coaches. I do what you want as far as the bullpen is concerned. Let's leave it at that."

Martin muttered a few more words and returned to his seat. Later on that flight, Holmquist, who continued drinking with Martin, kept standing up and shouting "Sit down!" at the players. When the plane arrived at Newark, he confronted Bill Madden at the baggage carousel and attempted to pick a fight with him. Madden had written some critical articles about Martin, and it was obvious that Holmquist wanted to show his boss just how far his loyalty went—as far as taking a pop at a writer. Before he got the chance, however, pitching coach Mark Connor and publicity man Joe Safety rushed to intervene, and Holmquist was pulled away, cursing at Madden. A few days later, a sober Holmquist apologized to Madden in the dugout in the presence of most of the players and coaches.

Unfortunately, too many of Martin's drunken encounters went further than the Torborg incident. His problem was that he always positioned himself for trouble by seeking out the hotel bar. Sometimes he would be looking for trouble, and other times trouble would come looking for him. One night in 1977, though, Martin was sitting with Moss Klein and publicity director Mickey Morabito at a bar in Toronto when a drunken patron came over and tried to start something up.

"Let's get out of here and go someplace else where they don't know me," Martin said.

Years later, Klein reminded Martin of that.

"Yeah," said Martin, "but I can't spend my whole life running away from people. What am I supposed to do? Sit in my room and drink by myself? It isn't fair."

Martin's long courtship and eventual marriage to Jill Guiver in 1988 seemed to have a positive, mellowing effect on him—when he was home. His wife, a stunning blonde nearly 30 years younger than he, appeared to exert some control over him. Yet once Martin resumed managing and got loose on the road trips Jill didn't make, he was unable to avoid trouble again.

The most celebrated case in point, of course, was the Lace incident in Arlington, Texas, which ultimately led to Martin's firing as Yankee manager for the fifth time. Following a 7–6 loss to the Rangers on May 6, 1988, Martin showed up at the bar at the Arlington Hilton, the Yankees' hotel. In his group were Mickey Mantle, Mantle's son, and Mike Ferraro, one of the Yankee coaches. After several drinks the group headed over to Lace, a topless nightclub about five minutes away.

The most accurate version of what happened at Lace seems to be this: After getting thoroughly sloshed, Martin was left alone at Lace as the Mantles and Ferraro went their separate ways. Martin then proceeded to get into an altercation with another patron in the men's room and was grabbed by a bouncer and another man. They were leading him outside, arguing anew, and Martin was unceremoniously tossed out the back door. He fell and hit his head on a stucco wall, suffering severe cuts on his ear and the side of his head. Martin claims he was punched by the bouncer once outside, but police reports do not verify that version.

In any event, Martin was a bloody mess. He eventually got a taxi ride back to the Hilton—only luck was not on his side that night. Often Martin's late-hour altercations escaped detection, and cuts and bruises were explained away. This time there were dozens of witnesses waiting on the Hilton's front lawn as he staggered out of the taxi. A fire alarm had gone off in the wee hours of the morning and everyone—including Steinbrenner—had been evacuated from the building.

If the Yankees hadn't been 20–9 at that point, Martin would have surely been fired on the spot. But because of the club's fast start, Steinbrenner publicly defended Martin while privately making plans to replace him a few weeks later.

Another victim, so to speak, of the Lace episode was Kevin Manahan, a reporter for the *Newark Star-Ledger*. Moss Klein had taken the weekend off, and Manahan, making his first Yankee road trip, would never forget it.

After covering a difficult first game that Friday night in which Martin and Don Mattingly were both ejected and a five-run Yankee rally fell short, Manahan had a quick drink at the hotel bar and went to bed. An hour later, he was awakened by the fire alarm and had to get dressed and walk down the back stairs out into the parking lot. When he returned to his room, Manahan got back into bed and was just falling asleep when his phone rang. On the other end was an hysterical woman who identified herself as Jill Martin, Billy's wife. She kept calling Manahan "Gene," while demanding to know what had happened to Billy. Manahan, in a groggy state, had no idea who this woman was or what she was talking about. He eventually hung up on her and went back to sleep.

Manahan was awakened early the next morning by a call from one of the other reporters, who filled him in on the Lace episode. It all suddenly began to get clearer to Manahan what had happened. Jill Martin, who was home in New York, had been alerted to Billy's latest crisis and telephoned the Arlington Hilton, asking for Gene Monahan, the Yankee trainer. The operator connected her instead with Manahan.

The next two days were a horror for a young reporter. Covering the games, both Yankee losses, was an afterthought. There were trips to Lace to interview any employee or customer who might have information about the fight. There were trips to the Arlington Police Department for updates and interviews. And there were dealings with Martin, who, in the best of times, could be rough on reporters he didn't know. In the middle of all this confusion, the Yankees activated 39-year-old batting coach Chris Chambliss, who had one at-bat and struck out.

When Manahan returned home the following Monday, he had some blistering words to Klein about what he could do with the Yankees.

"I was with this crazy team three days," Manahan said, "and I get blown out of bed by a fire alarm and woken up by an hysterical woman who kept calling me 'Gene.' I wound up spending half the weekend in the men's room of a strip joint, interviewing the bathroom attendant. I'm on a first-name basis with half of the Arlington Police Department. All in three days. No wonder nobody wants to make any of these damn road trips."

It is, of course, quite true that not all of Billy Martin's troubles came from the bottle. His scenes in dimly lit bars in front of a handful of late-night imbibers often paled in comparison to the spectacles he performed with umpires in broad daylight or at well-lit night games, often before millions of television viewers. It can be said with authority that Martin's two biggest bugaboos in all his managerial stints were booze and the men in blue.

By the time Martin returned to the Yankees in 1983 for Billy III, his ump bashing was such a prominent part of his dossier that the Yankee publicity department, with Steinbrenner's approval, used a drawing of Martin involved in a heated dispute with an umpire on the cover of the media guide. Martin didn't appreciate the idea and voiced his displeasure about it frequently that spring. Then, in the second inning of the first game of the season against the Mariners in Seattle, he was on the field arguing again with the umpires. He disputed three calls in that game, which the Yankees lost, 5–4, and afterward said, "Seattle's best player out there today was the second base umpire [Dan Morrison]."

The highlight of Martin's celebrated bumps with the umps that '83 season occurred on July 31 at Chicago's Comiskey Park. Martin was ejected in the fifth inning by umpire Dale Ford for arguing about the number of warm-up throws catcher Butch Wynegar should get when he replaced Rick Cerone behind the plate. (Cerone had just himself been ejected for arguing a close play at the plate.)

After the game, won by the Yankees, 12–6, in 11 innings, Martin was in a rage in his office, and it was clear that he had been working himself into it with the help of alcoholic refreshment as the game dragged on. This had not been the best of weeks for Martin, anyway. The notorious pine-tar game had been played one week earlier, July 24, and Martin thought he had staged one of his grandest moments of managerial one-upsmanship by getting George Brett's game-winning homer against the Yankees "canceled" because of apparently too much pine tar on his bat. Kansas City appealed the decision, and a couple of days later, American League President Lee MacPhail, citing "the spirit of the rule," overruled the umpire crew and let the home run stand. The game was to be completed on August 18 (with the Yankees going down meekly in the ninth to lose, 5–4).

Before the game at Comiskey Park, Martin had been seething over MacPhail's ruling, and he held a pregame meeting in an attempt to snap the

Yankees out of what he felt was a MacPhail-induced slump. "There's no question we were cheated," Martin told the players. "MacPhail changed the rules against us. But we have to battle back and show we're true Yankees."

Imagine: the pine-tar game marked one of the few times Billy Martin felt the umpires had ever made the right decision, and now the league president had overruled them! Martin was clearly in no mood to be crossed by the umpires now.

So even though the Yankees had come back to beat the White Sox, Martin severely criticized home plate umpire Ford, with whom he had had several previous run-ins through the years. After listening to Martin's charges, reporters went to Wynegar, known to be an honest guy. When Wynegar corroborated Martin's version, indicating Ford had seemingly "been out to get Billy," reporters Klein and Madden decided to get Ford's side.

The umpire, of course, had a completely different version of the incident. The number of warm-up throws for Wynegar had nothing to do with the ejection, he said. "Billy just wanted to keep arguing over the previous play. I told him twice, 'Let's play.' But he was making a farce of the game, so I ran him."

Madden and Klein returned to Martin's office, armed with Ford's comments. Martin was still pacing around the office, complaining bitterly about MacPhail and muttering about the umpires "being out to get the Yankees." Murray Cook, who had recently been named Yankee general manager, had accompanied the team to Chicago and was standing outside the office, peering in and wondering about the man who was in charge of running this team.

Klein told Martin what Ford said—and quickly regretted it. Martin's rage intensified to the point he was downright frightening. He stood toe-to-toe with Klein, as if the reporter had turned into an umpire, and began bellowing: "Ford's a stone liar, a flat-out, stone liar! He doesn't know the rules! I'm calling the umpire a liar, and I know the commissioner and MacPhail will call me in on it. But I'm telling the truth!"

Martin then calmed a bit, backed away, and continued his tirade against Ford. "He's a crew chief? He couldn't be chief of a one-man Indian tribe. He doesn't know the rule book. They ought to call the rule book the funny pages. All it's good for is when you go deer hunting and ran out of toilet paper."

As pointed out earlier, the reporters suspected Martin had been drinking in his office during the game, although nobody could be certain. One thing was certain, though: Cook was convinced his manager was nuts. He had watched the entire scene in silent disbelief, and when Klein and Madden headed out of the office, he stopped them and asked, "Does that happen often?" They assured him it happened only a couple of times a week, and Cook shook his head.

That proved to be only one of many wild and crazy episodes involving Martin and the Yankees that 1983 season. Remember, in addition to doing battle with the umpires and bar drunks, Martin was forever butting heads with Steinbrenner, too. His ongoing squabbles with the principal Yankee owner came to a head—and nearly resulted in his firing—during a tumultuous Yankee road trip to Milwaukee and Cleveland in early June.

The Yankees had lost their final game of the home stand to the Indians on June 8, 6–5, giving them five losses in their last six. Steinbrenner ordered Martin to work the team out on the off day in Milwaukee the next day. Having fought Steinbrenner so many times in the past about these workouts and always gotten nowhere, Martin told the Boss "Okay." What he didn't tell Steinbrenner, however, was that he would make the workout voluntary for everyone, including the coaches.

Martin, himself, did not even get to Milwaukee until late that afternoon. As he told Bill Madden the night before, "I'm flying out on my own, with my girlfriend, Jill. Why don't you join us? I'll meet you at the bar of my hotel at one o'clock."

Madden showed up at one o'clock, and sure enough, Billy was waiting at the bar. They had a couple of drinks while waiting for Jill to come down with her luggage and then were driven out to La Guardia Airport by Martin's chauffeur. While they sat in the limousine, Martin told Madden about the nonworkout.

"I'd appreciate it if you don't write anything about the workout today," he said, "because there isn't one. George just doesn't understand that the players need the off days to get their rest. Rather than argue with him, I just said 'Okay' and told the players they could work out, take a little hitting if they wanted."

Madden fully intended to honor Martin's request about not mentioning the workout. Unfortunately a series of crazy events that followed made it impossible.

The first night, the Yankees beat the Brewers handily, 7–1, behind the pitching of Shane Rawley. What the reporters didn't know, however, was that not all was so tranquil and easy in the Yankee dugout that night. Seems that in the middle of the game, Martin had become engaged in a shouting match with one of the County Stadium security guards about getting Jill safe passage out of the ballpark. While Martin was screaming at the guard, Rawley was suddenly getting hit hard by the Brewers. According to dugout witnesses, pitching coach Art Fowler tried to get Martin's attention back on the game and his pitcher.

"Billy! Billy! Rawley's getting in trouble!" Fowler yelled. "What do you want to do?"

"Get Gossage up," Martin yelled, then returned his attention to the security guard who, it was later learned, was transferred from dugout duty the next day.

The Yankees lost the next night, 6–2. Sunday, getaway day, was a beautiful, warm afternoon. As the reporters gathered in the press box for the start of the game, they looked down to the Yankee dugout where, sitting in the box right next to it, was Jill. She was wearing a halter top and shorts, and it was hard for anyone in the ballpark not to take notice of her. Martin certainly did. He sat on a towel on the top step at that end of the dugout for the entire game, and periodically he would reach over to her to take a note that she would pass over the fence with her toes.

The reporters were both amazed and amused at this blatantly outrageous behavior by the Yankee manager. Don Carney, the director of the WPIX local telecast to New York, later confessed that he ordered his camera crew not to pan to Billy or Jill during the game. Afterward the reporters got together and decided it would be best for all concerned if they ignored Martin's bizarre behavior. "The club is going fairly well. Billy, to this point, had been acting fairly sane," they reasoned. "Why stir up a lot of shit that will just make working with Martin unbearable for the rest of the season?"

Alas, they should have known you could never make pacts of that sort involving Billy Martin, because in Billy's case, things never went unnoticed. When the team got to Cleveland (after losing two out of three in Milwaukee), Madden got a call in his room from the Yankee publicity man, Ken Nigro.

"Listen," said Nigro, "I don't know what you want to do about this, but I just got a call from Henry Hecht in New York. He asked me all kinds of questions about Billy's behavior on this trip. I don't know if he's on to something or what, but you might want to try and find out."

Madden was worried now. Hecht, who worked for the rival *New York Post,* had been Martin's principal antagonist among the traveling New York press corps during Billy I and II. Now he was doing baseball columns, having relinquished the Yankee beat to newcomer Mike McAlary. All Madden could think of was Hecht writing a scathing column, detailing all of Martin's transgressions on the trip. The *Post* was the *Daily News'* main competitor, and Madden would have a hard time explaining to his editor why someone in New York would know more about what was going on with the team in Milwaukee than he.

Madden wondered if maybe McAlary had tipped Hecht off to take himself off the hook about looking the other way during the note-passing caper. At any rate, Madden called Klein and told him all bets were off regarding the pact.

"I've got no choice, Moss," Madden said. "If Hecht knows anything, you know he'll write it because it'll be bad for Billy."

Klein agreed.

Madden knew that Hecht had long enjoyed a good relationship with Steinbrenner, so the first person he called was the principal Yankee owner.

What transpired in that phone conversation ultimately ended Madden's relationship with Billy Martin forever. Steinbrenner, it seemed, was aware that Martin was acting erratically and not paying enough attention to his job. He was upset that Martin had brought his girlfriend on the road trip, and one of the coaches had told him about the aborted workout. More important, as far as Steinbrenner was concerned, the Yankees were playing badly and starting to slip out of the race.

"I'm probably gonna have to make a change," Steinbrenner told Madden.

Madden was stunned, but not nearly as much as by what Steinbrenner said next.

"What do you think about Yogi managing the team? That's who I'm thinking about. He'd be perfect, I think."

"Yogi Berra to manage the Yankees!" Madden thought. "Holy shit! Now what do I do?"

Figuring that Steinbrenner had surely broached his Yogi idea with others, Madden knew he couldn't sit on this. He wrote his story that day saying that Martin was facing the firing squad again and that Yogi would be named to replace him. Madden noted that Martin's demise was the product of his erratic behavior on the present road trip, which included allowing himself "to be distracted by his girlfriend during the course of Sunday's game in Milwaukee." The *Daily News* ran it on page one, accompanied by a huge Bill Gallo cartoon of Yogi Berra.

Well, it didn't take long for all hell to break loose. In particular, Mike McAlary was livid—and justifiably so. It turned out he hadn't said anything to Hecht, who had merely been on a "fishing expedition" in calling Nigro to get some dirt on Martin. So McAlary felt betrayed and immediately after that first night's game in Cleveland, he rushed down to the clubhouse to tell Martin what Madden had written.

Martin exploded.

"He wrote *what?*" he screamed. His face quickly flushed purple and the veins in his neck began bursting out. "How the hell could he write that? Doesn't he know I'm married? I'm married!"

Meanwhile, the players, hearing all this commotion coming out of the manager's office, thought Martin had really gone crazy now. They had no idea what he was ranting about and waited anxiously for the writers to come out of the office and fill them in.

The next day Steinbrenner flew into Cleveland, as did Martin's agent, Eddie Sapir. The two met with Martin at the Pewter Mug, and Steinbrenner agreed to give Martin a reprieve—with the condition that Billy change his ways and start instilling discipline in the team. That afternoon when Madden came down on the elevator into the lobby of Stouffer's Hotel, he was astounded by the chaotic scene that awaited him.

The lobby was mobbed with crews of television people, all running into each other as they scurried about in search of someone to interview. In the middle of it all was Eddie Sapir, shouting to one and all: "Billy has been vindicated! Reports of the girl are unfounded!"

What a circus. Madden could only laugh. Reports of the girl unfounded? Guess nobody talked to any of the 50,000 fans at County Stadium or the 50 or so press and TV people who were there on Sunday.

The Martin-Steinbrenner craziness kept up, though. As Madden and Klein boarded the team bus after the last game in Cleveland, a forlorn-looking Art Fowler, Martin's pitching coach, revealed to them that Steinbrenner had fired him. "I guess somebody's gotta be the scapegoat," he said sadly. "That seems to be my job around here."

The team returned to New York for a quickie three-game home stand against the Brewers—but what a wild, wacky weekend it turned out to be. Despite his reprieve, Martin was furious over Steinbrenner's firing of Fowler. That Friday, Steinbrenner tried reaching Martin all day by phone at his apartment, to no avail. Billy, it seems, was in a bar downtown, drinking himself into a further fury. When he arrived at Yankee Stadium late that afternoon, looking bleary eyed and disheveled, he brushed past wary reporters, went into his office, and slammed the door.

Meanwhile, at the other end of the clubhouse, a young woman from the *New York Times* was conducting a survey of Yankee players on the All-Star team voting. After about an hour, Martin reemerged from his office. Upon spotting the lady researcher, who was now sitting on the table taking notes, Martin confronted her, demanding to know what she was doing. The woman, Deborah Henschel, explained her mission, only to be told rudely by Martin to "get your ass out of here." Later that day Henschel and the *Times* filed a formal complaint with both the Yankees and the American League, charging that Martin had called her, among other things, a "hussy" and a "slut." Martin did say in his subsequent testimony that Henschel was "wearing a low-cut dress with slits up to here" and that she didn't look like she was a working reporter.

So now there was a whole new Martin brouhaha. Steinbrenner, after receiving a call from the *Times'* corporate relations department, announced there would be "an immediate and thorough investigation of the incident." He summoned third base coach Don Zimmer, trainer Mark Letendre, and pitcher George Frazier, all of whom were in the clubhouse at the time of the Henschel-Martin exchange, to give testimony.

All of them said they never heard Martin use those words, but Zimmer, who was by now thoroughly disgusted with working for Martin and covering up his late arrivals at the ballpark, admitted he wasn't within earshot of the incident. A few days later, Zimmer told Madden confidentially: "I can't wait for this year to be over. When it is, I'll be out of here so fast you won't even know I've gone." He kept his word, too. On the final day of that season, in Baltimore, Zimmer dressed in less than three minutes and raced out the door to the parking lot, where his wife was waiting in the car—with the motor running.

The Great *Times* Researcher Investigation thus exonerated Martin. In his official statement to that fact, American League President MacPhail noted with detached amusement that "this was apparently [Henschel's] first assignment of this nature as she is not a member of the *Times'* sports department. But I might also note that the timing was unfortunate, as Mr. Martin was under considerable extra pressure because of news stories reporting that he was about to be discharged. It was a case of bad timing all around."

Having survived all these crises, Martin somehow made it to the end of the year before he was fired again by Steinbrenner. The man named to succeed him was Yogi Berra.

Ah, but old Billy Martin adversaries, like Billy Martin, never seemed to go away, and nearly five years later, Martin was back at it again with the umpires and their union chief Richie Phillips, who had been a principal in the 1983 Dale Ford affair hearing.

In what would turn out to be the final days of Billy V in 1988, Martin was suspended and fined $1,000 for a dirt-throwing, dirt-kicking tirade against rookie umpire Dale Scott on May 30 in Oakland. The umpires all felt Martin had gone too far this time. As crew chief Richie Garcia said, "Let's put it this way, if my eight-year-old daughter picked up sand and threw it in someone's face, she'd be punished."

In the view of Phillips, the three-game suspension and $1,000 fine levied against Martin by American League President Bobby Brown was far too lenient. So Phillips and the umpires declared war on Martin.

"Billy Martin," said Phillips, "is going to have to sit in the dugout from now on with hands folded and his lips closed like a choir boy. We will no longer tolerate his tap-room behavior." In other words, the umpires were threatening to eject Martin if he so much as came on the field to argue a call or hollered at them from the dugout.

Martin, naturally, was outraged. So too was Steinbrenner, but only outwardly. "The umpires don't own the game," he said, "the owners own the game." Privately Steinbrenner was once again growing weary of Martin's constant foibles. And based partly on the counsel of his longtime special assistant/troubleshooter, Clyde King, he was coming to the conclusion that bringing Billy back again had been a terrible mistake.

From Oakland, the Yankees went to Baltimore for the final leg of what had become an exhausting trip for everyone. Martin had decided to take his suspension for the three weekend games in Baltimore. There was an off-day on Thursday, however, and Martin apparently spent most of it drinking. When Madden strolled into the Marriott Hotel bar around 10:00 P.M. , he saw Martin sitting there with a couple of other reporters and shortstop Rafael Santana.

Slurring his words and barely able to stay on his bar stool, Martin babbled on semicoherently about how the umpires were getting totally out of line. "They think *they're* the game!" he kept saying. "They've got too much power."

The reporters were more concerned about Martin getting into a fight and ruining what was left of their off day. No one wanted to start interviewing bar patrons, waitresses, and cops at 1:00 A.M. So Madden took it upon himself to escort Martin out of the bar, onto the elevator, and up to his room. There was a sigh of relief from the others when he returned to the bar. A while later the bartender brought over Martin's bar tab.

"I got that," said Santana, who two months earlier had been publicly trashed and humiliated by Martin for dropping a double-play relay at second base in Toronto. The reporters couldn't help but laugh over the irony.

The end of Billy V came suddenly. As usual, he was making the worst of a bad situation, giving Steinbrenner more than enough ammunition to fire him. He was officially given the hook on June 23, following a disastrous three-game series in Detroit in which the Yankees lost all three in sudden death. Reliever Cecilio Guante, who had been grossly overused all season by Martin, gave up game-winning homers in the first two games, including a stunning two-out, ninth-inning grand slam to Alan Trammell that gave the Tigers a 7–6 win in the second game.

But the unofficial firing of Martin actually had come on June 19, during a Sunday afternoon loss to the Indians in Cleveland. Steinbrenner had dispatched Clyde King to follow the team and observe it on this road trip. King was especially aghast at Martin's handling of the pitchers.

That Sunday in Cleveland, Martin all but blew a game for the sake of making a point with the front office about a pitcher he didn't like—Tim Stoddard. For weeks Martin had been imploring the front office to trade or release Stoddard, and he made little use of the hulking right-hander. Nevertheless, he brought him into this game in the sixth inning, with the Yankees trailing, 4–3. From his first pitch it was clear that Stoddard had nothing, but Martin allowed him to face eight batters all told, the results being two hits, five walks, a run-producing wild pitch, and one out. By the time Martin finally made a move to the bullpen, Cleveland's lead was 7–3 with the bases loaded and nobody out.

Martin sent for Charles Hudson, who hadn't been instructed to start warming up until Stoddard was in the process of walking the final batter he would face. Although Hudson told bullpen coach Jeff Torborg he wasn't ready, Martin waved him in anyway. The first batter Hudson faced, light-hitting catcher Andy Allanson, hit a grand slam. King, sitting in the press box, shook his head in dismay.

Afterward Martin snapped at reporters' questions regarding his use of Stoddard. "I can't read his mind," he said. "I didn't know he was gonna walk all those guys. They say he's capable of pitching up here, so I let him pitch." Privately, though, Martin indicated that he felt he had made his point, telling one coach: "They gotta release him now. I showed them how bad he was. He's finished."

Eventually Martin would prove to be right, as Stoddard was released in August. But Martin's treatment of him that June 19 didn't finish Stoddard—it finished Martin. That night, King reported to Steinbrenner and told the owner Martin was once again out of control. "My advice to you is that we make a change," King said, "but only if you make it quickly. It's not too late to save the season, but it's getting close to it. The pitching is a mess, and the team morale is slipping fast."

King's advice to Steinbrenner was to find a man who had the presence and stature to come into a volatile situation with so many high-salaried, huge-ego superstars and restore order. As usual, King had done his homework, having scoured the major league scene for just such a man. His suggestion: Dallas Green.

Steinbrenner was in full agreement, having grown sick of the bar scenes, the umpire bouts, the battles with new general manager Bob Quinn, the irrational use of the pitchers, and the breakdown of team discipline. The only thing was he didn't want to bring in Green in the middle of the season. As always, he was afraid of adverse fan reaction to the firing of Martin. And in Steinbrenner's mind Green wasn't a big enough name in New York to replace Billy. Instead, he wanted to first attempt to talk Lou Piniella into coming back. Just as Piniella had helped Steinbrenner sell the hiring of Martin to a skeptical public by agreeing to serve as general manager, he was eventually used to ease the firing of Martin.

Sadly for the Yankees, with each successive term as Steinbrenner's manager, Martin was less and less effective and more and more burned out. It was a situation rife with irony since even stronger than his need for alcohol was his need to manage the Yankees.

Steinbrenner overlooked Billy's first need and preyed on the second. He kept bringing Billy back because he thought it was good showbiz. There was never any thought of what it was doing to both Billy and the proud Yankee tradition of stability and order.

Hire Billy. Fire Billy. Hire Billy again. Fire Billy again. This was the Yankee circus of the 1980s, with Steinbrenner the ringleader and the once-defiant Martin thrust (however willingly) into the role of a performing seal. The fans love Billy, the Boss rationalized, and they'll come out to watch the Yankees because Billy creates excitement and puts fannies in the seats.

What Steinbrenner never seemed to understand was that each time he fired Billy, it took a little more out of Billy. It is awfully hard for anyone—fans, players, or media—to take someone seriously when he's fired five times from the same job. The minute Steinbrenner brought Martin back for another go-round, speculation would begin as to when Billy would be getting fired.

But if Steinbrenner refused to see what a travesty all the Billy Martin firings had become, Billy didn't see it either. Much like an old fighter (which he *was* too often in saloons across the country) Billy could not see that his skills had been eroded by too many last calls and too many firings. He could not see that he was not the same cunning, calculating, and combative manager he'd been in 1976–77. He could not see that he had become a caricature of himself.

In the end, many in Billy's legion of fans from the '70s grew weary of the circus act Steinbrenner had turned Billy into in the '80s. Those who remained Billy's loyalists didn't want to hear the media reports of his drinking and losing control. They would just as soon have killed the messenger.

So be it. For them, let Billy Martin be remembered for 1952—when he made the World Series-saving catch of Jackie Robinson's windblown pop fly against the Dodgers. Or 1953 when he hit .500 against the Dodgers to earn World Series MVP honors. Or Billy I, when he truly was a great manager who derived much of his success from being able to defy and deter Steinbrenner's interference. For Billy's diehard fans, Billy II-V and all the sad speculation of a Billy VI blur into memory like so many midnight cocktails.

CHAPTER 2

On the Rocks
with a Twist of Lemon

Although a bulbous nose and bulging belly may have outwardly belied the fact, Bob Lemon was a man's man through and through. He was tough enough to have gone one-on-one with both Reggie Jackson and Lou Piniella when each stepped over the line with him. He was also a hard drinker who knew no curfews when it came to late-night imbibing, and rare was the sports writer or appointed coach/companion who could go the distance with him. He had no fear of failure and no illusions of his own self-importance as manager of the New York Yankees.

When Lemon took over the 1978 Yankees from Billy Martin the team was in a state of chaos, trailing first-place Boston by 9½ games on July 25. His quiet ways and "let's just have fun" approach were the perfect antidote to Martin's frenzied intensity. Years later, Graig Nettles, a great friend and admirer of Martin, marveled at the difference Lemon made on the ball club in 1978. "The way things were going with Billy and Reggie and all that stuff," Nettles said, "it wasn't a question of where we were going to finish but *if* we were going to finish. Most of us were accustomed to the craziness, but that year was setting new levels. Lem came in and all the bullshit stopped."

Nevertheless, there were some incidents during the Yankees' drive that Lemon had to defuse. Naturally he gave credit to another source: the newspapers, or rather the lack of them. The New York City newspapers went on strike beginning August 10, leaving only three papers, the *Newark Star-Ledger,* Long Island's *Newsday,* and the Westchester-Rockland Gannett newspapers, to travel with the Yankees.

"Without those back pages screaming about stuff every day, I was able to keep things quieter," Lemon said. "I hated to see the newspaper guys out of work, but the strike, coming when it did, did more for us than if we picked up a twenty-game winner."

The Yankees wound up going 48–20 under Lemon, but not without several controversies that occurred with far less fanfare because of the strike.

Ed Figueroa, a talented but temperamental Puerto Rican-born right-hander who finished with a 20–9 record, had been unhappy with Martin. He felt Martin didn't appreciate him and took him out of games too soon. But it didn't take long for him to find Lemon equally unsatisfying as a manager. In one particular game when Lemon came to the mound to take him out, Figueroa stormed into the clubhouse before the manager got to him to take the ball. Lemon made the change and proceeded directly to me clubhouse where he confronted Figueroa. According to one player who witnessed the scene, Lemon told Figueroa: "You go along with me, you'll win a lot of games and make a lot of money. You pull that shit again, though, and you're finished."

Figueroa became a dominant force after that on the '78 Yankees, especially down the stretch. By the end of the year he was crediting Lemon for making his season, and also taking the opportunity to knock Martin.

"Billy thinks he knows pitching," Figueroa said. "He don't know shit. He hurts pitchers because he doesn't know how to use them. And he screws pitchers up because he always wants to call all the pitches. He don't know what's right for me to throw. Lemon, he's a pitcher. He knows what to do."

If Figueroa was a likely bet to give Lemon trouble, then Reggie Jackson and Mickey Rivers—a pair of free spirits, but of vastly different kinds—were even more likely. True to their nature, both presented Lemon with problems that had to be dealt with.

Before a game against the Orioles on August 12 at Baltimore's Memorial Stadium, Lemon was sitting in his office with Moss Klein. He was fiddling with the lineup card, seeming more preoccupied than usual.

"You having trouble?" Klein asked.

Lemon flipped the card over to him and said, "How do you think this one is going to go over?"

Klein took a look and replied, "Not too good."

Batting eighth in the order was Reggie Jackson.

Lemon explained his reasoning: Reggie was in a 3-for-28 slump. A left-hander, Mike Flanagan, was pitching for Baltimore, and Reggie struggled against Flanagan's assortment of off-speed pitches. The other lefty hitters in the order, Chris Chambliss and Graig Nettles, were going good at the time and also had far better success against Flanagan than Reggie. Lemon didn't want three lefty hitters in a row, so he dropped Reggie all the way down.

"I've got to treat him like I would any other guy," Lemon said. "Let's see how he handles it."

Naturally Reggie didn't handle it well at all. To Reggie, being asked to bat eighth in the batting order was the same as if Lemon had gone on national TV questioning his manhood. Reggie, proud number 44, thought the only spot for him in the order was number four. He had barely learned to deal with the insult of batting fifth.

When the lineup was posted, Reggie took one look and headed for the trainer's room. A few minutes later, after he was convinced this was not someone's idea of a practical joke, Reggie went over to pitching coach Clyde King.

"I don't feel so good today," Reggie told King. "Tell the man I'm sick and can't play."

King, aware of the lineup, relayed the message to Lemon, who shrugged, crossed Reggie's name out, and replaced him with Roy White. That was Lemon's style. No fuss, no public outbursts.

Reggie was used as a pinch hitter during the game, which the Yankees lost, 6–4. After the game, reporters approached Reggie about the situation.

"I'm sick," he said.

"Sick from batting eighth?" the reporters pressed.

"Just plain sick," Reggie replied, motioning to the manager's office.

When Lemon was asked about the situation, he said simply, "He told Clyde he didn't feel good. I'm not gonna play a guy who isn't feeling good. I hope he gets a good night's sleep and feels better tomorrow."

The next day Reggie waited for the lineup to be posted. He was batting seventh. He played and kept on playing.

Rivers, of course, was a challenge for any manager. A lovable, if infuriating, character, he tested Lemon less than a week after the Reggie incident. Rivers was always seeking advances on his salary and was miffed when a request was denied during the Yankees' West Coast road trip in August. On August 18, in Seattle, he let his annoyance be known by failing to hustle on a couple of plays. Then, two days later, Rivers and Roy White showed up late for the finale of the Seattle series. They had been at Longacres Racetrack. Lemon, who had already made out the lineup with Rivers in his customary leadoff spot, was fuming by the time they arrived. To make matters worse, Rivers came in laughing and acting like nothing was wrong.

Lemon immediately called them into his office, slammed the door, and could be heard yelling: "I've had enough of your bullshit. You're not playing, and I don't know if you'll play again!" He then cut into Rivers' Longacres winnings by fining him $250.

Although Rivers caused minor problems periodically the rest of the way, he played hard for Lemon after that. So too did everyone else, as the Yankees completed one of the greatest comeback drives to the pennant in baseball history, culminating with their 5–4 victory over the Red Sox in the sudden-death playoff game. It was typical of Lemon, however, that he would downplay his personal role in the triumph. In fact, in the privacy of his office at Fenway Park, long after the crowds of reporters and well-wishers had cleared out, he revealed to Moss Klein he almost didn't let Bucky Dent go to bat to hit the dramatic three-run homer that was to rank among the greatest moments in Yankee history.

"I almost screwed the whole thing up," Lemon confessed. He went on to explain that if the inning had unfolded differently, he would have pinch-hit for Dent. With one out, Chris Chambliss and Roy White each singled. Lemon then called on Jim Spencer to hit for Brian Doyle, who was playing second base for the injured Willie Randolph. Spencer flied out and now Lemon wanted to hit for Dent, his number nine hitter. Because of the Randolph injury, however, he was out of infielders. "I needed Fred Stanley to go in for Doyle at second," he explained. "Otherwise, I'd have hit for Bucky and who knows what the hell would have happened. Shows you how smart I am."

The Yankees went on to win the World Series, but Lemon's roller coaster ride to the top crashed before he even had time to savor it. His son, Jerry, 26, was killed in a car accident in November. Lemon was never the same.

He returned as manager for 1979, but it seemed apparent to most people around the club that his heart really wasn't in it. There just hadn't been enough time to recover from the tragedy.

The Yankees got off slowly and were dealt a crippling blow when Goose Gossage tore a ligament in his thumb in a shower-room scuffle with Cliff Johnson, April 19. With the team continuing to play poorly in mid-June, owner George Steinbrenner showed up on a road trip to Minneapolis and Texas.

The flight to Texas, following a 4–2 loss to the Twins (after which Steinbrenner blasted the team for its "lackadaisical performance"), was a wild one with a lot of laughing and blaring of music out of the players' tape decks. All the while, Steinbrenner, seated in the first-class section across from Lemon, was steaming. The next morning Steinbrenner found Lou Piniella in the coffee shop and questioned him about Lemon. He later questioned Tommy John and, after talking to both players, came away with the same feeling the team had: Lemon just wasn't in the game.

Steinbrenner reluctantly decided to make a change, although he couldn't decide whom he wanted to take over as manager—Gene Michael, who was managing at Columbus, or Martin, who had been scheduled to return in 1980, with Lemon moving into the front office as general manager. He finally opted for Martin, deciding that the switch that had worked wonders in 1978 might work equally well in reverse now. In '78 the Yankees had needed a calming effect. This time they needed a jolt of intensity to shake them out of their doldrums.

But while all this was occurring, Yankee president Al Rosen, Steinbrenner's front office chief and Lemon's close friend from their playing days together in Cleveland two decades earlier, was reaching his breaking point with Steinbrenner. To dump Lemon after what he had accomplished only a year earlier was unconscionable as far as Rosen was concerned. To bring back Martin, whom Rosen detested, going all the way back to when they were bitter rivals as players, made the firing even more abhorrent. As Rosen once explained his feelings about Martin: "I couldn't warm up to him if I were embalmed with him."

Despite Rosen's vehement objections, Steinbrenner went ahead with the change. A few weeks earlier, he and Rosen had also clashed over the scheduling of a twilight game between the Yankees and Angels in Anaheim, in which hard-throwing Nolan Ryan wound up starting for California. When Steinbrenner discovered the game had been scheduled for a 5:30 P.M. start, meaning that Ryan's heaters would be that much harder to spot, he went into a rage and attempted to get it changed. During a conference call with Commissioner Bowie Kuhn, he ripped into Rosen for agreeing to a scheduling situation that, in his opinion, put the Yankees at such a disadvantage. He also said he knew nothing about it, blaming it on the incompetence of his baseball people, which further infuriated Rosen.

On the day of the All-Star Game in 1979, Al Rosen resigned as Yankee president. Ironically, Lemon had come to Seattle to serve as the American League manager, based on his having won the pennant in '78. Klein and Madden, after getting word of Rosen's resignation, rushed over to the dugout to get Lemon's reaction before the word got out. Lemon, of course, knew of his friend's resignation. When asked by Klein and Madden what reason Rosen might have had for quitting, Lemon replied: "You can take just so much shit. You take it up to here [pointing to his waist], and up to here [pointing to his shoulders], but when it gets to here [pointing to the top of his head], you got to get out before you choke to death."

Still, Rosen remained forever grateful to Steinbrenner for having brought him back into baseball when he needed a job. "I've always told George: 'I love you as a friend, I just can't work for you,'" Rosen said.

Unlike Al Rosen, Bob Lemon wound up having to work for Steinbrenner twice—and the second time proved far more painful an experience than the first. In the end it reduced a proud man to tears. In September of the strike-torn 1981 season, Steinbrenner fired Gene Michael as Yankee manager after Michael publicly challenged the Boss to either fire him or stop threatening him. Lemon was asked to take the reins again, and just like 1978, he guided the Yankees through the playoffs and into the World Series against the Dodgers. Unlike '78, however, the Yankees didn't win the world championship.

Thus few if any Steinbrenner-watchers expected Lemon to start the 1982 season as Yankee manager. The 1981 season really had ended badly for everyone connected with the Yankees. After winning the first two games of the '81 World Series from the Dodgers, the Yankees proceeded to drop the next four. The one final, enduring image of that World Series was Tommy John waving his arms in disgust at the TV cameras as if to say, "I don't believe it!" after Lemon had removed him for a pinch hitter in the fourth inning of the last game with the score tied, 1–1. The Yankees went on to get clobbered 9–2 in the finale, prompting Steinbrenner to issue a formal apology "to the people of New York and to Yankee fans everywhere."

Lemon's strategy was questioned openly in the dugout by his players earlier in the series, too. In game three, with the Dodgers leading, 5–4, in the eighth inning behind Fernando Valenzuela, the Yankees put their first two runners aboard on singles. With pitcher Rudy May due up, Lemon looked up and down the bench.

"Where's my bunter?" players later quoted him as saying.

Looking out at May, who could just as easily have bunted as anyone else, no one answered.

"Where's my fucking bunter?" Lemon reportedly repeated, only more emphatically.

Finally, after scanning the entire dugout, Lemon implored, "Where the hell is Murcer?"

Bobby Murcer, sitting at the end of the bench, was astounded. As the Yankees' number-one left-handed power hitter on the bench—and the man with the best chance of tying or winning a ball game with one swing of his bat—he never figured on being called upon to bunt. But called upon he was, and unaccustomed as he was to bunting, he squared around and popped into a double play, killing the rally. Years later Lou Piniella would kid Murcer by calling out to him across hotel lobbies or restaurants: "Where's my bunter?"

At least Murcer didn't have the temerity to challenge Lemon as Reggie Jackson did in the 1978 World Series. Everybody who witnessed that Series will certainly remember Reggie's memorable nine-pitch confrontation with the Dodgers' hard-throwing rookie right-hander Bob Welch. What is not generally known was the dugout confrontation that occurred between Reggie and Lemon after Reggie struck out to end the game.

Embarrassed over being beaten by a rookie and leaving the tying and potential winning runs stranded at first and second, Reggie's first instinct was to redirect the blame for losing the game. So as he entered the dugout, he complained about being distracted by having the runners going, even though with two out and a 3-2 count the runners had to be moving. Lemon heard Reggie's remarks and immediately charged him. Before he could land a blow, players and coaches intervened and pulled Lemon away. He had made his point, though. He might be a nice, laid-back guy on the surface, but he wasn't going to be shown up by anyone, even Reggie, some 20 years his junior and about the most physically imposing player on the ball club.

Anyway, inasmuch as Steinbrenner had fired Dick Howser in 1980 for losing the playoffs 3 straight to the Royals (after winning 103 games during the regular season and setting an all-time Yankee attendance record), there was every reason to expect that Lemon would similarly be discharged for failing to win the '81 World Series. But a funny thing happened to Lemon on the way to Steinbrenner's guillotine the second time: he stopped drinking. Or at least hard drinking.

When Steinbrenner finally got around to summoning Lemon to Tampa for a face-to-face meeting in December of 1981, he fully expected to tell the 61-year-old skipper he was through again. When Lemon showed up looking rested, restored, rejuvenated, and, most significantly, some 24 pounds lighter, Steinbrenner was genuinely stunned. Lemon, it seems, had sworn off his beloved Canadian Club after the World Series, embarking on a rather unique wine-only diet.

"It beats quitting," he explained.

Upon seeing this new Lemon, Steinbrenner changed his mind. He hired Lemon back and, at the winter baseball meetings in Hollywood, Florida, a few days later, announced: "This time he'll get a full season, no matter what."

It should be noted that Steinbrenner was not the only person surprised and elated by Lemon's new diet. Lemon was never one to drink alone, and if he asked you to join him, you didn't say no. The problem was once you joined him, there was no way you could keep pace with him. The man, quite simply, was a champion drinker.

During spring training in 1982, when Lemon had been ordered by Steinbrenner to stay away from hard liquor, he set out on a massive wine-drinking spree. At the Galt Ocean Mile Hotel Bar in Fort Lauderdale one night, Moss Klein asked Lemon if he was developing a taste for wine. Considering the quantities of it he had been consuming that spring it certainly seemed like he was enjoying its pleasures.

"I hate the fucking stuff," Lemon said.

"Well, why then do you keep drinking it?" Klein asked.

"I'm trying to drink the state dry," Lemon replied. "I'm gonna drink all the wine in Florida and then the asshole [Steinbrenner] will have to let me move on to something else."

One night Lemon went to dinner with Klein and Bill Madden at a little French restaurant across the street from the Gait. When the waitress came over, Lemon decided to break his regimen and ordered a Canadian Club and water—only to be told that wine was the only alcoholic beverage served by the restaurant.

"For crissakes," Lemon said, "does the asshole own *this* place, too?"

Madden spent many a late night keeping company with Lemon at the bar. Of all the Yankee managers he'd covered, he was especially fond of Lemon. He found him to be great company and oftentimes insightful on the ways of life in the baseball business. On one particular night, however, Madden tried—unsuccessfully—to elude the skipper. It was around 12:30 A.M. and Madden had just completed writing his *Daily News'* game story in the Yankee Stadium pressroom. In the adjoining dining room/bar, Lemon had been having a few drinks with one of his coaches, Mike Ferraro, who was fading fast and looking to make his exit.

Madden, too, was tired and ready to head home to New Jersey. But as he stealthily made his way across the dining room toward the exit door, he heard a voice behind him.

"Where ya goin', 'Meat'?"

It was, of course, Lem.

"Headin' home," Madden replied.

"What's your hurry?" Lemon said. "The night is still young."

"Yeah, but I'm tired. Gotta get up early tomorrow."

"Since when are you too tired to have one?" Lem asked. "You young guys today can't go the distance."

Madden, realizing he was being taunted, looked around the room. Lou Napoli, the pressroom bartender, had long since gone home and the few people left in the room were, for the most part, sucking on the ice cubes from their last call.

"I'd really love to, Lem," Madden said, "but even so, Louie's gone and the bar is closed. There's nothing here to drink."

Undaunted, Lemon summoned Madden over to his table. Madden, figuring he'd just sit a few minutes while the manager finished his drink, obliged. It proved to be a fatal mistake. For as soon as Madden sat down, Lemon reached down under the table and produced a full bottle of Canadian Club.

Setting the bottle on the table, Lemon grinned: "My bar is *never* closed, 'Meat.'"

To the best of anyone's knowledge, Madden's departure at 3:30 A.M. was—and still is—the record for the latest any writer ever left the Yankee Stadium pressroom.

There's an epilogue to this story: Lemon never did reveal the "source" of his endless supply of spirits. However, "reliable sources" later confirmed that the bottle of Canadian Club he'd produced from under the table was pilfered from Steinbrenner's private stock upstairs.

It did not take long into the 1982 season to see that Lemon was going to have a hard time sticking to his new diet. His tolerance was tested by Steinbrenner from day one of spring training, when the Boss brought in the famed Olympic hurdler, Harrison Dillard, to conduct special running drills. Over the winter Steinbrenner, in a stroke of inspiration, decided to restructure the Yankees from a team of traditional left-handed power to a team of speed. He let Reggie Jackson go as a free agent and, to replace him, acquired Ken Griffey and Davey Collins, a couple of outfielders who had been principal catalysts in the Cincinnati Reds' run-and-gun game.

Griffey was to replace Reggie in the outfield, but with Dave Winfield, Jerry Mumphrey, Lou Piniella, and Bobby Murcer all also vying for playing time in the outfield, Lemon had no idea what he was supposed to do with Collins. Meanwhile, the New York press was quick to ridicule this latest Steinbrenner scheme. "Bronx Bombers now Bronx Burners," they joked.

Steinbrenner, growing increasingly irritated by the jokes being made about his team, called Lemon and the coaches into his trailer for meetings nearly every day. Oftentimes they would last as long as a couple of hours.

The Yankees went 9–16 that spring, a portent of what was to come in the regular season. By the end of the spring, the look of rejuvenation was gone from Lemon's face. The constant phone calls, meetings, and beratings—not to mention the state of confusion the camp was in—were fast taking their toll on him. It was becoming increasingly apparent he wasn't going to get that "full season." Less than a week into the season, Bob Lemon was wishing he wouldn't.

After losing both ends of a much-delayed opening-day doubleheader against the White Sox (a freak April snowstorm in New York forced postponements of the Yankees' scheduled opening series against the Rangers and prompted Steinbrenner to schedule workouts at West Point), the Yankees embarked on a three-city road trip to Detroit, Texas, and Chicago.

By the time they hit Chicago, they were 3–3 on the trip and 3–5 overall. But Steinbrenner was unrelenting in his harassment of Lemon and was already leaking stories to the press that he had made a mistake in bringing Lemon back.

On the off day in Chicago, April 19, Lemon arranged to take the traveling writers corps and his coaches to dinner at Jimmy Gallios' Miller's Pub, a popular, informal sports hangout. Because there were nearly a dozen people in the party, everyone split up into different taxicabs from the hotel.

Lemon was among the last to get down to the lobby—as it turned out he had been on the phone with Steinbrenner—and he wound up sharing a cab with Bill Madden. The cab-driver, who evidently didn't speak English, nodded affirmatively when Madden instructed him to take them to Miller's Pub. As they headed out into the Chicago night, Lemon turned to Madden.

"I've had it, Meat," he said. (He called everyone "Meat.") "I can't take it anymore."

"What do you mean?" Madden asked.

"I've had it with this guy," Lemon repeated. "No matter what I do, I can't please him. I'm going to quit."

"Are you serious?"

"As serious as I've ever been. I don't need this aggravation. Life is too short. I'm only telling you this because you've been a good friend. I can't take it anymore."

By now neither Madden nor Lemon had noticed the cabby had been driving around for more than 10 minutes and obviously had either misunderstood Madden's instruction or had no idea where Miller's Pub was. If Lemon considered Madden a good friend, the feeling was mutual. And so Madden abandoned his job as a reporter at this moment and offered some friendly advice.

"Don't quit," Madden said.

"Why?" Lem asked.

"Because if you do, you're liable not to get your money, and I'd hate for that to happen to you. If nothing else, the aggravation he's put you through has to be worth something. Play it out, let him fire you, whatever. But don't quit."

"I'll think about it," Lemon replied. "But right now I want to have some fun with my friends. Let's have a few drinks. Hey, where the hell are we anyway?"

Madden looked out the window and recognized nothing. He yelled at the cabby.

"Hey, what the hell's the matter with you? I said Miller's Pub! Where are you taking us?"

Somehow the cabby finally found Miller's Pub. After many rounds of drinks everyone, with the notable exception of Lemon, finally had some ribs. It soon got to be midnight and most of the party headed back to the hotel.

"It's still early, Meat," Lemon said to Madden. "You and Mikey [Mike Ferraro] come with me. I got a great place I want to take you. Ever hear of Billy Goat Tavern? It's a place all the newspaper guys go. Stays open all night."

Just what Madden and Ferraro wanted to hear. But they knew Lem was hurting and wanted to be around friends he could talk to. So off they went to the Billy Goat Tavern, a rundown little bar underneath a railroad trestle in what looked to be the middle of nowhere. It was now after one when the three got out of the cab. There was no one around, and Madden was certain they would never find their way back to the hotel from this place.

Lemon instructed the cabby to wait for them and marched across the street to the Billy Goat.

"You guys are gonna love this place," he repeated. "You make your own hamburgers here!"

Madden looked at Ferraro, who raised his eyeballs.

They were in the Billy Goat about a half an hour, drinking and talking, when the cabby came in and spotted Lemon. "Hey, mister, I'm not waiting out there anymore. Are you comin' or what?'"

Lem reached into his pocket and pulled out a $50 bill. "Here," he said to the cabby, "take off. We're stayin'."

Madden and Ferraro both sighed. Now Madden was positive they were stranded. Their last hope of being rescued had been shooed off by Lem, who was now, finally, making his own hamburger.

"I'll sleep on what you guys suggested," Lemon said. "I've never been a quitter before. It's just . . ." He didn't finish but just let the sentence trail off.

It was sometime well after 3:00 A.M. when they walked outside the Billy Goat Tavern. No sooner had they hit the street when a lone, empty taxicab pulled around the corner.

"I told you this was a popular place," said Lemon.

The Yankees went on to win both games in Chicago, then came home and lost three of four to the Tigers. Even though they won the fourth game to put them at 6–8, Lemon was taken out of his misery by Steinbrenner. He had an inkling when he found out that Gene Michael had been summoned from his West Coast scouting duties to New York by Steinbrenner. Sitting in his office with Madden before the game, Lemon asked, "Is something in the air?"

"I understand Stick's been called back to town by Steinbrenner," Madden said.

"Well then," Lemon said, "I guess this is it. Like the jilted husband, I guess I'll be the last to know."

That day, after the game, Steinbrenner made it official. Lemon was out again as Yankee manager and Michael was in again. To the surprise of many, Lemon showed up at Yankee Stadium the next morning to face the press. As he sat in the pressroom, though, patiently answering ail the embarrassing questions, his emotions—always in check—suddenly got the best of him. For the only time in Madden's memory, he saw Bob Lemon on the verge of weeping.

"Are you relieved?" some radio guy asked him.

Wiping his eyes, Lemon looked up and replied: "I was disappointed, not relieved. I thought I might go nine this time, but I didn't even get out of the first inning. I had a bad spring, so why didn't I get it then?"

As he watched this good and decent "man's man" being nearly reduced to tears, Madden could think of only one thing. He wished he had kept his mouth shut a week earlier in that taxicab and not advised Lem against doing what he wanted to do. He wished Lem had gone ahead and told Steinbrenner to shove the job, back in Chicago. If he had, he wouldn't have had to go through this public humiliation. And he still would have gotten his money.

They all did.

As it turned out, though, there was a postscript to all this. After his second firing, Lemon went back home to Long Beach, California, where he was made a permanent West Coast scout by Steinbrenner. Supposedly, as his reward for taking over the team twice in times of crisis—and for conveniently forgetting the promise of being named general manager for 1980—Lemon was told he would forever be the Yankees' highest-paid scout. His salary: $35,000. That, of course, was quickly eclipsed when Steinbrenner began firing subsequent managers such as Billy Martin and Michael and had to pay them off as well as high-salaried scouts.

Then, in the winter of 1988, Steinbrenner called in Lou Piniella, then the team's general manager, to go over the team's scouting budget.

"We're getting a little top-heavy in our salaries," he said. "I want you to pare the budget. We don't need Lemon anymore. Start with him."

"I can't do that to Lem," Piniella said.

"Well then," said Steinbrenner, "have your assistant do it."

So it was left to Bob Quinn, the assistant general manager, to phone Lemon on the West Coast to tell him his services were finally being terminated for good. After diplomatically beating around the bush for a few minutes, Quinn concluded his monologue to Lemon by saying he was being let go.

"What the fuck are you talking about, Meat?" Lemon said. "Don't you know? I've got a lifetime contract."

CHAPTER 3

Little Big Man

Dick Howser was a latter-day Don Quixote. Throughout his entire one-year reign as Yankee manager, it seemed he was always jousting at windmills far bigger than he. Though small in stature (he listed at five-eight but actually seemed much shorter), Howser was big on bravado and the courage of his convictions. History tells us he was the most successful of all Steinbrenner managers in terms of regular-season accomplishment. Under Howser, the 1980 Yankees won 103 games—the most of any Steinbrenner-owned Yankee team— and set a one-season attendance record that stood until 1988. Along the way, though, Howser had to fight off one challenge after another to his authority.

Certainly Howser's size and his long association with the Yankees as a loyal coach, subservient to a foursome of managers before him, were against him in his efforts to be taken seriously. Just as certainly, his might and mettle were tested early and often, by such opponents as Graig Nettles, Ed Figueroa, Luis Tiant, Lou Piniella, Bobby Murcer, and ultimately and inevitably, the principal Yankee owner, George Steinbrenner. Howser jousted with them all and, like Don Quixote, emerged victorious until the end, when he was caught up in the Steinbrenner windmill that gets all Yankee managers.

The first player to joust with Howser was Graig Nettles, one of the many proud veterans from the Yankee glory years of 1976 through 1978 who was now beginning his decline. Nettles, 35 that 1980 season, had missed most of spring training with a fractured pinky and got off to an even worse start than was customary for him (4 for 27 with just 2 RBIs on a wrong-field double). The Yankees had a slow start, too, dropping six of their first nine games in 1980. In the course of three games in early April, Howser pinch-hit three times in the late innings for Nettles. The third time, Nettles came back to the dugout, slammed down his bat and helmet, heaved his batting glove, and proceeded to punch out some lights in the runway that leads to the clubhouse. When the game ended and the Yankees returned to the clubhouse, Nettles had dressed and departed, a violation of club rules.

Howser used quiet diplomacy to defuse this problem. When asked by reporters what he planned to do about Nettles, he replied: "If our record was 6–3 instead of 3–6, I probably would have let him bat. I don't blame him for being miffed. I guess I'd be mad, too. But I'm not concerned about it. I'll have a talk with Graig and let him know why I did it. He's just not ready yet."

A few days later Ed Figueroa presented the next challenge to Howser, going into one of his familiar pouts after being removed from the starting rotation with just three starts. But Figueroa had injured his arm in spring training and, as it turned out, was all but finished because of the injury. Against the advice of the front office, Howser had decided to take Figueroa north with the club from spring training and started him off in the rotation despite his suspect physical condition. When Figueroa struggled with a 6.00 ERA, 2 losses, and just 1 strikeout in his first 12 innings, Howser replaced him with left-hander Tom Underwood, who went on to win 13 games that season. It was another sign that Howser would not be held hostage by the past. He would give the Yankee veterans their due, but ultimately he was going to do what he felt was right for the 1980 Yankees, not the '78, '77, or '76 Yankees.

It was in June that Howser had his first public joust. This time the opponent was Luis Tiant, whose glove-throwing rage after being removed from a game in the eighth inning with a 4–0 lead against the Blue Jays brought out the previously suppressed fire in Howser. There were about 25,000 fans in the stands at Yankee Stadium that day. Tiant had pitched brilliantly, holding the Blue Jays to two hits when Barry Bonnell tripled and Alvis Woods walked on four pitches with two out in the eighth. Out came Howser, much to Tiant's surprise. Once he realized Howser was going to call in Goose Gossage to finish the game, Tiant, another of the prideful veterans on the Yankees, dropped the ball and stormed off the mound before Howser could get there. And when he got to within a few feet of the Yankee dugout, Tiant heaved his glove into the seats.

Howser, furious at being publicly shown up in front of 25,000 fans and his 24 other players, followed Tiant down the runway and into the clubhouse where he engaged in a shouting match with the 40-year-old pitcher. At the end of it, Howser shouted, "That'll cost you $500." Later, a still-seething Howser told a couple of reporters: "I wish it had been $5,000, but I don't want to spend all winter in court battling a grievance. I've got better things to do with my time. We've got a good club here. If I put up with that, I'll lose the respect of everyone out there."

As the season moved on, the Yankees began to jell under Howser. A 19–7 May and a 19–9 June put them comfortably in first place, but all was still not love, honor, and obedience between the veteran players and their rookie manager. In particular, Lou Piniella and Bobby Murcer, two of Howser's closest friends on the ball club when he was coach, began creating monumental headaches for him as manager. With Reggie Jackson in right field having his finest season as a Yankee, and Bob Watson, Jim Spencer, Oscar Gamble, Piniella, Murcer, and rookie Joe Lefebvre, Howser had no shortage of bats. The problem was keeping them all happy and finding them all enough playing time. For the most part, Howser did a lot of platooning, which worked well except in the minds of Piniella and Murcer, who could be heard grumbling in the clubhouse almost daily.

Years later, Howser never forgot what he felt was a betrayal by two players he expected to be leaders and allies in his maiden voyage as Yankee manager. His relationship with Murcer never healed. With Piniella it took an unexpected confrontation—and subsequent apology—in the bar of the Pontchartrain Hotel in Detroit in 1981 to forgive and forget. In a quirk of fate, the Yankees had just checked into the Pontchartrain, while the Royals, whom Howser was then managing, were in the process of checking out, having played the Tigers that day. Piniella was in the bar having a drink with Bill Madden when Howser strolled in. At first the greetings between Piniella and Howser were warm and light-hearted. But Howser had obviously had a few drinks already, and when Piniella said something about how happy he was to see his former manager doing well in Kansas City, away from the constant turmoil that was the Yankees, Howser couldn't resist getting in his digs. "You and Murcer sure didn't help that situation for me," he said firmly. "I haven't forgotten that, either."

Piniella, realizing Howser was serious, turned serious himself. "You know, Dick," he said, "of all the things I've done in this game, that's the one thing I'm ashamed about. I was wrong, dead wrong. I'm not afraid to tell you that right here, in front of Billy. This isn't for print, but I really came to respect you as manager that year, Dick. You were right, and I was wrong to question you like I did. I want you to know that."

As it turned out, the Nettles, Figueroa, Tiant, Piniella, and Murcer incidents that 1980 season were mere brushfires for Howser compared to the holocaust that burst out over three cities in mid-August in one of the wackiest road trips in Yankee history. Despite the Yankees' fast rise into first place under Howser, they were unable to shake Earl Weaver's Baltimore Orioles, who were similarly playing at a .600 pace from June on.

On August 14 the Yankees went into Baltimore for the start of a pivotal 5-game showdown series with Orioles. It was also the start of a grueling 13-game, four-city road trip that continued on to the West Coast. The trip started badly when the Yankees lost three of the five games to the Orioles, including the last two, which shaved their lead to a scant half game. It was enough to throw Steinbrenner into panic. His response was to issue a stinging criticism of Howser as well as the players. It was Steinbrenner's first public vote of no-confidence for his manager, whom he second-guessed for failing to have a slumping Eric Soderholm sacrifice after Bob Watson had led off the ninth inning of the final game in Baltimore with a single.

"I could not believe my ears when he [Howser] did not have Soderholm bunting," Steinbrenner said in a phone call from his Tampa office to Bill Madden in Seattle the next day. "There seems to be an old axiom among baseball people that you have to play for the win on the road. That's a lot of crap! You've got to play for the tie first, and Howser should've had Soderholm moving over the runner.

"Dick Howser is my manager and he's done a helluva job to keep us in first place the way he has. But as a fan, I have the right to question his strategy. He knows his job rests on the bottom line, and the bottom line is winning. You've got to give Earl Weaver all the credit. He's a wizard, and our guy's a rookie manager. He said he wasn't gonna let Reggie Jackson beat him, and he didn't. But he also did it by pitching to him, not just by walking him—and look how many times Reggie struck out [seven, while going 2 for 17 in the five-game series]. I wouldn't invite Weaver to Christmas dinner, but you've got to give the devil his due."

Naturally it didn't take long for word of Steinbrenner's blast to reach Howser, and when it did, Howser was genuinely hurt. He was also genuinely annoyed and wasn't about to let Steinbrenner show him up any more than he would any of his players. So after winning the first two games in Seattle and feeling perhaps a little cocky, Howser told Moss Klein and Bill Madden to stay a little longer in his office.

"There's something I want to say…" he began, then looked over to his close friend, batting coach Charlie Lau. "I don't know, Charlie, should I?"

"Say it!" Lau implored.

"Should I?"

"Say it! Get out your notebooks, men."

As Howser began again, Madden and Klein took out their notepads.

"You know," Howser started, "now that I'm competing against a rookie manager [Maury Wills, who was in his first year managing the Mariners], I know it's very important for me to win."

Klein and Madden immediately got the drift. The sarcasm was dripping out of Howser's mouth.

He went on: "I'd hate like hell to be intimidated here after being intimidated in Baltimore by the other guy this week. If I can't be manager of the year, maybe I can at least be rookie manager of the year. Hell, that would really be something to win—especially in my first year."

He was grinning widely now, as was Charlie Lau. Klein and Madden couldn't help but chuckle, too. This was, after all, terrific stuff. Howser was lashing back at Steinbrenner, but ever so subtly. As the season wound down, he would do so a few more times, too, always stopping short of a direct blast at the Boss. For their part, Madden and Klein would frequently needle Howser, asking him if anyone had invited him to Christmas dinner yet. Steinbrenner, however, considered the battle lines drawn. Howser had taken him on in the newspapers, and now he was just waiting for the right opportunity to exact his revenge.

In the meantime Steinbrenner implemented a series of roster moves and personnel shufflings while the team was in Seattle and did not ask for Howser's approval of them. His first move was to bring in Clyde King to serve as a personal pitching coach for Ron Guidry. (Through the years Steinbrenner frequently has brought in King to work with the pitchers, always over the manager's head. It is a move that is perceived by both the manager and the players as Steinbrenner's "planting" of a spy in the clubhouse. King has understandably felt uncomfortable in this role, but as a self-acclaimed "company man," he has remained Steinbrenner's most loyal servant.)

It seemed that Guidry had been struggling, and the decision was to send him to the bullpen for a while.

Bill Madden was sitting in the Seattle press box, having just filed his story of Howser's response to Steinbrenner, when he got word of Guidry going to the bullpen. Spotting Guidry warming up, playing catch along the first base line, he rushed down onto the field to ask him about it.

"Are you really going to the bullpen, and if so, whose idea was it?" Madden asked as he began approaching Guidry.

"Is this an interview?" Guidry yelled back, "because if it is, you have to stay over there behind the white line. Go ahead, ask me what you want."

Hollering his questions to Guidry, some 20 feet away, was the strangest interview Madden could remember ever having conducted. But it soon got even crazier when Jim Spencer strolled in from first base and interrupted.

"There's something I want to say, too," Spencer said. "I have a prepared statement for you."

"Wait a minute," said Madden, "what's your problem?"

"Don't you know?" Spencer said. "They flew in a first base glove for Murcer today. They want him to play first base."

"Well," said Madden, "you'll just have to wait your turn. I have to finish up with Guidry first."

When he got done with his long-distance interview with Guidry, Madden turned to Spencer, who by now had pulled a piece of paper out of his pocket and began reading from it.

"My rebuttal to Mr. Steinbrenner is that I've been a professional first baseman for sixteen years now and I've always done the very best I can. I cannot be motivated by a person who does not know a thing about baseball. I wish Bobby Murcer all the luck in the world, but if he can learn in one week what it took me eighteen years to learn about first base, then I tip my hat to him."

By now it was clear to Madden that this was going to be one of those days. Everybody was popping off, and Madden was running out of notebook paper and wondering how in the hell he was going to get all these zany developments into one concise *Daily News* story. His next stop was the dugout where Howser was sitting, watching the team take infield practice.

"What the hell is going on around here, Dick?" Madden asked.

"What do you mean?" replied Howser, grinning from ear to ear. "Everything's normal."

Howser went on to say that Guidry had volunteered to go to the bullpen and that it wasn't going to be a long stay. He also said he didn't mind King's presence, even though he had to find out about it in the newspapers and not through Steinbrenner.

"Well then," asked Madden, "what about the experiment to make Murcer a first baseman?"

"George always has the statistics," Howser said, alluding to the fact that Steinbrenner was evidently trying to get Murcer more at-bats, "but it's still my prerogative to do what I want. He obviously feels Murcer can help us as a first baseman."

"What do you think, Dick?"

Howser just smiled.

"Well, when do you think we can expect to see Murcer playing first base?"

Howser smiled even wider. His expression told you everything you had to know. The first base glove for Murcer was never seen again.

The next day the trip moved on to Anaheim, but the Looney Tunes weren't over yet. Seems that Steinbrenner, concerned about the lack of infield depth, recalled second baseman Brian Doyle from Columbus and ordered Chicken Stanley to be put on the disabled list. Only thing was, Chicken didn't know he was hurt. A few minutes before game time, he came right into the press box and sought out Madden and Moss Klein.

"I want you guys to know," he said, "they're putting me on the disabled list against my will. There's nothing wrong with me. Go ahead and write it."

Klein looked at Madden. "Do you believe this trip?" he said. "They're all going crazy. Now they're even coming up into the press box to tell us things."

Throughout all the craziness, Dick Howser guided the Yankees to a first-place finish. But in the playoffs that year, the Yankees were swept by the Royals, which meant Howser had failed to make Steinbrenner's "bottom line." It is doubtful anyone who watched those games will ever forget two indelible moments: George Brett's gargantuan three-run homer off Goose Gossage into the third tier of Yankee Stadium's right field seats, the decisive blow in the final game; and Steinbrenner blustering and waving derisively at Howser's third base coach, Mike Ferraro, after Willie Randolph was thrown out at home plate attempting to score all the way from first in the eighth inning of the second game. It had taken a perfect throw from Brett to get Randolph, after Royal left fielder Willie Wilson overthrew the cutoff man, but Steinbrenner, who was sitting among the Yankee wives, was incensed.

The Ferraro flap ultimately led to Howser's firing as Yankee manager, for despite the playoff sweep, Steinbrenner obviously felt he needed a little more ammunition to pull the trigger on Howser.

Immediately after the playoffs Steinbrenner went into seclusion, refusing to discuss Howser's future. But then, a few days after the World Series, word leaked out of Tampa that Don Zimmer, a good friend of Steinbrenner's, had been offered the job of Yankee third base coach. Howser, who had defended Ferraro vigorously after the Steinbrenner blowup over the Randolph play, was called at his home in Tallahassee, Florida, and asked for his comment on the Zimmer report.

"George still hasn't talked about it," he said, "but I would think I should be given the courtesy of approving or disapproving the coaches that are added to the ball club. You know, I have to work with these guys every day. Certainly as manager I should be able to say who's going to coach and who's not going to coach."

Well, that did it. Now, in Steinbrenner's eyes, Howser had openly challenged him.

"I don't appreciate Dick Howser popping off like this," he said. "Howser I can't figure out. I'm very upset. I'm very disappointed in him. My staff is in agreement with everything I have projected, and we're not quite ready to have Dick Howser start running the New York Yankees totally yet."

The die was cast, but a few more days of silence passed before Howser and general manager Gene Michael were summoned to Tampa for a meeting with Steinbrenner at the Boss' hotel, the Bay Harbor Inn. The three met for a couple of hours, after which it was agreed that Howser would not return as manager and would be replaced by Michael. As a "sweetener" to go quietly, Steinbrenner agreed to pay off the mortgage on Howser's new house in Tallahassee.

About a half hour later, though, on his way to his farm in Ocala, Steinbrenner suddenly had second thoughts. It was not revealed at the time, but he pulled his car over on the highway and called Michael back at the Bay Harbor to tell him he wanted Howser to come back.

"I've thought about it, Stick, and it just isn't right," Steinbrenner said. "Dick deserves to come back. Tell him I've thought it over and decided that. Tell him we want him to come back."

Michael was delighted by the Boss' change of heart. For one thing, he had gotten to enjoy the general manager's job, even when so often it meant serving as a buffer between Steinbrenner and Howser. For another, he believed in his heart that Dick Howser was the best man to manage the New York Yankees.

So as soon as Steinbrenner hung up, he rushed down to the Bay Harbor Bar to meet with Howser.

"George has thought it over, Dick," Michael said. "It isn't right what we decided on tonight. He wants you to come back."

But Howser's downcast mood was not at all brightened by this sudden 360 by the Boss.

"I'd rather leave it this way, Stick," he said.

Michael was taken aback. "Why? He wants you back. I want you back. We've been a good team, you and I, and I know we can do it all next year."

"I just don't want to go through it again," Howser replied.

"These last few weeks, especially, my stomach's been upset and I just haven't felt good. No, let's leave it as it is."

A day later, Steinbrenner called a press conference at Yankee Stadium. Even by Yankee standards, this was a classic exercise in absurdity.

As reporters filed into Steinbrenner's huge office at the stadium, the Boss sat behind his round desk. To his left was a table with three trays of bite-sized roast beef, ham, and turkey sandwiches, the kind with toothpicks in them to hold them together. Across the room, against the window that faced out onto the field below, sat Dick Howser. He was sitting almost sideways so as not to have to face Steinbrenner. Throughout the press conference he seemed to be staring blankly out the window as Steinbrenner spoke.

"Does anyone want some sandwiches?" Steinbrenner began. "A drink anyone?"

No one responded, so Steinbrenner continued. He explained that Howser had decided "not to return" as Yankee manager because of a lucrative offer to go into real estate in Tallahassee. Michael would be stepping down as general manager to take over for Howser.

According to Steinbrenner, the reason it took so long for this decision to be made was "because Dick wanted to make sure he was doing the right thing."

To that, someone asked Howser why he didn't want the job anymore.

"I have to be cautious now," he said slowly. "It's just...that the other thing popped up."

Steinbrenner went on to say that "at no time" had there been put any conditions or "rules or commands that Dick had to live by to return as manager. The door was open for him to return, but he chose not to accept."

"Were you satisfied there were no conditions?" somebody asked Howser.

"I'd rather not comment on that."

Finally Moss Klein turned to Howser and asked, "Dick, were you fired?"

"I'm not going to comment," Howser said again.

Steinbrenner then jumped in. "I didn't fire the man," he insisted. "I think it's safe to say Dick Howser wants to be a Florida resident the year round."

Howser said nothing. After a few more uneasy minutes, the reporters began to put away their notebooks. Just as they were about to get up, somebody suddenly asked Howser if he had any advice for his friend Stick Michael.

"Yeah," he said with a return of his old wit, "my advice to him would be to have a strong stomach and a long contract."

With that, everyone got up and left. As he stood behind his desk, watching them all filing out, Steinbrenner, looking almost forlorn, was shaking his head.

"Nobody ate any sandwiches," he said.

It should, of course, be noted that Dick Howser's stay as a Florida real estate entrepreneur lasted all of eight months. On August 31, 1981, he gave up his lifelong dream of staying in Florida "the year round" and accepted the job as manager of the Kansas City Royals. Four years later, he managed the Royals to the world championship.

Tragically, he scarcely had time to savor his greatest triumph. On July 18, 1986, after complaining of headaches and a stiff neck, Howser was discovered to be suffering from a malignant brain tumor. He fought a gallant fight, even coming back and managing the Royals the following spring. But on June 17, 1987, he died in St. Luke's Hospital in Tallahassee. He was 51. Among the eulogies paid to him that day was this statement from George Steinbrenner:

> Firing Dick Howser and not re-signing Reggie were the two biggest mistakes I ever made with the Yankees. It's true Dick and I had our problems. He resented me making suggestions. He was an intensely proud individual—a tiger. In a way, we were a lot alike. And we both knew we couldn't work together.

CHAPTER 4

Take This Job and Stick It

Considering how close they would become, and how many roles Gene Michael would play in George Steinbrenner's kingdom, the incident that initially brought "the Stick" to the Yankee owner's attention was strange. Hilarious, in retrospect, but strange.

In 1973, a few months after he had purchased the Yankees, Steinbrenner attended a game in Texas. He was a pure novice when it came to baseball—some would say this hasn't changed after all these years—and he positioned himself in the stands to watch his team take infield practice.

Naturally Steinbrenner was expecting a drill that would make General Patton proud—a slick study in precision and discipline, preferably with a John Sousa march playing in the background to provide cadence. Imagine, then, the horror in Steinbrenner's eyes when he watched one player prance onto the field and throw his glove frantically into the air, only to have a hot dog fly out of it!

Steinbrenner had no idea who the player was, but he made a note of the uniform number and told manager Ralph Houk he wanted the player severely disciplined, benched, or even traded for this blatant act of frivolity. Once he realized the Boss was serious, Houk called Michael, the guilty player, into his office and told him, between laughs, that he was deep onto Steinbrenner's shit list.

Michael was often the victim of pranks such as the hot dog caper because he had a phobia about small crawly, creepy creatures. Players are quick to pick up on these phobias and torment their teammates about them—as Phil Rizzuto learned a generation earlier. The hot dog had been placed in Michael's glove by Hal Lanier, who, years later, wound up managing the Houston Astros.

So it was, then, that Lanier could be credited with bringing Gene Michael to Steinbrenner's attention, because from that day on, the owner closely monitored the tall, slim shortstop. As time passed, though, Steinbrenner no longer viewed Michael as a hot dog man. Instead, he saw a shrewd, intelligent baseball man with a sharp personality. "A bright young executive type" is the way Steinbrenner described him.

Thus, when Michael's career ended, Steinbrenner brought him back to the Yankees, first as a "walkie-talkie" scout in the press box in 1976, then as a coach, a minor league manager, and in 1980, as general manager. As general manager, Michael played a vital role. He was the middleman between Steinbrenner and manager Dick Howser. Michael and Howser were close friends, and Michael succeeded in bearing the brunt of Steinbrenner's verbal assaults on his manager before relaying the owner's often illogical suggestions to Howser. But when Steinbrenner decided to fire Howser after the Yankees were swept in the 1980 playoffs at the hands of the Royals, he turned to Michael, his all-purpose man.

As soon as he became manager, Michael learned the painful lesson: in Steinbrenner's mind, the least-knowledgeable person in the entire organization is the manager. And who's to say he's not right since so many of them have taken the job, knowing they would have no support from the owner and inevitably be fired.

As Michael once said to Moss Klein, sitting in a bar during one of those stormy periods in 1981, "In every other job I've had with him, he seemed to respect my opinion to some degree. But when you become his manager, it's like your IQ drops by 50 percent. All of a sudden you don't know anything."

Michael ran into immediate problems as Steinbrenner's manager when spring training began in 1981. Reggie Jackson was late reporting to camp, touching off your typical Yankee tempest. Of course, Steinbrenner wanted Michael to rip Reggie to the reporters. It would make for good back-page publicity back in New York, and it would also serve to knock Reggie down a couple of pegs. Michael was clearly on the spot and he knew it. "If I don't rip him real bad, then I'm in trouble, but if I do what Steinbrenner wants, then I lose Reggie," he said one night in the hotel bar. "It's a can't-win situation, but I guess I'm going to have a lot of these, aren't I?"

He was never more right. The '81 season was a strike-shortened year, and the Yankees wound up winning the first half title without realizing they were doing so. Since they were in first place when the strike began on June 11, they were awarded the first-half "title" and an automatic berth in the playoffs, no matter what happened in the second half. They couldn't lose. Was there ever a better situation to be Steinbrenner's manager? Ask Michael. He lasted 27 more days.

Even though the divisional playoff spot was clinched, Steinbrenner was in even more of a panic than usual when the Yankees began the second half playing lethargically. As the days went on, his calls to Michael to wake the team up became more frequent. There were meetings and more meetings. And complicating the situation was a prolonged slump by Reggie. Steinbrenner was ordering Michael to bench Reggie and to pinch-hit for him. Michael began to snap under Steinbrenner's pressure—so much so that one night he even used Aurelio Rodriguez, a lifetime .237 hitter, as a pinch hitter for Reggie.

Finally, on August 26, Steinbrenner ordered Reggie to undergo a complete physical examination. On the surface, Steinbrenner could say he was merely trying to determine if there was a reason for Reggie's slump. But as Reggie said and others suspected: "He's just trying to embarrass me. There's nothing wrong with me."

The badgering from Steinbrenner finally reached the breaking point for Michael. In late August the Yankees were in Chicago, not a good town for Yankee managers as history has shown. On August 27 they dropped the opener of a three-game series to the White Sox, 3–1. The next day, reporters gathered in the locker room before the game, awaiting Reggie's return from his physical. When Reggie arrived, however, he refused to talk and headed straight for the trainer's room. While the reporters waited, Michael sent publicity director David Szen to bring the group to his office.

Everyone just assumed Michael was going to say something about Reggie, Moss Klein even gave him his cue by asking the first question: "What can you tell us about Reggie?"

"Reggie's fine," Michael said, "but I don't want to talk about Reggie. I have something else to say."

As the reporters looked at each other quizzically, Michael pulled out a few sheets of yellow legal paper and began reading from them: "I heard from George again today. I'm tired of getting the phone calls after games and being told it's my fault that we lost. I thought I knew what I was getting into when I accepted this job, but I didn't expect it to be this direct and this constant.

"When I was general manager last year, George used to tell me he was going to fire Howser, but he never told Howser. But with me, he keeps telling me: 'Stick, I think I'm going to have to let you go.' So when he said it to me again today, I said: 'Fine. Do it now. Don't wait. I don't want to manage under these circumstances. Fire me and get it over with or stop threatening me. I can't manage this way. I've had enough.'"

Michael continued, ripping Steinbrenner more openly than any manager had yet dared. "I don't think people know what it's like to work for him," he went on. "I don't think it's right that I should constantly be threatened by him and yelled at in front of my coaches. He can take the job, but he's not gonna bring me down."

Steinbrenner was attending the game at Comiskey Park that night, and the writers, after exiting Michael's office, headed to the stands to find the early-arriving Yankee owner. Steinbrenner, seated with several of his upper-society friends, was clearly annoyed to be confronted by a group of reporters, and he subsequently showed no emotion when informed of Michael's remarks. "He has said enough for everybody already," Steinbrenner said. "Any discussion I have with my manager is supposed to be between my manager and me. If he thinks this will help him, that's his problem."

That night, back at the hotel bar, Michael told Klein he had no intention of quitting. "I'm not trying to force his hand, either," he said. "I know I'm going to be fired for this. But I just think people should know what it's like to work for him."

Later that night when Klein and a couple of the coaches adjourned to Michael's suite, the endangered manager began loosening up, laughing at the description of Steinbrenner being bothered by the reporters in the stands in front of his friends. "You know what my ultimate fantasy is?" he said. "Someday I'd like to buy a ball club and hire him as my manager. I think that would be fun."

The next eight days, however, were not fun for Michael. They were the ultimate Steinbrenner manager torture. Instead of firing Michael immediately, Steinbrenner kept his manager hanging, while completely shutting him off from communication from the front office. General manager Bill Bergesch and others were ordered not to speak to Michael, and Steinbrenner himself was unavailable to reporters. It was an eight-day cold war that ended when Steinbrenner telephoned Bob Lemon in Long Beach, California. Lemon's wife, Jane, answered the phone and said her husband was at the barber's. Steinbrenner got that number and called Lemon in the barber's chair and asked him to come back as manager.

The following week, after a cooling-off period, Michael was invited to Yankee Stadium to meet with Steinbrenner. The owner, feeling remorse as he always does when he fires a manager, told Michael he still regarded him "like a son." Accordingly, he asked Michael to take a front office job. But Michael, still smarting over being fired as manager after guiding the Yankees to a strong enough early showing to earn a spot in the postseason playoffs, said he still felt he had been a good manager.

"Sure you are," said Steinbrenner. "But why would you want to stay manager and be second-guessed by me when you can come up into the front office and be one of the second-guessers?"

As so often happens with Steinbrenner managers, Michael found himself back in the second-guess seat 14 games into the 1982 season when the owner decided to sack Lemon for the second time. It was April 26, an off day in New York, when Steinbrenner made the change. The next day the California Angels were due in town, and there were many who suspected Steinbrenner chose this time to fire a manager in order to overshadow the return of Reggie Jackson to Yankee Stadium. Jackson had joined the Angels as a free agent the previous winter after Steinbrenner virtually ignored him, never offering him the chance to return. In later years Steinbrenner would concede this was the biggest mistake of his career as Yankee owner and blamed it on Charlie Lau, the late former Yankee hitting coach, who, when asked his opinion of Reggie as a hitter, said he had "one, maybe two good years left."

On the night of April 27 it was the Yankees and Gene Michael, in his second debut as Yankee manager, who were completely overshadowed by Reggie—much to Steinbrenner's utter dismay and embarrassment. Coming into the series, Reggie had been in a slump, and Steinbrenner had privately been telling friends: "See, we knew he was through."

He wasn't—not by a long shot, which is precisely what he hit that night when he connected on a Ron Guidry fastball and blasted an electrifying homer off the upper deck facade in right field to seal a rain-shortened 3–1 Angels' victory. As Reggie circled the bases in delighted triumph not felt since his three-homer dramatics in the final game of the '77 World Series, the 35,458 fans rose to their feet, looked to the owner's box on the mezzanine level behind home plate, and began a spontaneous chant: "Steinbrenner sucks! Steinbrenner sucks! Steinbrenner sucks!"

Said Reggie: "The fans made a vocal expression that George made a mistake letting me go. They were able to say something a little more directly than I could."

The Yankees thought the incident was a riot. After the game they were laughing and high-fiving as if they had won—hardly an auspicious start for Gene Michael's second coming as Steinbrenner's manager. "What were they chanting?" dead-panned Rick Cerone. "I couldn't quite make it out."

Guidry, after saying little to the horde of reporters, called Klein and Murray Chass of the *Times* over to his locker. "I had to sort of try and keep from smiling," Guidry said. "I was keeping my glove over my face. It was about really the only fun I had in the game."

Oh, but what a commotion was brewing upstairs. Steinbrenner was beside himself over this display of public humiliation. Less than 10 minutes after the game was called by the umpires, Steinbrenner called a meeting of the manager and coaches in his office. The meeting was hysterical—literally.

As Michael and his coaches sat down, Steinbrenner began pacing around his office, repeating over and over, "This is the worst thing that's ever happened to me.... How could this happen?... How could the fans do this after all I've done for them and this team? I was humiliated. My family was humiliated.... I can't believe this..."

As he paced and rambled, Michael and the coaches were desperately trying to keep from laughing. At one point, though, Steinbrenner spotted coach Jeff Torborg suppressing his laughter with his hand over his face and exploded in rage: "You think this is *funny?* You think this is a goddamned *joke!* Didn't you hear what they were saying? 'Steinbrenner sucks, Steinbrenner sucks!' You think that's funny? How would you like it if they were chanting 'Torborg sucks, Torborg sucks'?"

With that he dismissed them, one of the few times a manager and his coaches left a postgame meeting with Steinbrenner with smiles on their faces.

Guidry, meanwhile, was called on the carpet by Steinbrenner the next day. After reading Guidry's comment to Klein and Chass, the owner was outraged at what he called a "betrayal." When Klein and Chass showed up in the clubhouse that day, Guidry called them over.

"Remember what I said to you guys last night?" he said. "Well, I didn't say it."

Klein and Chass both gave Guidry puzzled looks.

"Listen," Guidry added, "I know it isn't right, but it seemed like it would avoid a lot of problems all around if I just denied ever saying it. He called me in this morning and was going crazy over what I said. So when he calmed down a little, I said, 'I think those guys misunderstood me. I didn't say it that way.' You guys quoted me accurately, but please, let's just let it go."

Unfortunately for Gene Michael, things never got better and "Stick II" lasted all of 86 games. He was fired on August 4 with a record of 44–42. At a terse, impromptu 1:00 A.M. press conference in the Yankee Stadium press room following a doubleheader loss to the White Sox, Steinbrenner marched in and announced that Clyde King would be replacing Michael as manager. "I will answer no questions," he said and marched out. Earlier that night, in the sixth inning of the second game, in which the Yankees were slaughtered, 14–2, Steinbrenner ordered Bob Sheppard, the public address announcer, to read a statement saying that all fans in attendance would be entitled to free tickets to any future Yankee game.

"When I heard that," Michael said, "I knew I was gone again."

Ironically, after Steinbrenner had fired Michael the first time, in September of '81, he announced the following December at the winter baseball meetings in Hollywood, Florida, that Michael would return as manager for the '83, '84, and '85 seasons, with Lemon staying on for 1982. That afternoon, Michael, Dick Howser, and Billy Martin were all sitting around the bar at the Diplomat Hotel joking about the Yankee revolving manager's chair.

"You're coming back for '83, '84, and '85?" Howser said to Michael. "Well, then, I've got '86, '87, and '88."

"Okay," chimed in Martin, "and I've got '89, '90, and '91!"

"The crazy thing about all of it," said Michael, "is that I never got to 1983 because I got hired and fired again in '82!"

CHAPTER 5

Managing à la King

Clyde King was unlike the rest of George Steinbrenner's managers in one distinct respect: he was a tee-totaler. He wouldn't even walk into a bar, unless, of course, it was a salad bar. And Clyde hardly ever cursed, either. His general expression of surprise or dismay was "Garden peas!" But if Clyde didn't drink, smoke, or curse, he more than made up for all those abstinences by his appetite for food—almost any food.

Clyde loved to eat. Lots. Often. Rapidly. Among his favorites were ribs, cole slaw, pork chops, and desserts—especially ice cream. King dined frequently with Madden and Klein and loved regaling them with his stories of the old days in Brooklyn when he pitched for the Dodgers. He also loved evaluating the current players with them, probing them for their opinions. And while the end of the meal would have signaled adjournment to the bar with the other Yankee managers, with King it meant his special dessert order: "Pie a la mode with ice cream."

"But, sir," the waitresses would all reply, "'a la mode' *means* 'with ice cream.'"

"I know that," King would say, laughing, "but I want my ice cream with ice cream!"

And he'd always get it that way, too. One time, in Dino Cassini's, a favorite Italian restaurant of King's on 32nd Street near Madison Square Garden, Madden watched in awe as Clyde finished off a salad, a huge helping of spaghetti and meatballs, and then consumed two giant bowls of peach melba a la mode, each time asking the waiter to put "a little extra whipped cream on the top."

During Steinbrenner's 1:00 A.M. announcement of Gene Michael's firing following the Yankees' August 3 double-header loss to the White Sox in '82, the Yankee owner referred to King as the "interim manager." Obviously it can be said that *every* Yankee manager is an interim manager, especially those who served between Billy Martin's escalating Roman numerals. But King was truly interim in that there was no contract extension in his case. He was merely getting a pay boost—from his $35,000 scouting salary to $100,000 as the manager.

The Yankees were out of the race when King took the reins in 1982, and Steinbrenner basically wanted Clyde to oversee the final 62 games to get the feel of the team's problems and provide more insight for the inevitable off-season purge. Or as Bob Lemon, the first of the three 1982 managers, said when asked if he thought an "overhaul" might be in order after the season: "An overhaul? There's gonna be a damned holocaust!"

Clyde, a smooth talker who knew every angle, had been Steinbrenner's behind-the-scenes guy since 1974, when he joined the organization as a scout. He had been a pitcher for the old Brooklyn Dodgers in the forties and fifties, getting by on moderate talent and loads of smarts. Roy Campanella called him "professor" because of his studious, bespectacled appearance and his knowledge of every trick in the game. With Campy's help, Clyde cooked up numerous schemes to aid his pitching (his "bubble gum" pitch and his quick-pitching of players such as Willie Mays were just two).

After a few stints as pitching coach for several teams, and as manager of the Giants and Braves, King joined the Yankees with a reputation as a "pitching doctor." His knowledge of the mechanics of pitching enabled him to dissect the reasons behind pitchers' problems. Or at least Steinbrenner felt so. King quickly became a top adviser to Steinbrenner and also gained a reputation among others in the organization, deservedly or not, as Steinbrenner's in-house spy. Steinbrenner frequently moved him into uniform as a "co-pitching coach" whenever the staff was struggling, and King's frequent arrivals when Art Fowler was pitching coach inevitably created friction with Billy Martin. Fowler was always Martin's hand-picked pitching coach, a comrade-in-arms whose loyalty to Billy knew no bounds and no last calls. When Steinbrenner brought in King to work with Billy's pitchers, Billy rightfully perceived it as the Boss jabbing at him. It was also rightfully perceived as the first step toward Billy's demise as manager.

King had started the 1982 season as a scout. On June 11 he was named pitching coach, replacing Stan Williams, much to the upset of manager Gene Michael. On July 19 Steinbrenner elevated King as a "special assistant." Two weeks later he made him the manager, a position King accepted "reluctantly, but willingly."

After a few weeks on the job, however, King got the old managing bug again. There was no pressure on him to win because Steinbrenner had conceded the season as a lost cause. King was evaluating talent and attitudes, but at the same time he began asserting himself more than the players expected. In Kansas City, when Oscar Gamble was loafing, King laced into him in front of all the other players in the dugout, ordering him to "get the hell out of here and don't come back until you're ready to play."

Maybe if the Yankees had started winning steadily during those final two months Steinbrenner would have viewed King as a manager. But the team was consistently mediocre. As Piniella summed it up after one particularly awful loss to the White Sox in New York: "We stink. We absolutely stink." Nobody was blaming Clyde, but he knew his remote chance of coming back to manage for the start of a season in '83 was dwindling with each succeeding loss. Still, he held out hope.

For sure, King had a special way of dealing with the tough losses. Bob Lemon once said: "I never bring the tough losses home with me. I leave 'em at a bar somewhere along the way." Well, Clyde would leave *his* in a restaurant whenever he could. He didn't like fast-food joints, though. Fast food, to him, meant food eaten quickly. And when there wasn't a suitable restaurant or coffee shop open late, he would order room service.

The late September Yankee weekend in Milwaukee of '82 was especially discouraging to King. More than enough to drive a man to eat...and eat. The Yankees were swept in a three-game series at County Stadium by the Brewers, who were headed to their first pennant. The scores of those games were 14–0, 6–4, and 14–1, completing an eight-game road trip that started with five losses in Baltimore. An 0–8 journey against the two top teams battling for the AL East title took away the Yankees' chances of even being September spoilers. As Graig Nettles said when asked which team, the Brewers or Orioles, was better: "It's hard to tell. They both look good, but you have to remember they've been playing us."

It was after the Saturday night loss to the Brewers that King invited Klein and Madden to join him in his suite in the Pfister Hotel, where the Yankees stay in Milwaukee. The way to tell when Clyde was especially upset was when he needed company to eat.

Klein and Madden finished working, returned to the hotel, and went to Clyde's room. What awaited them was truly a touching sight: Clyde had set up a little table in the room with three places set with knives and forks and napkins and glasses. It was like a kid setting up a make-believe party. As Klein and Madden entered the room, Clyde informed them the food was on its way. "A feast," he proclaimed.

As the minutes passed, Clyde began getting a little impatient. Suddenly there was a knock at the door. Room service indeed! Clyde had arranged to have barbecued ribs with coleslaw, beans, and potato salad delivered. The works. And there was a very special delivery boy: Yogi Berra.

"I think you got enough here," Yogi said, standing in the doorway with three huge bags.

"Won't you stay?" Clyde said.

"Nah," said Yogi, "I already ate. Besides, I can see you got some things you want to talk about."

So Yogi left—without even so much as getting a tip.

While they ate, there wasn't much talking. But after the ribs had been consumed, Clyde began unveiling certain plans he had for the ball club. He would elaborate later with the same two writers when the team was in Boston, but this was the first real inkling that he was really hoping to be asked back as manager. He started off in his usual manner, asking Klein and Madden some questions about the team that he already had the answers to. He asked them what they thought of Catfish Hunter and what they thought of Roy White. Could these guys, not with the Yankees at that time, be good coaches? Clyde was laying the groundwork for his coaching staff. The talk about coaches and players that might be available went on for a long time. Klein and Madden left the suite in the wee hours of the morning, firmly convinced that Clyde was anxious and ready to return as manager. A week later, over lunch at a place in Boston called Charlie's Eating and Drinking Establishment, he went further.

As the three of them finished their lunch and Klein and Madden ordered coffee, Clyde pulled out a large yellow notepad. On it he had mapped out all the changes he planned to suggest to Steinbrenner regarding players and coaches. He even had prospective free agents he was going to recommend signing as well as trade proposals. He had Hunter and White listed as prospective coaches along with Billy DeMars, who was then still the Phillies' highly regarded batting coach.

"I don't know if we can get all of these people," Clyde said, "but this is what I'm gonna recommend to Mr. Steinbrenner. Believe me, boys, I've done my homework here. Right now we're not a very good ball club. I think he realizes this. We have a lot of work to do, but I think with these changes, we can win next year. What I'd like is to manage a couple of more years, then step aside and give it to a younger man after we've gotten this team back to what it was again."

On their way back to the hotel after lunch, Klein and Madden could not help but be pleased by the prospect of King returning as manager. If there was anyone Steinbrenner seemed to have faith in, it was King, and maybe, for once, there wouldn't be the constant adversarial relationship between the owner and the manager that ultimately led to turmoil and failure.

But as they each got to their rooms, Klein and Madden found telephone messages waiting for them. They were, ironically, from two different Oakland writers, but the message was the same: "You might be interested to know that the A's today gave Steinbrenner permission to talk to Billy Martin."

It seemed that Martin had done the impossible: he had worn out his welcome in his hometown after almost single-handedly turning the Oakland A's around from a moribund team in ruins (after Charlie Finley had sold and traded off all their good players and fired all their top scouts) to a division champion in 1981. A's President Roy Eisenhardt had simply grown tired of Billy's foibles, and Billy, as was his wont, was doing everything to get himself fired. The last straw was when he trashed his office at the Oakland Coliseum in a drunken rage.

All Klein and Madden could think of was poor Clyde. At almost the same time he was going over his master plan with them for rebuilding the team, Steinbrenner was laying the groundwork to bring back Billy Martin for the third time. When the two reporters called him in his room to tell him of the news from Oakland, King was speechless.

Shortly before the seventh game of the World Series in St. Louis, the A's announced out of Oakland that Martin had been fired. By mid-November, Martin's return as Yankee manager was a foregone conclusion, although there had been no official word from Steinbrenner. He avoided questions, saying no decision had been reached and that King was still the manager.

King thus still held out hope, especially since there was the real possibility that Steinbrenner was delaying the final decision to see if Martin could make it through the off-season without getting involved in any embarrassing drunken bar fights. If that was the reason, then history was on King's side, because Martin would surely wind up getting plastered in some bar and have his name spread all over the papers for popping some guy. And then Steinbrenner would talk about "Yankee image" and "the best interests of the team," etc., etc., and turn to King.

But on one Saturday afternoon that November, Klein decided to make a checkup call to King, just to make sure he hadn't received any word from Steinbrenner. King hadn't, he said, and they continued talking. As they talked, King's wife, Norma, came in with the mail and handed a Yankee envelope to Clyde. Obviously it was a check, and Clyde, without interrupting the conversation, opened it as he was speaking. Then Klein heard him mutter, "That no good—"

Klein asked what happened. Very likely, if King hadn't been on the phone, he probably wouldn't have revealed what he found in the check. But his angry reaction got him talking. The check was for an amount based on his $35,000 scouting salary—not the $100,000 managing salary he was supposed to continue receiving at least until the end of the year.

Steinbrenner and his accounting people were doing their off-season payroll paring, and since Steinbrenner had no intention of bringing King back as manager, he reduced him back to the lower pay scale. To continue paying him for the final six weeks of the year would have amounted to an extra $7,500 or so. But despite King's loyal service, Steinbrenner obviously wasn't impressed. King eventually called the accounting department to tell them of their "mistake" but was informed that the salary change came "from the top." Billy Martin was not named manager until January, but Clyde King's hopes of returning ended that day when his check came in the mail.

Still, King was shrewd enough to continue getting his checks from Steinbrenner long after his brief managerial stint. By 1989 he'd climbed again to a yearly salary of $100,000, the result of his having been severed as Steinbrenner's general manager in 1986. Behind the scenes he still held considerable influence, too, although that appeared to be dissipating somewhat in 1989.

Indeed, King seemed to fall out of power with Steinbrenner at about the same time he fell out of a tree house in his backyard in Goldsboro, North Carolina. He'd had the tree house built for his grandchildren and was doing some work on it in mid-April while taking some time off from his scouting duties.

He fell nine feet, suffering a fractured collarbone and other injuries, but when Steinbrenner was first informed of the accident, he raged: "What the hell was he doing at home? He's supposed to be scouting."

By midseason the 63-year-old King had recovered and was back on the road as an advance scout. But by that time his advice was no longer being sought by Steinbrenner. King's offense? It was he who'd recommended to the Boss that Dallas Green be hired as manager.

CHAPTER 6

It Ain't Over Till It's Early

Most people around the Yankees, even the ever-skeptical press corps, were naive enough to think it would be different for Yogi Berra. Oh sure, when Yogi was hired by Steinbrenner to manage the Yankees for the 1984 season nobody thought it would be for more than a year or so. It's just that because Yogi was so beloved by everyone in New York—Yankee fan or foe—everybody figured Steinbrenner would be far less ruthless and relentless in his callous treatment of him as manager than he had been with any of his predecessors. For a while Steinbrenner *did* tread carefully with Yogi, avoiding any public display of nonsupport or criticism. If there is one thing Steinbrenner fears most—and has paid dearly for—it is to have a popular former employee such as a Billy Martin, Lou Piniella, or Yogi go public on him. For that reason Steinbrenner has paid hundreds of thousands of dollars to his former managers to remain with the organization as "advisers" and scouts. As all of them would have to admit, it is nothing more than hush money.

Yogi Berra never got hush money, which, in the eyes of many, made him the most honorable of all Steinbrenner managers. Where Yogi made his mistake was gradually letting Steinbrenner know that going public about anything just wasn't his style. Once Steinbrenner realized that Yogi could be berated, harassed, and threatened just like all the others and wouldn't say anything publicly about it, Yogi's mystique was shattered. In a way, though, he still got the best of Steinbrenner. When he was fired in April of 1985, he told Klein and Madden that he was through as a Yankee "as long as Steinbrenner owns the team."

Yogi was Steinbrenner's manager for all of 1984 and 16 games of 1985, the interim between Billy III and Billy IV. Actually, Steinbrenner had come close to making Yogi the manager on two earlier occasions. In June 1977, after Martin had been involved in that dugout scene with Reggie Jackson at Fenway Park in Boston, Steinbrenner was preparing to make a move but was talked out of it. And in June of '83, when Martin was beginning to self-destruct again, neglecting his job while carrying on with his girlfriend, Steinbrenner was about to turn to Yogi. Instead, he backed off and let Martin finish the season before giving the job to Yogi.

Why did Steinbrenner choose Yogi? Because there really wasn't anyone left in the "Yankee family" whom Steinbrenner hadn't used up and who fit the Boss' main criteria for a manager: a "name" guy who "can put fannies in the seats."

So in December of 1983, at another of those farcical press conferences at Yankee Stadium, Steinbrenner announced that Martin, who was hospitalized in Minneapolis at the time because of a liver condition, was being "shifted" to the role of consultant and scout. Not fired, mind you, but "shifted." Martin's attorney, the flamboyant New Orleans judge Eddie Sapir, attended the press conference in Martin's behalf and told everybody that "Billy accepted this move like the true Yankee that he is." Why didn't Martin complain? Because Steinbrenner, using a different sort of hush money, promised him that his uniform number, 1, would be retired during the season. Bill Madden later noted that Steinbrenner's idea of Yankee tradition is firing a man four times as his manager, then retiring his number and erecting a plaque in his honor alongside those of Babe Ruth, Lou Gehrig, Joe DiMaggio, and Mickey Mantle.

So there was Berra, seated in Steinbrenner's office during the press conference, listening to Steinbrenner trying to come up with reasons for making this change. "What I want is commitment," Steinbrenner said. "All I know is, no matter what time of day I walk into that clubhouse, no matter how early it is, there are always two guys in there—Pete Sheehy [the clubhouse man] and Yogi Berra."

Klein couldn't resist. "Did you ever consider giving this job to Sheehy?" he asked.

Unfortunately for Yogi, 1984 became the year of the Tiger before his Yankees ever had a chance to flex their muscles. Detroit got off to a record 35–5 start, and Yogi's Yankees were never in contention. As the situation grew more and more hopeless, Steinbrenner began calling more and more meetings. One of them was particularly memorable.

It was in July, just prior to the All-Star break. Steinbrenner summoned a weary Berra and his coaches into his office at Yankee Stadium. As they sat there, Steinbrenner launched into one of his tirades, directed mostly at Yogi. "You guys have really let me down," he said. "I gave you what you wanted. This is your team and look at it—look what's happening!"

One of the coaches said later that he was watching Yogi, who was staring downward, clenching his fists in an effort to control himself. But after another mention of "this is *your* team," Yogi exploded in rage.

"It was almost scary," said the coach. "Most of us had never seen Yogi that mad. He's always such a calm guy. Nothing seems to get him that excited—at least outwardly. But, man, this was something!"

Yogi jumped from his seat and fired a pack of cigarettes in Steinbrenner's direction. The pack hit the table directly in front of Steinbrenner's seat and a few cigarettes popped loose and landed on him. Nobody moved.

Yogi, now cursing freely, shouted: "This isn't my fucking team, it's *your* fucking team! You make all the fucking decisions. You make all the fucking moves. You get all the fucking players that nobody else wants. You put this fucking team together and then you just sit back and wait for us to lose so you can blame everybody else because you're a fucking chicken-shit liar."

There was silence, and Yogi stormed out of the room. As the coach said: "We all wanted to applaud and walk out, but nobody dared say a word. We didn't know what was going to happen next. A minute went by, and Yogi came back. He started screaming again. Then he leaned over the desk, with his arms on it, looking like a gorilla, and he kept cursing at Steinbrenner. Every phrase had the word 'liar' in it. All the while, though, George kept his cool. He never seems to get into shouting matches. He said a few things, very calmly. Then Yogi, having yelled himself out, left the room. You know what George said? 'I guess the pressure of losing is getting to him.' That's all. End of meeting."

Steinbrenner didn't fire Yogi over that meeting, figuring he'd get around to it at the end of the season. He would come to regret waiting, though, because the Yankees staged a second-half rally, going 51–29 after the All-Star break, the best second half record in the majors. They did it with a bunch of young kids called up from Columbus by General Manager Clyde King with Yogi's complete endorsement. Among them: third baseman Mike Pagliarulo, shortstop Bobby Meacham, outfielders Vic Mata and Brian Dayett, and a delightfully goofy pitcher named Joe Cowley. Although they were too far out to challenge the runaway Tigers, the strong second-half finish by the Yankees, coupled with the transfusion of young talent, created public support for Yogi's retention and high hopes for 1985.

The day before spring training '85, Steinbrenner showed up in Fort Lauderdale and had a meeting with Yogi and the coaching staff. Afterward he announced to reporters: "Yogi Berra will be the manager for the whole year. A bad start will not affect Yogi's status." It sounded as if Steinbrenner was still apprehensive about the power of Yogi's popularity, but Yogi knew better. When asked for his reaction to being given a vote of confidence for the whole season, he retorted: "That's what he told me. You don't think it means anything, do you?"

It certainly didn't. The last manager who had been guaranteed "the whole year" was Bob Lemon in 1982, and he was fired after just 14 games that year. Yogi lasted longer. He was fired after 16 games in '85, with a 6–10 record and a team beset by injuries.

Before that, it was long spring training for Yogi. All spring, Steinbrenner was calling meetings, and they began to take their toll on everyone. The season opened in Boston, with the Yankees losing 9–2. The next day was worse, 14–5. When reporters left the press box to head down to the clubhouse, Steinbrenner was waiting on the rooftop of Fenway Park, outside the box of Red Sox' co-owner Haywood Sullivan. During the course of a rambling talk on the Yankees' obvious failures, Steinbrenner stated several times that the next day's game was "crucial." To the best of anyone's memory, it was the first time the third game of the baseball season had been called "crucial." Nevertheless, the Yankees lost, 6–4, and after that it was just a matter of time before Yogi's "whole year" would become another false Steinbrenner promise.

The reporters knew it, and Yogi knew it. The Yankee players knew it, too, but they managed to win their next four in a row and five of the next six. But Steinbrenner was just waiting for another skid. The Yankees then lost three in a row, beat Boston at Yankee Stadium, and lost the first two games of a three-game weekend series in Chicago. Saturday night, after the second loss to the White Sox, Steinbrenner telephoned General Manager Clyde King, who was with the team in Chicago. He informed King that he had already had talks with Martin and Sapir and that he was going to make a change after the next day's game. Martin would be waiting for the team in Texas, the next stop on the trip after Chicago.

Yogi didn't know anything, but the reporters, most of them conditioned to the ill winds of a Yankee manager firing, had a good idea. But when they rushed downstairs to the clubhouse, Yogi simply complained about the umpires and the game-winning walk Cowley issued to White Sox shortstop Ozzie Guillen.

Finally, Clyde King arrived, having been delayed in the elevator. He had been appointed by Steinbrenner to give Yogi the bad news that everyone else already seemed to know. King entered the cramped manager's office and asked reporters to leave and closed the door. The reporters then began telling the players what was transpiring.

By the time King reopened the door, the scene in the clubhouse was bedlam. The firing of Yogi and the return of Martin represented twofold bad news for most of the players. Don Baylor kicked over a trash container in the middle of the room. Don Mattingly retreated to the trainer's room and was flinging metal containers against the wall. Only Rickey Henderson, whom Martin had always spoiled in Oakland, was pleased. A spring training ankle injury had kept Henderson out of the first 10 games of the season for Yogi, but now he was whistling and singing in the shower room while getting angry glares from the other players.

Steinbrenner, making himself unavailable as usual under these sort of uncomfortable circumstances, issued a press release: "The level of play dictated a change had to be made."

The players, asking for copies of the release, were muttering. "The level of *play?* After 16 games—10 of which Henderson, the newly acquired superstar catalyst, didn't play?" One by one, after tearing up the releases in disgust, they entered Yogi's office, shaking hands, hugging the deposed manager, and in a couple of cases, weeping. There had never been a scene like this at any previous Steinbrenner manager firing.

Yogi, true to his nature, refused to criticize Steinbrenner. "It's his team," he said. "He can do with it what he wants. It was going to happen sooner or later, so we might as well get it over now."

That afternoon, on the plane to Arlington, Texas, Moss Klein sat with Dale Berra, Yogi's son, who had been acquired from the Pirates in December of '84 in what was largely viewed as a gimmick—a father/son-manager/player scenario. Ironically, Dale had been one of the bright spots of Yogi's 16-game tenure in '85, batting .343 as the right-handed platoon for Pagliarulo at third base. Dale had been crying when he said good-bye to his father in the manager's office at Comiskey Park, and he was still red eyed on the plane. "He told me," Dale said, "'You have your career ahead of you, I've already had mine.' He said, 'Billy Martin's a good man. You've known him since you were a kid. Just play hard for him, that's all he asks. Don't worry about me. I'll be home watching what you do.'"

For Dale and the players this had been a full day of emotion and upheaval. For the traveling beat writers it was only half over. For when the Yankee charter arrived in Texas, waiting for them at the Arlington Hilton would be Billy Martin and Eddie Sapir.

But when the Yankees arrived at the hotel, the craziness that always seemed to accompany Billy Martin wherever he went had already started. The hotel's three elevators were all broken, and the hotel was in a state of mass confusion as everyone had to tote their luggage up some 15 to 20 flights of stairs, depending on which floor they were on. (It is interesting to note that this is the same hotel that forced the evacuation of everyone out onto the front lawn in May of 1988 as a drunken and battered Billy Martin stumbled out of a taxicab after being beaten up in Lace, a topless bar.)

The reporters were in a particular rush to get to their rooms since most of them had not yet filed "Part I" of the Yogi-Billy switch, which had been gathered "on the run" in Comiskey Park as the team made the getaway flight to Texas. It was thus a bedraggled-looking group of writers who arrived in Sapir's and Martin's suite. There was a huge platter of cheese and fruit on the table and a bar with a few bottles of spirits, glasses, and an ice bucket off to the side.

"Help yourself, folks," Eddie Sapir said. "Anybody want a drink?"

If ever there was a time a reporter might have wanted to have a drink with Billy Martin, this was it. Nevertheless, everyone passed and let Sapir go on with what, by now, had become the most hollow and repetitive dissertation in modern Yankee history.

"This time," Sapir said, "it's going to be different. Billy and George really *understand* each other now."

"That's right," echoed Billy. "George and I have talked a lot and we have an understanding. The main thing is, we both want to win."

The next day Steinbrenner was angered by what he called the "emotional" responses to Yogi's firing by the players and the media. He issued periodic statements through his publicity director Safety. The highlight: "I didn't fire Yogi, the players fired him. The way the team played is the reason Yogi is no longer the manager. Today's players have changed because of long-term, guaranteed contracts. Players have soft jobs and they're lazy. I keep hearing about this guy and that guy being unhappy. Well, if they're not happy, let them get jobs as cabdrivers, firemen, or policemen in New York City. Then they'll see what it's like to work for a living."

Later in the day, after having gotten even more worked up over all the sympathy for Berra, Steinbrenner issued another statement, calling the reaction of the players "almost humorous."

"I could care less what the players think," he said. "They're the ones who cost Yogi his job."

A couple of months later, Yogi, in his first public appearance since the firing, went to Cooperstown for the Hall of Fame induction ceremonies. Madden was there, too, and they talked privately while Yogi sat under a huge tent signing autographs.

"Have you gotten over it yet?" Madden asked.

"Would you?" Yogi said. "Sixteen games . . ."

Madden said something about Yogi being better off, but he could see and sense the man's wounded pride.

"I hope we'll be seeing you around the park," Madden said.

"Not as long as he's there," Yogi said.

He kept his word, too. After taking a job as a coach with the Houston Astros at the behest of his close friend, Astros owner John McMullen (who was once a limited partner of Steinbrenner's in the Yankees), Yogi no longer had any reason to ever visit Yankee Stadium during the summer. Then, on August 21, 1988, Steinbrenner gave him one: the Yankees decided to honor both Berra and Bill Dickey, the two catchers whose shared uniform number, 8, had been long since retired. The occasion was to erect plaques in the two catchers' honor to be hung in Monument Park along with all the other Yankee Hall of Famers—and of course, Billy Martin. It was announced that the Berra family would be on hand to take part in the ceremonies, but when the day arrived, none of them showed. Bill Dickey was honored alone.

Much to his regret, Steinbrenner came to realize Yogi was a man of his word, as his estrangement from the Yankees lasted 14 years. It wasn't until January 5, 1999, that Steinbrenner and Berra finally reconciled, with the Boss making a visit to Yogi's museum at Montclair St. University in New Jersey to personally apologize for the way that long-ago firing was handled.

CHAPTER 7

A Lou-Lou of a Mess (Parts I and II)

Gene Michael, Steinbrenner's "favorite son" before Lou Piniella, learned the hard way that you forfeited that status once you became Yankee manager. Then you became just like all the other bozos before you—or as Michael put it: "All of a sudden, after always relying on your expertise, George suddenly thinks you don't know anything."

Lou Piniella thought it would be different for him. He really did. He was, after all, even closer to Steinbrenner than Michael because of his having grown up in Tampa, Steinbrenner's adopted home town. And even during his playing days, Piniella and his wife, Anita, had often socialized with the principal Yankee owner and his wife, JoAnne. Steinbrenner loved Piniella, so much so that he even tolerated Piniella's irreverence at Yankee organization meetings. At one particular meeting, Steinbrenner was enraged over leaks to the press and ordered lie detector tests taken by everyone in the organization to determine the culprit. "I'll take one as long as you take one, George," cracked Piniella as everyone in the room broke into laughter. Only Piniella could get away with things like that—before he became the manager, that is.

Actually, Piniella got a taste of what managing the Yankees was all about a year before officially taking the job, and briefly decided he'd never do it. It was in midsummer of '85, during another period of Billy Martin turmoil, that Piniella became the interim Yankee manager for four days. It was enough not only to discourage his managerial ambitions, but also to cause him to consider other avenues of employment outside of baseball.

On July 28, before the final game of a series against the Texas Rangers at Arlington Stadium, Martin was experiencing severe back spasms. He consulted Dr. B. J. Mycoskie, the Rangers' team physician and an old friend of Martin's from when he'd managed in Texas. Dr. Mycoskie gave Martin a shot to relieve the spasms but, in the process, wound up creating a more serious problem by puncturing Martin's right lung, causing a 25 percent collapse.

By the second inning of the game, Martin was in severe pain. The game-time temperature was a sweltering 105 degrees, and the Rangers were already rolling toward an eventual 8–2 victory over the Yankees. Martin, at the insistence of trainer Gene Monahan, went to the hospital where the diagnosis of the punctured lung was made.

During the game, up in the press box, a report circulated that Martin had left the ballpark, disgusted with the Yankees' performance. Considering Martin's past history, such an incident wasn't out of the question. But by the time the game ended, Martin had returned and was in the clubhouse, in obvious pain. He was receiving care from Monahan, and as the team prepared to leave for Cleveland on the chartered flight, Martin returned to the hospital.

Piniella was the obvious choice as acting manager since it had already been announced by Steinbrenner that he was being "groomed" by Martin to take over in the future. And Martin had said that Piniella would be sitting next to him in the dugout at all times, "learning how to manage." Piniella, for his part, usually kept his distance and was uncomfortable about the "grooming" status, because he knew Martin never wanted to think in terms of successors.

But now, with the Yankees opening a five-game series in Cleveland and Martin remaining under doctors' care in Texas, it was left to Piniella to show how much he had learned. There was, however, a catch: Martin would stay in touch with the team by telephone during the games, by special arrangement between Steinbrenner and Peter Bavasi, then the Indians' team president. From his hotel bed in Texas, Martin would be able to instruct Piniella by phone, patched into the dugout from the Indians' switchboard. The most ironic part of this arrangement, though, was that the player chosen to be the middleman on the phone hookup was troubled catcher Butch Wynegar, who despised Martin and would eventually come to feel the same way about Piniella.

On July 29, the series opener, Bavasi arranged for an extra switchboard operator to field Martin's calls. Wynegar, who was on the disabled list but traveling with the team, manned the phone at the end of the dugout and relayed Martin's instructions to Piniella. Only the Yankees could come up with an idea as nutty and complicated as this. The situation was ripe for high comedy, and it truly was a laughing matter—to everyone but Lou Piniella.

That first night actually wasn't so bad because the Yankees won, 8–2. Martin, according to Piniella, "called about eight or nine times," offering advice on shifting outfielders against certain hitters and on calling pitchouts at certain times.

But the fun-loving, mischievous Bavasi couldn't resist the opportunity to inject more chaos and confusion into baseball's most chaotic team. "I told the operator to connect Billy with extension 311 a couple of times," Bavasi confessed. "That's our dugout. I figured Billy would get a little excited being given Pat Corrales [the Indians' manager]. But when I checked with the operator later, she said all Billy told her was, 'My dear, would you please connect me with the right dugout this time.' That didn't sound like Billy. He must have been sedated."

In fact, despite the Yankees' official announcements, it turned out Martin wasn't even in the hospital. His condition under control, he was permitted to roam the streets for a few hours at night and wound up—where else but?—in a bar. As Piniella said later, "The whole thing was really ridiculous."

Soon it got even more ridiculous. The publicity about Martin's phone calls planted ideas in the minds of hundreds of would-be managers around the country. The next night, a doubleheader, impostors were calling, identifying themselves as Billy Martin and asking for the Yankee dugout. The harried operator dutifully put the calls through, and Wynegar and Piniella were besieged by phony Martins. "I was getting guys telling me to put the hit-and-run on when there wasn't even anyone on base," said Piniella.

The Yankees won the opener but lost the second game. By now Piniella no longer saw any humor in the Yankees' dial-a-manager caper. Let Martin reach out and touch someone else, he thought. Martin himself had called just once during the doubleheader according to Wynegar, who said, "There was loud music in the background, and I could hardly hear him."

The next night was even worse and Piniella's patience was really wearing thin. The Yankees lost again, 6–5. The calls had been shut off, but when Martin did manage to get through, Piniella suspected his collapsed lung was being filled with alcohol. "I'm trying to manage, and I got Billy on the line saying, 'Lou, why do these players hate me?'" Piniella related years later.

After the return flight to Newark Airport following a 9–1 loss to Cleveland, Moss Klein stood next to Piniella as they waited at the baggage carousel. Piniella, clearly dejected, finally said, "Well, you might as well know, I'm through. I won't be at the ballpark tomorrow, or any other time. I've seen enough of managing. I've decided I don't want to manage, so what's the sense of staying around as coach? If I don't want to manage, I don't have any future in the game. So I'm getting out. I just wanted you to know."

Through the years, Klein had been through more than a few of Piniella's "retirements" as player. Always they were the stuff of the moment, after a particularly bad game, and none lasted more than 12 hours—especially after Piniella would get home and tell Anita. But this one seemed serious. It was too late to phone the office, with the last deadline having passed by now. So Klein suggested to Piniella, "Why don't you sleep on it? This was a tough series, and right now you're frustrated. You'll feel different in the morning."

When Piniella's baggage arrived, he grabbed it and reiterated, "You won't see me tomorrow."

The Yankees opened the home stand against the White Sox the next night, and Klein had been planning to take a day off after the two-week road trip. But the threatened absence of Piniella forced him to go to Yankee Stadium.

Martin was back and the media was occupied with him. Only Klein realized that the batting coach wasn't at the ballpark. This time Piniella had been true to his word. So Klein telephoned him at home. Anita Piniella, sounding upset, said to call back in a little while, that she was "having a problem with Lou this time." But Anita, who had always succeeded in talking Lou out of his retirements as a player, came through again. Less than an hour later, Piniella answered the phone and said he had already heard from Martin and would most likely be back the next day. Piniella asked Klein not to write about the incident because it would cause too much unnecessary commotion and he had decided to come back anyway.

As it turned out, though, there was an upheaval on the Yankee coaching staff that night after all. The Yankees lost the game to the White Sox—their fourth straight defeat—and Steinbrenner, upset by the team's slump, reacted in characteristic fashion. He fired the pitching coach, Mark Connor, who would eventually be rehired as pitching coach when Piniella became the manager for real.

After the entire incident, Piniella still wasn't sure why he had returned. "I have to be crazy to want to manage this team, absolutely crazy!" he said. "There's no reason to want to do this. I can make more money running my restaurants the right way. But I can't help it. I still want to be Yankee manager one day."

That day came on October 17, 1985, but not before the Yankees staged one of their classic witch-hunts, culminating it with another of their farcical cross-country conference calls that upstaged the World Series (by now another Yankee tradition). Remember now, Steinbrenner had already preordained Piniella as Martin's heir apparent whenever Billy IV should eventually be terminated. But when the season ended, with the Yankees having fallen out of the race in late August and Martin having become engaged in two celebrated barroom scraps at the Cross Keys Inn in Baltimore, Steinbrenner said he was leaving the decision of manager for 1986 up to Clyde King, the general manager, and his assistant, Woody Woodward. "They will have absolutely no stipulations or input from me," Steinbrenner added.

Sure.

King, the straight-arrow, devout southern Baptist, certainly had no use for Martin, whom he regarded as a pitiable little scoundrel ruined by the evils of booze. But just as certainly, no one ever believed that Billy Martin could be fired as Yankee manager by anyone other than the principal Yankee owner.

Nevertheless, King, like Diogenes, went through the motions of conducting a search for right man for the 1986 Yankees. He said he planned to talk to recently fired Pirates manager Chuck Tanner, who was quickly signed by the Atlanta Braves to a five-year, $2-million contract. He said he seriously considered Bobby Cox, who had resigned as manager of the Blue Jays, only to likewise end up with the Braves as general manager. And at one time, during the middle portion of the World Series in St. Louis, King said he was looking at former Mets manager Joe Torre but then hinted that he himself might, in fact, be a candidate for the job.

If nothing else, that served to keep reporters guessing right up to the announcement that came a few days later, when the Series had moved back to Kansas City. Because of the shortage of hotel accommodations in Kansas City, most of the beat reporters were quartered in Lenexa, Kansas, some 30 miles from Royals Stadium. It was there where Yankee PR man Joe Safety put through the conference call to announce "King's decision" to replace Martin with Piniella. Like all the other Yankee press conferences to announce a change of managers, this one was replete with burlesque touches.

In making the announcement, King insisted that Steinbrenner "had no input or stipulations" as to whom he chose as manager. He then relayed, in complete seriousness, the phone conversation he had with Steinbrenner once the decision was reached. King: "Boss, we've made our decision." Steinbrenner: "Who is it?" King: "Lou Piniella." Steinbrenner: "That's fine." King: "Boss, are you happy?" Steinbrenner: "I sure am."

Listening to King detail this conversation, one could only picture Steinbrenner sitting anxiously in his office during all those days leading up to the announcement and saying to himself: "I wonder who Clyde will choose?"

"And what is Billy Martin's status?" someone asked King.

"I have no idea," said King.

As Lou Piniella would find out, this was by no means the last of Billy Martin in his Yankee career. Not long into the 1986 season, Billy was back, sitting upstairs at the stadium in Steinbrenner's private box, second-guessing

Piniella and telling the Boss how *he* would do it if *he* were managing. After one of these sessions in the owner's box at Comiskey Park in Chicago, one of the people present told Bill Madden: "It was really sad to hear this. Martin just can't help himself. George would get him going, criticizing some move Lou would make, and Billy would chime right in."

To be sure, it was to be a rude awakening for Piniella, although he started off brimming with confidence, while making every effort to assert himself as his own man and not the Boss' puppet. In that respect, one of the most memorable of all the days of Piniella's term as Yankee manager was the very first one. It was the first spring training game in Fort Lauderdale, March 8, 1986, a beautiful, sun-splashed Saturday afternoon. The spring training opener is always a festive occasion, the start of a new season and the unveiling of new faces—which in the Yankees' case usually begins with the manager.

On this day Steinbrenner had as his special guests Chrysler president Lee Iacocca, New York real estate mogul Donald Trump, and the Boss' longtime buddy Bill Fugazy, the limousine man. Prior to the game, Steinbrenner marched them through the clubhouse as if to alert the players to the importance of this game. Piniella, however, was not concerned with the parade of celebrities in his midst. Since it was only the first game of the spring, a lot of his regulars weren't yet in "game action" shape. As a result, his first official lineup as manager of the New York Yankees did not include Don Mattingly, Dave Winfield, or Rickey Henderson. Instead, Piniella fielded a team comprised mostly of raw rookies with names such as Jay Buhner, Darren Reed, Orestes Destrade, and Phil Lombardi—hardly familiar faces to Steinbrenner, let alone Iacocca, Trump, or Fugazy.

Happily for all concerned, the Yankees won the game, although you could not have known that by Steinbrenner's mood afterward. One can only presume the Boss was embarrassed by not having any of his multimillion-dollar superstars on display for his important friends. If so, it was only a fraction of the embarrassment Steinbrenner was to feel when his entourage got downstairs to the VIP parking lot adjacent to the Yankee executives' trailer. It is a tiny lot with room for only about a dozen cars. Off to the right, backed up against the fence, was Donald Trump's Lincoln Continental. Directly in front of it, blocking it in, was an older Datsun.

Once it was discovered that Trump was going to be unable to get his car out, the parking lot attendants furiously began pushing it forward and maneuvering it around the "offending" Datsun. Trump did not seem at all upset by the inconvenience of waiting for his car to be liberated, but Steinbrenner was furious.

"Whose car is this?" he demanded.

The parking lot attendants all shook their heads. They thought one of the public relations department interns might have parked it there, but they weren't sure. At last, Trump's car was moved free, and he went on his way. But Steinbrenner was nowhere close to being mollified. He summoned a couple of state troopers into the lot and ordered them to run a check on the Datsun's license plates to determine who the owner of it was.

Meanwhile, standing off to the side, next to a pair of Cadillacs, one white and one maroon, were Steinbrenner's wife and children. They were waiting to leave, but Steinbrenner had now become obsessed by this vacated Datsun.

"I know," he said at one point, "let's let the air out of his tires."

Somebody was quick to talk him out of that, diplomatically pointing out the irrationality of such an act, even if committed by the principal Yankee owner. It would, after all, merely make the car harder to move and wouldn't help at all in locating the car's owner. After about another 20 minutes or so, as Steinbrenner paced back and forth between his trailer and the Yankee clubhouse, the intern who had parked the Datsun and gone off with the keys was produced. Before he could get into the car, however, he was told by one of the attendants that he had to see Mr. Steinbrenner.

"Let me just move my car first," the kid said.

"No," said the attendant, "you have to see Mr. Steinbrenner now."

The kid got out of the car, turned, and saw Steinbrenner pacing toward him. It was like a scene out of "Gunsmoke," with everyone hovering off to the side while Marshal Dillon faced off on Main Street against the desperado at the other end. At 20 paces George fired.

"But, Mr. Steinbrenner—" the kid protested.

"You're fired," Steinbrenner repeated.

But that was not quite the end of it. At last, Steinbrenner got in his white Cadillac and began following his wife and family, in the maroon one, out of the lot. But as JoAnne Steinbrenner weaved her way through the horde of fans hovering around the gate, a big Volkswagen minibus, driven by Gerri Meacham, the wife of the much-maligned shortstop Bobby Meacham (who had once been demoted all the way to AA ball by Steinbrenner after committing an error that cost the Yankees a ball game) began coming in the gate. JoAnne Steinbrenner alertly put on the brakes and then backed up to yield the way to Gerri Meacham's bus. As she did, she backed right into Steinbrenner's car.

Fortunately, there was no damage done, except maybe to George's ego. Even the intern came out of it okay. He was told to stay away from the camp for a day and then came back and worked the rest of the spring. If Steinbrenner saw him, he never said anything, and three years later the kid was hired to work in the front office in New York.

During the early part of that '86 spring training, Piniella, as a first-year manager, would hang around after a routine meeting with Steinbrenner in the executive trailer. After one particular session of second-guessing and suggestions, the Boss was in a chipper mood. Piniella had an idea.

The Yankees were playing an exhibition game against the Orioles at old Miami Stadium the next day. Steinbrenner's seat location Piniella knew all too well: it was right next to the Yankee dugout, a few feet from where the manager usually hung out during the game.

"George, I have an idea for you tomorrow that you're going to love," Piniella said. "How would you like to be the manager?"

Steinbrenner's initial reaction was one of puzzlement.

Piniella proceeded: "From where you'll be sitting, you can give all the signs just as well as I can. I'll give you a few signs now. We'll make them easy. And tomorrow, you take over. You tell me the lineup, you decide how you want to handle the pitching, and you give the signs to Stick—hit and run, bunt, steal, whatever you want to do."

Steinbrenner thought for a moment and smiled. "Okay," he said. "Let's do it."

He was to show up at Miami Stadium early, give Piniella his lineup and go over the signs with the Stick, third base coach Gene Michael. And without anyone knowing it, George Steinbrenner was going to be Yankee manager for the day.

Piniella, of course, relished the idea. Maybe a little on-the-job experience would show the Boss just how tough managing really was, how many options there were to consider, how many decisions to make.

Michael, however, wasn't so keen about it. "How can you do this to me?" he protested to Piniella that night. "If a guy gets thrown out stealing, he's gonna say I got the sign mixed up! Whatever goes wrong is gonna be my fault. And God help me if I *miss* one of his signs!"

The next day, the Yankee bus arrived at Miami Stadium three hours before the 1:30 game time. Piniella, figuring that Steinbrenner hadn't slept that night in the excitement of his "official" managing debut, expected the Boss to be waiting for him when he got off the bus. But George wasn't there. An hour passed. Two hours. Game time approached and Piniella filled out the lineup, still waiting for Steinbrenner to appear. The game started and still no Boss.

Finally, about 10 minutes into the game, Steinbrenner appeared at his seat next to the dugout.

"George," said Piniella, "what happened? I was waiting for you to do the lineup. You can still do the signs. I'll give you a few and—"

Steinbrenner smiled back at him. "Oh, no, you don't," he said. "You're not gonna trick me that easy. I figured out what you're up to. You're the manager. You do the managing. I'm the owner. I'll do the second-guessing. That's the way it's supposed to be."

A couple of weeks after that, Piniella got his first indoctrination as to just how little say Yankee managers have in personnel decisions. Steinbrenner called a meeting of Piniella, the coaches, and the rest of the Yankee high command on March 28 to decide on the final squad cuts. In particular, a decision had to be made on 45-year-old Phil Niekro. Despite. Niekro's age, Piniella wanted to keep the pitcher. Niekro had, after all, won 16 games in each of the previous two seasons for the Yankees. The rest of the coaches and staff agreed, and when a vote was taken, it was 11–1 to keep Niekro, with only Clyde King, the man who had recommended signing Niekro two years earlier, dissenting. Steinbrenner then looked at his son, Hank, who had come aboard that spring as one of part of George's nebulous, ever-changing group of "baseball people."

"What do you say, Hank?" Steinbrenner asked.

"I say we let him go," Hank replied.

"I agree," Steinbrenner said. "That makes the vote 12 to 11," he declared, giving himself ten votes.

Piniella, according to witnesses, blew up.

"What are you even bothering to ask our opinion for?" he shouted at Steinbrenner. "You know what you're gonna do anyway."

He then stormed out of the trailer and, as reporters couldn't help but notice, was in the foulest of moods the rest of the day. At the end of it Piniella called Phil Niekro into his office and told him he was being released.

The first "cut" of Piniella's career in baseball management proved to be about the toughest. He and Niekro had been sort of kindred spirits those previous two seasons as a couple of "over-40s" in a young man's game. Piniella, of course, was a coach, but he still hung out after the games with the players, especially the older ones like Niekro. He jokingly referred to himself as "the midnight coach" in charge of checking curfews. One night in Kansas City, Piniella was at the Longbranch Saloon, a bar in which he is a part owner. It was about 2:00 A.M., closing time, and he was sitting at the bar with Bill Madden. The place was almost empty, but Madden, glancing across the room, spotted Niekro sitting behind a partition having a drink.

"Hey, Lou," laughed Madden, "look over there. It's 'Father Time' [the nickname the writers gave Niekro]. He's pitching tomorrow. Some 'midnight coach' you are."

"Ah, hell, Billy." Piniella sighed. "I can't tell Knucksie to go to bed. He's *older* than me."

Piniella's anger over having to release Niekro was understandable. There was no finer person to pass through the Yankees in the '77-to-'89 period than "Father Time."

Aside from learning the hard truth that managing for George Steinbrenner means being constantly harangued and second-guessed—even for one who has previously enjoyed "favorite son" status with the principal Yankee owner—Piniella's first year in the hot seat was largely uneventful. It could be said with considerable justification that the Yankee season was doomed that March afternoon in Dunedin when Britt Burns, Steinbrenner's most celebrated off-season acquisition, went limping off the field in an exhibition game against the Blue Jays, never to pitch again. Burns, who, it turned out, was afflicted with a degenerative hip condition, had won 18 games the previous season with the White Sox and was being counted on as a mainstay in the Yankee starting rotation.

The pitching staff was in a constant state of flux all season long, as Piniella juggled frantically to keep the team in contention, but the end result of all of it was a record-setting season for reliever Dave Righetti, who was called upon to save 46 games, and a second-place finish, 5½ games back. It was only that close because of a season-ending four-game sweep over the pennant-winning Red Sox.

During the course of the season, while the Yankees floundered out of contention, Steinbrenner could periodically be heard saying it was a mistake to give Piniella the manager's job without his having had any previous managing experience. In the beginning of September, Steinbrenner's longtime confidant Howard Cosell blasted Piniella both on his radio show and in his column in the *New York Daily News*.

The crux of Cosell's attack was that there had been "10 or more games" in which Piniella screwed up as manager and cost the Yankees victories. Cosell, of course, never did detail precisely which 10 games those were. What *was* interesting about the attack was that in the midst of it, Cosell recited Mike Easler's batting average with runners in scoring position. Since no one in the Yankee publicity department had provided him with this information, one could only marvel at Cosell's intimate knowledge of Yankee personnel.

Piniella, meanwhile, was understandably angered and hurt—especially since it was evident to everyone that Cosell was merely serving as Steinbrenner's stalking horse. But when Piniella confronted Steinbrenner about it, the Boss denied having anything to do with the Cosell attack.

In 1987 Steinbrenner was far more direct in his attacks on his onetime "favorite son." Although Steinbrenner conceded the Yankees' strong finish in '86, culminating with the four-game sweep of the Red Sox, had been sufficient reason to give Piniella another season as manager, it wasn't long before both of them were butting heads out in the open—much to the delight of the back-page headline writers in the New York tabloids.

The 1987 Yankees played to a familiar script—too little pitching and too many injuries—and together those two elements doomed Piniella. All told, Piniella used a record 48 players in 1987, including 15 different pitchers in his constantly fluctuating starting rotation. Twelve different players went on the disabled list, most notably Rickey Henderson for 55 games and Willie Randolph for 26.

Remarkably, the Yankees were in first place at the All-Star break, 55–34, with a three-game lead over Toronto. It all began to crumble, though, in August with a 2–8 road trip and the infamous "missed phone call."

On Sunday, August 2, before the team left for Cleveland, Piniella was called up to Steinbrenner's office at Yankee Stadium, where the two got into a heated argument. Steinbrenner wanted Pat Clements, a left-handed reliever whom Piniella liked, demoted. In Clements' place Steinbrenner wanted to bring up Al Holland, another lefty reliever whom the Boss had signed as a free agent a year earlier as a favor to his friend, agent Tom Reich. Holland's arm was about shot, and in fact, his manager at Columbus, Bucky Dent, had recommended he be released. But Steinbrenner had his own ideas.

Once Piniella arrived, the Boss revealed that he'd been looking through his binoculars at Clements warming up in the bullpen. "I've never seen an athlete so scared," Steinbrenner said. "I know athletes. I coached football at Northwestern." In the ensuing conversation the Boss countered Piniella's reservations about Holland by saying, "Well, maybe he'll do better getting major league hitters out. I don't care. He's coming up and that's it."

The next night in Cleveland, the Yankees lost, 2–0, to the Indians. During the course of the game, Steinbrenner called the press box and told public relations director Harvey Greene to inform Piniella "to be in his room for a phone call from me at 2:00 P.M." the next day. Greene followed orders and passed on the message to Piniella, who fully intended to oblige, even though he had a lunch date for Tuesday and figured Steinbrenner was merely harassing him.

Piniella's lunch date was with Bobby Murcer and two of Steinbrenner's limited partners in the Yankees, Michael Friedman and Eddie Rosenthal. The four of them decided to go across the street from the Yankees' hotel to a place called the Pewter Mug. After a while Piniella glanced at his watch.

"I've got to go soon, fellas," he said. "The Boss is calling me at two o'clock."

"Fuck him!" said the two minority owners. "Let's go to shopping, unwind, and have some fun. You deserve it."

Piniella thought about it and agreed. Fuck him, indeed. He probably won't call anyway.

Ah, but on this occasion, Steinbrenner *did* call. And when Piniella wasn't there to take the call, there was hell to pay. It did not help Piniella's cause that the Yankees played horrendously Tuesday night, losing, 15–4, to the Indians. Prior to the game, the coaches, under orders from Steinbrenner, had put catcher Mark Salas through a grueling two-hour drill behind the plate—in full gear in 95-degree heat. (Steinbrenner was upset with Salas for committing a passed ball in Monday's loss, but the workout hardly helped. He committed three more passed balls in the 15–4 loss. About the only Yankee who had a worse night was Holland, who surrendered five walks and six runs in 1⅔ innings of nonrelief.)

On Wednesday Piniella called General Manager Woody Woodward to discuss bringing up a catcher.

"I'm not allowed to talk to you," Woodward said.

"What do you mean?" Piniella said.

"Just what I said. I can't talk to you. Nobody here is allowed to. I suppose you're just gonna have to straighten it out with him."

Piniella was incredulous that Steinbrenner could be so petty. He obviously didn't remember all the times in the past when the Yankee manager had been unceremoniously cut off from the front office. Above all, though, he wasn't going to call Steinbrenner. Instead, he decided it was time to get everything out in the open and he knew exactly how to do it.

The Yankees won the last game in Cleveland and moved on to Detroit. Prior to the first game against the Tigers, Piniella called the reporters together in the clubhouse.

"I just wanted you people to know we've been trying to get a catcher [Joel Skinner] up here for three weeks now," he said. "Lately I've intensified my efforts, but he still hasn't made the Columbus shuttle."

"Have you talked to Woody about it? What does he say?" the reporters asked.

"Woody's been told not to talk to me."

Hooo boy! Did that ever do it! Saturday, after the Yankees lost twice to the Tigers, Steinbrenner issued a rambling and profane two-page statement through Greene, rebutting Piniella's charges, sort of, while going public with sensitive front office discussions involving Rickey Henderson's hamstring injury.

Beginning with the missed phone call, Steinbrenner said:

> The simple fact is Piniella didn't even come back from lunch—if that was where he really was—to get a call from his boss at two o'clock. He didn't bother to call me or to get word to me that the time was inconvenient for him. I don't know of too many people—even sportswriters—who, if their boss told them to be available for a call at a certain time, wouldn't be there.
>
> As for me not talking to Piniella, that's pure horseshit, ask Woody. I told Woody to put the plan to bring Skinner up in full action. Everything was set, but I just wanted to talk to Lou about it briefly. The fact is Piniella was all for the Salas-[Joe] Niekro trade. I opposed it, but I let Woody and Lou make the deal. Now all of a sudden, Skinner is the answer to our problems and Salas is a "bum."

With that, Steinbrenner segued into the Henderson problem, which no one had even been thinking or talking about of late:

> As for the Rickey Henderson matter, I was leaving that in the hands of our team doctor and trainer until Woody called me and said Piniella wanted to disable him right now because he was "jaking it," his teammates were mad at him, and he [Piniella] wanted guys to play and he would win it all without Henderson. I said I wouldn't disable a man as punishment, and despite what Piniella thinks, I don't think we can win it without Rickey Henderson. I said we should talk to Lou. We did, and Piniella told us he wanted Henderson traded as soon as possible.

If Piniella thought Steinbrenner had truly gone nuts, he wasn't alone. In the past Steinbrenner had issued some wild statements and said some ridiculous things, but the reporters all agreed that this was the most outrageous. With his statement he had destroyed any credibility Piniella could have hoped to maintain with the sensitive, handle-with-care Henderson, driving a wedge between the manager and one of the team's star players. Steinbrenner was saying the club couldn't win without Henderson, but after airing all of the behind-the-scenes dirty laundry about how Piniella and the front office wanted to deal with Rickey's injury, how did he think Piniella could ever get Henderson motivated to play again?

Piniella was predictably enraged but managed to keep his emotions in check. He told reporters he would "have something to say tomorrow "That night he had dinner with Murcer and TV broadcaster "Hawk" Harrelson. Over a few bottles of wine, Harrelson and Murcer succeeded in convincing Piniella not to fire back at Steinbrenner.

"It'll just make things worse," said Harrelson. "You've always been above it. Don't go crawling into the gutter with him now."

The clincher, however, was when Piniella called Woodward, whom he considered a good friend, and asked him if he'd back him up if he blasted Steinbrenner.

"I just can't, Lou," Woodward said. "I hope you can understand my position."

A footnote here is that, at the end of the season, both Piniella and Woodward had letters of insubordination placed in their files from Steinbrenner. Piniella's was for failing to be in his room in Cleveland. Woodward's was for taking his daughter to college. It seems Woodward had informed Steinbrenner he was going to need to take a couple of days away from the office to enroll his daughter at Florida State. Riding in a cab with his daughter from Yankee Stadium to the airport that day, Woodward had a message relayed to him by the cabdriver.

"Are you Mr. Woodward?" the cabby asked.

"I am."

"Well, they're tellin' me you're wanted back at the stadium. We gotta turn around."

There was no way Woodward was going to cancel out on his daughter for the sake of one of Steinbrenner's whims. He informed the cabby to keep going to the airport.

"Don't worry," Woodward said, "I'll call the stadium when we get to the airport."

By now the cabby was becoming fascinated by this potentially explosive episode unfolding around him, and obviously familiar with Steinbrenner and the Yankees, he was beginning to think he might become part of history.

"Let me go with you when you make the call," he said. "I'll watch your bags."

Woodward laughed.

According to other front office sources, when word got around that Woodward did make the call to say he wasn't turning around and coming back, the front office employees all burst into applause.

Unfortunately for Piniella, Hawk Harrelson was wrong about one thing. Things *did* get worse. For even though Piniella didn't blast back at Steinbrenner, the Boss wasn't through firing *his* salvos. Undoubtedly infuriated upon reading of the players burning his statement in the clubhouse in Detroit, Steinbrenner waited until the Yankees were blown out 10–1 in the first game in Kansas City, the last leg of the road trip. After that game he called Greene with yet another release, in which he said: "I'm glad to see the players so firmly behind Lou Piniella. If this is their idea of support, then I'm happy not to have it."

The night before, when the team arrived in Kansas City from Detroit, Piniella had called Woodward at home and tried to resign. Woodward was understanding and supportive but wouldn't accept Piniella's resignation.

"Maybe he doesn't want you to manage right now, but I do," Woodward said. "You're the best man for the job."

But with the Monday night debacle in Kansas City and yet another blast from Steinbrenner, Piniella was now at his lowest ebb as Yankee manager. After the game he went straight to the Longbranch and was deep into the Remy Martin when Bill Madden arrived around midnight and joined him at a table.

"Why is he doing this to me, Billy?" Piniella said. "Doesn't he want to win? This is a mess now. He's killed whatever chances we had of winning. But do you know what really gets me? I really loved this guy. He did a lot for me and my family, and I can't forget that. But I can't forget this, either."

The perverse thing about it all was that Steinbrenner really loved Piniella. By not being in his room to take the phone call, Piniella, in Steinbrenner's eyes, had gone from a favorite son to a prodigal son and, as such, had to be punished. Piniella's friends urged him to call Steinbrenner and extend an olive branch.

"That's all George wants—for you to make the first move," they told him.

What you had, though, was one tough Spaniard and one stubborn German, and never the twain did meet until it was too late to salvage the season or save Piniella's job.

Steinbrenner and Piniella talked on the phone during a late August trip to the West Coast, and agreed to meet when the team returned. Then they talked again toward the end of the trip, in a hilarious conversation.

Tommy John, at 44, was doing more than his share to help the pitching, getting by with his usual style—and guile. His outing against the California Angels on August 24 at Anaheim Stadium was particularly entertaining. John was pitching against Don Sutton; both wily veterans were notorious for having plenty of tricks up their sleeves...and in their gloves, pockets, caps, and anyplace else they could put them.

On this night Sutton was a bit clumsier than usual, and WPIX-TV cameras picked up some apparent evidence of his doctoring the ball. Steinbrenner, at home in Tampa, was watching the game and was outraged. He telephoned the ballpark, got through to the dugout in the third inning, and began lecturing Piniella.

"Don't you see what Sutton's doing out there?" Steinbrenner said. "You can see him plain as day. Why aren't you doing something? Get him thrown out."

Piniella answered calmly, "George, do you know what the score is?" he said. Steinbrenner knew the Yankees were leading, 1–0. Piniella continued: "George, if I get the umpires to check Sutton, don't you know that the Angels are going to check TJ? They'll both get kicked out. Whatever they're doing, TJ is doing it better than Sutton. So let's leave it alone for now."

The Yankees won, 3–2. And as one scout said that night, "Tommy John against Don Sutton. If anyone can find one smooth ball from that game, he ought to send it to Cooperstown."

On Friday night, August 28, Piniella and Steinbrenner met at Yankee Stadium and cleared the air over the "missed phone call." (Piniella never did tell Steinbrenner he had been having lunch with the limited partners, however.) It was clear, too, from Steinbrenner's statements to the press afterward that Piniella would not be back as manager.

"After the season, we'll evaluate the job he did," Steinbrenner said. "Lou knows he will judged by the bottom line, and injuries are no excuse. He's not a great manager. How many great managers are there? But I never said he was a bad manager."

Piniella still couldn't understand that once he agreed to manage for Steinbrenner, he was held in the same low esteem by the Boss as all his predecessors had been. Steinbrenner so much as admitted that in an off-the-record conversation with Bill Madden after Piniella was fired and "shifted" to general manager that winter.

"I know Lou still wants to manage," Steinbrenner said.

"But he's too smart for that. Managing's an awful job, and Lou's above it. He belongs in the front office."

If only both of them had remembered that when, inevitably, Steinbrenner had to get rid of Billy Martin again in June of '88.

Toward the end of '87, with the handwriting on the wall, Piniella vowed to all his close friends that he would never work for Steinbrenner again once the ax fell. Thus when he agreed to become general manager and made the rounds of all the talk shows, arm and arm with Martin, his friends felt betrayed. It was generally felt that Piniella had sold out. It was sickening to them to see him participating in this public "love-in" charade with Martin, the man who had stabbed him in the back while he was the manager.

In a way Piniella did sell out. Steinbrenner gave him a three-year contract that meant security to his family, who didn't want to leave the New York area. Then, too, Steinbrenner's and Piniella's love-hate relationship was once again working itself out. Suddenly Steinbrenner was acting like a daddy again, and

Piniella, relieved not to be manager anymore, put all the hate from the past August out of his mind.

That was a fatal mistake because, much to the shock and regret of his friends, he allowed Steinbrenner to seduce him into taking the manager's job again on June 23, 1988. All winter long and all that spring, even after he relinquished the general manager's job to become a special assignments scout, he had vowed there would be never be a "Lou II." He wasn't back on the job 10 days before he realized he had made the biggest mistake of his career.

In convincing Piniella to take over from Martin, Steinbrenner tore up Piniella's contract and gave him a new three-year deal at $400,000 per. He also told him he would have a far freer hand in running things than he had in Lou I.

"I'm going to have full control," Piniella said confidently at that hastily called June 23 press conference. "It's quite evident that by him asking me back he has confidence in my ability."

Maybe he believed that and maybe he just wanted to believe it. But on July 3, just 10 days after his return, Piniella's worst fears were realized.

All it took were a couple of calls from the Boss, complaining about Piniella's failure to use Dave Righetti in an extra-inning loss to the White Sox, and Lou knew he had made a terrible mistake.

"It's right back to where it was last year," he said. "I had to be crazy to come back to this."

If only he knew *how* crazy. From that point on, things just got worse and worse. Piniella's best pitcher, John Candelaria, quit on the team in late August, refusing to pitch with torn cartilage in his knee. As the pitching collapsed and injuries to Willie Randolph, Wayne Tolleson, and Mike Pagliarulo decimated the infield, the team began playing horribly.

In late August, following a loss to Seattle, Don Mattingly issued an uncharacteristic tirade, venting his frustration. The remarks were directed at Steinbrenner, and the owner was furious. He wanted an apology the next day and said as much to Mattingly's agent, Jim Krivacs. But Mattingly had no intention of apologizing.

Steinbrenner had a statement drawn up the next day in which he criticized Mattingly, charging that the star was making excuses for his own shortcomings in the disappointing season. The statement included comments from Piniella—comments that Piniella hadn't made. Steinbrenner wanted Piniella to authorize the statement and sign it. Piniella refused—knowing that the refusal would finish him as manager. The message he received from Steinbrenner was clear: either you're working for the players or you're working for the owner. But Piniella wanted no part of the statement, and it was never released.

Only an equally prolonged slump by the front-running Red Sox kept everyone in the American League East pennant race until the final days of September.

But when the Red Sox swept three out of four from the Yankees in Boston to open up a 6½-game lead on September 18, it was obvious to one and all that "Lou II" had been a terrible mistake. There had also been rumors that Steinbrenner had not filed Piniella's contract with the league office, and when Bill Madden decided to follow up, he found out more than he wanted to know.

On September 19, Madden called Steinbrenner in Tampa and inquired about Piniella's status.

"It's true I haven't filed the contract," Steinbrenner said. "But I have my reasons."

"Are you at liberty to reveal them?" Madden asked.

"Yes," said Steinbrenner, "but you can't write this because it's a very sensitive matter."

Steinbrenner then explained that in the course of launching an in-house investigation of marketing director Arthur Adler (who had resigned a month earlier in a messy dispute over monies owed to him), it was discovered that some $10,000 worth of Scandinavian furniture had been sent to Piniella as payment to the Yankees by a company for its radio commercials.

"Do you see what I mean?" Steinbrenner said. "If Lou's been stealing from me, I've got to let him go from the entire organization. He's like a son to me and I'm certainly not going to prosecute him, but he's got to go."

Madden was dumbfounded.

"There's got to be an explanation for this, George," he said.

As it turned out, there was, but even though it had been assumed Piniella wouldn't be back as manager if the Yankees didn't win, Madden now knew it was a certainty. At the same time, Madden got a call from a close friend of Dallas Green's informing him that Green had been having ongoing talks with the Yankees about taking over as manager and that "the deal is all but done."

Armed with all of this, Madden wrote a front-page story in the *Daily News* that said a big Yankee shakeup was coming, with Piniella to be fired as manager and replaced by Green. (Green, it should be noted, had been rumored to be in line for the job ever since Madden had revealed Green would have been offered the job back in June had Piniella not agreed to come back.) Because he had promised Steinbrenner never to reveal to anyone—Piniella especially—the business about the furniture, Madden could not write the real reason Piniella wouldn't be back.

Meanwhile, Piniella was crushed by the story and particularly upset at Madden, whom he had considered a close friend.

"Couldn't you have waited until we were eliminated from the pennant race before writing this?" he asked Madden.

"I wish I could have," Madden explained weakly. "But there were circumstances that prevented me from sitting on it."

For a week Madden felt sick about having to write what he did. It was, without question, the toughest story he ever had to write, and what made it worse was not being able to ask Piniella about the furniture. To do so, he knew, would set Lou off and betray a confidence with Steinbrenner. So all he could do was wait for Steinbrenner to confront Piniella' about it.

On September 26, the Yankees went to Baltimore, and Piniella revealed to reporters he had met with Steinbrenner over the weekend in New York and "cleared the air" about a few matters. Madden was relieved, but not nearly as relieved as when he got Piniella alone under the grandstand before the game.

"Did George ask you about any other things—off-the-field things—that are upsetting him?" Madden asked delicately.

"You mean the furniture?" Piniella said.

Madden suddenly felt like a 100-pound weight had been lifted from his shoulders.

"Yeah, the furniture."

"Do you believe the son of a bitch thought I stole from him? What the hell is ten thousand dollars' worth of furniture to me? I'm making four hundred thousand!"

Piniella then explained that the furniture had been a gift to him in lieu of payment for doing a five-minute pregame show for WABC radio in 1986. Even though most managers are paid up to $50,000 extra for doing similar pregame shows, Piniella was asked to do his gratis, primarily because WABC had paid a record amount for the Yankee radio rights and was looking to get back whatever perks possible on their investment. When Piniella refused, citing the intrusion on his time, Adler arranged a compromise in which he would be paid in merchandise instead of cash.

According to Adler, Steinbrenner had approved the arrangement. Piniella thought the matter was resolved, especially after Steinbrenner added a year to his contract when he fired him again at the end of the season. But a couple weeks later Piniella got a bill from the Yankees for $10,000.

A final bit of irony to the furniture flap surfaced the following season when Piniella was interviewed by the Toronto Blue Jays for their manager's job. It turned out that Steinbrenner refused to let Piniella go unless the Blue Jays compensated him with one of four of their top-rated young pitchers, Duane Ward, Todd Stottlemyre, David Wells, or Alex Sanchez. But before the talks got to that point, the Blue Jays discussed the parameters of the job with Piniella.

They explained to him their feelings about the importance of the manager dealing with the press and the fans.

"Very likely," they told Piniella, "we'd want you to do a radio show for us. It'll help tremendously in the public relations area, and it'll afford you some extra income."

"That's fine with me," replied Piniella, "as long as you don't pay me in furniture."

Sometime later, Barry Halper, the noted baseball memorabilia collector who is also one of Steinbrenner's limited partners in the Yankees, told Piniella of an incident late in the 1985 season that proved to be an accurate forewarning of what was to come. It seemed that *The Sporting News,* having learned of Halper's extensive collection of old baseball uniforms, decided to do a cover story with Yankee players all modeling the uniforms of Ty Cobb, Cy Young, John McGraw, Pud Galvin, *et al.* Piniella, Rickey Henderson, Willie Randolph, Don Baylor, and John Montefusco were among the players asked to pose in the uniforms, and Steinbrenner himself agreed to don a top hat, tails, and cane as the model for Jacob Ruppert, the Yankee owner in the twenties.

As he descended on the Yankee Stadium elevator to the room in the basement where the shoot was to take place, Steinbrenner asked Halper if all the players were present and accounted for.

"Everything's okay," Halper said. "We just had to make a couple of last-minute substitutions. Randolph, Baylor, and Piniella didn't make it."

"What?" exclaimed Steinbrenner. "Well, I'll take care of that. The next time Randolph wants any favors for his family, he can forget it. And Baylor, the next time he asks for extra tickets, he pays for them himself."

A minute or so went by, and Steinbrenner didn't say anything else. Finally Halper spoke up.

"What about Piniella?" he asked. "You didn't say anything about him."

"Don't worry," said Steinbrenner. "I'm gonna really fix him. I'm gonna make him the manager."

CHAPTER 8

The Misfits

Many of them have come with high hopes, filled with excitement about playing for the team with the grand and glorious tradition—the team of Ruth, Gehrig, DiMaggio, and Mantle—in the media capital where fame and fortune beckoned. Within weeks they were gasping for air, searching for sanity, longing for a trade.

Others have come with built-in trepidations, having heard all the horror stories through the baseball grapevine. But within weeks they learned firsthand that the stories didn't begin to do justice to the reality of life as a Yankee.

It is a proven fact that life as a Yankee isn't for everyone. In truth, those who have been able to handle the pressure and prosper during the Steinbrenner era are more the exceptions than the rule. Others have managed to get by, checking off each passing day on the calendar like in the old prison movies. These were the Ken Griffeys, the Jack Clarks, the Rick Rhodens, who willingly took the Boss' money, performed reasonably well for their wages, and looked forward to the day they could play out those contracts someplace else.

And then there have been the Misfits, that ever-growing group of players who simply couldn't adapt to the Yankee way of life—the topsy-turvy, helter-skelter, bizarre world that can be so pressurized, so tumultuous, so devastating to the psyche. Indeed, for some of them it seemed as though they had crashed through the looking glass and landed in an upside-down kingdom where instability was the norm and where a heavyset man, dressed as the King of Hearts, was running around shouting, "Off with their heads!"

The misfits share a common disadvantage: they come up to the big leagues through other organizations, where there had been the normal pressure to succeed, the normal sense of urgency to win. The longer a player has spent in those organizations, the more difficult the adjustment in coming to the Yankees. Those who came up through the Yankee system or were acquired at a young age, before having much of a chance to see how other players lived, have a better chance of surviving. Basically they don't know any better.

But with the rare exceptions, those who have come from other teams and were even slightly tense or had the tiniest tendency to worry or fret, are doomed to be misfits. There have been the misfits who came in trades, having no choice in the matter. And there have been the misfits who came for the money, accepting free-agent windfalls, often against the advice of others, and living to regret it.

The parade of misfits through Steinbrenner U. has included players and personalities of all types, and their demises took various forms. Some Misfits, such as Roy Smalley, were actually useful players as Yankees. But they were bumped around, tampered with to the point of total confusion, never coming close to the stardom they had attained with other teams. Other Misfits were given only the briefest of chances, then dismissed, shaken by the experience. Billy Sample was in that group. So too were Toby Harrah, Dave Revering, Mark Salas, and Dale Berra, Yogi's kid.

Then there were the extreme cases of misfits, those who came to the Yankees when they appeared to be in their prime, but who became utter failures—for various reasons. Put Steve Kemp, Omar Moreno, Eric Soderholm, Ken Holtzman, and Rawly Eastwick in that category.

Finally there have been those who march at the head of the parade, singular sensations in the Yankee misfit category.

Doyle Alexander and Rick Reuschel, longtime winners who became colossal losers as Yankees but escaped to become winners again elsewhere—and in Alexander's case, to have several last laughs at the expense of his former captors.

There was Butch Wynegar, who couldn't stand it anymore and simply packed up and went home. Steve Trout and Ed Whitson worked themselves into such states that all sense of reality disappeared for them and they found themselves living nightmares in pinstripes. And who can forget Cecilio Guante, the Dominican relief pitcher who spent a year and a half with the Yankees, all the while maintaining he didn't speak English? But on the day he was liberated, traded to the Texas Rangers, he packed his bags and walked out of the clubhouse, shouting, "Free at last! Free at last!"

Davey Collins, a prince among the misfits, spoke for all of them, and all the ones to come, toward the end of his one season as a Yankee in 1982: "Once you leave the Yankees," Collins said, "once you recover from the shock and start feeling like your old self again, you realize that anything you do from that point on in your life is never going to be as difficult."

With those words as introduction, we present some of the more notorious Yankee misfits and their sad stories.

Steve Trout

Lou Piniella will never forget the solemn, assuring words delivered by George Steinbrenner on July 12, 1987. Piniella was sitting in the manager's office at Yankee Stadium going over his lineup for the Yankees' game against the White Sox that afternoon when the red phone on his desk rang.

"Lou," came Steinbrenner's voice at the other end, "I just won you the pennant. I got you Steve Trout."

Steve Trout. Was there ever a player more totally ill-equipped to handle the pressures of New York and the craziness of Steinbrenner's Yankees than this bewildered left-hander from the Chicago Cubs? By season's end both Piniella and his pal Gene Michael were joking that Trout may actually have gotten both of them fired.

When the deal was announced that Trout was going from the Cubs to the Yankees for a trio of young pitchers, right-handers Bob Tewksbury and Dean Wilkins, and left-hander Rich Scheid, Michael, who was then the manager of the Cubs, was outraged. As flaky and unpredictable as Trout might have been, he had also been one of Michael's best pitchers and, in fact, was coming off a pair of shutouts. Michael's immediate reaction to the deal was to rip his boss, Cubs president Dallas Green, for "giving up on the season."

Green did not take kindly to Michael's remarks, and the two of them jibed at each other the rest of the season until Michael resigned as Cubs manager in September. Unfortunately for Michael's close friend Piniella, it didn't take long for Trout to demonstrate that Green was right in getting rid of him and his $1 million salary.

Poor Trout. He had pitched his entire major league career in Chicago with second-division White Sox and Cubs teams, and suddenly he was thrust into a new environment—New York, the Yankee scene, and a pennant race, all of which were completely foreign to him. It did not take long for Piniella to realize Steve Trout was not going to win the pennant for him.

"I didn't really know anything about him until we went to Texas right after the All-Star break and he was waiting for us there," Piniella recalled. "After talking to him in my office, I was more confused than ever. Then when I went out and watched him warming up on the side, I got the feeling we had ourselves a real problem here. After a while I said to [pitching coach] Mark Connor: 'When's he gonna cut it loose?' Connor looked at me and said: 'That's it, Lou. He's done.'"

After Trout's first two outings, in which he surrendered 10 runs and 14 hits over 11 innings, Steinbrenner, never one to worry about putting a little extra pressure on his players, said, "The next start will tell about this guy." Fortunately for all concerned, the Yankees were on the road at the time, and Trout never saw Steinbrenner's comment. It was after he pitched six scoreless innings in a no-decision effort against the Royals in New York that a local reporter asked him, "Were you thinking about what Steinbrenner said?"

"What did he say?" Trout asked.

When told that Steinbrenner had said this start was crucial, Trout replied, "Oh, God, I'm glad I didn't know that."

That turned out to be the high point of Trout's Yankee experience. In Trout's next outing, against the Indians, he lasted just 3⅔ innings, surrendering five walks and making three wild pitches. In his defense, he didn't get a whole lot of support from his catcher, Mark Salas, who was charged with a passed ball in the game. At one point in the game, Hank Greenwald, the Yankee radio broadcaster, remarked in his best dry wit after one of Trout's pitches: "That was a great catch. I guess it's kind of sad, though, when you say that and you're talking about the pitcher throwing the ball to the catcher."

The next day, as an after-effect of having to catch the wild Trout, the beleaguered Salas was charged with three more passed balls. Looking back on those games, Piniella couldn't help but find the humor—however sick—in the sad state of Yankee events. "Watching Trout and Salas out there," Piniella said, "I thought maybe they were betting on the game. If they were, I wished I'd have known about it. I wanted to get in on the action! I told Salas the next day: 'You must be having fun out there. You've gotten to know everybody sitting behind home plate on a first-name basis.'"

By now Piniella had come to the hard realization that the man who was supposedly going to win the pennant for him wasn't even going to be able to start for him. Trout was completely coming apart and was in fear of even going to the mound. In an effort to help him regain his confidence (not to mention his sense of direction), Piniella assigned pitching coaches Mark Connor and Stan Williams and scout Eddie Lopat, the former Yankee standout left-hander of the fifties, to work with Trout in the bullpen.

It was to no avail. On August 9 in Detroit, having lost two of the first three games in their four-game series against the Tigers, the Yankees were blown out in the getaway game, 15–4, to fall out of first place. Dennis Rasmussen was the starting pitcher and struggled early. Looking for someone to provide him with some quality long relief, Piniella phoned the bullpen to get Trout up.

Talk about being caught between a rock and a hard place! Each time Piniella got up on the top step of the dugout in anticipation of coming to get Rasmussen, Trout would throw a ball over the catcher's head in the bullpen. (It wasn't until after the game that Piniella learned that one of Trout's errant pitches had struck a spectator in the stands and that the fan required medical treatment.) Rasmussen, too, was all over the place with his pitches, and here was Piniella's potential relief man sending his pitches into orbit.

Piniella was finally left with no choice but to bring Trout in as the game quickly got out of hand. As Piniella was returning from the mound, having made the change, Kirk Gibson, who was in the on-deck circle as the next Tiger batter, shouted over to him, "Why me, Lou?" Not surprisingly, Trout didn't last more than an inning.

The night before, Piniella was sound asleep in his room at the Pontchartrain Hotel when his phone rang about 3:30. It was the night manager inquiring as to who was in room 407.

"I don't know," said Piniella. "What's the problem?"

"Well," the manager said, "he hasn't slept there in three nights and we were concerned that whoever is supposed to be in that room was either sick, missing, or something even worse."

In retrospect the night manager wasn't far wrong. Piniella said he'd look into it, but before going back to sleep, he got out his rooming list and checked to see who was in room 407. It was Trout.

The next day, in the clubhouse, he confronted Trout about it. Trout explained that he'd been staying at his mother's house, which did not satisfy Piniella.

"The problem was," Piniella recalled a year later, "Trout said the same thing when we were in Chicago and Minneapolis. Now, either his mother had a lot of homes or he had three mothers."

Trout made a few more starts for the Yankees, his most memorable coming on August 28 in New York against the Seattle Mariners. As soon as he took the mound for the start of the game, it was clear to everyone in the ballpark he was totally lost. As they played the national anthem, Trout stood there, staring out at the flag. He was the only player on the field who had his hat on.

Trout never won a game for the Yankees. His line for 14 appearances in 1987 reads: 0–4, 6.60 ERA, 51 hits, 37 walks, 27 strikeouts, and 9 wild pitches in 46⅓ innings. As Piniella said, "It's very upsetting for a manager when he goes out to talk to his pitcher and the guy says, 'Lou, I'm not worth a shit. Get me out of here.'"

That winter, getting Trout "out of here" was precisely what Piniella did. As the general manager now, Piniella and Yankee vice president of baseball administration Bob Quinn attended the winter meetings in West Palm Beach. It was there that the seeds were sown for the trade of Trout to Seattle, although Steinbrenner seemed to think Piniella and Quinn were just having a good old time of it in sunny Florida at the Yankees' expense.

Their first day at the meetings, Piniella and Quinn were approached by Bobby Cox, the general manager of the Braves, who was interested in a young third baseman in the Yankees' minor league system named Hensley Meulens. Cox had a pretty good left-handed pitcher, Zane Smith, whom he was willing to trade, and as everybody, especially Piniella, knew, the Yankees desperately needed pitching.

"Let's play golf today," Cox said, "we'll talk while we play."

After completing 18 holes, during which they were able to combine business with pleasure, Piniella and Quinn arrived back at the clubhouse only to find three pink telephone message slips for each of them. All of them, of course, were from Steinbrenner, in Tampa.

"Tell you what, Bob," said Piniella, "you take care of the greens fees and I'll take care of the pink slips."

As expected Steinbrenner was extremely upset over not having been able to reach his two executives all day.

"Goddamn it, Lou," Steinbrenner railed to Piniella, "don't tell me you were out playing golf all day! I didn't send you to these meetings to play golf. I'll tell you this: Next year you're not going."

As if there was ever a "next year" for any of Steinbrenner's general managers.

Anyway, the next day, Piniella and Quinn got together with Seattle Mariners President Chuck Armstrong and his general manager Dick Balderson. Before getting down to discussing the parameters of the Trout deal, the four exchanged small talk about their respective owners—Steinbrenner and his counterpart with the Mariners, George Argyros.

"How's your George?" Armstrong asked.

"Oh, just fine," said Quinn. "We're forbidden to play any more golf here. How's *your* George?"

"Great," said Armstrong. "You may have heard. We're operating now under Seagull Management."

"What's that?" asked Quinn.

"You know," said Armstrong, "George flies in, he eats a little bit, then he shits all over everybody and flies out."

About a month later, on December 22, Piniella traded Trout and outfielder Henry Cotto to the Mariners for another left-hander, six-foot-eight Lee Guetterman, and a minor league right-hander named Clay Parker. It didn't matter that Guetterman didn't have a fastball to match his size. This was your classic "addition by subtraction" trade with the Yankees ridding themselves of another misfit.

Ed Whitson

The forerunner to Steve Trout was Ed Whitson. Eddie Lee Whitson, a high-strung, beer-guzzling pitcher from Johnson City, Tennessee, was miserable as a Yankee. That description applied to his state of mind as much as his pitching.

Whitson, who had been happy pitching in San Diego with the Padres, was another in that long list of players who couldn't resist Steinbrenner's money but who couldn't deal with the pressure of playing for it in New York with the Yankees. He signed as a free agent after the 1984 season, receiving an outrageous five-year, $4.4-million contract. It did not take long for Whitson to regard that contract as a pact with the devil—and without an escape clause.

Whitson was 29 when he signed with the Yankees, and was coming off the finest season of his otherwise mediocre seven-year career, with a 14–8 record for the Padres. From the very beginning with the Yankees, when he strained his back while pulling on his socks the day before his first scheduled start in April of 1985, nothing went right for Whitson.

Now, if Whitson had had a manager who was compassionate and understanding, who knew how to handle his delicate psyche and who made him feel welcome and needed, maybe things could have turned out differently. But 16 games into the 1985 season, that manager, Yogi Berra, was fired. And Whitson's manager became Billy Martin.

The day after Martin took over, pitcher John Montefusco, the perceptive veteran, made a prophetic assessment of the Whitson-Martin relationship. Talking to Moss Klein in the clubhouse in Arlington, Texas, Montefusco said: "Watch out for Martin and Whitson. I know Whitson. I've been on teams with him before, with the Giants and Padres. There's no way—no way in hell—that Whitson will be able to deal with Billy. There's gonna be bloodshed, believe me."

That was still in the future, but the Martin-Whitson pairing was on shaky ground from the outset. Whitson hated Martin's approach, the way he berated pitchers for their mistakes, the way he ignored most players except for his few favorites. And Martin had little use for Whitson, whom he regarded as an overpaid, underachieving waste.

Whitson did little to change Martin's thinking in the early months of the season. In his first 11 starts, through early June, Whitson was 1–6, with a 6.23 ERA, and had become the object of the fans' taunts at Yankee Stadium. The fact that he was so visibly upset by the fans' reactions only encouraged more of the same treatment. The Yankees were struggling and the fans had found their target.

Whitson was so rattled by the fans that even in a loss to Toronto on June 11, when he pitched well and received some positive reaction, the fans were on his mind more than the result. That night, his fine outing had prompted occasional chants of "Ed-die! Ed-die! Ed-die!" from the Yankee Stadium crowd, and Whitson was touched.

"I didn't know what was going on," Whitson confessed. "I couldn't believe they were on my side."

A few lockers down, Dave Righetti heard Whitson talking about the fans. "I told him," said Righetti, "that all the beer vendors in the stadium are named Eddie. The fans were calling for beer, not for Whitson."

But Martin wasn't interested in Whitson's catharsis with the fans. "We lost again," he snarled, "and all this guy cares about is if the fans like him. Tell him he can go sit in the stands from now on."

Whitson actually improved from that point and pitched reasonably well for a while. The Yankees also regrouped, and after trailing Toronto by as much as 9 games on August 8, they moved back to within 1½ games of the first-place Blue Jays a month later.

But after winning the opener of a crucial four-game series against the Blue Jays at Yankee Stadium on September 12, the Yankees lost the next three. Whitson started the final game, which was to make the difference between being 2½ games out or 4½ out. He was bombed, chased in the third inning of an 8–5 loss.

The Yankees suddenly started going to pieces, and Martin, who had a history of doing the same in such troubled times, started to self-destruct, thus setting the stage for the historic confrontation between the manager and the pitcher.

Following the three losses to Toronto, the Yankees had a makeup game against the Indians the afternoon of September 16. Although they were now 4½ behind with 20 games to play, they still had a chance, and every game was vital. That day, they took a 5–3 lead into the ninth inning, only to lose, 9–5, as Martin allowed ineffective reliever Brian Fisher in to absorb the entire six-run shellacking. Righetti was standing in the bullpen, hands on hips, waiting for the call that never came.

Martin never clearly answered the questions about his decision to stay with Fisher, simply insisting that the young pitcher wasn't being hit hard. Now the Yankees were five games behind as they headed for Detroit for a three-game series. In the opener of that series, Martin allowed Ron Guidry to keep pitching while the Tigers blasted five homers off him in six innings en route to a 9–1 rout.

The next night Martin's thinking became even more bizarre. With the score tied, 2–2, in the sixth inning, runners at first and third and two out, Martin told hitting coach Lou Piniella to order lefty-hitting Mike Pagliarulo to bat right-handed against lefty Mickey Mahler. Granted, Pagliarulo had struck out twice previously in the game against Mahler, but this hardly seemed the time to be experimenting with batting from the other side of the plate. Pagliarulo hadn't batted right-handed in a game since he was in college. Martin also had several right-handed hitters on the bench but later said he wanted Pagliarulo to stay in the game because of his defensive value.

Piniella relayed the orders to Pagliarulo. At first Pagliarulo thought Piniella was kidding, attempting to break the mounting tension in the Yankee dugout. When he realized Piniella was serious, Pagliarulo dutifully walked up to the plate and took his place—in the right-handed batter's box.

Detroit catcher Bob Melvin, after doing a double take to make certain it was indeed Pagliarulo, said, "What the hell are you doing?"

Replied Pagliarulo sheepishly, "I'm *trying* to get a base hit."

Naturally he didn't. He looked at a called third strike. "I just couldn't pull the trigger," Pagliarulo explained later.

Don Baylor, watching in stunned disbelief from the bench, later said, "I figured Billy had a trick play on, but after Pags took the third strike, I was thinking, 'Well, when's the trick gonna happen?'"

The Yankees lost the game, 5–2, and lost the series finale to the Tigers the next night, 10–3. By the time they arrived in Baltimore for the final leg of the road trip, Martin was in a bad state. Prior to the series opener against the Orioles, he told reporters he was passing Whitson over for his scheduled turn the next day because Whitson had a sore arm.

Whitson, told of the change and the "sore arm," started laughing. He was actually giddy, apparently having gone beyond the edge in his tension-filled season and his hatred for Martin. After holding out his arm for reporters to inspect, he called them over later to show them an old *Playboy* magazine that was laying around the clubhouse. He was laughing hysterically, pointing to the "Miss May" centerfold. The previous week, during a loss to Toronto, Steinbrenner had called Dave Winfield "Mr. May"—a sarcastic reference to Reggie Jackson's title of "Mr. October."

"Do you think Winfield is a friend of hers?" Whitson asked the reporters, pointing to the centerfold girl. "Mr. May and Miss May!" Then he went looking for Winfield to introduce him to the centerfold.

But if Whitson seemed to be nearing the edge, so too did Martin. That night, Martin inadvertently called for a pitchout, which became a key factor in the Yankees' 4–2 loss to the Orioles. Martin had a sign on with catcher Butch Wynegar for the pitchout—he would stand at the top step of the dugout and scratch his nose.

But with the score tied at 2–2 in the seventh, a runner on first and a 2-0 count on the Oriole batter, Lee Lacy, Martin gave the sign without realizing it.

Wynegar, who couldn't understand why Martin would call a pitchout in that situation, creating a 3-0 count with pitcher Rich Bordi already struggling with his control, knew better than to defy the short-fused manager. So the pitchout was called, the runner at first wasn't going, and Bordi wound up walking Lacy to bring up the Orioles' two best hitters, Cal Ripken and Eddie Murray. Both of them hit RBI singles, sending the Yankees down to their eighth loss in a row.

After the game Wynegar told reporters they better ask Martin if they wanted to know anything about the pitchout. And Martin actually laughed when giving his explanation. He said he hadn't been thinking about where he was standing, and that he scratched his nose "because it itched."

Later that night, at the hotel bar, Martin was itching for something else—a fight. And after a few drinks he found one, which turned out to be the prelim bout to a wild weekend for him and Eddie Lee Whitson.

Martin was sitting at the bar with pitching coach Bill Monbouquette, whom he otherwise had little use for, when two couples approached him. "One of the girls said the other couple had just gotten married," Martin said, "so I bought them a bottle of champagne."

The two couples left, but later on, about 1:45 A.M., the newlyweds returned and talked to Martin awhile. The groom excused himself and went to the men's room, then came back and took his new wife to a table. But a few minutes later the guy was back. Martin was talking to reporters when he felt this poking on his shoulder. As he turned, the groom said to him: "We've got to talk. You said something to my wife."

"Get lost, pal," Martin said, and turned around.

But the guy wouldn't leave. Instead, he pressed on: "You told my wife she has a pot belly. I just married her this afternoon."

Martin replied, "I did not say she had a pot belly. I said this woman here [pointing to another woman at the bar] had a fat ass."

At that point, the man poked Martin again, and Martin shoved him back. Quickly a few players who had been observing the scene intervened. Rich Bordi restrained Martin, while Dave Righetti and Rickey Henderson got in front of the offended groom. The manager of the bar told the guy to leave, and Martin shouted, "We'll take this outside."

Martin went outside a few minutes later but returned quickly. "He sure got away in a hurry," he said. The next day, before the game with the Orioles, Martin was still complaining about the groom's speedy departure. "I didn't get him, but that doesn't mean I didn't want to. I was in the perfect mood. That guy caught me right, the way things are going. I don't care where I sit, it can be in a bullet-proof room. Someone's always gonna come along. And no matter what, it's always my fault, right?"

That night, following a Yankee victory that ended an eight-game skid, Moss Klein returned to the Cross Keys Inn from dinner with friends Andy and Anita Leiter. They were standing in the lobby when Martin came along. He had been drinking. Ignoring Klein's friends, he began telling the reporter he had been "set up" the night before in the bar, that the groom who had tried to pick a fight with him had been hired by Steinbrenner to get Martin in trouble again and give the Boss a reason for firing him. Then Martin walked off—in the direction of the bar.

Klein walked the Leiters to the parking lot, and Anita made a prophetic remark. "If I were you," she said, "I'd stay in the bar tonight. It looks like he's itching for another fight."

When Klein walked into the bar and looked around, he saw Whitson at the same table he had been at hours earlier, when Klein had been waiting to meet his friends. Whitson had a few friends with him, and the whole table was covered with beer bottles. Meanwhile, about 100 feet away at the bar, Martin was talking with broadcaster Frank Messer and Dale Berra and his wife. Klein took a table directly behind the area of the bar where Martin was sitting, but in the L-shaped room, he couldn't see Whitson's table.

Klein was joined by *Newsday* reporter Marty Noble and two women, Betsy Leesman, a Yankee employee, and her friend, who was in town as a babysitter for Bob Shirley's kids. After a while Betsy said, "Hey, Billy just got up," and Klein jokingly said, "I'll go see if he's leaving."

But as Klein turned the corner, he saw Martin and Whitson grabbing each other. Who started the fight? Klein had missed the key moment, as it turned out. Martin later insisted he had gone over to the table to aid Whitson, who was being bothered by somebody else. Whitson claimed that never happened.

The fight was quickly in full progress. Berra, Ron Hassey, and coach Gene Michael, aided by Whitson's friends, were trying to separate the two combatants as they rolled onto the floor. When they got up and were being restrained, Klein tried to talk Martin into leaving.

"Billy, you better get out of here," Klein said. "If you get into another fight, you know George will be out to get you."

In addition to trying to be helpful, Klein was also being selfish. He was so tired of doing Martin fight stories and Martin firing watches. That's what conies from covering the Yankees. Beat writers get to the point where they actually root against stories happening, just to get a break from the craziness.

But Martin, who was under control in comparison to the wild-eyed, raging Whitson, wouldn't leave. He kept saying, "That guy's crazy. He's crazy! I just tried to help him. What's the matter with him? Can't he hold his liquor?"

That, in turn, only served to further incite Whitson, who kept screaming and cursing at Martin. And Martin, never one to back away from a good fight, kept advancing as Whitson was being pushed back, out of the bar and into the lobby. Martin then made a blunder of getting too close and Whitson, who was wearing cowboy boots, kicked him squarely in the groin. Martin doubled over, then screamed, "Okay, now I'm gonna kill you. Now you did it."

The restrainers, joined by the hotel security men, rushed Whitson outside, in front of the hotel. Martin followed. There was a brief scuffle between Whitson and Berra, in which Whitson tore Berra's V-necked sweater and Berra responded by slugging him in the mouth, producing a split lip. It was far more damage than Martin would do.

Whitson broke loose, charging Martin and tackling him on the concrete pavement in front of the hotel entrance. They flailed away at each other on the ground before being pulled apart again by the security men. Martin was now bleeding from the nose and holding his right arm which, it was later discovered, was fractured. He was screaming, "He's finished. He's gone." And Whitson was screaming back, "You tried to bury me. You tried to ruin me!"

Finally a police car pulled up, and Martin headed back inside to the bar. But after a while he told Klein he was going out to find Whitson. He stopped at the front desk, asked for Whitson's room number, and got onto the elevator. But in an incredible bit of bad timing, as Martin got off the elevator on the third floor, Whitson was getting off the elevator right next to his. A shouting match started before Whitson's friends and hotel security people hustled him back to his room.

Bill Madden, who was staying on the third floor, was on the phone to his office, relaying all the events of the barroom and parking lot when he heard this new commotion.

"Hold on a minute," he said, "they're starting up again. Right here in the hallway."

A while later Madden came out of his room and saw Martin standing in the hallway in his underwear, holding his arm. He was a pathetic sight, but even more pathetic was what he was saying.

"I'm goin' down there and kick the shit out of that son of a bitch," Martin said. "He's in his room hiding from me. But I'm gonna get him out here."

Fortunately someone talked Martin into going to bed. The next day, he showed up at Memorial Stadium with his arm in a cast and sling, looking more bedraggled than usual. Whitson had been sent home by General Manager Clyde King, and Woody Woodward, King's assistant, had arrived on the scene to investigate the incident at Steinbrenner's behest.

Sitting in his office, Martin said he was "disappointed I didn't get a punch in. Too many people were holding me and getting in my way." He sneered at Whitson's tactics. "I can't fight feet. Maybe I ought to go to one of those karate schools in the off-season."

Someone asked Martin to compare the fight with some of his other notorious capers, particularly the parking lot scuffle he had with one of his pitchers in Minnesota, Dave Boswell, in 1969. "At least Boswell fought with his fists," Martin said. "This guy fights like a sissy, with his feet. But I guess it's similar because they both went cuckoo."

But when asked about his angry shouts that Whitson was finished as a Yankee, Martin said: "If he can pitch, he'll pitch. I never said I have to like my players. And if I have to yank him out of a game, I'll do it. But I'll watch his feet."

In the end Whitson outlasted Martin, who was fired right after the season. Nevertheless Whitson still desperately wanted out. All through spring training the following year, his agent, Tom Reich, urged Steinbrenner to trade the troubled pitcher, whose problems with the fans only worsened after the Martin fight.

One day that spring, Whitson spoke openly of his fear of the fans. "I have to get out of here," he said. "The issue has become a matter of safety for my family. If I get off to another bad start, someone might blow my head off."

Madden couldn't help but recall an incident in 1985 when he approached Whitson for an interview while the Yankees were waiting for a plane in the Ontario, California, airport. As he asked Whitson about his trying times with the fans, the pitcher began to cry. He talked of the "personal hell" he had been going through, but when he began to talk about his family, he couldn't go on.

On another occasion Whitson had told of the night a carload of rowdy fans followed his car out of the Yankee Stadium parking lot, taunting him and threatening him. He ran a red light to escape them, fearing they were going to follow him home. Whitson had also talked about finding carpenter's nails under the tires of the family car in the driveway of his house in Closter, New Jersey. Midway through the 1985 season, he began sending his wife and daughter home to Columbus, Ohio, when the Yankees went on roadtrips, and three days after the season he sold the house.

Whitson said he had "shoeboxes full of hate mail, but that didn't bother me after a while. It's the people who come up to your car window, the ones who threaten you and find out where your house is. That's the scary part."

Still, Whitson didn't get his wish for a trade right away in 1986. Steinbrenner was finding it difficult to trade a pitcher who was making nearly $1 million a year and who, at least on the surface, appeared to be going nuts. Meanwhile, the fans were getting on him even more as 1986 began, and Whitson became increasingly more paranoid.

During pregame drills he always wore his warmup jacket on the field, no matter how hot it was, because he didn't want early arriving fans to spot his uniform number and begin harassing him. Then, before the game, he would often take the long route to the bullpen, going through a passageway and a tunnel underneath the stands, rather than walk on the field. When he was in the bullpen, he became increasingly jumpy. Loud noises would unnerve him, another reliever said. After a few pranks the fun-loving bullpen crew of Righetti, Shirley & Co. realized how deathly afraid he was and tried to defend him from the taunts of the fans.

Meanwhile, Lou Piniella, who had replaced Martin as manager, couldn't figure out what to do with Whitson. First he decided not to use him in games at Yankee Stadium. Then he changed his mind. But when he saw the fear in Whitson's eyes at the prospect of taking the mound at the stadium, he again decided Whitson would be strictly a "road" pitcher.

When Whitson did pitch, he was ineffective. "Physically," said Piniella, "there's nothing wrong with him." Asked if Whitson's problems were therefore strictly mental, Piniella replied, "That's a good assumption."

As bullpen coach Jeff Torborg explained, "He has a good arm and good stuff, but he's such a high-strung individual, he obviously can't relax here. He gets so emotionally worked up that he can't function."

That was an understatement. During an early-season loss at Yankee Stadium in '86, his first appearance there since the Martin fight in September, Whitson's fear of the fans intensified. But when he pitched well against the Royals in Kansas City on April 21, he told Piniella he would be ready for his next turn five days later—at Yankee Stadium against Cleveland.

Piniella had already decided to use Bob Shirley in that game, afraid to start Whitson at the stadium. But he changed his mind, encouraged by Whitson's optimistic reaction from the Kansas City game. On the morning of April 26, two hours before the Saturday afternoon game against the Indians, Yankee trainer Gene Monahan rushed into Piniella's office.

"We've got a problem, Skip," Monahan said. "Whitson is hyperventilating."

"What?" exclaimed Piniella.

"He's hyperventilating," Monahan repeated. "You better take a look at him."

Piniella hastily followed Monahan into the trainer's room. Sure enough, there was Whitson, sitting on the table, sweating profusely, gasping for breath, white as a sheet. There was no question Yankee phobia had struck again.

Piniella located Shirley and told him he'd be pitching and returned to his office. Ten minutes later Whitson came in.

"I'm fine, Lou, I'm really fine. I want to pitch."

Piniella asked him if he was sure, and Whitson again insisted he was okay. Piniella replied, "Okay, you're in there. You're my starter."

The words were barely out of his mouth when Whitson began hyperventilating again. Piniella threw up his hands and called in Monahan.

"What the hell kind of shit *is* this, Gene?" he asked. "When he calms down—*if* he calms down—tell him he's scratched. For good."

The fans, who had been expecting Whitson, were chanting "Ed-die, Eddie" before the national anthem was played. They were obviously disappointed when the ballyhooed "Return of Whitson" was canceled. So was Shirley. All the confusion got to him, and he gave up three runs in the first inning, retiring only one batter before an exasperated Piniella yanked him. After the game Whitson was gone. The official "injury" report released by the Yankees said that he had suffered a "pulled rib cage muscle" and had a "stomach virus."

Finally, on July 9, 1986, Eddie Lee Whitson's wish came true. He was traded back to the Padres for reliever Tim Stoddard. The Yankees were playing in Texas that night. When Whitson was informed of the trade shortly after 2:00 P.M., he checked out of the hotel and rushed to the airport in time for a 4:00 P.M. flight to San Diego. While standing on the checkout line at the Yankees' hotel, he was singing "Happy Days Are Here Again!"

Back with the Padres, Whitson became a happy and effective pitcher again. And despite all his troubles with the Yankees, he somehow managed an overall 15–10 record for his year and a half with them. Of course, that record was highly misleading. He had a 5.38 ERA, allowed an average of 14.38 base runners per nine innings, and gave new meaning to the Rolling Stones' hit "19th Nervous Breakdown."

Davey Collins

Nobody epitomized the wild and crazy 1982 Yankee season more than Davey Collins, the leader of the misfits. The mild-mannered, moderately talented Collins was a study in confusion from the day he made the ill-advised decision to sign with the Yankees as a free agent. And as the tumultuous season progressed, with no less than 47 players, 3 managers, 5 pitching coaches, and 3 batting coaches passing through the Bronx scene, Collins remained genuinely stunned by the goings-on. It should be said, however, that his early-season amazement turned to amusement by midseason.

Collins had no business coming to the Yankees. He was a well-paid victim of George Steinbrenner's panic-button plan to turn the Yankees into a "speed" team for 1982—defying the tried-and-true tradition of building Yankee teams around left-handed power.

Although Collins didn't sign with the Yankees until December 23, 1981, the official beginning of his Yankee career was October 28, the night the World Series ended with the Yankees losing to the Dodgers. Before the game had ended, a grim Steinbrenner prepared a terse statement: "I want to sincerely apologize to the people of New York and to Yankee fans everywhere for the performance of the Yankee team in this World Series. I also want to assure you that we will be at work immediately to prepare for 1982."

The next day, Steinbrenner called a press briefing and explained his newly hatched plan. "I'm tired of sitting around and waiting for someone to hit a three-run homer," he said. "To be a big-inning team, you have to have speed. And we'll be going for more speed."

Thus Steinbrenner embarked on a mission to turn the Bronx Bombers into the Bronx Burners. Home runs were out, speed was in. First he traded for potential free agent Ken Griffey, a left-handed hitter who customarily stole more bases in a season than he hit homers. His next step was the signing of Collins.

Basically, Steinbrenner just overwhelmed Collins. Both the Kansas City Royals and Toronto Blue Jays were attempting to sign him. A 29-year-old slap-hitting outfielder, Collins had stolen 79 bases for the Cincinnati Reds in 1980 and was generally regarded as an artificial turf player whose hitting was best suited to high hoppers off the turf that he could leg out for singles.

The Royals and Blue Jays both had artificial turf playing fields and both had clear-cut spots for Collins. But in mid-December Steinbrenner contacted Collins' agent, Richie Bry, and informed him of his desire to sign Collins. Bry knew what that meant: no matter how high the bidding went, Steinbrenner would make the best offer.

Which he did—a whopping $2.475-million, three-year package that was ludicrous even in those free-spending, free-agent days for a player of Collins' limited ability. Collins was both overwhelmed and confused. He knew the Yankee outfield was overcrowded with talent. Dave Winfield, Griffey, and Jerry Mumphrey all had spots set, and Lou Piniella and Bobby Murcer were still around as reserves. What's more, Steinbrenner still had not officially let Reggie Jackson go as a free agent. First base was occupied by Bob Watson.

So even though Collins was eager to take the Boss' generous offer, he also wanted to play. He called Steinbrenner directly to ask him about the situation, and Steinbrenner responded with a promise. "You'll get more at-bats than Winfield," the Boss said. "Don't worry about it."

Collins, unfamiliar with Steinbrenner's campaign-promise approach when dealing with free agents, accepted the word of the principal Yankee owner—as well as his money.

Less than a month later, Reggie Jackson signed with the California Angels after having been virtually snubbed by Steinbrenner. Years later Steinbrenner would call that one of his biggest mistakes as Yankee owner. And years later Davey Collins would say his decision to sign with the Yankees was *his* biggest mistake. In effect, Collins was to be taking the place of Reggie, an exchange that history would not smile on.

Collins reported to spring training in late February, about to begin a season he would never forget. His first day in camp he was told he was going to be a first baseman, and he worked every day the rest of the spring with coach Joe Altobelli, a former first baseman.

Meanwhile, the camp had been turned into a circus by Steinbrenner. Consider the development of March 2, less than a week before the exhibition games were to begin.

The Yankees showed up for the workout, only to be informed there would be no workout—at least not in the usual sense. Instead of hitting, throwing, pitching and base-running drills, the players were told to don their sweat suits and head to the back field to run 45-yard sprints under the direction of Harrison Dillard, the former Olympic hurdling champion, who had been imported by Steinbrenner as a special spring training instructor. Dillard's assignment was to teach the Yankees to run. He was to scrutinize the running styles of all the players and then offer tips on how to improve each one's technique.

"You can't underestimate the importance of speed," said Steinbrenner, who reminded his players that he had been a champion hurdler in his college days at Williams.

"They must have used ankle-high hurdles in those days," cracked Graig Nettles.

The Yankees' "Day at the Races" was a fitting sequel to the Marx Brothers comedy. Bobby Brown, the talented young outfielder, turned in the best time, sprinting to the finish line in 5.18 seconds to beat Jerry Mumphrey. Brown, however, blundered after the race. Back in the locker room, Steinbrenner went over to Brown and jokingly said, "You better get ready for the Olympics."

But Brown, who wanted to be traded, ruined his chances of getting on Steinbrenner's good side by muttering, "How about getting me ready to play somewhere else." Steinbrenner, annoyed, turned away, saying, "We're working on that." One month later Brown was traded to Seattle.

Oscar Gamble, who had been excused from the races because of a muscle pull, got in the spirit while watching the others sprinting across the outfield grass and insisted on running. Gamble didn't have any running shoes with him, and instead of going all the way back to the clubhouse, he ran in his socks. He turned in the second-fastest time with a 5.19 clocking.

Collins, meanwhile, had come through with flying colors for Steinbrenner in the sprint. He was paired against Winfield and edged him out, even though Winfield jumped Yogi Berra's command of "Go!" and had a head start. Steinbrenner went out of his way to congratulate Collins, who was now beginning to realize this was anything but your ordinary baseball team.

"I don't think any team ever had a spring training workout like this one," Collins said, shaking his head.

And to think that that was one of the more orderly days for Collins. When the exhibition games started, Collins could never figure out which way to go. Despite his daily work with Altobelli at first base, Collins was usually used in the outfield by manager Bob Lemon, and he was ordered to play in B games, then hustle back to play in the A games.

As Lemon confided to Bill Madden at one point, "They gave me this guy and told me to play him, but what the hell am I supposed to do with him? We've got guys better than him at every position."

The Yankees began to struggle, and Steinbrenner began to panic. There were nightly postgame meetings in the executive trailer behind the ballpark, with the weary Lemon and his coaches trudging in and out while JoAnne Steinbrenner paced the darkened parking lot waiting for her husband.

Soon Steinbrenner was ordering double-session workouts and special drills, warning his players that their complaints of fatigue would fall on deaf ears. The principal Yankee owner was beginning to sense that the team he had put together was missing something—mainly power—but bristled at the mounting criticism and jokes being made of his Bronx Burners. The more criticism, the more workouts. Young players were being banished to Columbus, older players were being overworked, trades were being made. Lemon, who would be fired 14 games into the season, was probably the first manager ever to get on thin ice in spring training.

All the while, Collins was sitting back observing his new world in disbelief. He realized he didn't fit, and his insecurity was magnified by the taunting he took from teammate Rick Cerone. Cerone was quick to sense Collins' worry and began inventing daily trade rumors, coaxing the writers into telling them to Collins. Always they were trades to bad teams—which further served to unnerve Collins.

Collins was staying at the team's spring training headquarters hotel, the Gait Ocean Mile, and would often sit on the beach with Moss Klein in the late afternoon.

"Why do they want me here?" Collins would ask Klein. "There's no role for me here. This is the craziest team I've ever seen."

Collins would ask Klein to check with Lemon about his plans. But Lemon had no answers.

"I guess he's gonna play somewhere," Lemon said. "Will he be traded? You got me, Meat. They don't tell me what's going on here. I'm just the manager."

Collins lasted the entire 1982 season, which was a lot longer than Lemon lasted, but Collins' question—"What am I doing here?"—was never answered. He played first base, he played all three outfield spots, he was the designated hitter, and he was a pinch hitter and a pinch runner. He made it into 111 games, but no, he didn't get as many at-bats as Winfield. In fact, he ranked seventh on the team in at-bats. The one category he ranked first in was confusion.

Collins simply couldn't believe the Yankee operation of shuttling so many players, managers, and coaches in and out like commuters at Grand Central Station. The 47 players set a record that year. The speed concept was quickly abandoned, and the power game was restored when Steinbrenner went out and acquired aging, faded slugger John Mayberry from Toronto. Nothing, of course, worked. The Yankees finished with a 79–83 record, their worst since 1967.

The capper to all this chaos and confusion for Collins, the point when he stopped being amazed and started being amused, came on May 13. Two days earlier, catcher Cerone had suffered a broken thumb in a play at the plate against the California Angels in Anaheim. With Barry Foote the only remaining catcher, Juan Espino was called up from Columbus. The next night was the series finale at Anaheim. Espino joined the team but didn't play. He merely warmed up the pitcher between innings.

That night the Yankees completed a trade for Minnesota catcher Butch Wynegar, who joined the team the next day in Oakland. Collins was sitting by his locker in the Oakland clubhouse that day. When Klein walked in, Collins called him over.

"Which one's Espino?" Collins asked, a question that would serve as the keynote address for that '82 season. "I haven't met him yet."

Klein laughed. "You're too late, you missed him," he told Collins. "He was on the flight here from Anaheim, but he was sent back to Columbus today. Wynegar's here. Espino's gone."

Collins shook his head, that familiar wide-eyed expression coming across his face. "This place is unbelievable," he said. "There's nothing like it anywhere."

After the season Collins was mercifully traded to Toronto. He had two fine seasons with the Blue Jays, the team he wished he had signed with in the first place. So anxious was Steinbrenner to dump Collins' contract on the Blue Jays and erase his mistake of signing him, he compounded it by agreeing to throw into the deal a minor league first baseman named Fred McGriff. Even though McGriff was from Steinbrenner's home town of Tampa, the Boss knew nothing about him. He found out six years later when McGriff hit 34 homers for the Blue Jays.

As it turned out, Steinbrenner admitted to Collins some guilt pangs over everything that happened in 1982. A few weeks after he was traded to Toronto, Collins received a letter from the principal Yankee owner. "He just wanted to wish me luck with Toronto and thanked me for giving him 100 percent as a Yankee under trying circumstances," Collins said. "He said he felt bad that things didn't work out with the Yankees. And he admitted it was a strange year."

Collins' travels took him to Oakland in 1985, Detroit in 1986, and back to Cincinnati in 1987 after a brief spring training stop with Montreal. He later joked to Klein: "If I bought a house in every city I played in, when it comes time to retire, I'd have a ready-made real estate business."

By 1988 Collins had been with eight teams in an 11-year career, but nothing would ever dim his memories of 1982.

"That year was an experience I'll never forget," he said. "I wouldn't want to go through it again, but it gave me stories to tell the rest of my life."

Doyle Alexander

It is doubtful if there was ever a more sour person to pass through the Steinbrenner asylum than Doyle Alexander, the much-traveled right-handed pitcher. Maybe that was because Alexander knew he was a misfit with the Yankees and resented not being somewhere else where he could just go out and pitch and be left alone. Actually, Alexander had two tours of duty in The Bronx, neither of them of his own choice, which undoubtedly had a lot to do with his sullen disposition.

In 1976 Alexander was traded to the Yankees in midseason from the Baltimore Orioles and wound up the surprise starter in the first game of the World Series against the Cincinnati Reds, as Billy Martin had run through all his more highly regarded starters in the playoffs versus Kansas City. Alexander was bombed for nine hits and five runs in six innings in that game and, if nothing else, was probably satisfied he had pitched his last game as a Yankee.

Shortly after the season, he filed for free agency and fled to Texas and the perennially last-place Rangers. After a couple of years in Texas, Alexander moved on to Atlanta and eventually San Francisco, where he was about as far away from the Yankees as one could hope for.

As he did almost every place he went, however, Alexander became embroiled in a contract dispute in the spring of 1982. And like all of Alexander's previous employers, the Giants decided they didn't want the headache of trying to re-sign disgruntled Doyle. So they called the Yankees and Steinbrenner, who were more than willing to take Alexander back…so willing that they signed him to a new four-year contract worth $2.2 million.

It took a few days to complete the trade because of Alexander's contract demands, but on March 30 the deal was announced that Alexander was coming back for a couple of minor league prospects, pitcher Andy McGaffigan and outfielder Ted Wilborn. Bill Madden had been tipped off about the trade a day earlier and called manager Bob Lemon in his hotel room at the Gait Ocean Mile to ask him about it.

"I hear you've got yourself a new starting pitcher," Madden said.

"Oh, yeah?" said Lemon. "Who am I getting?"

"Doyle Alexander," replied Madden.

There was a brief moment of silence at the other end of the phone.

"Just what I need," said Lemon, "another hemorrhoid."

With that, Lemon said he wanted to go back to watching "Barnaby Jones," his favorite TV show, which helped him take his mind off the ever-growing loony bin he was being asked to preside over that spring.

The next day, as word of Alexander's second coming circulated around the Yankee camp, Lemon's sentiments seemed to be shared by a few others. Moss Klein was talking to Graig Nettles in the clubhouse and told him how Steinbrenner predicted Alexander would win 15 games for the Yankees.

"Fifteen?" said Nettles. "Hmmm. How many years did George give him?"

"Four," said Klein.

"Yeah, well," deadpanned Nettles, "in that case he *might* win 15."

As it turned out, Nettles' dire assessment wasn't even close to the mark. Alexander won one game for the Yankees in his second go-round with them. Then again, he didn't make the four years, either. He was released after a year and two months with them, only to resume his career as a quality pitcher with the Toronto Blue Jays.

Alexander was anything but a quality pitcher for the Yankees. Whether he just didn't want to be there or whether he just couldn't adjust to life in the Yankee fishbowl, Alexander could do nothing right in pinstripes.

After missing most of spring training because of his contract dispute, Alexander stayed behind in Fort Lauderdale to pitch himself into shape and didn't make his first start until April 24. He never could seem to get on track, though, and was largely ineffective in his first two starts.

In his third start, against the Mariners in Seattle, he was the victim of a five-run third inning in which four of the runs were unearned. Furious over having to come out of the game at that point, Alexander came into the dugout and punched the wall, breaking a knuckle on his pitching hand. The self-inflicted injury knocked him out of action for six weeks, and he got no sympathy from the Yankee high command.

"I don't feel sorry for him at all," said Yankee manager Gene Michael. "It was a dumb thing to do...one of the dumbest things I've ever seen. How a pitcher who's been around as long as he has can punch a wall with his pitching hand is beyond me. We needed him. He was important in our plans, and he's not only hurt himself, he's hurt the team."

Initially Alexander agreed with Michael's harsh assessment of the mishap and, instead of waiting to be fined by the club, offered to return a month's pay to the Yankees for his mistake. But then union chief Marvin Miller and the Players Association stepped in and said that would be a dangerous precedent for a player to set. Alexander agreed and informed the Yankees he was rescinding his offer.

The Yankees wound up fining Alexander $12,500 for his painful experience, but that was not the end of it. Toward the end of his recuperation period, Alexander went to Columbus, the Yankees' AAA farm team, to pitch his way back into shape. When Steinbrenner requested him to stay awhile longer in the minors to be certain he was ready, however, Alexander refused.

Steinbrenner was incensed. He ordered Alexander's activation on June 9 and told manager Michael to pitch him right away. Alexander pitched that night against the Athletics in Oakland and was pummeled for five runs and five hits, retiring only four batters. Afterward Yankee general manager Bill Bergesch issued a stinging indictment of Alexander that had obviously been dictated by Steinbrenner.

"George said he is sorry he signed Alexander off the recent series of events," Bergesch said. "If we could trade him tomorrow, he [Steinbrenner] said he would authorize me to do it. What Doyle Alexander did tonight was disgraceful, but typical of the selfishness of some of the modern-day ball players."

Michael followed that up by announcing that Alexander was going to have to pitch his way back into the rotation by going to the bullpen.

"It's their team, and they can do with it what they want," said Alexander. "I'm not looking for a verbal war with these guys. I'm available to pitch if they want me."

It seemed impossible that Alexander's season could deteriorate any further than that point. Nevertheless, he continued to pitch poorly, while blaming his performance—perhaps with some justification—on his irregular pitching schedule.

On August 10 Alexander reached his nadir as a Yankee, and Steinbrenner reached his zenith as a statement writer. The Yankees were playing the Tigers in Detroit, having won four of their last five games under new manager Clyde King. On Alexander's first pitch of the game, Tiger second baseman Lou Whitaker homered into the left field seats. Two more homers would follow in a six-hit, six-run barrage that drove Alexander to the showers after just three innings.

From his home in Tampa, Steinbrenner furiously dictated a statement to Bergesch that, even by the principal owner's standards, was outrageous. Usually the reaction in the press box to Steinbrenner statements is either ridicule or disinterest, but this one brought looks of astonishment from one and all before the hilarity began to set in.

"After what happened tonight," Steinbrenner said, "I'm having Doyle Alexander flown back to New York to undergo a physical. I'm afraid some of our players might get hurt playing behind him. He steadfastly refused to go back to Columbus another time to pitch his way back into shape. That's okay if you back it up with solid performance. But Alexander has given up eight homers in 38 innings, and in his last two starts he's given up 11 runs in five innings. Obviously something is wrong and we intend to find out."

After the game reporters flocked to Alexander for his reaction to this latest and most stinging blast from Steinbrenner.

"It's obvious I'm not pitching well," Alexander said calmly. "I'm not pitching the way I can, and I regret that for the fans and my teammates."

What about the physical?

"I think it's a good move," Alexander said, adding much to the surprise of everyone that he agreed to do it. "But I want to make it plain this is with a medical doctor, not a psychiatrist. A lot of people are going crazy around here, but I'm not there yet."

Goose Gossage echoed that remark by saying, "Doyle's getting a physical, but George needs a mental."

As for Steinbrenner's fears for the safety of his players when Alexander was pitching, Nettles gave assurances that wasn't a problem.

"I wasn't worried," Nettles said. "Maybe I might have been if I was sitting in the left field stands."

Alexander finished the '82 season with a 1–7 mark and 6.08 ERA. Undoubtedly Steinbrenner would have liked to follow his inclination earlier in the year and trade the disappointing pitcher, but with that record and that salary, Alexander had virtually no value on the trade market. As a result, when spring training began in February of 1983, he was back with all the other Yankee pitchers in Fort Lauderdale.

This time Billy Martin was on hand as Yankee manager, his third stint. Billy, of course, remembered Alexander from the pitcher's first tour of duty with the Yankees. He hadn't been particularly fond of him then, and he wasn't now, although he realized Alexander was probably going to have to be on his staff because of the big contract. Anyway, Alexander surprised one and all when, in his first start of the spring, he threw three shutout innings against the Orioles.

After Alexander had completed his outing, Bill Madden ran down to the clubhouse to solicit his thoughts about a new start and a new season. Madden kept asking Alexander questions but got no response. Finally Alexander looked up and said, "You're probably wondering why I'm not answering your questions. The reason is I haven't forgotten all the things you wrote about me last year, and as far as I'm concerned, I have nothing to say to you."

"I only wrote what I saw," said Madden. "You had a lousy season.... I think even you would have to admit that. I didn't rip you unfairly. You had a bad year and I wrote it."

"It doesn't matter," said Alexander. "You continue writing, I'll continue pitching. Your job is to observe me and write it. I'm not going to help you by giving you quotes. You just observe."

The rest of that spring and into the season, Madden and the rest of the writers observed Alexander struggle some more as Martin pitched him irregularly. At last, on May 31, Dour Doyle's tribulations as a Yankee came to an end. He was released, with Steinbrenner obligated to pay the remaining $1.5 million on his contract. His overall record for the year and a half he spent with them the second time was 1–9, with a 6.16 ERA, and of the 24 games he appeared in, the Yankees lost 21.

Unlike so many of the Misfits who never recovered from their Yankee experience, Alexander went on to have the last laugh at his tormentors' expense. Three weeks after the Yankees released him, he signed with the Blue Jays and won 17 games in each of the next two seasons for them. Alexander's last victory in 1985 was a five-hit, 5–1 effort against the Yankees that clinched the American League East title for the Blue Jays. The final irony of that was the Yankees were eliminated by a man whom they were still paying.

Two years later, after Alexander had worn out his welcome in Toronto (as well as Atlanta a second time), he surfaced in Detroit with the Tigers. Acquired in a trade on August 12, he proceeded to go 9–0, with a 1.52 ERA, the rest of the year and almost single-handedly pitched the Tigers into the American

League playoffs. A few weeks prior to Alexander's trade from Atlanta to Detroit, the Yankees were looking for a pitcher as well. Braves general manager Bobby Cox offered them Alexander, but they turned him down. Instead, they got Steve Trout.

Roy Smalley

Roy Smalley always seemed to be a stranger in a strange land during his 2½ seasons with the Yankees. He never really fit on the field, and he never fit too well in the clubhouse with the other players. Neither ill fit was his fault.

As a player, Smalley was mostly the victim of poor planning and panic-stricken moves that characterized the Yankees' upside-down blueprint in 1982. He was acquired to play shortstop for a team that already had a shortstop, Bucky Dent—and this despite scouting reports that his increasingly limited range dictated that he should be a third baseman or, better yet, a designated hitter.

Smalley could hit, there was no question about that. In fact, he set the Yankee all-time record for home runs by a shortstop in 1982, hitting 16 of his 20 homers while he was playing short. But there were those who said he should have simply brought his bat instead of his glove when he had to play the position, because his painfully narrow range prevented him from reaching many grounders.

When Clyde King was Yankee manager and growing tired of watching balls skip through the infield as Smalley made futile efforts to get to them, he described him this way: "When I watch Smalley playing shortstop, I think of those old movies of the Mummy. You know, when the guy is wrapped up with all those bandages and walks so stiff he can hardly move. That's my shortstop. The Mummy."

Smalley had another name in the clubhouse: Tootsie. When the Mummy unwrapped the bandages at shortstop, he would put on some fancy threads, a wardrobe that went far beyond most of the players' jeans-and-T-shirt attire. California cool and all the latest in designer fashions were the standard Smalley attire.

Rick Cerone, a noted clubhouse needler, pinned the moniker Tootsie on Smalley, mocking his elegant, ultrastylish clothes and dazzling colors. The movie *Tootsie,* for which Dustin Hoffman won an Oscar in the role of a frustrated actor who finds success disguised as an actress, was popular at the time, and Cerone decided that Smalley's stylish look, in hues of mauve, lilac, and powder blue, was more befitting a model—or maybe a cheerleader—than a ball player.

Traditionally, if a player shows he can be riled by kidding, then the kidding becomes relentless. Those who have phobias about crawly creatures, for example, are tormented constantly. Gene Michael had such a phobia, and even when he advanced to the status of manager, the pranks continued. One day in Chicago, a player—most suspected Cerone—put a frog in a cup Michael was about to drink from, and the manager bolted from his chair as if he was on fire.

Smalley didn't laugh off the Tootsie remarks, so there was no end to them. "Tootsie couldn't take it," Cerone said years later. "I guess if it didn't bother him, we would've quit it. But he would always get mad."

Even when Smalley was eventually traded to the White Sox, the taunts continued. The first time the Yankees played in Chicago after Smalley's trade, Cerone immediately spotted him during batting practice and, noting the White Sox uniform colors, shouted across the field, "Hey, what a great trade for Tootsie. Now he gets to wear red shoes!"

Smalley certainly didn't help his case one day in Minnesota when he told a local reporter that "most of the guys on the team use Walt Garrison as their model for what to wear. They think Giorgio Armani is a soccer player."

Indeed, most players wore the type of jeans that Garrison, the former Dallas Cowboy running back, promoted in commercials. And most had no idea who designer Armani was. But that comment just encouraged further stunts—such as the time in Kansas City when several players showed up early to plant a black negligee in Smalley's locker, under his uniform.

The word was passed around, and a dozen players, along with a few reporters, were waiting for Smalley to take his uniform off the hanger, to reveal the negligee. When he did, the cries of "Tootsie!" began. Once again, rather than join in—or at least acknowledge the locker room attempts at humor—Smalley sneered and continued dressing, ignoring the laughter.

In many ways, Smalley was reminiscent of the character of Winchester in "M*A*S*H." He was clearly more refined, more intelligent, more well-spoken than most of his teammates, and he certainly didn't make any attempt to be one of the guys. He was good friends with Butch Wynegar, who had been his teammate in Minnesota, and to a lesser degree he was close with Don Baylor and Dave Winfield and a few others. Most of the rest—well, they could just pull their schoolboy pranks, snicker all they wanted. Smalley didn't seem to care.

The writers, however, were especially fond of Smalley. He was great to them, a breath of fresh air, with his ability to expound on any given subject. He was consistently cooperative, extremely perceptive, and unusually articulate. And he was as amazed as anyone at George Steinbrenner's methods of operating the New York Yankees. While all the other players would mostly shake their heads at that, Smalley would offer clever remarks.

One time he explained Steinbrenner's handling of the team this way: "It's like a dog who has a favorite toy. You know, the way a dog will keep chewing at the toy, tearing at it, kicking it around. Eventually the toy just starts falling apart. I don't mean to compare Mr. Steinbrenner with a dog, but the way he handles this team, well…we're the toy."

The image seemed perfect.

Smalley's treatment on the field, the way he was periodically benched and misused, bothered him far more than the sophomoric pranks in the locker room. From the beginning he was in a bad spot. When he was acquired from the Twins the day before the 1982 season opener, Bucky Dent was still the shortstop and considered the one rock of stability on the Yankees. And Graig Nettles was still the third baseman.

The problem was that Dent was originally supposed to go to the Twins as part of the package for Smalley. But at the last minute Twins owner Calvin Griffith said he didn't want Dent, and the Yankees substituted a minor league shortstop named Greg Gagne. Suddenly, here was Smalley, taking playing time from Dent, a former World Series hero and a favorite among the Yankee fans. An early-season injury to Nettles temporarily solved the problem, although Smalley wound up playing 89 games at shortstop and 53 at third base that '82 season.

By late June Smalley was already sick of the situation. Nettles had returned, and Michael was using an unpredictable rotation at shortstop. "The way we've been used has hurt Bucky and has hurt me," Smalley said. "We've both been accustomed to playing all the time, not worrying about being benched if we go hitless for two games. They've turned it into a contest—who can do the most in fifty at-bats or less. They should just make up their minds."

Smalley, who had been a solid player for the Twins for six years before coming to the Yankees, eventually became the regular shortstop when Dent was traded to the Texas Rangers in August.

The 1983 season was even more confusing for Smalley. Billy Martin had taken over as manager. Back in 1975, when Martin was the Texas manager, he had actually given Smalley his first break as a rookie with the Rangers, but it soon became apparent to Martin that Smalley had deteriorated as a shortstop. Martin started using young Andre Robertson, who became a sensation. Smalley was used irregularly, a few games at short, a backup for Nettles at third, and an occasional first baseman.

When Robertson was severely injured in an automobile accident on August 18, Martin wanted Bobby Meacham, a rookie who had had a standout spring training, to take over as shortstop. In July Meacham had been called up for less than 24 hours before general manager Murray Cook traded for all-purpose infielder Larry Milbourne. Since Cook had done the acquiring, Martin had no use for Milbourne, and that turned out to be a break for Smalley, who started playing regularly at short.

When Smalley would make errors, however, Martin would go into rages. On August 27 Smalley made two ninth-inning errors at Anaheim Stadium, enabling the Angels to rally for two runs and a 7–6 victory. Martin was livid. In the press room after the game, as he downed drinks, he complained loudly to Moss Klein, blaming Cook for the loss.

"If we had Meacham," Martin said, "I could've got Smalley out of there. But I'm not gonna use Milbourne, so I have to stay with Smalley, and he can't play shortstop. The genius general manager is costing us the pennant."

Martin's point was driven home with Steinbrenner two weeks later. The Yankees had surged to within four games of first-place Baltimore going into a September 10 double-header with the Orioles at Yankee Stadium. But the Orioles swept the doubleheader, effectively eliminating the Yankees. In the opener, with the score tied 2–2, Smalley made an error, his second of the game, and that opened the door to a six-run Oriole inning.

On the press elevator going down to the basement of the stadium after the game, Steinbrenner said, "You don't win pennants without a shortstop." Clearly Smalley's days at the position were numbered.

But before Smalley's ultimate escape from the Yankees, there was still a stretch of confusion and torment in store for him.

By the time the 1983 season ended, Smalley knew he was no longer regarded as a shortstop. That job would be Robertson's if he was able to make the comeback from his injuries. Meacham was next in line. But there was a spot for Smalley as the third baseman, with Nettles eligible for free agency and Steinbrenner apparently undecided about re-signing him.

Then, in early November, Nettles re-signed. That effectively blocked third base, leaving Smalley the backup again. At the winter meetings in Nashville, his path was further blocked when the Yankees acquired utility infielder Tim Foli from the Angels.

Smalley wanted out. He had told general manager Cook he'd like to be traded, but that didn't get any results. So Smalley became more outspoken than usual. When Klein asked him about the acquisition of Foli, Smalley said: "I have to wonder whether George talks to his general manager. Murray Cook knows I want to be traded. What he doesn't understand is my biggest worry is that I won't be traded. I want to go. Nobody seems to know what's going on here. It's just characteristic of the way the Yankees operate."

Five days later Cook telephoned Smalley, who assumed he was about to be told he was traded. As he braced himself, Smalley heard Cook talking about a contract extension!

"I was shocked," Smalley said. "Even though I learned at that point never to expect logical developments with the Yankees, I couldn't understand this one."

Smalley had one year remaining on his contract, making the offer of an extension all the more surprising. But Steinbrenner had decided Smalley could help as a backup at first base and third base and would eventually replace Nettles, who was nearing 40.

"I was told," said Cook, "to get Smalley signed…to overwhelm him with dollars. I wasn't sure how he was going to fit, but I was supposed to sign him right away."

Smalley, 31 at the time, didn't need much convincing when Cook made the five-year $3.9-million offer. Suddenly the future of the Smalley family was secure. His amount of playing time, or whatever position he played, didn't seem that important anymore. Like so many free-agent Misfits who took Steinbrenner's money, however, Smalley would soon discover that money didn't buy sanity.

By the time spring training started, new manager Yogi Berra had decided to give Smalley a shot at the first base job. What about the backup to Nettles? Why, that plan was aborted by the February acquisition of third baseman Toby Harrah from the Cleveland Indians, another move that nobody could quite figure. After all, Steinbrenner had just signed Nettles for two years at big money and Smalley for five years at even bigger money, what did he possibly need with another third baseman? In addition, the Yankees were hurting in the bullpen with the loss of Goose Gossage to free agency, and they used a reliever, George Frazier, to get Harrah.

Nevertheless, Yogi figured he was supposed to find playing time for Smalley. "I don't think George is paying him that much to sit around," Yogi said, echoing Bob Lemon's remarks about Davey Collins, a Yankee Misfit of a couple of years earlier.

First base appeared to be open, although there was this kid named Mattingly who had shown flashes of being a pretty decent hitter as a rookie in 1983. "Mattingly will get playing time," Yogi insisted. "He'll be my swing man, a backup at first and in the outfield."

Smalley went to work at first base. He wasn't especially impressive, though, and when he had a shaky day in a March 21 game against the Mets—with Steinbrenner watching—the rumblings began. Steinbrenner told the writers that Mattingly should be the first baseman, a choice that history would certainly support. In fact, Steinbrenner called a meeting at the Bay Harbor Inn in Tampa following the loss to the Mets to inform Berra of the switch that was about to be made. Yogi, resenting Steinbrenner's interference, resisted at first. But the Yankees were 5–12 in the Grapefruit League, and Steinbrenner was ready for changes.

Smalley was less upset than Yogi. "I just think it's pretty funny that George and his—quote—baseball people are ready to make a change because of a few spring training games," Smalley said. "Panic is setting in. If we were 18–2 instead of 5–12, the world would indeed be rosy."

Smalley admitted he would have been more upset if he hadn't been armed with the financial security of the five-year contract. "They made an expensive decision during the winter to go with me at first base," he said. "If George wants to panic, that's up to him. I just think we should recognize that it's funny they made this expensive decision and now they're willing to chuck it all on the basis of a few exhibition games."

But then there was an added twist. On March 26 Steinbrenner called another emergency meeting. The Yankees were continuing to struggle, and as Nettles said, "There's panic under the Big Top."

Not only was Steinbrenner dissatisfied with Smalley, he didn't like Ken Griffey in center field, another spring training experiment. So Griffey was being returned to first base, Mattingly was back to the role of first base-outfield swing man, and Omar Moreno was restored to center field. Smalley? He was the number-three third baseman behind Nettles and Harrah.

Oy vey! Smalley was informed of his further-reduced status that morning, when he, Harrah, and Griffey were summoned to a Steinbrenner-ordered "punishment workout" at Fort Lauderdale Stadium. Smalley was handed a fielder's glove to replace his first baseman's glove, and Griffey was presented with a first baseman's glove. Harrah was invited, Smalley said, "because he made an error yesterday."

Smalley found the juggling humorous, describing the maneuvers as "typical panic moves." But he didn't appreciate the negative remarks Steinbrenner had made about his defense, or the implications the owner was making about "Smalley being complacent."

"I'm not paid to make decisions on who should play where," said Smalley. "But what I don't like is the philosophy of the owner. Just because he pays large salaries doesn't mean he's entitled to demean and denigrate a player's ability."

Ironically, Mattingly would make almost that same statement four years later when he blasted Steinbrenner for giving the players money but no respect.

Yogi, meanwhile, just shrugged at all the moves, saying, "The way we've looked, we had to do something. But everything is subject to change."

That went without saying.

And a few days later everything changed again. Nettles, who had incurred Steinbrenner's wrath when the Boss got wind of his comments in his forthcoming autobiography, *Balls,* was traded to the San Diego Padres after weeks of verbal warfare with the Boss. Smalley was elevated to platoon status with Harrah at third base.

By mid-July, however, the Yankees were hopelessly out of the pennant race and the decision was to go with young Mike Pagliarulo at third base. On July 18 the Yankees did what they should have done two years earlier: they traded Smalley to the White Sox.

"I'm very pleased to be going to Chicago," Smalley understated. "Each of the three years I spent with the Yankees presented a different kind of confusion. I handled things as best I could. I'll remember my time with the Yankees as being a very interesting period. Regardless of anything else, when you're with the Yankees, you stay on your toes. That's a necessity."

Nearly four years later, the Yankees entered Smalley's life again, providing an appropriate finish to his career. He had been traded by the White Sox to the Twins before the 1985 season, returning home. He put in three useful seasons with the Twins, mostly as a designated hitter, culminating his last season with an appearance in the 1987 World Series, the first Series in his 13-year career.

At the time of their deal with the White Sox, however, the Twins had an agreement they could return Smalley any year, prior to March 1. After the 1987 season, with two years still left on that contract extension the Yankees had thrust on him, the Twins decided the time to return Smalley had come.

The White Sox, meanwhile, thought they had the same arrangement with the Yankees, dating back to their 1984 deal for Smalley. Thus it appeared in early February of 1988 that Smalley would be coming back to the Yankees for one more stint as a Misfit.

Amazingly, he welcomed the idea. He was prepared at that stage of his career, to be a part-timer serving as a left-handed pinch hitter and occasional DH. At first the Yankees seemed interested, until they signed free agent Jose Cruz to fill their need for a lefty hitter off the bench. While the Twins had their "return-to-sender" Smalley clause in writing with the White Sox, the White Sox had received only a verbal agreement with Steinbrenner to send him back to the Yankees.

As late as February 20, Chicago general manager Larry Himes assured Smalley he would be going to the Yankees.

"We basically don't need you here," Himes said. So Smalley, anticipating his trip to the Yankee camp, contacted a Fort Lauderdale real estate agent about a spring training apartment.

Days passed and Smalley remained in limbo. While he waited back home in Edina, Minnesota, Jack Clark arrived at the Yankee camp and incurred some problems with his apartment rental. The real estate agent asked Klein about Smalley's status.

"I don't think he's coming," Klein said.

"Well then," she said, "I'll just move Clark into his apartment."

Klein called Smalley to inform him of this latest development.

"Tell Jack I was glad to help," Smalley said.

And Smalley never did come to the Yankee camp. Once it became apparent they were not going to accept him, he reported to the White Sox' camp and was subsequently released. The Yankees did agree to pay part of the remaining $1.6 million due him.

A few teams contacted him, but he chose to retire. He finished with a .257 lifetime average, 163 homers, and 694 RBI. As might be expected, he said he would always remember his Yankee years as "the strangest and most interesting of my career."

Steve Kemp

In many ways, the all-time Steinbrenner Yankee Misfit was Steve Kemp. Both Kemp and his agent, Dick Moss, should have foreseen that back in December of 1982 when they chose the Yankees over a half-dozen other suitors in the free agent market that winter. Kemp, after all, was a left-handed hitter who didn't pull the ball, which in Yankee Stadium can be a serious impediment. With its nearby right field porch, Yankee Stadium has forever been a home run haven for left-handed hitters—as long as they had the ability to pull the ball and hoist it over the wall some 320 feet away.

At any rate Steinbrenner was determined to have Kemp, and when he came waving $5.5 million over five years, Kemp and Moss did not think about the Yankee Stadium power alleys or how the Orioles, with their more conventional ballpark and organization, might be a better fit. Curiously, at the announcement of the signing, Steinbrenner chose to single out Kemp's running ability rather than his hitting. "He runs down to first base every time like he's running a hundred-yard dash," said Steinbrenner. "I like guys like that."

If nothing else, the Kemp signing touched off a firestorm among the rest of the baseball owners and alienated Steinbrenner from his brethren like nothing he had done before. Orioles owner Edward Bennett Williams, who claimed he was never even given a chance by Moss to bid on Kemp, accused Steinbrenner of "stockpiling hitters like nuclear weapons."

So right from the beginning Steve Kemp's Yankee times were marred by controversy. All too soon, however, controversy gave way to pain, frustration, and ultimately, failure.

In the fourth game of the '83 season, Kemp was involved in an outfield collision with Jerry Mumphrey and Willie Randolph in Toronto and felt something pop in his right shoulder. Although X-rays revealed only a bone chip and Kemp kept on playing, his shoulder was never to be the same again.

By the end of 1984 the Yankees had given up on Kemp. That winter, Steinbrenner had his eyes on a new free-agent outfielder, Rickey Henderson, and Kemp was considered an unwanted extravagance. The problem was what to do with him. Who would take that contract, with three more years at $1 million per?

The "who" turned out to be the Pittsburgh Pirates. Quite likely, the vast majority of baseball executives were relishing Kemp's failure in New York, if only because it was costing Steinbrenner so much. No one wanted to see anyone take Kemp off Steinbrenner's hands. But the Pirates had someone they wanted to get rid of just as badly—Dale Berra, who also had a big contract with three more years to run on it. The Pirates could find no takers for him—until, that is, they talked to the Yankees, for if there was one person in baseball who loved Dale Berra, it was Yogi Berra.

During the course of the winter meetings in Houston in December of 1984, Pirate general manager Harding Peterson spoke with Bill Madden about Kemp.

"Can Kemp play at all?" Peterson asked.

"It's hard to tell," said Madden. "He's been hurt so much, he's never been able to get going. I'll say this for the guy, he plays hard and gives it his all. He's just had no luck. But why would you want to take a chance on him with that contract?"

"Because," said Peterson, "I can't stand looking at Dale Berra playing third base anymore."

But if Peterson had grown exasperated by Berra's infield play, the general manager would soon find Kemp to be no million-dollar bargain either. Berra may not have been an All-Star and may not have been worth anywhere close to what he was being paid, but as an infielder who could play short or third and who could hit a little, he was a useful player.

Kemp, on the other hand, was simply burned out from his Yankee experience. The injuries, the benchings, and the loss of his confidence had taken too much of a toll. He made two aborted comeback attempts, with the Padres in 1986 and the Texas Rangers in '87 and '88, and even though he was still being paid that $1 million per year, he went back to the minor leagues to try to rediscover his skills. When he was released early in '88 by the Rangers, Kemp finally gave it up. He was 33 years old.

Joe Cowley

Joe Cowley was probably the only person to have a spell cast over him *after* he played for the Yankees. That is not to say he wasn't a Looney Tunes in his two seasons in pinstripes. One can never forget the prophetic words of Yankee PR man Joe Safety the day Cowley was recalled from Columbus by the Yankees in midseason 1984.

"I just met this guy Cowley who we called up," Safety told Bill Madden. "You're undoubtedly gonna love him, but I gotta tell you—he's goofy, man."

Safety was right on both counts. The writers did love Cowley, and yes, he *was* goofy, man. It was hard not to like Cowley, although he certainly tried the patience of his teammates and his managers.

For instance, there was hardly a funnier sight than Yogi Berra going out to the mound to either talk to Cowley or remove him. Yogi was five-seven and Cowley six-five. But when Yogi got to the mound, Cowley would inevitably put his hand on Yogi's shoulder, giving the impression that it was *he* who was consoling the manager—not the other way around.

Billy Martin, as one might expect, got especially exasperated with Cowley but later admitted he could never figure him out. One time, Martin came to remove Cowley from a game and was taken aback when the big right-hander greeted him by saying, "Don't feel bad, Skip. You're making the right move getting me out of here."

"I couldn't even get mad at the guy," Martin said. "He's such a cuckoo bird."

It is perhaps fortunate that no one will ever know if Reggie Jackson would have been as tolerant of Cowley's flakiness the afternoon of August 21, 1985. The night before, in perhaps his finest moment as a Yankee, Cowley struck out 13 batters against the Angels, including Reggie three times. As was his custom in the years after he left the Yankees, Reggie liked to come over to the Yankee clubhouse to say hello to his old teammates—which he did the following day after being rung up three times by Cowley. Seeing Reggie across the room, Cowley blurted out: "Is that Reggie over there? Geez, how many times did I strike *him* out last night?"

Reggie, who was busy in conversation, didn't hear him. And because everyone who did hear him realized that Cowley was just being Cowley (i.e., goofy), his remark was never repeated to Jackson.

Right from his initial appearance in the Yankee clubhouse, it was apparent to just about everyone that Cowley was a different breed. He was a Misfit, all right, but he probably never knew it. He had been a career minor leaguer in the Atlanta Braves system when the Yankees liberated him by signing him as a six-year minor league free agent, November 22, 1983. On his first day as a Yankee, he talked about his 10 years with the Braves organization and the brief trial he had with them in 1982.

"It was right here in New York," Cowley said. "I was lying in my hotel room watching TV when I suddenly realized we were playing a day game, not a night game. I rushed out the door, got a taxi, and told the driver to take me to Shea Stadium. But the guy didn't speak English. I wound up getting fined three hundred dollars."

Cowley was a big (210 pounds), strapping country boy from Lexington, Kentucky. During the off-season he worked as a deputy sheriff back home in Kentucky—an occupation that seemed especially misfitting. In his brief time with the Yankees, things were turned around: the long arm of the law was always in pursuit of *him*. That's because John "the Count" Montefusco was intent on tormenting Cowley.

"It had to be done," Montefusco explained years later. "Cowley was so far off the wall he was begging to have things done to him."

One of the first things Montefusco did to Cowley was to arrange for the Florida state troopers, on patrol at the Yankees' spring training camp in Fort Lauderdale, to stage a mock arrest of Cowley one March day in 1985. A few minutes after a physician from the baseball commissioner's office had addressed the Yankee players about drug abuse, a trio of somber-faced troopers marched into the clubhouse and confronted Cowley at his locker.

"Mr. Cowley," said one of the troopers solemnly, "I'm sorry to have to do this, but we have a warrant here for your arrest."

Cowley was dumbfounded.

"Wha...what's this all about? I haven't done nuthin'," he said and began walking away.

The trio of lawmen followed, however, and explained to Cowley that he was being arrested for reckless driving. It seemed, they said, that when he had driven out of the parking lot a couple of days earlier, he had run over an old lady who was standing by the gate attempting to get an autograph.

Cowley didn't know what to say. A look of terror came over his face when the trooper got out a pair of handcuffs and told him to put out his wrists.

"Please," Cowley begged, "don't arrest me in my Yankee pinstripes. At least let me get into my civvies."

As Cowley attempted to lead the troopers into a back room, the rest of the players in the clubhouse, who had been watching the scene from a distance pretending not to notice, broke out laughing. Cowley looked around, saw the troopers were laughing, too, and knew he had been had.

Later that spring, Montefusco decided to take the tormenting of Cowley a step further—by sending him a paternity suit. Montefusco found out about a girlfriend Cowley had had in Columbus, and went to the trouble of finding where she lived. He then contacted a lawyer who lived in the girl's state and asked him to draw up some phony paternity papers.

"After thinking it over, though, we decided not to go through with it," Montefusco said. "We figured Cowley was crazy enough. If we did anything more to him, he might go over the edge."

For all his flakiness, Cowley went 9–2 that first half-season with the Yankees and 12–6 in 1985. The players, managers, and coaches all felt he could have done even better if he had been able to keep his concentration on the mound. But once he'd get a three- or four-run lead, Cowley had this infuriating habit of walking batters or giving up cheap hits on dumb pitches. Don Baylor, the acknowledged clubhouse leader and judge and jury of the Yankees' kangaroo court, fined Cowley repeatedly for such transgressions.

In the middle of one game, after Cowley walked the leadoff hitter in the fifth inning, with a 5–1 lead, he saw Baylor standing on the top step of the Yankee dugout glaring at him. "I know," he yelled at Baylor, "I owe you ten for that one."

Baylor just shook his head.

"The problem with Cowley," Baylor remembered, "was that he lived on his own planet, and occasionally he'd let us visit it."

And while on the subject of visitors, there was the time when Montefusco decided to make up for all the fun he'd had at Cowley's expense.

"Joe," he said one morning, "what are you doing this afternoon?"

"Nothing," said Cowley, "why?"

"'Cause I'm gonna send a girl up to your room," said the Count. "Only thing is, you gotta call me after she leaves and let me know how it went."

Later that afternoon, Cowley called Montefusco's room and told him the girl had just left.

"Well, how was it?" said the Count.

"Terrific," said Cowley. "One of the best I've ever had!"

"Man," said Montefusco, rolling in laughter now, "you just made my day. That was the best forty bucks I ever spent!"

"I don't get it," said Cowley. "What's so funny?"

"What's so *funny?*" said the Count. "I'll tell you what's so funny. That was a *transvestite!*"

There was dead silence at the other end of the phone, as Cowley was obviously in a state of shock over once again being had by Montefusco.

"The rest of the guys were afraid this would really do it to Cowley," said Montefusco, "so after a few minutes I told him I was only kidding…that she was really what she was supposed to be. Actually, I think she was more leery of Cowley. She had her boyfriend…or pimp or whatever…waiting right outside the door for her."

The Yankees finally grew tired of trying to visit Cowley's planet and shipped him to Chicago in one of their many trades with the White Sox in December of 1985. The White Sox' general manager at the time, "Hawk" Harrelson, had always been a free-spirited flake himself, and in Cowley he saw a kindred spirit. Darned if Cowley didn't enhance his reputation for the unpredictable by tossing a no-hitter against the California Angels, September 19, 1986.

That proved to be his final flirtation with success, however. In the spring of 1987 Cowley suddenly started walking batters in the first inning. He lost all sense of the strike zone, and the White Sox traded him to the Phillies. With the Phillies things got even worse. He was sent to their AAA farm in Old Orchard Beach, Maine, and went 3–9, with a 7.86 ERA and 76 walks in 63 innings.

Just what was responsible for his inability to find the plate is anyone's guess. "I tell you," Cowley said after being released, "I have no idea, other than the voodoo theory. I think someone took a voodoo doll out on me, and I don't know why."

Montefusco swears it wasn't him.

Goodbye Columbus

Before Columbus, there was Tacoma. Before Tacoma, there was Syracuse. Through the years the places have changed, but their meaning and purpose to young Yankee prospects has remained the same. To those who know them only as ports-of-call on the minor league baseball map, their names may be Columbus, Tacoma, and Syracuse, but to those who have known the meaning and purpose of being banished there, they might just as well be Siberia, Purgatory, and Devil's Island.

Mind you, being traded is accepted, even welcomed, by many young Yankees. At least a trade, even to a dismal second-division team, means getting a legitimate chance at success on the major league level. But being banished to Columbus (or any of its predecessors) means being buried within the Yankee organization, most often forgotten with no escape. Almost as cruel a fate is boarding the interminable shuttle between the Yankees and Columbus. Like the mythical Charlie on the MTA, who was immortalized in song by the Kingston Trio in the 1950s, there seemed to be no way off for those poor souls like Dave LaRoche, Bobby Brown, or Bobby Meacham. They were baseball's version of stunt men: with no real parts, they were just fill-ins who never got a real chance.

Indeed, no minor league franchise has seen quite so many aging veterans pass through its clubhouse doors as Columbus. Back in 1983, when Steinbrenner was upset at the early showing of the Yankees, he threatened them with Columbus. "If we don't start winning soon," he said, "there'll be some big changes made. I can lose like this with the kids at Columbus."

The "kids at Columbus" that year included such fuzzy-cheeked "youngsters" as 31-year-old Barry Foote, 32-year-old Rowland Office, 32-year-old Butch Hobson, and 41-year-old Bert Campaneris, all of whom had long since seen their best days as major leaguers. The real kids at Columbus always knew their best chance was to attract the attention of another major league team. College activists of the sixties had a slogan: "Don't trust anyone over 30." The Yankees of the seventies and eighties seldom if ever trusted anyone *under* 30.

Bobby Brown, an outfielder whose frequent trips on the Columbus Shuttle earned him the names "Yo Yo" and "Uptown, Downtown, Outta Town Bobby Brown," once explained: "At Columbus it was always a matter of just waiting and hoping that some team, somewhere, would need you. As a young player, you knew the chances of the Yankees wanting you were slim, and the chances of staying around long once you got called up were even slimmer."

Homegrown Yankees? After the death of Thurman Munson in 1979, Ron Guidry was the only Yankee who had never played for another organization. Then Don Mattingly came along in 1983. And even Mattingly was the victim of the usual treatment at first: after first making the team to open the 1983 season, he was returned to Columbus after seven at-bats in 23 games. He was recalled again in June, and his success temporarily opened the door for other Columbus products. Shortstop Andre Robertson moved in, along with pitcher Ray Fontenot.

And in 1984, when the Yankees fell out of the race early, manager Yogi Berra and General Manager Clyde King convinced Steinbrenner to promote a whole platoon of Columbus players, shortstop Bobby Meacham, third baseman Mike Pagliarulo, outfielder Brian Dayett, and pitcher Joe Cowley. Most of them enjoyed some degree of success, playing key roles in the Yankees' 51–29 record after the All-Star break that year. As one pundit so brilliantly put it: "It took Columbus six months to discover America, but it took Steinbrenner 12 years to discover Columbus."

But that was essentially where the talent flow from within dried up. In the succeeding years the Yankees and their pitching staffs, weighted with over-35 veterans, flirted with pennant contention early, only to fade consistently in the dog days of August; there was no infusion of infectious and enthusiastic youth to provide the needed spark.

The annual practice of relinquishing their first and second amateur June draft picks every year by signing veteran, established free agents finally took its toll on the Yankee farm system. Whatever prospects there had been in those years from 1985 through 1988 were traded, and when Steinbrenner sought to overhaul an aging and crippled infield of Willie Randolph, Rafael Santana, and Mike Pagliarulo in the winter of 1989 (not to mention an ancient and arm-weary starting rotation), there was no one at Columbus—or even the next two levels lower in the farm system—to step in. Thus there was more of the "quick-fix" solution, as free agents Steve Sax, Dave LaPoint, and Andy Hawkins were signed for contracts totaling $10.175 million.

Jim Beattie

Jim Beattie learned about life as a Yankee prospect the hard way. Beattie, a highly touted young pitcher, received a double-barreled assault: first, he was verbally blasted by Steinbrenner, then he fell victim to the free-agent recruits. By the time he was traded to Seattle in 1979, Beattie had left his best games on the Columbus shuttle. He was relieved to go, but the Yankees had burned him out.

Beattie was at first regarded as a jewel when the Yankees grabbed him in the fourth round of the June 1975 draft. A six-foot-six right-hander out of Dartmouth, he was an intelligent, studious all-around athlete who had majored in art and achieved all-America honors in both baseball and basketball. He spent three years honing his skills in the Yankee farm system before arriving on the Yankee scene on April 18, 1978. He was 23, with a world of potential.

One week later he made his major league debut and beat Baltimore's future Hall of Famer Jim Palmer, 4–3. He won his next decision, 4–1, over the White Sox, then struggled in his next few starts, which resulted in his getting his first lesson in Yankee-style banishment.

On June 21, in the finale of a series against the high-flying Red Sox at Fenway Park, Beattie was rocked for five runs in two innings, and Boston rolled to a 9–2 victory to knock the Yankees eight games out of first place.

To make matters worse, George Steinbrenner was at the game. The principal Yankee owner sat in a box near the Yankee dugout, watching grim-faced while subjecting President Al Rosen and General Manager Cedric Tallis to a steady barrage of expletives directed at Beattie, manager Billy Martin, and pitching coach Art Fowler. Steinbrenner told Rosen and Tallis that something had to be done, that "Martin and Fowler are messing up our pitching." With the Scoreboard taunting him with its 7–0 Boston lead after four innings, he settled on a scapegoat.

"Get Beattie out of here, he isn't ready," Steinbrenner told his stunned front office chiefs. "I want him on a plane to Tacoma."

Rosen and Tallis assumed the move was to be made after the game. They were wrong.

"Don't just sit there," Steinbrenner told Tallis. "I told you what to do. Go down and tell him to get to Tacoma...now!"

And so it was that in the fourth inning of the game, while Beattie sat glumly in the clubhouse, knowing he had let the team down in a key game, Tallis delivered the crushing message as diplomatically as possible.

"It's not the kind of a thing you ever forget," Beattie said years later.

After the game Steinbrenner approached reporters and didn't hesitate to inform them of Beattie's demotion. "Did you see Beattie out there?" he said. "He pitched like he was scared stiff."

To his credit, Beattie did not let this public humiliation bring him down. Clyde King, the ever-present Yankee troubleshooter in charge of wayward pitchers, joined him in Tacoma and worked with him on a new, no-windup delivery. Beattie appeared in three games at Tacoma, had a 2–0 record, including a no-hitter, and was called back to the Yankees on July 13.

In his second tour of duty with the Yankees that '78 season, Beattie became an important figure in the miracle stretch drive. Over his final seven starts, he was 4–2, with a 2.68 ERA, including a victory over the Red Sox in the famous "Boston Massacre," the Yankees' four-game sweep at Fenway Park in September.

After the Yankees went on to defeat the Red Sox in the dramatic postseason playoff to win the American League East, Beattie's fortunes took an even greater upward swing. With the experienced Yankee starters unavailable after the stirring drive, Beattie was selected by Martin to open the American League championship series against the Kansas City Royals. He responded with a strong showing, giving up one run and two hits in 5⅓ innings and combining with Ken Clay, another future outcast, for a 7–1 victory.

Then, to top off his five-week Fantasy Island tour, Beattie beat the Dodgers, 12–2, in game five of the World Series for his first major league complete game.

After all that he obviously had it made, right? With most teams, maybe, but not with the Yankees.

On November 13, 1978, less than four weeks after Beattie's World Series triumph over the Dodgers, the Yankees signed free-agent right-hander Luis Tiant, taking him away from the Red Sox. Nine days later, they signed free agent Tommy John, the Dodger ace who had won two games against the Yankees in the past two World Series. Tiant, 38, and John, 35, joined a rotation that already included Ron Guidry, coming off a 25–3 season, Ed Figueroa, coming off a 20–9 season, and Catfish Hunter, a future Hall of Famer. Obviously there was no room for Beattie, World Series hero or not.

Sure enough, on April 2, three days before the 1979 season opener, Jim Beattie, who was not supposed to be on the team, wasn't. He was summoned to manager Bob Lemon's office, passing the housing sign-up list on the bulletin board on his way. He and Martha, his wife of six months, would be apartment hunting in Columbus, new site of the Yankees' AAA club instead of house hunting in New Jersey.

Beattie was called back a month into the '79 season—under some rather bizarre circumstances. Goose Gossage had been injured in that famous shower-room scuffle with Cliff Johnson, and Beattie was being asked to switch from a starter to the bullpen closer role. Then after a couple of relief outings, that plan was scrapped, and he was used as a starter again.

Not surprisingly, the momentum he had gathered at Columbus—4–0, with an 0.51 ERA—got lost in the shuffle. Beattie struggled as a starter, was sent back to Columbus, and recalled again. He finished the season with a 3–6 record and a 5.21 ERA. On November 1, 1979, he was traded to Seattle in a six-player deal that brought center fielder Ruppert Jones to the Yankees. Beattie was still only 25, and the Mariners expected great things from him. But a series of injuries short-circuited his career, and he became another of those young Yankee prospects who were left to think what might have been.

Ken Clay

Shortly before the official end of Jim Beattie's Yankee career came the unofficial end of Ken Clay's Yankee hopes. Clay had been signed by the Yankees out of E. C. Glass High School in Lynchburg, Virginia, where he had been an all-around sports star. He was the Yankees' second pick in the June '72 amateur draft and spent the next three years working his way up through the Yankee minor league system. In 1975 Clay and Beattie were teammates at Syracuse and regarded as the two top pitching prospects in the organization. There the similarities ended, as Clay was more of an outgoing party guy than the serious, bookish Beattie.

Clay's one moment in the sun as a Yankee was shared, appropriately, with Beattie; they combined on a two-hitter to beat the Royals in the opener of the 1978 American League playoffs. Clay's contribution to the effort was $3\frac{2}{3}$ innings of hitless relief.

Like Beattie, though, Clay found it difficult to heap more success on his initial success, and 1979 proved to be a lost season for him. For most of the season he was used erratically by the Yankees, as a spot starter, long reliever, and most often, a bullpen spectator. His demise occurred on September 1 against the same Kansas City team he had subdued in the playoffs the previous year. On this night Clay let the Royals get back into the game after the Yankees had scored five runs in the first inning. When Billy Martin came to the mound to make a pitching change in the third inning, Clay protested. That made Martin even angrier, and it caused an equal reaction from the principal Yankee owner's box.

The Royals went on to win the game, 9–8, but Steinbrenner didn't wait for the result. In the fourth inning he ordered public relations director Mickey Morabito to round up the writers and bring them to the owner's office.

Now, over the years these impromptu midgame gatherings in Steinbrenner's office have produced many humorous anecdotes. Obviously the hastily called sessions were prompted by fits of anger by the principal owner, and Steinbrenner would therefore be at his irrational best and in his sputtering glory. The 1979 season had been a complete disaster for Steinbrenner and the Yankees, beginning with Goose Gossage's thumb injury, then Thurman Munson's death in a plane crash, August 2, and the team's inability to sustain any sort of a winning streak. By September 1 it had all come to a head, and Clay, in his moment of frustration, was caught in the eye of the hurricane.

"We've given Ken Clay many chances, and he has laid a big fat egg," Steinbrenner told the assembled writers. "He doesn't have any heart. If he can't pitch with a 5–0 lead, then he doesn't belong in the majors."

That was not the end of it, though. Steinbrenner was just warming up.

"Ken Clay," he continued, "has complained about not getting a chance, but he doesn't deserve any more chances. He has let his team down too many times already."

Then, making it perfectly clear just how he viewed Clay, Steinbrenner reached into his professed area of expertise—horse racing—and spouted these immortal words: "He's a morning glory. That's a term we use for a horse who is great in the morning workouts, who looks beautiful but who can't do it in the race. The horse spits the bit, and Ken Clay has spit the bit."

With that, Ken Clay, pitcher, was reduced to Old Paint, glue factory candidate. Clay appeared in a couple of meaningless games in September, then was stationed at Columbus in 1980 until being traded to Texas in August of that year for veteran Gaylord Perry, whom the rebuilding Rangers were just trying to unload.

This once-glittering Yankee pitching prospect wound up with a 10–24 career record. A likable, fun guy, he would nevertheless forever be remembered as the player Steinbrenner compared to a horse, the pitcher who "spit the bit."

Mike Griffin

Mike Griffin's story was similar to Beattie's and Clay's. He was a young pitcher, regarded for a time as a top prospect, who made the unpardonable mistake of flopping in a spring training game against the Mets—with Steinbrenner watching. The result: a stern dismissal, a banishment to Columbus, and a trade to the Cubs—all by the time he turned 24.

Griffin had come up through the Texas organization, signed in 1976 as an 18-year-old out of Woodland High in northern California. After three seasons in the Rangers' system, the tall right-hander was traded to the Yankees in November of 1978 as part of the 10-player deal that also brought Dave Righetti into the Yankee system and sent Sparky Lyle to Texas. Righetti was the key player as far as the Yankees were concerned, but Griffin turned out to be a surprise. After pitching impressively in the AA and AAA minor league levels for the Yankees in 1979, he was a late-season call-up—in time to hear the Ken Clay morning glory story.

In the spring of 1980 Griffin won a spot on the Yankee staff, following the ill-fated steps of Jim Beattie by winning the James P. Dawson Award as the top rookie in spring camp. Griffin opened the season in the Yankee starting rotation and won his first two decisions, beating Toronto and Detroit. But within a month, after a few mediocre outings, he began to learn firsthand of the Yankee high command's impatience with young pitchers. By June he was back in Columbus.

He returned in mid-September for the stretch drive (as the Yankees won the American League East), and he had even moved ahead of Righetti, who had spent the entire 1980 season at Columbus, compiling an unimpressive 6–10 record. The following spring, Griffin found himself in a battle with Righetti and Gene Nelson for one of the last spots on the pitching staff, and he was losing it.

On the sunny afternoon of March 22, 1981, at Fort Lauderdale, Griffin reached the end of his Yankee days. The Yankees were hosting the Mets, a precarious time for any young Yankee player, what with Steinbrenner's obsession with beating his crosstown rivals, even in a spring exhibition game. On this day the principal Yankee owner was in a particularly foul mood, owing to a comment by the Mets' general manager, Frank Cashen. A few days earlier Cashen had described Yankee Stadium as "Fort Apache, Yankee Stadium"—an allusion to the popular, violent cop movie of the time, *Fort Apache, the Bronx*. Cashen had intended the remark as an off-the-record joke, but the comment was prominently displayed, with Cashen's picture, in Sunday's *New York Daily News*. The newspaper arrived at Steinbrenner's trailer at Fort Lauderdale only minutes before the Mets' team bus pulled up that morning.

Steinbrenner was in a lather. "If Frank Cashen made that comment," he said, "it doesn't surprise me, because I've never thought very much of Frank Cashen. He's not much of a man to say that. I don't want a remark by a man I have so little respect for to upset my fine relationship with Nelson Doubleday and Fred Wilpon (the Met owners), but if Mr. Cashen cares to come and discuss the comment with me in a room somewhere..."

Steinbrenner added that he had contact with the commissioner's office about imposing a fine on Cashen, just as he had the previous year when he objected to an advertising campaign by the Mets that included comments about the Yankees. The Mets were fined $5,000 that time, with Jerry Delia Femina, the head of the advertising firm, happily contributing after having received hundreds of thousands of dollars' worth of free publicity.

Cashen wouldn't comment on the remark, knowing he couldn't deny it. He was understandably annoyed that a reporter had used what had clearly been meant as an off-the-record joke, and was embarrassed by the situation. Steinbrenner, who must have been waiting for an apology, flared anew when told of Cashen's "no comment."

"Frank Cashen wouldn't have the guts to say whether he really said it," Steinbrenner said, "but I believe he did."

With that, Steinbrenner adjourned to his private box atop Fort Lauderdale Stadium to watch what he considered to be a personal duel between his team and Cashen's team, with the winner gaining the admiration and respect of the entire New York metropolitan area. Alas, Dave Kingman ruined Steinbrenner's day. Kingman, the powerful slugger who had been reacquired by the Mets from the Cubs in February, hit two monstrous homers, a 430-foot drive off Rudy May in the fourth inning and a towering 480-foot blast over the left field wall against Goose Gossage in the ninth. The homer against Gossage iced the Mets' 9–5 victory and had the fans buzzing. It undoubtedly impressed the tens of thousands of viewers back home, too, since the game was televised locally in New York.

Griffin, meanwhile, had held Kingman to a double but gave up five other hits in the Mets' five-run seventh inning. That was more than Steinbrenner could tolerate. When the game ended, the reporters scurried over to his rooftop suite, knowing this would be a day when the principal owner's rantings would be particularly entertaining.

The rooftop serenades by Steinbrenner became legend in Yankee spring training lore. Every spring he watched most of the games from his lavish box, adjacent to the press and TV boxes. He sat in a customized high-back swivel chair, often entertaining his influential friends. Poor performances by his gladiators on the field were taken as personal affronts, as if the players had purposely tried to embarrass the principal Yankee owner.

On those days the reporters didn't have to be invited to visit him. They knew from experience when the principal owner was ready to start providing fodder for back-page stories or to begin "singing his tunes" as the beat writers have come to describe those rooftop serenades. The long-standing joke when the Yankees were struggling was to make a visit to "Mr. L. Tunes" (the "L," of course, signifying "Looney") and drop a few quarters into the jukebox. Usually a simple "What did you think of the performance of So-and-so" would suffice for a good 15 minutes' worth of tunes and fill several pages in a reporter's notebook.

And so as the fans exited the ballpark that day, many still pointing to the area where Kingman's second homer had landed and arguing about the distance, the reporters knew Mr. L. Tunes would be ready to sing. First, Steinbrenner criticized the team in general. Then he zeroed in on Rick Cerone, the catcher, who had struck out with the bases loaded, made a throwing error, and presumably called for the pitches that Kingman crushed out of the ballpark. Graig Nettles and Jim Spencer also came in for criticism before Steinbrenner apparently concluded his diatribe by saying: "The team was embarrassing. Now's the time to screw down the hatches. I want to see some improvement."

As the reporters were preparing to depart, Steinbrenner suddenly added Griffin's name to his cast of sinners. "And Mike Griffin has fooled us long enough," he said. "We found out about him today. That does it for him. He won't be pitching for us this year. He has to go back to the minors and work his way up again—if he can."

That was it. When the reporters got down to the clubhouse, Griffin was sitting disconsolately in front of his locker, knowing he had failed at the worst possible time. He knew the law of the Yankee jungle, and he knew what was coming. The next day he was sent to Columbus. A few months later, when the major league clubs were on strike, he was traded to the Cubs.

Bobby Brown

The same day Mike Griffin was demoted to Columbus, March 23, 1981, another young Yankee was also sent down, and while Griffin's banishment was expected, the demotion of Bobby Brown, the multitalented outfielder, was a stunner. But like Griffin, Brown had been the victim of poor timing: Steinbrenner was on the warpath following the loss to the Mets, and with the season opener approaching, he was determined to make changes.

Brown, coming off a strong 1980 season in which he hit .260 with 14 homers and 27 stolen bases in 137 games, had been slumping in the exhibition games, hitting just .111. And on the day after the Mets' game, he committed an error in center field in a 7–5 Yankee loss to the Braves at West Palm Beach. Steinbrenner had been at that game as well, and following the 45-minute bus ride back to Port Lauderdale, Brown was summoned to the trailer of general manager Cedric Tallis. When the unsuspecting outfielder was informed of the news, he was outraged. His immediate response was: "Columbus? Over my dead body!" Other players, including Ruppert Jones, Brown's competition for the center field job, succeeded in calming him down and convincing him to report to the minor league camp in Hollywood, Florida.

As fate would have it, Brown was back sooner than he expected because an injury to Reggie Jackson opened up a spot on the opening day roster. During his 10-day absence, however, the Yankees had acquired a new center fielder, Jerry Mumphrey.

Brown spent the 1981 season on the Columbus shuttle, setting a modern Yankee record for frequent-flyer miles between New York and Ohio. In all, he made three round trips, while appearing in only 31 games for the Yankees. The great promise he had shown in 1980, when injuries to Jones had created playing time for him, never surfaced again.

"Bobby was a tough guy to figure out," said Gene Michael, who managed Brown at Columbus and was his biggest booster among the Yankee high command. "All that talent, but something always seemed to be missing."

Columbus president George Sisler called Brown "the greatest minor league player I've ever seen," and there were many others who felt there ought to be a special league between AAA and the majors for guys like him. "He's proven to be too good for triple A, but he's just not good enough to play in the majors" was a familiar assessment of Brown.

Indeed, before he came to the Yankees in June of 1978, Brown had played six years in the minor leagues and been cut loose by three different organizations. He could run, throw, hit for power, and was a switch-hitter with seemingly a world of potential, but nobody seemed to feel he was for real. It was just that he always seemed to do the wrong thing at the wrong time—like turn the wrong way on a fly ball or botch a routine play after making a sensational one. Inevitably he would frustrate managers.

When Billy Martin replaced Bob Lemon as Yankee manager in June 1979, the plan was for Brown to be given the regular center field job and be groomed as a star of the future. After a few games with Martin, Brown's star plummeted. "He can't play center," declared Martin.

Eight days after Martin's return, the Yankees reacquired Bobby Murcer from the Chicago Cubs, and Brown was sent to Columbus. At the AAA level that season, he hit .349 and was named co-Most Valuable Player in the

International League. The Yankees eventually traded Brown to the Mariners before the 1982 season, and a year later he landed in San Diego, where he got to play in the '84 World Series as a reserve outfielder for the Padres.

Perhaps the most fitting epitaph to Bobby Brown's career was provided one day during spring training in 1981 by Jim Spencer. Spencer, who was 34 at the time and nearing the end of his fine career, didn't look at all like an athlete, let alone a Gold Glove-caliber first baseman. He had a flabby look more suited to a player for a pickup softball team, but he was a greatly coordinated first baseman and left-handed hitter.

Spencer, fully aware of his appearance, was standing in the Yankee clubhouse in Fort Lauderdale, talking to Moss Klein, when Brown strolled by clad only with a towel wrapped around his waist. Glancing at Brown's glistening, perfectly proportioned, muscular physique, Spencer thought to himself of all the blunders and funks that had plagued Brown as a Yankee. Finally, after a minute or so, Spencer shook his head and said: "You know something, Bobby? If we could put my head on your body...man! We'd be a superstar!

Dave LaRoche

It turned out Bobby Brown's record as the all-time travelin' man on the Columbus shuttle was short-lived. In 1982 along came Dave LaRoche, a typically flaky left-handed relief pitcher who provided some welcome humor that season by turning the dreaded Columbus roller-coaster into a season-long comedy act.

Unlike most of the shuttle's previous passengers, LaRoche was a seasoned veteran. He was 33 and had been in the big leagues for 11 seasons when he joined the Yankees in 1981 following his release by the California Angels. A onetime bullpen ace, he settled in as a middle innings mop-up man with the Yankees and was with them most of that season.

But in 1982, with lefties Rudy May and Shane Rawley being used mostly in relief, LaRoche was needed only occasionally. In between, he was shuttled to and from Columbus; with four trips in a three-month stretch, he symbolized the heightened lunacy of that season, when the Yankees used a then-record 47 players. All told, 19 players saw action with both the Yankees and Columbus that 1982 season, and nobody dissented when LaRoche appointed himself honorary captain of the Columbus Yankees.

LaRoche was called up on April 26, appeared in a game on May 4, and was sent back to Columbus the next day. But before LaRoche cleared waivers to go back, Doyle Alexander punched out the dugout wall in Seattle and landed himself on the disabled list with a broken knuckle. Thus LaRoche was told to stay around. He stayed for three days and was sent out to Columbus again. But three weeks later, he was back again, only to be sent down again even though he had a 22-inning scoreless streak in progress. "I figured I was safe at *least* until I gave up a run," LaRoche said.

The Yankee players, accustomed to instability, could not help but be amused at LaRoche's continual comings and goings.

"LaRoche is like *Sporting News*," cracked Graig Nettles. "He comes out once a week."

Dave Collins, a first-year Yankee who watched the team's steady stream of player maneuverings in a state of perpetual amazement, said: "I hardly know LaRoche, but I've never shook hands with anyone so much in my life. I'm either always telling him 'Good luck in Columbus' or, a few days later, 'Welcome back, good to see you again.'"

The highlight of LaRoche's adventures on the Columbus shuttle came on May 10 when he had been told to report to Columbus, only to have his orders rescinded when Alexander broke his hand. Having just arrived back at Columbus when he was resummoned, LaRoche decided to drive back to New York and catch a flight to California from La Guardia so he'd have a car available when he got home from the West Coast road trip.

The drive took longer than LaRoche had expected, and in his urgency he neglected to check his gas gauge. At about five o'clock in the morning, he was crossing New York's Tappan Zee Bridge when he ran out of gas. He pushed the car into a safe area, then spotted a neighborhood gas station. "What a break!" he thought. Except the station was closed.

Hoping somebody might be sleeping in the back, LaRoche started banging on the door. An early-rising neighbor spotted LaRoche smashing on the door of the gas station and called the police, thinking he was trying to break in.

LaRoche, meanwhile, gave up on trying to rouse anyone from the gas station and went to a nearby pay phone to call a friend. As he was on the phone, three squad cars pulled up. At the sight of all this commotion he had caused, LaRoche could hardly stop laughing. Only with the Yankees could you get into a crazy predicament like this. When he was finally able to talk, he showed the cops his identification, presumably recounting stories of his famed "La Lob" blooper pitch to them, and succeeded in getting them to drive him to the airport. He arrived at Anaheim Stadium in plenty of time for that night's game but, of course, wasn't needed. Nor did he pitch in either of the other two games in Anaheim. When the Yankees headed on to Oakland, LaRoche was told to report back to Columbus. Meanwhile, his car remained unofficial police property in New York...until, of course, his next return in early June.

LaRoche completed the '82 season with the Yankees and was told, he insisted later, that he had a $100,000 offer to return the following year, even if it meant another season of jet-hopping on the Columbus shuttle. The Yankees would make sure the shuttle provided soft drinks and peanuts, he presumed. So he showed up in spring training in '83 as a nonroster invitee. As he might have expected, he was asked to go back to Columbus at camp's end. For $50,000. LaRoche reminded General Manager Bill Bergesch of the $100,000 verbal agreement, but Bergesch chose not to remember it.

Offended by the Yankees' memory lapse, LaRoche returned home to Fort Scott, Kansas, to be with his wife, Patty, who was pregnant. He stayed in shape that summer by playing softball, and sure enough, when the Yankees decided they needed a lefty reliever in late July, they called LaRoche. He reported to Columbus, worked his way into shape by pitching in seven games, and joined the Yankees on August 12. Billy Martin, however, was no more of a LaRoche fan than he was a Bobby Brown fan. He had no use for these refugees from the Columbus shuttle.

For the most part, Martin ignored LaRoche, pitching him in only one game, and that one being one inning of a lopsided loss to Oakland on August 23. It turned out to be the final appearance of LaRoche's major league career. He was sent back to Columbus a week later, to make room on the roster for John Montefusco, who had been acquired from San Diego. No one was quite certain as to how many times that made it for LaRoche on the Columbus shuttle, but as he said, "It's gotten to be fun, and I'll miss it. For one thing, I got to know all the stewardesses on US Air on a first-name basis now."

Tucker Ashford

Tucker Ashford, a personable young infielder from Tennessee, was another Yankee who got to know Columbus well. Like Griffin, his ultimate banishment from the Yankee scene occurred on the rooftop of Fort Lauderdale Stadium during that looniest of Yankee springs, 1982.

The spring of '82 was the period when Steinbrenner had decided to transform the Yankees into a speed team. From the beginning that spring, Stalag Steinbrenner was a zany asylum with ex-Olympic hurdling champion Harrison Dillard conducting running drills in the outfield. And when the team began losing on a regular basis, there were nightly meetings in Steinbrenner's trailer office, with manager Bob Lemon and his weary coaches trudging in and out.

Ashford was a mere footnote to that camp, a forgotten victim. His crime: two errors in a March 21 game against the Orioles, leading to three unearned runs and an 8–1 Yankee loss. The timing of his flubs was awful, because Steinbrenner had just begun to roar. The day before, he had complained about the Mets again because their latest advertising promotion was: "See the Mets.

We Don't Lack Power." It was, of course, another putdown of the Yankees' speed-team concept, and Steinbrenner was seething.

Ashford wasn't even supposed to be in the lineup that day against the Orioles. But Graig Nettles fouled a ball off his right shin and came out of the game. Ashford replaced him at third base, made his two errors, and had his Yankee career terminated.

During the game, Steinbrenner was pacing in his box. By the fourth inning he was livid, as the Yankees were headed to their 10th loss in 13 spring exhibitions. He telephoned the dugout and told Lemon he wanted to talk to Vice President Bill Bergesch, who was seated in the box next to the dugout. Bergesch was summoned, listened briefly, then returned to his seat. An inning later, another call. This time Bergesch had been given an order that required immediate attention. He had been told to make a large sign and post it in the locker room during the game, where everyone would see it: "All players not in B game Monday must be in uniform at 11:00 A.M."

Since the 11:00 A.M. reporting time was five hours earlier than the regular reporting time for night games, there was considerable grumbling from the players. As Nettles said, "The big guy is going wacky again, isn't he?"

Unbeknown to Tucker Ashford, he would not have to concern himself with this latest bit of wackiness by the principal Yankee owner. Because Steinbrenner, after seeing those two errors, had made the decision to banish Ashford. Up on the roof after the game, Mr. L. Tunes sang his farewell melody to Ashford, who until that day had been regarded as a backup to Nettles, with a good chance of making the team.

Steinbrenner started his rooftop refrain that day by criticizing the team as a whole and Lemon in particular. "Something is missing," he said. "Some guys look like they're out there sleepwalking. It's the manager's job to get them motivated. We're going to practice and practice and keep practicing until we get it right. I don't care if guys are tired. When you're making $500,000 and $600,000 a year, there's no such thing as battle fatigue."

In that respect Steinbrenner was right, but the fact that he failed to mention was what was missing on this team—mainly the two baseball basics: team chemistry and power. The Yankee team Steinbrenner had put together in 1982 was a mess, a hodgepodge of free agents, trade refugees, holdover fading sluggers like Bobby Murcer and Lou Piniella, and of course the new "speed" players. There was no cohesiveness, no stability, no direction and, perhaps most significant, no Reggie.

Then as Steinbrenner began to leave the rooftop, he had one parting shot: "We've seen enough of Tucker Ashford."

Three days later, veteran third baseman Butch Hobson, another in a long line of Misfits to join the 1982 Yankees, was obtained in a trade with the Angels. To make room for Hobson, Ashford was outrighted to Columbus. A hard-nosed former star with the Boston Red Sox (as well as a onetime Alabama quarterback under Bear Bryant), Hobson's skills had eroded considerably from numerous injuries. In addition, he carried with him a $400,000-per-year contract that was to run for three more years—which is why the Angels were more than eager to take nothing in return from the Yankees for him.

Bobby Meacham

While so many Columbus shuttlers have had experiences they'd never want to tell their grandchildren about, no "war story" is more rife with disappointments and setbacks than Bobby Meacham's.

For six years, from 1983 until his trade to Texas in December 1988, Meacham was the embodiment of all the turmoil and torment that have befallen all those bright-eyed Yankee prospects. During those six seasons Meacham did it all—or rather *had* it all done to *him.* He was a Columbus-New York frequent flyer in 1983, being called up four times, twice for a one-day stay; he was exiled in 1984, dropped all the way to AA ball for making an error in the fourth game of the season; he went from being the Yankees' regular shortstop in 1985 (playing the final two months with a hand injury at the Yankees' request) to a utility infielder at Columbus in less than a year; and ultimately he was traded to Texas.

Amazingly, Meacham managed to keep his sanity through all this turmoil and torment. A deeply religious player and a prominent member of the Baseball Chapel, he could just as often be seen sitting in front of his locker reading the Bible as a newspaper or a press guide. Meacham seldom showed anger and always seemed to look for the brighter side of things (when inevitably there wasn't one). Throughout it all he insisted he wanted to stay with the Yankees, hoping he'd get yet another chance.

His first season with them should have convinced him. He made four trips on the Columbus shuttle in 1983, twice being summoned to New York for a one-day viewing. His July 16 trip was especially interesting. It was Old-timers' Day at Yankee Stadium, and Meacham, having shuttled in from Columbus, sat around and watched all the legends. Immediately after the game he was informed he was going right back to Columbus because infielder Larry Milbourne had been acquired from the Phillies. Milbourne, it should be noted, will forever be remembered for his parting quote when the Yankees traded him to the Twins a year earlier. Said he: "I'm going from one crazy owner [Steinbrenner] to another crazy owner [Calvin Griffith]."

In 1984 Meacham made the Yankees with a strong showing in spring training and began the season sharing the shortstop job with veteran Tim Foli. He made it through the first four games. In the eighth inning of the fourth game, he committed a two-out error against the Rangers in Arlington, Texas, which allowed the go-ahead run to score from third base, as the Yankees lost, 7–6. That was the Yankees' third straight loss, and Steinbrenner was in a predictable rage.

When manager Yogi Berra returned to his room after the game, he received the dreaded phone call from the principal Yankee owner. "We're getting rid of Meacham," Steinbrenner barked into the phone.

Berra couldn't believe what he was hearing. Four games into the season and his shortstop was being demoted! And not just to Columbus, either, but to Nashville, the Yankees' AA farm! It seemed that Andre Robertson, the previous season's regular Yankee shortstop until he suffered a near-fatal neck injury in an automobile accident, was rehabilitating at Columbus, so it was deemed that Meacham should go a class lower in order to play every day.

Berra tried arguing with Steinbrenner, insisting that it was a bad move. Steinbrenner didn't want to hear it and soon the conversation became heated, with Yogi shouting into the phone almost as loudly as Steinbrenner. A Yankee official in the next room, hearing the normally mild-mannered Berra yelling, thought there was a fight in progress, that Yogi must have caught a burglar in his room. Yogi *was* upset about a theft, but it was the theft of his shortstop.

Meacham took the news graciously the next day after being informed by Berra. When Moss Klein caught up to him at the hotel as he was checking out, Meacham said: "I know Yogi didn't want to make the move. But I'm not the type to pout. I was surprised at first, but I've been told by lots of other guys never to be surprised at anything that goes on here."

Berra, meanwhile, was uncharacteristically testy when asked about Meacham. There were none of his usual smiles or shrugs that day. "It's not my doing," he said evenly, "and I don't want to talk about it."

Meacham's replacement was Keith Smith, a 22-year-old infielder who had appeared in one exhibition game that spring. When he arrived at Arlington Stadium, he was surrounded by reporters and was understandably bewildered. "It's hard to believe I'm here," said Smith, who was there for all of 10 games and four hitless at-bats before going back to Columbus.

As Smith talked to reporters, a bemused Lou Piniella, who was nearing the end of his career, looked on. A while earlier, Piniella had noticed the clubhouse man removing Meacham's nameplate from above the locker and replacing it with a new one inscribed "Smith."

"I feel like I'm lockering next to the tomb of the unknown soldier," Piniella said.

But veteran Willie Randolph, who had seen too many of these banishments of young players through the years, didn't see any humor in this one. Randolph had taken a special liking to Meacham, his keystone partner most of the spring. And he was uncharacteristically outspoken when asked for his opinion on it. "Something like this can be very detrimental for a young player," Randolph said. "And it puts extra pressure on every kid in the organization. It could get to the point where kids won't want to come up because they're scared of the pressure."

Steinbrenner was stung by the criticism and defended the demotion by explaining that "it was important for Meacham to be playing every day because we might need him."

Meacham was at Nashville only a few days before moving up to Columbus, as Robertson was called up to the Yankees. On June 15 the Yankees called Meacham back to New York, and from there he settled in as their regular shortstop. He was the regular all through 1985 as well, playing 156 games despite being hampered by a dislocated tendon in his left hand the final two months. He played in persistent pain and was unable to hit left-handed, but at the Yankees' request he put off necessary surgery until after the season.

Although the hand injury caused his batting average to plummet to .218 by season's end, Meacham was still the Yankees' regular shortstop when the 1986 season began. However, he had been making some errors—as had the entire Yankee infield—and Steinbrenner was beginning to get impatient again. After a Yankee loss to the Angels on June 2 (in which Meacham made one error and Randolph two), Meacham was benched by manager Lou Piniella.

"Why I've been singled out, I don't know," Meacham said. "Other people are making errors, too."

Meacham sat for three games, played for one game, sat for three more, played once more, made an error, and *poof!* was once again "disappeared" to Columbus. The date was June 15. Meacham was not shocked by the move, for a couple of reasons. One, nothing the Yankees did to him was surprising anymore, and two, the night before, when he came back to the Yankee hotel, he saw Ivan DeJesus standing around in the lobby. DeJesus was one of those "kids" the Yankees had stashed away at Columbus, a 33-year-old veteran of 10 major league seasons who had most recently been picked up after being released by the Montreal Expos in spring training.

DeJesus became the Yankees' fourth shortstop that season, and before the year ended, two more would be acquired in trades, Paul Zuvella and Wayne

Tolleson. Meacham, meanwhile, returned to Columbus only to find the Yankees had one more cruel trick in store for him. When he left, Piniella told him he just needed to play regularly for a while at Columbus to get his game back and his confidence restored. When he arrived at Columbus, though, he was informed that the organization wanted him to play second base, that they now viewed him as a "utility player."

In less than a year, Meacham had gone from the starting shortstop for the Yankees to a utility infielder at Columbus. He was only 25 years old.

Meacham returned to the Yankees on September 1, when the rosters were expanded. But even though the Yankees were out of the race, he wasn't given a chance to play. Over those last five weeks, he made two late-inning appearances at shortstop, then started the final game of the season.

"What they're doing to Meacham is downright criminal," Randolph said. "Why don't they just trade him or let him go so he can have a chance?"

Still, Meacham didn't ask for a trade, and the Yankees didn't make one for him. What they did do was heap another dose of humiliation on him before demoting him once again to Columbus.

Meacham reported to spring training in 1987, having spent three weeks at Bucky Dent's camp working with the former Yankee shortstop in an effort to restore his confidence. Although manager Piniella and team officials said there would be "competition" for the job between Meacham and Wayne Tolleson, Meacham was used more at second base when the exhibition games began. Then, in a game against the Expos in West Palm Beach on March 23, Meacham made two errors. The Yankee infield as a unit committed six errors on the rock-hard infield of West Palm's Municipal Stadium that day, but Steinbrenner, who was watching the game in the stands, waved in disgust and singled out Meacham. After the game Steinbrenner told General Manager Woody Woodward to "get rid of Meacham. He's scared stiff out there."

Finding any takers for Meacham in his present state of reduced value was virtually impossible. Instead, he was sent to Columbus again. The beneficiary was Zuvella, who had been used sparingly all spring and who had made four errors. "I can't say I'm not surprised," Zuvella said. "Nobody has said 'boo' to me all spring. I guess that's just the way they do things around here."

This time the demotion hit Meacham hard, and he finally lost his composure. He knew Piniella had wanted him and had encouraged him. But Piniella knew it was a lost cause trying to plead Meacham's case with Steinbrenner. Piniella had no use for Zuvella, who had been awful when given the chance at shortstop in 1986. Steinbrenner didn't care. He just wanted Meacham out.

After receiving the news from Piniella on April 2, Meacham sat in front of his locker in Fort Lauderdale, his eyes red and near tears. Pitcher Dennis

Rasmussen, his closest friend on the team, sat next to him, consoling him while motioning the writers away.

Upon regaining his composure, Meacham said: "I'm shocked this time. I played well enough to make this team. It seems obvious they just don't want me around. They're messing with my mind now."

Later that day, Moss Klein called Meacham, figuring this would be the time, finally, when Meacham would demand a trade and tear into Steinbrenner. Instead, Meacham had swung back the other way. "Maybe I'm crazy to want to play for this team," he said. "That's what my friends and family have been telling me. But for some reason I want to stay. I just don't think they want me."

And still it was not over for Meacham. The Yankees had a few more surprises for him. After the usual discombobulated 1987 season—a couple of months at Columbus, a couple of stints with the Yankees, a trip to the disabled list—he was back in 1988. This time he made the team and didn't get sent to Columbus at the drop of the first ground ball.

After being used as a backup at second base and shortstop, Meacham suffered a pinched nerve in his neck just before the All-Star break. He was placed on the 21-day disabled list on July 14 and began reporting to Yankee Stadium daily for treatment. He thought he was making steady improvement, too, but on August 3, as he sat home watching the Yankees' game against the Brewers in Milwaukee on TV, he heard one of the announcers say between pitches, "Well, I see where they placed Bobby Meacham on the 60-day disabled list today."

"I was absolutely stunned," Meacham said. "I was just about ready to come back. I had seen a chiropractor, and he gave me the go-ahead. The Yankees knew that. And then they knock me out for the whole season."

Why was the move made? Because the Yankees, hit by a series of injuries, were at the limit allowed for players on the 21-day disabled list. When they needed room because of an injury to Randolph, they simply bumped Meacham to the 60-day list, effectively ending his season.

For once Meacham blew his stack. He confronted General Manager Bob Quinn about it in the trainer's room a few days later, and as one Yankee said, "I never knew Meach could yell like that!"

The move was made, though, and Meacham's only recourse was to file a grievance. After considering it, he decided against it. "I'm not in the position to be making waves around here," he told Klein. "I'm not worried about the reaction here. I figure they can't do anything else to me. They've done it all already, and this was the topper. But if I file a grievance, other teams will figure I'm a troublemaker and nobody will even want to trade for me. Getting traded, that's my only chance of ever having a career."

So Meacham kept quiet, and on December 5 his prayers were answered when the Yankees traded him to Texas for outfielder Bobby Brower. The Rangers had just signed their shortstop Scott Fletcher to a whopping $3.9-million contract, but they told Meacham they had plans for him at second base. Those plans lasted all of one day. The next day Meacham's hopes were dashed again— just a different team doing it—as the Rangers announced they had traded for Indians slugging second baseman Julio Franco. As Yogi Berra might have told Meacham, it was "deja vu all over again."

What is it like to be young and a Yankee in the Steinbrenner era?

A pitcher named Roger Erickson probably best summed it up for Meacham, Beattie, Clay, and all the others. After his demotion by the Yankees in spring training 1983, Erickson, then 26, said: "They told me I'm their future. I told them, 'I don't want to be in your future. It's frustrating enough being in your present.'"

CHAPTER 9

The Survivors

In the world of George Steinbrenner's Yankees, only the fittest survive, and only the those with the thickest skins and the toughest psyches have been able to cope. They are that unique breed of individuals who, as Kipling put it, have the ability to "keep their heads about them when all of those around them are losing theirs."

Happily for Yankee fans, there have been enough of them in the Steinbrenner era to have formed the nucleus of two world championship teams, four American League pennant winners, and five division titlists. Unfortunately all of those glories came prior to 1982, which explains why most of the Yankee survivors are no longer on the active major league scene.

There was Sparky Lyle, the flaky reliever who laughed at Steinbrenner and wrote a best-selling book about his zany exploits, and Bobby Murcer, the homespun lefty power hitter from Mickey Mantle's Oklahoma who was traded and reacquired by Steinbrenner, then later hired and fired as a broadcaster. And there were Chris Chambliss and Roy White, those two quiet pillars of dignity and grace on those '76, '77, and '78 championship teams. And Catfish Hunter, the guy who taught them all how to win. In the winter of 1988, three of the most enduring Yankee survivors of all had either been exiled or were on the verge of it. Willie Randolph, the team's second baseman since 1976, was ignored when he became a free agent, the Yankees having decided to sign the younger Steve Sax, the Dodger second baseman, who'd also become a free agent. (Ironically, Randolph wound up replacing Sax with the Dodgers.)

In addition, new manager Dallas Green made it clear he didn't want either Tommy John, 45, or Ron Guidry, 38, on his pitching staff. Only an eleventh-hour reprieve by Steinbrenner, who invited them to spring training, gave them a chance at one last hurrah with the Yankees. But Guidry's hopes were dashed by a spring training elbow injury, and he retired in July after a futile comeback attempt in the minors. John, meanwhile, made the team with an impressive spring training and was even the winning pitcher on opening day. But that was, in effect, *his* last hurrah. He struggled thereafter and was released on Memorial Day with a 2–7 record.

Guidry, Randolph, and John had one element in common when it came to surviving with the Yankees: Steinbrenner seldom drew them in his line of fire. Don Mattingly, the Yankees' sole pillar of stability as the decade ended, was similarly charmed. With the exception of a much-written-about broadside fired at the Boss at the close of the 1988 season, he usually kept out of the public fray with Steinbrenner, preferring to let his bat do the talking. It was a strategy that was perhaps destined to earn him a designation as the Yankees' ultimate survivor.

Those who follow in these pages had different survival skills. They were the ones who tested the heat and lived to tell about it.

Reggie Jackson

No one has ever passed through the Yankee scene more equipped or adept at handling the chaos and craziness of the Steinbrenner Bronx Zoo than Reginald Martinez Jackson. Hell, Reggie didn't just handle it, he *thrived* on it. He said as much in his very first one-on-one interview as a Yankee: "I'm the straw that stirs the drink." Was he ever. More prophetic words were never spoken.

Everything Reggie did—from his running battles with Steinbrenner and Billy Martin to his spectacular home runs (and equally spectacular strikeouts) and his colorful and often outrageous quotes—was done with a flair and a sense of grand theater. Reggie loved being on stage and for someone like him, New York was the only stage. In later years both and he and Steinbrenner admitted that many of their public verbal sparrings were, in fact, staged with the idea of keeping the Yankees on the back pages of the New York tabloids.

Not that the two didn't frequently go at it with genuine passion. One suspects that the real reason Reggie was let go as a free agent after the 1981 season stemmed from a clash of egos with Steinbrenner. Among Steinbrenner's Yankees nobody is bigger than Steinbrenner (which would certainly explain the Boss' running feud with the player who succeeded Jackson as the Yankees' number-one star, Dave Winfield).

Reggie thrived under pressure and in front of the largest audiences, as clearly documented by his World Series heroics, especially the three home runs he hit in the final game of the '77 Series against the Dodgers. But George Frazier, a happy-go-lucky relief pitcher who could be considered somewhat of a Yankee survivor himself, recalled one of the most awesome displays of Reggie power under pressure being played out in a virtually empty theater.

"It was the 1981 season, my first year with the club," Frazier said. "Reggie was struggling, and George ordered him to undergo an eye check and a complete psychological test. It was humiliating to Reggie, and he was really pissed about it. But because he was going so bad at the time, he wasn't dealing from his usual strength. So he didn't fight it.

"Anyway, we were in Detroit when Reggie came back from all the testing. It was early in the afternoon when he walked into the clubhouse and asked Jeff Torborg to get a couple of bags of balls and throw batting practice for him. Jeff agreed, and then Reggie turned to me and asked me if I wanted to shag. I told him, 'Sure.' So he said, 'Okay, then go sit up in the upper deck.'

"Well, what happened next was the most unbelievable display of hitting I ever saw. Of the two dozen or so balls Torborg threw to him, there wasn't but two that didn't leave the ballpark and most of 'em landed in the upper deck. When I came back down to the clubhouse, Reggie was waiting for me.

"'Go tell "the man" what you think of my eyesight,'" he said.

That was the worst of times for Reggie as a Yankee. His batting average and run production were off dramatically, his body was beginning to feel its 35 years, and now Steinbrenner was wounding his pride even deeper by ordering him to undergo all these tests. In a strange sort of way, though, it also became among the best of times for Reggie because of the special kinship he would form with Travis John.

Travis, Tommy John's three-year-old son, had been the object of an entire nation's prayers that summer after falling from a second floor window and landing on his head. He was in a coma for 17 days, hovering between life and death. What is generally not known about the Travis John story was that Reggie Jackson was a daily visitor at the young boy's bedside and is given credit by Sally John, Tommy's wife, for helping bring Travis out of the coma.

"We'll never know for sure what triggers what in those kinds of situations," said Sally, "but Reggie, who was going through a lot of personal problems of his own during that time, came into the hospital this one day and grabbed one of those Muppet puppets that [Muppets creator] Jim Henson had sent over. He put it on his hand and started shaking it in front of Travis' face, all the while moving its mouth and talking for it. He was making jokes about George and things. All of a sudden, you could see the corners of Travis' mouth form into a tiny, little grin. It was the first time he had shown any sign of movement."

Slowly Travis John made what could be called a miraculous recovery, and happily, he bears no after-effects today from the near-fatal accident. He also retains a lifelong friend in Reggie Jackson, whom he unknowingly also helped through a bad time.

Come the World Series against the Dodgers, Travis had made a complete recovery, and Steinbrenner approached Sally John about having him throw out the first ball for the second game. At first she had some reservations, but as Steinbrenner explained it: "We've been getting a hundred calls a day asking about Travis, and this will give us the opportunity to show everyone how he's doing. It'll be a wonderful way to honor his battle back to recovery and an inspiration to everyone."

Sally agreed, but there was still one big problem: Tommy John was scheduled to pitch that night for the Yankees and it was his feeling that the emotion of walking Travis out onto the field before the game would be simply too much for him. For a stand-in, he turned to Reggie, who was later accused by many of his detractors of having seized on Travis' first-ball ceremony for his own personal aggrandizement.

It turned out to be Reggie's final appearance in the World Series spotlight, and the memory of it is preserved forever in a picture that hangs on Travis John's bedroom wall. It is of Travis being hugged by Reggie after making his pitch from the Yankee Stadium mound. On it is inscribed: "To Travis, a great friend in one of my fondest moments. Your friend forever, Reggie Jackson."

"We really needed that love and support on the human level that we got from Reggie," said Sally John.

Because so many of the other Yankee stars—Thurman Munson, Graig Nettles, Ron Guidry, Sparky Lyle, et al.—found his flamboyance and craving for attention a bit overbearing, Reggie had few close friends on the ball club. Most everyone remembers the Reggie-Billy Martin blowup on national TV in Fenway Park in Boston on June 18, 1977. But a less-publicized Reggie encounter occurred a month later when he locked horns with Sparky Lyle in a dugout episode in Kansas City.

It was July 16, a Saturday night, and the Yankees were in the process of losing to the Royals. Reggie's awful play in right field in recent weeks had been a source of disgust not only to Martin but to the Yankee players as well.

In the seventh inning the Royals' Hal McRae led off against Lyle and hit a fly ball to right. First, Reggie misjudged it, breaking in while the catchable ball sailed over his head beyond his reach. Then he rumbled it when it caromed off the wall, and dropped it as he tried to pick it up. Finally, he corralled it but double-clutched as he made his throw. McRae, meanwhile, circled the bases and was generously awarded a triple with an error charged to Reggie for allowing him to score.

In the first inning of the game Reggie had also dropped a fly ball by George Brett, and when he returned to the dugout, Lyle was waiting for him.

"Why don't you get your head out of your ass and start playing," Lyle said.

"You talking to me?" Reggie said.

"Yeah, you look like a clown out there."

Reggie took a few steps toward Lyle before the other players intervened. No punches were thrown, and the Yankees did their best to cover up the incident. None of the beat writers found out about it that night, but before the next day's game Murray Chass of the *Times,* and Moss Klein were standing in the dugout when a security guard, making conversation, said to them, "Any upshoot on that Reggie-Lyle fight last night?" The two reporters, after a momentary silence, assured him they'd find out and later thanked him for his inadvertent tip.

"Seems like there's something crazy going on with this team all the time," the guard said. He didn't have to tell the reporters that.

By the end of 1977 Reggie was still having his defensive troubles in right field but was at least making more of an effort at it. One night, following a late-September rainout in Toronto, a group of players were hanging around the lobby of the Hotel Toronto. Dave Kingman, who had spent most of the year in the National League with the Mets and Padres, had just been acquired by the Yankees to help in the stretch drive, and the other players—Lyle, Munson, and Paul Blair—were asking him about the differences between the two leagues. It was right about then that Reggie happened along and started asking Kingman about some of the National League pitchers.

Kingman mentioned Tommy John (then with the Dodgers), who had missed the entire 1975 season and part of '76 with an arm injury but came back to go 20–7 in '77.

Munson, using Kingman as a set-up man, asked, "Didn't he have some sort of complicated surgery?"

Kingman noted that, yes, John had undergone a procedure in which a tendon was transplanted from his right arm into his damaged left elbow.

That was all Munson needed. "You see, Reggie," he said, "there's hope for you after all." Then, turning to Blair, the superb defensive outfielder, he said, "Hey, Paul, would you agree to have your hands transplanted to Reggie? Then maybe he could catch something."

Everybody broke up. For a moment, though, Reggie didn't smile. Had this happened earlier in the season, there might in fact have been a brawl in the hotel lobby. But Reggie had adjusted and realized Munson's needling was a sign that he was being accepted. So he joined in the laughter.

More often than not, Reggie would seek out the lesser lights of the ball club for companionship on the road. (His closest friend was backup catcher Fran

Healy, who stayed on with the Yankees as a broadcaster for a few years after being released in 1978.)

In Milwaukee in 1981, Reggie invited Frazier to have dinner with him one night in the English Room, a swanky, gourmet restaurant on the lower level of the Pfister Hotel. It is the sort of place where the maitre d', a rotund, engaging fellow named Frank Bonfiglio, does all the tableside cooking in a tuxedo.

When the two players arrived at the restaurant on this night, Reggie, who was wearing a sweater, was told by the head-waiter he would have to put on one of the "in-house" jackets the restaurant kept for just such an emergency.

"No problem," said Reggie, "I'll take this one," and grabbed a coat that looked to be at least two sizes too small for him.

Upon slipping it on, he stretched his arms—and proceeded to tear a huge hole down the seam in the back. As many of the other patrons in the restaurant looked on in astonishment, Reggie calmly sat down at the table and wore the jacket, hole and all, through his entire meal. When he was done eating and had paid the bill, he got up from the table and stretched again, once with his right arm and then with his left arm, both times tearing off the sleeves. He then strolled over to the headwaiter and handed him back the coat—in three pieces.

"Thanks for the jacket," he said matter-of-factly, and walked out.

For the Yankee beat writers, having Reggie on the team added an extra dimension to the coverage. He was the most controversial and most quotable player ever to wear a Yankee uniform. The George-Billy-Reggie triangle was an almost-daily headache that played out in soap opera fashion over the back pages of the tabloids. As such, losing access to Reggie was unthinkable, but it happened to Moss Klein for more than a month during the tumultuous 1979 season.

When Martin replaced Bob Lemon on June 18, 1979, Reggie was predictably upset. He wanted nothing to do with Martin and felt that Steinbrenner had betrayed him by bringing Billy back. In fact, a few days before the move was made, Reggie telephoned Steinbrenner to express his opposition to the change. Steinbrenner, for the first time, became upset with Reggie for attempting to influence his decisions.

When Martin returned, Reggie was injured with a slight hamstring pull. It seemed obvious, though, he was nursing the injury to avoid playing for Martin. He missed the first 10 games of Martin's return, during which time Klein wrote a column referring to him as "Reluctant Reggie."

The first day back from the road trip, Klein walked into the Yankee clubhouse and heard Reggie yell at him from across the room: "My name isn't Reluctant Reggie!"

Klein shrugged and Reggie came closer, now loudly expressing what he thought of the column. Finally he told Klein not to bother talking to him again.

Although aware of how difficult it would be to cover the Yankees without talking to Reggie, Klein nevertheless kept his distance. If a quote from Reggie was vital for a story, Klein chose to follow the postgame horde of reporters to his locker and listen in. But those occasions were rare. Basically Klein was determined to ignore Reggie.

A case of unfortunate timing made the situation even worse. Klein's older brother, Dave, also a reporter at the *Newark Star-Ledger,* did a freelance story for *The Sporting News* in early July. The story was a cover piece about Reggie, accompanied with a huge caricature of Reggie, labeled "Super Mouth."

A few days before *The Sporting News* came out, Klein hesitantly approached Reggie to inform him of the article and to assure him that this wasn't a "family attack" on him. Reggie nodded, and that was it. But the next day *The Sporting News* surfaced in the Pfister Hotel lobby newsstand. You couldn't miss Reggie's picture—and Reggie didn't.

That night, following a loss to the Brewers, Klein was seated next to Chass of the *Times* on the team bus to the airport for the flight to Chicago. Two rows back was Reggie, who began shouting: "Moss Klein speaks! Moss Klein knows it all! Moss Klein, the expert!"

Klein waited a few minutes as Reggie's taunts continued. Finally he turned to Reggie and said, "You're a jackass." Klein could not figure out why he used that term, since it wasn't one he ordinarily used. But Reggie, who hadn't heard his retort too well, yelled, "What did you call me? A black what?"

Klein cringed. Now this was becoming a racial incident. He turned to Reggie again and said: "I called you a jackass. *Jackass,* that's *all.*"

Graig Nettles, sitting in the row behind Reggie, suddenly chimed in: "This sounds like a very intelligent conversation."

After the flight to Chicago, as everyone started to deplane, Reggie started up anew. "Moss Klein the expert, who's probably making twelve thousand dollars a year."

At that point Frank Messer, the broadcaster, interjected, "Hey, Reggie, I thought you always said money wasn't the measure of a man."

As it turned out, Klein's troubles with Reggie came to an abrupt end a few days later. After the series in Chicago Munson was killed in the crash of his private plane. Three days later Klein was in the Yankee clubhouse following a Sunday-afternoon game against the Orioles, talking to Fred Stanley, the utility infielder. The team was flying to Canton, Ohio, the next day for Munson's funeral, and Steinbrenner had invited all the beat writers to attend. As the two were talking, Reggie approached them.

Klein stiffened as Reggie came right up to him.

"Are you going to the funeral?" Reggie asked.

Klein nodded affirmatively.

"That's good," Reggie said. "I'm glad." Then he walked away, leaving Klein stunned.

But Stanley, aware of the feud, explained that at the team's chapel meeting that morning, the chaplain had given an emotional talk about the foolishness of holding grudges. Munson, the chaplain said, probably held grudges in life and never had a chance to resolve them because of his tragic death. From that day on, Reggie was nothing less than obliging and warm toward Klein, and the two maintained an excellent relationship.

If there was one common thread that ran through Reggie Jackson's career, it was winning. He earned the nickname "Mr. October" for his batting heroics as a Yankee in the World Series, but by the time he came to the Yankees, he was already an old hand at postseason play. And when he left the Yankees for California in 1982, it looked as if winning and baseball in October were still going to remain a part of him.

Unfortunately, the postseason jinx of the Angels and their long-suffering manager Gene Mauch (neither of whom ever made it to the World Series) proved mightier than Reggie's winning mystique, and twice in his five years of wearing a halo, in 1982 and '86, he came up a loser in October as the Angels twice blew leads in the American League playoffs.

It was after the final game of the 1986 American League playoffs between the Angels and Red Sox that Bill Madden and Reggie ran into each other at the bar at the Copley Plaza Marriott in Boston, where the Angels were staying. Reggie was in a philosophical mood, discussing his future, which, he knew, was no longer with the Angels. He talked about the possibility of maybe going back to the Yankees but then quickly dismissed it.

"You know," he said, "George and I have probably become better friends now than at any time since when I signed with him. But I can't go back there. I know that. It would never work."

As the night wore on closer to last call, a guy approached Reggie at the bar and started taunting him. He was clearly looking to start something, and Reggie had had enough drinks that he was willing to oblige. Madden, foreseeing an ugly scene he wanted no part of, intervened.

"Ignore the guy, Reggie," he said. "Or at the very most tell him to blow off."

"Why?" said Reggie. "He's asking for it."

"You're right," said Madden, "but to start something here would be to reduce yourself to Billy Martin's level. Do you want to do that?"

Reggie smiled. "I get your drift," he said. "Let's get out of here."

Reggie Jackson wound up his career where it started—with the Oakland Athletics—in 1987. But that was not quite the end of his would-be association with the Yankees.

In early July of 1988 a report surfaced that Reggie, through an intermediary, had told Steinbrenner he would be willing to make a comeback—if nothing else in order to provide the Yankees with some veteran leadership down the stretch. The intermediary was one William Goodstein, a player agent who did not represent Jackson. Goodstein was a notorious publicity seeker, and he seized on a conversation he had had with Jackson (in which Reggie apparently said half-seriously that he would consider making a comeback) and leaked it to the press.

Steinbrenner, when contacted about the report, was embarrassed because it made him look like a desperate publicity seeker himself.

"Look," he told Madden, "nobody feels worse about Reggie not ending his career with the Yankees than I do. I made a huge mistake. But I would never want him to come back now and embarrass himself. This whole thing is ridiculous, and I don't want anything to do with it. I want to remember Reggie like every other Yankee fan wants to remember him—for hitting those three home runs in the last game of the '77 World Series…for being the guy who led us."

Nevertheless, Goodstein continued to insist the Jackson comeback story was legitimate and went as far as to say Reggie was willing to go to Columbus, the Yankees' AAA farm team, to work his way into shape. It did not matter that neither of Reggie's longtime agents, Matt Merola or Steve Kay, professed to know anything about this comeback story. And when finally Reggie was located for comment on it, he laughed.

"You can stick a fork in me," he said. "I'm done."

Publicity had always been his game, but Mr. October was smart enough to see the foolishness of trying to be Mr. September.

Graig Nettles

They called him Puff, Captain Midnight, and Mr. Quip, and at any given time any of those monikers fit Graig Nettles like a well-worn third baseman's glove. His Yankee teammates often joked about his elusiveness. One moment he would be part of a crowd in a bar or restaurant, and the next, *puff!* he'd be gone, not to be seen again until the next day in the clubhouse.

Perhaps that's why it was so unusual that Nettles was one of the ringleaders in one of the wildest off-the-field capers in Yankee history. Of all people, he certainly had a proven record of knowing when to disappear before the long arm of the law arrived. But on this occasion, a balmy September evening in Boston in 1983, Nettles, along with a half-dozen other Yankee merrymakers, wound up being confronted by a cordon of gun-toting cops on the roof of a bank.

It seems that Jay Howell, a relief pitcher in the free-spirited mold of all good relievers (who would go on to far greater infamy by altering the texture of baseballs with pine tar in the '88 National League playoffs), had erected this giant slingshot out of rubber tubing and funnels. As Howell noted with considerable pride, it had the capacity to fling water balloons great distances. All that was needed was a proper launching pad to put this marvelous invention into practice.

Now, immediately adjacent to the Boston Sheraton, where the Yankees stay, is a bank that rises high above the city and has a long, flat roof. One of the more ingenious Yankees—it was never revealed who—discovered a way to get up on the roof of the bank, and it was there that The Great Slingshot Caper took place.

With Bob Shirley serving as the "point man," leaning over the edge of the building citing targets, Howell, Goose Gossage, Dave Righetti, George Frazier, and Nettles took turns firing the water balloons out of the slingshot. Into the Boston night the balloons sploshed off buildings and sidewalks, startling pedestrians as far as two or three city blocks away.

At one point, Shirley spotted a couple coming out of a J. P. Hillary's Restaurant on Boylston Street, two blocks away. On his command the slingshot was immediately aimed in that direction, and the balloon was fired. Incredibly, it landed right in front of the couple, so close to them that the woman thought she had been struck by a beer bottle. They quickly ran for cover and called the cops. Unbeknown to the couple or the Yankees, however, the cops were already en route to the bank because one of the players had unknowingly set off a burglar alarm.

Suddenly, what looked to be an entire squadron of Boston cops, wielding guns and nightsticks, came busting onto the roof, shouting, "Freeze! Police!" Sobriety immediately gripped the Yankee party, and Nettles, never at a loss for a quip, said: "This is just terrific. How can I ever tell this to my kids. I get arrested on the roof of a bank in the middle of the night, and I'm not even robbing the damn place."

Somehow, the Yankees, who had hidden the slingshot behind an air conditioning duct, convinced the cops they were just having a couple of beers and taking in the sights on the roof. The cops agreed to let them go without making any report—but warned them to keep their future parties restricted to their rooms.

Somebody had to go back on the roof to retrieve the slingshot, though, and once they did, they couldn't resist the temptation of firing off a few more water balloons. This time Frazier took the slingshot over to a little square across the street from Daisy Buchanan's, the favorite saloon in Boston of most of the ball players and sportswriters. It was 2:00 A.M., and everyone was coming out of the joint when a couple of Yankee players spotted Frazier across the street.

"No!" they shouted. "Don't do it, George! Are you crazy?"

As a matter of fact, Frazier was, and ignoring their pleas, he fired off a balloon that whistled across the street and shattered the huge picture window of Daisy Buchanan's into a thousand pieces. Without a word, but knowing he had really done it this time, Frazier marched into the place, reached into his pocket and threw three 100-dollar bills onto the bar.

"That's for the window," he said.

By then, Graig Nettles had long since gone *puff!* into the night, but of all his Yankee misadventures, the night of the water balloons was the one he remembered best.

"All I know," he said, "is that I'm thirty-eight years old and the captain of the team, and here I was up on the roof of a bank, drinking beer and shooting water balloons all over the city. With the Yankees, I guess, you needed those kinds of diversions."

As far as the writers were concerned, Nettles provided more than his share of "diversions" in his 11 years with the ball club. He had as many run-ins with Steinbrenner as Reggie; they just weren't always as volatile. Then again, there was the time he and Reggie had their celebrated run-in after the 1981 playoffs in Oakland—which only served to prove how absolutely crazy the Yankees are and how there is never a time when a reporter covering this team can let his or her guard down with them.

The Yankees had just swept the A's (managed by Billy Martin) in the playoffs to earn a spot in the World Series against the Dodgers. Things couldn't be going better. The team was peaking at precisely the right time, Steinbrenner wasn't threatening to fire anybody, and everybody was in a buoyant mood. So buoyant that Steinbrenner hastily put together a party at Vince's, a restaurant not far from the Oakland Coliseum, to celebrate the team's decisive three-game sweep over Martin and the A's.

The reporters were invited to attend, too, but were more intent on getting their stories written and catching an overnight flight back to New York. Besides, what could possibly go wrong at a victory celebration that Steinbrenner was throwing?

What indeed?

That night the four senior beat writers, Murray Chass, Moss Klein, Phil Pepe, and Bill Madden, all flew home together, content in the knowledge that all was for once tranquil in Yankeeland. When they got to Chicago to change planes, however, Chass called home to tell his wife what time he'd be arriving at Newark Airport. A few minutes later he caught up with the other three at the check-in area.

"You're not gonna believe this," he said. "Reggie and Nettles got in a fight at the victory party last night."

"You're right," said Madden, "I don't believe it."

"Honest," said Chass, who couldn't help but laugh now at the absurdity of it all. "My wife said [veteran columnist] Dick Young was at the party and has a front-page story in the *Daily News* today. Everyone in New York is talking about it, and here we are, the four veteran writers who are supposed to know everything about this team, and we don't know anything about one of the biggest stories of the year."

So what was to be a nice, peaceful, uneventful off day suddenly became another reporter's nightmare. Phone calls to bartenders and hotel personnel had to be made, airport vigils were now the order of the day, since the Yankee team flight would be coming in later. The World Series was now secondary to another Yankee brouhaha.

The Jackson-Nettles fight was. precipitated when Reggie brought in a large group of friends to the party and sat down at a table that had been temporarily vacated by Nettles' wife, Ginger, and his 12-year-old son, Michael. When Ginger and Michael returned and asked for their seats back, an argument ensued. Reggie got up and sought out Nettles, who was at the bar, and one thing led to another with Reggie knocking a bottle of beer out of Nettles' hand, and Nettles slugging Reggie and knocking him to the floor.

At that point Steinbrenner rushed over and started yelling at both the combatants to cut it out. "We're disgracing the Yankees in front of these people and this city!" he screamed. "Stop it now. Stop it immediately!"

Both Reggie and Nettles later expressed embarrassment over the incident, and details of the fight remained sketchy. But a patron in the restaurant that night had a tape recorder and recorded much of the inflammatory rhetoric for posterity; Amid all the commotion, Reggie's voice is heard most clearly on the tape, screaming: "I ain't liked the dude for ten years. I don't care if I play in the World Series. I don't have a contract. I can go anywhere. I ain't drunk. I ain't gonna take this stuff anymore."

When order was restored, Steinbrenner told Reggie to tell his friends to leave. Reggie took that as an insult, an indication that Steinbrenner was siding with Nettles, and that's when he said to the Boss, "You'll regret this."

More than Reggie, though, Nettles seemed to relish sparring with the Boss. There was one time in Boston when Nettles spotted Steinbrenner sitting in the Yankee clubhouse before a game—on Nettles' stool. This was right after

Steinbrenner had been making statements about Nettles getting fat and slowing down.

"George is right," Nettles said, pointing at Steinbrenner, "Nettles *is* getting fat."

It was also Nettles who foiled Steinbrenner's most painstaking attempt at enforcing security measures in spring training 1982. The Yankees were playing exhibitions over on Florida's Gulf Coast and staying at Steinbrenner's Bay Harbor Inn in Tampa. A midnight curfew was in effect, and Steinbrenner would be damned if any of his players was going to violate it in his own hotel. Just to be sure, he had house detectives prowling the lobby as well as each of the hotel's three floors.

Now this was a challenge that Nettles couldn't resist, and along with a couple of other players, he tied together a bunch of sheets and towels, secured them around the grating on the balcony of his room (which happened to be in the back of the hotel), and slid down the side of the building into the shrubbery. After a few hours of late-night reveling at one of Tampa's livelier watering holes, the players returned—well after midnight—climbed back up the knotted sheets, and went to bed without ever being found out by Steinbrenner's house dicks.

Nettles had his share of contract hassles with Steinbrenner, too—mostly because he was a victim of incredibly bad timing. In 1976, for example, Nettles was in the midst of a slump when his agent negotiated a three-year contract for him. At the time, it looked like a good deal, even though he was to be a free agent at the end of the year. Shortly after signing the contract—worth approximately $140,000 per year—Nettles snapped out of his slump and went on to lead the American League in homers. Then that winter, the first wave of free agency hit baseball, and Nettles looked around and saw countless players with half his ability suddenly being offered millions of dollars by the baseball owners.

The following spring he staged a brief two-day "protest" walkout from the Yankee training camp, prompting Steinbrenner to issue the first of many "Nettles is nearing the end of the-line" pronunciations.

"An extension," said Steinbrenner, "is out of the question. At the end of this contract, Nettles will be thirty-four, and in the option year he'll be thirty-five. It is not good business to think about extending a contract to a man of that age."

Nettles, of course, was still playing at age 44 and was the regular third baseman for the Padres in the '84 World Series at 40. But Steinbrenner did not relent about his age after that spring training dispute, saying frequently that Nettles was "in the twilight" of his career.

Nettles was quick to zing the Boss for that, every time he made an exceptional play in the field—such as the third game of the 1978 World Series, when he bedazzled 56,447 fans at Yankee Stadium as well as a national TV audience of millions with three sensational diving plays against the Dodgers. (Dodger manager Tommy Lasorda called it "one of the greatest exhibitions of fielding I've ever seen.")

Ironically, it was right before that game that the Rawlings glove people had canceled Nettles' contract with them. Nettles had been complaining about their refusal to get his gloves into the stores so he could make some royalties off them, and he finally resorted to writing to the president of the company about it. Former Braves first baseman Frank Torre, the Rawlings representative, was annoyed at Nettles going over his head and came into the clubhouse at the World Series and told Nettles the company had decided not to renew his contract.

"I can honestly say that didn't give me the incentive to have the kind of Series I had," Nettles said. "But it was rather bad timing on their part."

As for Steinbrenner's "twilight" line, Nettles responded: "I guess maybe I should go to Japan next year where the sun sets a day later." Years later, when Steinbrenner traded him to the Padres, he revised the quip to "maybe playing for San Diego will help me because twilight comes later out there. With the time difference I could add three hours to my career."

And another time in 1980, when Steinbrenner criticized him as being "definitely fat and probably finished," Nettles retorted: "That irritated me, but I have to consider the source. It comes from a man who obviously knows nothing about how to control his weight. Two things he knows nothing about are baseball and weight control."

Ultimately, like all the Yankees—survivors included—there came the time for Nettles to part company with Steinbrenner. At least he finally got his big payday, though. After all the years of declaring Nettles was past his prime, slowing down or getting fat, Steinbrenner rewarded the veteran third baseman with a two-year, $1.8-million contract in November of '83. Nettles was 39 at the time, had been named team captain the previous season, and was going to be a free agent if Steinbrenner didn't re-sign him.

But two things happened that soured the Nettles-Steinbrenner relationship just when it looked as if they were finally going to live happily ever after together: (1) Nettles wrote a book that winter, and (2) Steinbrenner went out and traded for another third baseman, Toby Harrah. When the Nettles book came out that spring, containing all the old jibes at Steinbrenner, the Boss reacted with predictable outrage. Meanwhile, Nettles, though happy at last with his contract, was extremely unhappy about relinquishing playing time to Harrah.

Finally, on the last day of spring training, Steinbrenner traded Nettles to the Padres, intimating that he had become a negative influence with some of the younger players on the team, particularly Dave Righetti. Parting was not sweet sorrow, as Nettles assailed Steinbrenner, saying: "He tried to discredit me. It's too bad they couldn't just trade me and say 'good luck.' But that's the way the man does things. He deals in character assassination. He's done it before and he'll do it again."

One final bit of irony. In January of 1989, when Steinbrenner was involved in what most people viewed as a pretty thorough character assassination of Dave Winfield, he said in a private conversation to Bill Madden: "You know, Winfield is the most selfish athlete I've ever known. He's nothing like Reggie… or even Graig Nettles. Nettles may have said a lot of nasty things about me, but he played hard, gave me his all, and was all for the team. I'd take him back anytime."

Bob Shirley

At the winter baseball meetings in Honolulu in December of 1982, George Steinbrenner was flushed with pride over the signing of free-agent outfielder Steve Kemp away from the Chicago White Sox. Only thing was, Kemp was really Steinbrenner's number-two target in the free-agent market that winter. Target number-one was the Seattle Mariners' left-hander Floyd Bannister, who had earlier scorned Steinbrenner by letting it be known he had no desire to pitch in New York for the Bronx Zoo Steinbrenner Yankees. (Ironically, Bannister wound up signing with the White Sox, prompting a sour-grapes Steinbrenner reaction in which he ridiculed the two White Sox owners, Jerry Reinsdorf and Eddie Einhorn, as "those two pumpkins" and "the Katzenjammer twins.")

Now Tony Attanasio, one of the shrewder (if lower-key) agents in the business, was aware of Steinbrenner's unrequited lust for Bannister and had come to Hawaii with the idea of selling the Boss on someone just as good, if not as spectacular and overpowering. That someone was Bob Shirley, a junk-balling left-hander who, to that point in his career, had compiled a 53–74 record (and only one winning season) as a sometime-starter and long reliever over six seasons with three National League teams.

Attanasio, it seems, had prepared this elaborate "tout sheet" on Shirley that, if taken at face value, would lead one to believe that he was every bit the pitcher that Bannister was. "Okay, it was illusory of sorts," Attanasio would admit later, "but at the time you could make the case that Shirley, whenever he was used exclusively as a starter for ten or more consecutive games, compared favorably with Bannister as a starter."

Whatever, it was enough to convince Steinbrenner, who was determined to come home from the winter meetings with a left-handed pitcher to go with his left-handed power hitter. When Attanasio came back from dinner one night to the Sheraton-Waikiki, the winter-meeting headquarters, Yankee coach Don Zimmer was pacing up and down in the lobby, anxiously awaiting him. "George wants to see you right now," Zimmer said. "I can't tell you why, but you better get up to his suite immediately before he changes his mind."

That night, Steinbrenner signed Shirley to a three-year contract worth nearly $2.4 million. It is hard to say if Shirley was worth it (or worth the $500,000 extension he got for 1987). Overall as a Yankee, his record was 13–20, indicating he was grossly overpaid for his services. Then again, when compared with such free agents as Ed Whitson, Dave Collins, or Rawly Eastwick, all of whom were paid millions by Steinbrenner but couldn't last in New York even *two* seasons, Shirley could be considered a bargain. Certainly he provided useful service to the Yankees in his five years in pinstripes, and if his innings weren't as numerous as Attanasio promised Steinbrenner, well, that wasn't Shirley's fault. There was never a day he wouldn't take the ball, even in the worst of times.

Above all, Shirley was a survivor, maybe the ultimate survivor when you consider he was able to overcome, first, a less-than-overpowering or imposing repertoire of pitches and, second, two terms of Billy Martin, who was loath to use him in almost any situation. Through it all, Shirley marched to his own drummer, never making waves but frequently providing needed comic relief to a team under constant pressure from above.

He was the famed Vapor Man, who would show up at team parties covered completely with shaving cream—and nothing underneath. At one team party Dave Righetti came dressed in a toga, brandishing a long leash that went out the door. As curious onlookers waited to see what—or who—was on the collar at the other end of the leash, in crawled the Vapor Man, once again garbed only in shaving cream. The players erupted in laughter as Shirley, on all fours, began growling and lunging at horrified female onlookers.

Another of the more memorable Shirley capers occurred on the final weekend of the 1984 season in New York. The Yankees were playing out the schedule against the Tigers, who had long since clinched the division title and were in the process of merely getting their pitching set up for the playoffs. Accordingly, Tiger manager Sparky Anderson was shuttling in one pitcher after another every couple of innings on this day to give them all some work, and the bullpen car was constantly in use.

Because he had nothing else to do in the bullpen—having started and won the opening game of the series two days earlier—Shirley was sitting in the bullpen car, moving it forward and backward each time a pitcher was called in. But when Guillermo Hernandez, the Tigers' ace reliever (and the American League MVP and Cy Young winner that year), was called in, Shirley decided to pay him the ultimate respect: he drove him into the game himself.

The rest of the Yankee relievers broke up in laughter as they watched Shirley drive the car out of the bullpen with Hernandez sitting in the passenger seat. Dave Righetti quickly called the Yankee dugout to pass the word, and by the time Shirley had let Hernandez off and was circling back along the first base line, the rest of the Yankees were prepared for him. They began throwing spit cups, tobacco wads, and tape rolls out of the dugout at the bullpen car.

"It was just a whim, but I guess it was all pretty funny," Shirley said, "except Hernandez didn't seem to understand it. For one thing, he didn't speak very good English. When he got in the car, I wished him good luck in the playoffs, and he didn't say anything. He just looked at me kind of funny. I think maybe he didn't know who I was or what the hell was going on. The other Tigers did, though. When I drove past their dugout, they all stood up and applauded."

Another time, the Yankees were getting blown out by the Rangers in Texas when Shirley, who had been playing a trivia game with the rest of the relievers to pass the time in the bullpen, was called in to mop up. At the time he was stumped on a question: "Name the five states whose names end in *s.*" A native Oklahoman, Shirley had no trouble coming up with Arkansas, Kansas, Texas, and Illinois, but he was stumped on the fifth. He went into the game, still racking his brain for the fifth state. After facing three batters and retiring all three on scorched fly balls to the farthest reaches of the ballpark, he jogged off the mound. As he approached the dugout, revelation struck. He rushed to a phone at the far end and called the bullpen.

Righetti answered: "Okay, what is it?"

"Massachusetts!" Shirley replied triumphantly.

Actually, that had been a rather typical Shirley relief effort. He was not averse to using the entire ballpark to get batters out. Nor was he one to come into a game and blow away the opposition with heat. In 1985, in Toronto against the Blue Jays, Yogi Berra brought Shirley in to face Willie Aikens, a dangerous left-handed power hitter, with runners at first and second and one out. Shirley proceeded to walk Aikens on four pitches to load the bases, and then went 3-1 on the next batter, Damaso Garcia, before getting a break on what should have been ball four from plate umpire Greg Kosc.

"Ah, it was just a little high," Shirley said.

Bobby Cox, the Blue Jays' manager, thought it was more than just a little high and vented his feelings rather profanely at Kosc.

Shirley got his next pitch into the strike zone, finally, and Garcia pummeled it—right back to the box. In self-defense Shirley ducked and shielded his face with his glove, only to find the ball squarely in its pocket when the smoke cleared. Quickly regaining his composure, he calmly tossed the ball over to first to double up Aikens and end the inning. As he strolled back to the dugout with a contented smile of having fooled 'em once again, he was greeted by Berra.

"I think that's enough for today," Yogi said.

Yogi liked Shirley, though, primarily because he appreciated Shirley's willingness to always take the ball and never complain. Billy Martin, on the other hand, found Shirley to be an unnecessary evil. He had absolutely no confidence in him and, therefore, no use for him.

In one stretch of Billy IV in 1985, Shirley went 23 days without appearing in a game. As he put it, "The pressure was becoming excruciating." Martin finally sprung him to pitch the ninth inning of a 13–1 Yankee blowout of the A's in Oakland. The only reason it turned out Martin used him on this occasion was because Rich Bordi, the pitcher he wanted to use, had been given permission to go over to a San Francisco hospital to be with his wife, who was giving birth. When Shirley arrived at the mound, catcher Butch Wynegar asked him if he remembered the signs. And in the dugout Phil Niekro joked, "He's just in there icing his arm."

Shirley went on to retire the side on three routine ground-ball outs. When he came in, Martin said, "If you pitch like that all the time, I'll use you more."

After the game, reporters flocked to Shirley, who had kept a sign at his locker which updated his "days in captivity."

"It was nothing," Shirley said. "The only reason I got in there was because of something that happened in the Bordi bedroom nine months ago."

Alas, life under Martin was mostly idleness for Shirley, who continually had to come up with new ideas for passing the empty hours in the bullpen. Later that year the Yankees were in Anaheim playing the Angels. It had been a particularly uneventful game, and around the sixth inning somebody in the press box looked out to the Yankee bullpen in left field and began laughing. There, sitting all by himself in the empty bleacher seats above the bullpen, was Shirley. When Doug Holmquist, serving as the Yankees' "eye in the sky" coach in the press box, spotted him and phoned down to Martin, the manager's reaction was one of fury.

"Tell him to get the hell out of the seats!" Martin screamed into the telephone at bullpen coach Jeff Torborg.

"I suppose," Shirley said, "Billy thought I was getting some popcorn. All I was trying to do was get a better view of the ball game. All you can see from the bullpen there is the back of the left fielder's jersey."

Because Shirley was such a delightfully wacky free spirit, it was hard for any manager to stay mad at him—even Martin, who instead chose to ignore him. Lou Piniella tried the same practice—to no avail. By the time Piniella became manager in 1986, Shirley's charmed life as a major league pitcher had about run its course. He was 0–4, with a 5.04 ERA, and Piniella only kept him on the team because of his hefty contract and the need to have someone to pitch all those garbage innings in the early blowouts—of which there were many.

In good times or in bad, Shirley loved to drink, and even though he may not have gotten that much action in the games, he was always the center of activity on the team flights. In addition to volunteering his services to the airline crew as an extra steward, by the end of the flight he would always have somehow managed to squirrel away in his duffel bag the better part of the allotment of the minibottles of booze. Eventually the stewardesses would become baffled as to where all the liquor went. Fortunately everyone in the Yankee traveling party always knew where it was.

On one flight Moss Klein had a toothache and asked the stewardess if she had something for him to swirl around to numb the pain. The stewardess checked, returned, and said with a puzzled look, "I'm sorry—there's no liquor left."

Klein knew exactly where to go—to the rear of the plane and Dr. Shirley, who reached into his bag and produced three bottles of Amaretto.

"Here," he said. "This should take care of you. Take these and call me in the morning."

After the games, especially night games, you could always find Shirley in the hotel bar. Most often he could be found closing it. But unlike Martin, Shirley was a happy drunk, who never got into trouble. He just liked to sit over in a corner with Righetti or (earlier) Dale Murray and drink beer until somebody told him it was time to leave.

One particular night in Texas, though, he stayed too long at the fair, as the song goes. Every night at the Arlington Hilton bar (which is actually a disco), last call at 1:45 is announced by the music suddenly changing from loud rock to, of all things, a Viennese waltz. The Yankees had lost that night, and Piniella happened to be at the bar with a couple of his coaches, replaying his night's misery over a few vodkas. As the waltz came on, he looked out at the dance floor, only to see a solo figure gliding around the floor a la Fred Astaire—using a chair for a partner. It was Shirley.

Piniella glanced at his watch. "He probably thinks he's funny," he said. "And I guess he is. But tomorrow he's gonna find out that his funny just cost him $500."

Shirley paid the fine without complaint or comment. It was, after all, a mere pittance compared to what he earned for his five years with the Yankees. Throughout those five seasons, you could say he provided laughs aplenty for all who traveled the Yankee scene. You could probably say, too, that he had the last laugh.

Lou Piniella

"Sweet Lou" Piniella is probably most remembered for his hot Latin temper. His blowups at umpires, opposing players, and George Steinbrenner are the stuff of which legends are made. But those were always short-lived. What was enduring about him was his engaging sense of humor, and that, above all, was what enabled him to cope and survive better and longer than all the others.

Piniella came to the Yankees in December of 1973 in a trade from the Kansas City Royals for relief pitcher Lindy McDaniel. He remained as a player into the 1984 season, five times batting over .300. In four World Series he hit .319. He was a native of Tampa, Steinbrenner's adopted home town, and the Boss never made much of a secret of the fact that Piniella was his favorite of all the players.

Because Piniella was his favorite, Steinbrenner felt he had to act like a father to Lou at times. Piniella was always a happy-go-lucky sort who enjoyed all of life's pleasures, and Steinbrenner saw a need for discipline in him. That, of course, led to conflict between the two—the most vocal and volatile coming in the spring of 1982 with the Great Piniella Weight War.

The seeds of that weighty war of words were actually planted the previous winter. Piniella was asleep at his home in Tampa one morning in early January when his wife, Anita, came into the bedroom and told him that Hopalong Cassady was at the door to see him. Cassady, the former Heisman Trophy-winning running back from Ohio State in the fifties, had been hired by Steinbrenner as a special scout and sometime fitness instructor for the Yankees.

"What the hell does he want?" Piniella asked.

"I don't know," Anita said. "You better find out."

Piniella dragged himself out of bed and went to the door.

"What's up, Hoppy? What brings you here?"

"George asked me to come by and get you," Cassady replied. "He wants you to start getting in shape early this spring. He's concerned about your weight, especially now with you getting into your late thirties. It's harder to get it off. He wants me to work with you three days a week here in Tampa right up until spring training."

"You gotta be jokin'," Piniella said.

"No, George is serious about this, Lou. I'm just doing my job."

About then, Piniella thought about the new three-year contract Steinbrenner had given him. He remembered being so pleasantly surprised by the Boss' willingness to sign him up through the age of 40. But then there had been that one catch—a weight clause which Steinbrenner had inserted in the contract, calling for Piniella to be fined $1,000 for every pound he weighed above 200.

"Okay," shrugged Piniella. "When do we start?"

"How about right now," said Cassady. "I'm here."

So off they went to a nearby health club where a mini-marathon course was laid out with the tires, the rings, the chin-up bars, etc., as well as all the Nautilus equipment.

Piniella tried running the course just once that first day, worked out briefly with the Nautilus equipment, and said to himself: "This is crazy. I'll be so worn out by the time spring training comes I won't be able to lift a bat."

So he had to think quickly of a way out.

"What's the standard time I'm supposed to do this course in, Hoppy?" he asked.

"Oh, by the time you get it down to twelve minutes we can quit the workouts," Cassady replied.

"Well, let me ask you something, Hoppy." Piniella said. "What's that favorite brandy of yours again?"

"Why, Carlos Primero," Cassady said, "it's expensive as hell, why?"

"Well, I'll bet you a bottle of that you can't do this course in twelve minutes."

"Sure enough? Okay, I'll take that."

As Cassady began warming up, Piniella went over to a nearby refreshment stand and bought himself a glass of orange juice. When he came back, he took the stopwatch from Cassady and went up into the grandstand, where he found a newspaper.

"Okay, Hoppy," he yelled down. "Anytime you're ready."

"Let it go," said Cassady, who took off around the course as Piniella clicked the stopwatch.

As Cassady pumped and puffed around the course, Piniella sipped his juice and read the paper. At last he saw Cassady coming around the bend to the finish line.

"Great show, Hoppy!" he yelled. "Fourteen minutes! That's pretty damn good."

For Cassady the brandy bet had now become secondary to running the course in 12 minutes. He was determined to make the time. Two days later he picked Piniella up again, and the scenario repeated itself. Piniella took his juice and his paper into the grandstand and clocked Hoppy running around the course.

"You're getting better, Hoppy," he said when Cassady completed the course. "This one's just a little under 13."

Now they went over to the Nautilus equipment, and Piniella professed to feel a little uneasy using it.

"I've really never worked with weights before," he said. "I don't know if it's a good idea."

"Here, let me show you," said Cassady, who began demonstrating all the different weight lifts.

"Damn," said Piniella, "you're really in great shape, Hoppy."

"Watch," said Cassady, "I can do even more."

And that's the way the workouts went all that month. Cassady would run around the course while Piniella sat and looked on with the stopwatch, the newspaper, and his orange juice. Then they would go into the Nautilus room, and Piniella would watch Cassady work out with the weights. When they returned to Piniella's house, Anita looked curiously at Cassady, who was all sweaty and exhausted, and at her husband, who looked as fresh and rested as when he left. Cassady probably didn't care that he had failed in his mission to turn Piniella into a finely-chiseled physical specimen for spring training. Both he and Piniella could laugh privately at the thought of Steinbrenner sitting in his offices at American Shipbuilding feeling pleased at the thought of making both of them miserable.

But when Piniella got to camp in Fort Lauderdale in mid-February, Steinbrenner took one look at him and knew that he had done nothing about getting in shape over the winter. He ordered him on the scale, which Piniella tipped at 215.

"You've got a week to get down to two hundred," Steinbrenner said, "and if you don't, I don't have to remind you it'll cost you a thousand dollars a pound."

Well, now the fun began. Steinbrenner was determined to make Piniella pay the price—physically, mentally, and monetarily—for coming into camp overweight, and Piniella was just as determined to fight the Boss and lose his excess poundage in his own time. On February 22 Piniella was weighed again and was down to 207, but Steinbrenner had general manager Bill Bergesch tell him he was being fined $7,000.

Then the exhibition games began, and Piniella found himself being kept in them longer than any of the other regulars by manager Bob Lemon. It did not help either that the team was playing poorly and tempers were frayed all around. That became ever-so-evident one night when, after a Yankee loss in Fort Lauderdale, Piniella and Lemon had to be kept from punching each other out.

On Steinbrenner's orders that spring, the players all had to run laps in the outfield after every game before they could shower and leave. While he was doing his laps, Piniella spotted a baseball lying on the ground and picked it up and tossed it to some kids in the stands.

Suddenly, Lemon, who was in an awful mood anyway, started yelling at him. It seemed that Steinbrenner, in one of the many meetings he called that spring with the manager and coaches, had berated everyone about throwing baseballs into the stands. Piniella, unaware of this dictum, couldn't believe Lemon was getting on his case like this and charged the manager. Though 20 years older and nowhere near as physically fit as even beefy Lou, Lemon stood his ground and tried to get Piniella in a headlock before other players and coaches rushed over to pull them apart.

The time bomb that had been tick, tick, ticking away in Lou Piniella finally exploded on March 16. The Yankees were playing a B game against the Rangers in Fort Lauderdale in the morning, followed by an A game in nearby Pompano Beach that afternoon. Piniella looked on the bulletin board and saw his name listed to play in the B game. As it turned out, the game went 11 innings, and since most of the other regulars had already bused over to Pompano, Piniella played all of it.

He was exhausted when he stepped into the shower, his mind wandering to that first tall, cold beer at Shooter's. Suddenly his concentration was interrupted by the clubhouse attendant.

"You're wanted on the phone, Lou."

"Who is it?" Piniella asked.

"It's Lem. He's calling from the ballpark at Pompano."

Piniella got out of the shower and went to the phone.

"Hurry up and get dressed, Meat," said Lemon. "I need you over here."

"You gotta be jokin', Skip," said Piniella. "I just got done playing eleven innings!"

"No joke, Lou," said Lemon, now sounding very serious. "The Boss wants you over here. You gotta come over or it's my ass."

"Well, this is bullshit," said Piniella, "and you can tell him that. I'm not coming."

He hung up the phone and got back into the shower, only to be interrupted again by another call. This time it was Steinbrenner.

"Lou, you get your ass over here right now, or I'm gonna fine you a thousand dollars."

Piniella was livid.

"George, I'm not coming. Fine me, suspend me, do whatever you want, but this is a lot of shit and you know it. You can stick that game. I just got done playing eleven innings over here and that's all I'm gonna play today."

Two days later, just before the Yankees' game against the Braves in West Palm Beach, Piniella learned he had been fined another $1,000, running his weighty spring tab now to $8,000. The line was bad enough, but the fact that he had to find out about it from the writers really infuriated him.

Pacing up and down along the first base line, Piniella worked himself up and began blistering Steinbrenner. "I am utterly disgusted with George

Steinbrenner," he said. "All we have ever been told around here is that what happens within the Yankee family is supposed to stay there. It's a sad way for a player to learn he's being fined—through the press.

"I'm sick and tired of this. I was invited here early and I end up getting fined $1,000 a day. I'm not happy with the damn fines. I'm like Smith Barney. I've worked hard for my money. To be suddenly treated like Little Orphan Annie is ridiculous."

Steinbrenner, of course, relished the conflict, which created back-page fodder in the tabloids back in New York. He also had little sympathy for Piniella, who had been resisting his efforts at discipline for two months now.

"Sometimes Lou has to be treated like a nineteen-year-old," he said. "Everybody in Tampa will tell you that. I've got it in black and white. He knew about the weight clause. He knew what he was signing. If I'm a man and my employer was paying me three hundred fifty thousand dollars a year, which is more than the president of the United States is making, and there are ten million unemployed people out there earning nothing in this country, I'd sure as hell take seven pounds off to honor my contract.

"Someday Lou Piniella will be out of baseball and in business. Boy! He'd last five days in business."

As the spring wore on and the season began, all the furor over Piniella's weight became forgotten. The Yankees continued to play poorly, and Lemon was fired 14 games into the season. To the best of anyone's knowledge, Steinbrenner never did collect the fines from Piniella and the two resumed their father-son kinship that lasted right up until Piniella became manager in 1986.

Throughout his days as a player, he was always the one who got away with saying anything to the Boss. One time Steinbrenner, upset with the players' complaints about having to work out on an off-day, called a clubhouse meeting to air them out. "You guys are complaining about being overworked?" Steinbrenner said. "You don't even know what work is. You're not tough enough, any of you. I know what tough is. I've seen it down on the docks where the longshoremen work."

"C'mon, George," piped up Piniella from the back of the room, "the only time you've ever been down on the docks was to put gasoline in your father's yacht!"

If anyone else had dared to say something like that, they'd have been berated, fined for insubordination, and eventually traded. But Steinbrenner couldn't help but laugh himself at Piniella's irreverence.

Just as evident as his humor, however, was Piniella's hot temper, which, as demonstrated by the incident in West Palm Beach, frequently got him in hot water. By the tune he became manager, he had mellowed considerably.

He could still throw a tantrum with the best of them, though—like the day in Cleveland in August 1986 when he was ejected from a nationally televised game after putting on a spirited spectacle, kicking dirt, throwing his cap, and running back and forth at the umpires. When he returned to the hotel mat night, he remembered it was his wife's birthday. When he called her at home in New Jersey, her first comment was: "I'm forty-three years old and I'm married to a four-year-old."

Anita Piniella was always the voice of reason with Lou. Often, Piniella's impulsiveness and anger over a particularly bad game would lead to a spur-of-the-moment decision to retire. Then it would be up to Anita to talk him out of it. The Piniella retirements eventually became a running joke among the writers.

Piniella was ready to retire one night in Milwaukee after a tough game against the Brewers' crafty (some said shifty as well) left-hander Mike Caldwell. Bobby Murcer, Piniella's closest friend on the team, calmed him down by convincing him that Caldwell was throwing a spitter.

"Forget it, Lou," Murcer said. "The guy cheated. It's not your fault. They let him cheat. What can you do?"

A few minutes later Piniella, having gotten himself further worked up, called the writers over and bellowed: "How the hell do they let him get away with that stuff? He's a cheater!"

One memorable Piniella "retirement" actually lasted for several hours—because he made his "that's it, I'm finished" decision following the final game of a 15-day West Coast road trip and brooded about it all the way home on the plane to Newark.

That retirement started after the Yankees' June 15, 1980, game in Oakland against the Athletics, who were now being managed by Billy Martin, in between his second and third tours of duty with the Yankees. Piniella had been unhappy about his part-time status under new Yankee manager Dick Howser. In effect, Howser was platooning Murcer and Piniella, and both were griping about it. On that day the Yankees won, 8–2, but Piniella, who had replaced Murcer when Martin switched from a right-handed pitcher to a left-hander in the third inning, went hitless in two at-bats. Afterward he was fuming.

When the reporters came into the clubhouse, Piniella motioned Moss Klein over. Like all the other writers wanting to make the getaway flight home, Klein was in a particular rush this day. There was only an hour to get his story written if he wanted to make the team bus, and there was other business that had to be attended to. Because this was Martin's first year in Oakland, having been fired by Steinbrenner the year before, it meant having to check both clubhouses before going upstairs to the press box to write. As always with Billy, there was a budding controversy, too. Steinbrenner, it seemed, had chosen that day to issue a statement urging Martin to wear his Yankee uniform to the Yankees' Old-timers' Day festivities the following Saturday in New York.

So it was essential to check with Martin after the game, which Klein knew wasn't going to be fun. After just watching his A's lose their third straight to the Yankees, Billy didn't figure to be in a mood to talk about uniforms.

With all this in mind and the clock ticking away, Klein was a bit uneasy when Piniella called him over. And when Piniella started rambling on about his latest "retirement," Klein could see himself getting trapped in Oakland that night and missing the Yankee plane. He didn't want to ignore the story, but he knew from experience that Piniella's retirements never lasted. The time it would take to write an extra story about a Piniella retirement that would undoubtedly be over before the next day's game would cost the flight.

Klein thus interrupted Piniella.

"Look, Lou," he said, "I think you're making a mistake. You're too good to retire now. I'm not going to use it. Think about it. You'll change your mind."

Piniella was stunned that his "story" was being rejected, and he persisted.

"I'm serious about this," he said. "I've had it."

Murcer, meanwhile, was egging Piniella on, which was just what Klein didn't need. "I think you're right, Lou," Murcer said. "It's time to get into another business. What do you need this for. This guy [Howser] doesn't even let us play."

Time was running out. Klein had to make a decision.

"Lou, I'm not going to write this," he repeated. "If you're serious about it tomorrow after you've had a chance to sleep on it, I'll be happy to do the story, but right now isn't a good time for you to decide to retire."

The next day in New York, Klein came into the clubhouse and saw Piniella was already at his locker. When Piniella turned and saw him, he started laughing.

"Anita told me I'd be crazy if I retired," he said. "She told me she couldn't stand having me around all the time. So I'm back. But I am going to talk to Howser about getting more playing time. I'm too young to be a platoon player."

And Piniella would play for four more years, with several more near retirements. Finally, in June of 1984, he decided to hang them up for real. He was nearing 41 and had a painful shoulder injury. But as it turned out, when he finally made the decision, he waited one day too long.

The announcement was made on June 14 in Boston, with Piniella holding a press conference that afternoon in General Manager Clyde King's suite at the Sheraton-Boston. That night, he received a thunderous ovation from the Fenway Park fans after the announcement came over the PA system. Piniella then proceeded to get three hits in the game.

The original agreement with King was that Piniella would retire right after the game and become full-time batting coach so his place on the roster could be filled by a younger player. But the warmth and affection shown to him by the fans in Boston convinced Piniella that he should end his career in New York, at Yankee Stadium, and not on the road. Steinbrenner, naturally, approved wholeheartedly, knowing it would create another emotional "farewell" event at Yankee Stadium—the kind of extravaganza he loved.

That Saturday, June 16, was designated Lou Piniella Day, but in marked contrast to his supposed final appearance in Boston the day before, this was a disaster. Piniella went hitless in five at-bats, driving in one run with a ground ball out. He was choked up much of the game as the fans gave him long ovations every time he came to the plate.

"There were tears in my eyes every time up, and that made it hard to hit or concentrate," Piniella said. "I was just trying too hard. I was too anxious, and for a guy who's supposed to be a student of hitting, I did everything wrong."

Then, thinking about how his 0-for-5 collar had come on the heels of his next-to-last-day hitting heroics in Boston, Piniella laughed.

"It's funny," he said. "After all the times I almost retired, when I finally made up my mind to really go through with it, I wound up waiting one game too long."

Mickey Rivers

Mickey Rivers could have been a superstar. He could have been as good as he wanted, but the problem was he didn't always want to play. And when he did play, he didn't always want to make an all-out effort.

But for his three-plus years with the Yankees, until a frustrated George Steinbrenner traded him to Texas on August 1, 1979, Rivers was one of the most delightful characters ever to wear pinstripes. He was a survivor because anybody else who pulled the stunts that he pulled would have been exiled much sooner. But Rivers had all that talent, and he was also such a lovable guy that nobody—not Steinbrenner, not Billy Martin, not any of the front office executives whom he hounded for salary advances—could stay mad at him long.

Rivers came to the Yankees in a trade with the California Angels on December 11, 1975—the key date in the Yankees' return to the glory years after a decade of passive management by CBS had doomed them to their lowest ebb. On that day team president Gabe Paul pulled two deals at the winter baseball meetings, acquiring Rivers and pitcher Ed Figueroa from the Angels for outfielder Bobby Bonds, and getting second baseman Willie Randolph from the Pittsburgh Pirates (along with pitchers Dock Ellis and Ken Brett) for pitcher Doc Medich.

Rivers was exactly what the Yankees needed—a leadoff hitter with dazzling, intimidating speed. He was also an outstanding center fielder despite a weak throwing arm. He sparked the Yankees to the American League East title in 1976 and really deserved Most Valuable Player honors that instead went to teammate Thurman Munson. Had Rivers continued playing through the season, he'd have probably won the award. But as was his wont, in the final month of the season, with the title clearly in hand, he didn't feel like playing too often. As a result, his final numbers weren't nearly as impressive as they could have been.

But that's what Rivers was all about. When he felt like playing, he was something special. In some games you could almost tell in the first inning if he was in the mood to play, by the way he went down the line to first base. When he wanted, he could turn singles into doubles and doubles into triples. He would taunt fielders into making bad throws and upset a whole team with his baserunning antics. And he could cover vast areas in the outfield, catching up to balls that seemed uncatchable.

Those were the days when he would do his baton twirling with his bat after missing a pitch, and his notorious waddling walk to home plate when coming to bat. He was the fastest runner on the team and the slowest walker. In the clubhouse after winning games, he would play disc jockey with his stereo hookup, laughing and shouting to teammates. He was a sharp, street-smart guy who enjoyed pretending he was dumb, often testing people until they got to know him. And once he trusted someone, he was a friend to the end.

Rivers had a quick wit, too—one of the necessities of being a Yankee survivor. If any players got on him, he would put them down in a flash. Reggie Jackson learned that. On one of those rollicking team bus rides in the late '70s, Rivers was agitating Jackson in an effort to help Reggie become one of the guys. At one point, Reggie said: "Rivers, don't mess with me. I've got an IQ of 160." Rivers shot back, "You don't even know how to spell IQ!"

Another time Reggie was mocking Rivers when Rivers stopped him cold. "Reginald Martinez Jackson," Rivers shouted. "You got a white man's first name, a Puerto Rican's middle name, and black man's last name. No wonder you're so screwed up!" Reggie never lived that one down.

Rivers was the forerunner to Rickey Henderson. Not quite as talented, a little more temperamental, and a whole lot more of a freewheeling character. As he would do in his later tours of duty as Yankee manager with Henderson, Billy Martin tried to keep Rivers happy—not only because it was important to the team's chances but also because Martin genuinely liked Mick the Quick. Many times Martin would sit and talk with Rivers—before games, during games, and after games— trying to soothe him, often giving Rivers money out of his own pocket when those requests for salary advances were denied. But after a while, when those soothing sessions lost their effect and Rivers was back to his old tricks, Martin would lose patience, benching him, yelling at him, and levying fines that, of course, were never paid.

For the most part, Rivers' happy times outnumbered the darker ones. He had his own way of talking, and it took a trained ear to understand what he was saying. He had his own vocabulary, with words like "gozzlehead." What was a gozzlehead? Nobody ever knew.

A lot of Rivers' problems resulted from the racetrack. He loved the ponies, but they obviously didn't love him. He was a steady loser, necessitating all those requests for salary advances. When he had money in his pocket, he rarely kept it there. Racetrack winnings were quickly "reinvested," as he liked to say, or given to friends. The racetrack losses often led to problems, too—like the one in 1977 that must surely rank high in the annals of Yankee craziness.

Rivers had evidently had a domestic spat with his then-wife, Mary, who, in turn, decided to vent her anger and avenge herself by playing bumper cars in the players' parking lot. When she drove her car into the lot and located Rivers', she suddenly began crashing into it, backing up, banging it, backing up again and banging it some more. As she kept repeating this process, the parking lot attendant, who'd been watching in astonishment, finally rushed over and chased her out of the lot. Unfortunately, all the times Rivers' wife had backed her car up for another run at Rivers' car, she had crashed into the car behind her, which belonged to a reporter. The Yankees eventually settled for all the damages, with Martin urging Steinbrenner to avoid another crisis with Rivers because the team was in a pennant race and couldn't afford one of his funks.

Another time, as the Yankees were preparing to leave for a trip to Minneapolis on an off day, Rivers was a last-minute arrival. He was wearing a leather jacket and a pair of tattered jeans, hardly the coat-and-tie attire the Yankees require on team flights. Rivers immediately huddled with Martin. The manager, after listening a few minutes, broke into laughter and reached into his pocket and handed Rivers some money. It seemed that Rivers' wife, in another fit of pique over his domestic carelessness, had burned all of his clothes.

Needless to say, Rivers' marriage to Mary didn't last. But the humorous incidents that punctuated it didn't end with the parking-lot bumper-cars caper. On September 22, 1978, the Yankees, who were locked in that duel-to-the-wire pennant race with the Red Sox, were playing the Indians in Cleveland. When Rivers walked into the clubhouse before the game, a deputy sheriff from Cleveland Cuyahoga County was waiting for him—with a subpoena from the now-separated Mary for alimony payments.

When the deputy sheriff left, reporters approached Rivers.

"No big deal," he shrugged. "She just don't like some of the 'vestments I've been making."

Klein asked Rivers how long it had been since he'd seen his ex-wife.

"We had lunch today," Rivers replied. "She lives here. We went to the racetrack."

Keeping Rivers as interested in the ball games as he was in the racetrack wasn't an easy task for any manager, especially when the games weren't crucial. That's why spring training was an annual period of problems between Rivers and the manager. Rivers didn't like reporting to spring training, even though the Yankees' spring base, Fort Lauderdale, was just a short drive from Rivers' home in Miami.

In the spring of 1977, Rivers' second with the Yankees, he did not report until March 1. Baseball rules dictate that as the deadline for players' reporting, but by then most all of the other Yankees had been in camp nearly a week. That morning, with Rivers still having not been heard from, Martin put a note in his locker, informing him of his displeasure. About two hours into the workout, Rivers showed up. He went to his locker, saw the note, read it, and ripped it up.

"They're giving me hassles already," he said.

Then he revealed the reason for his unhappiness and his late arrival. "Members of the front office," as he put it, had been trying to change his style. They wanted him to take more pitches (he had walked only 13 times in 1976, a low total for a leadoff hitter) and bunt more often. Rivers resented these suggestions.

"That ain't my style," he said. "I do things my way. I don't need no pressure. I ain't gonna change. They don't want me the way I am, let 'em trade me. I do my job. I do what I'm supposed to do, and I do a lot better than other guys do what they're supposed to do. Why don't they tell the other guys to change? I like to concentrate on my strong points. Ain't no sense in working on my weaknesses. Why work at stuff I'm no good at?"

Armed with that logic, Rivers refused to join that first full-squad workout. "I'm mad," he said. "I'm being picked on. I don't need to talk to the manager. He didn't talk to me. I don't need no notes left."

When told that Martin had made arrangements to have Mickey Mantle, a special spring training instructor, work with him on drag bunting, Rivers said, "Mantle? I'll follow the programs, but I ain't changin' my ways."

Rivers returned to his happy-go-lucky ways after that, and things remained fairly peaceful until another incident on March 17. Martin, who was not pleased with Rivers' efforts in the first few spring games, included him on a trip to Vero Beach, a three-hour bus ride, for an exhibition against the Dodgers. Now Dodgertown is the prototype spring training complex, a magnificent expanse of orange groves, clapboard buildings, and narrow palm-tree-lined streets, all encircled by a lush green golf course. Mickey Rivers, however, was not at all impressed. He was instead thinking about all the other regulars who had been excused from the trip, getting a day off instead of spending six hours on a bus.

So when Rivers led off the game with a grounder to Dodger shortstop Bill Russell, he didn't run it out. He took a few strides in the direction of first base, then loped over to the dugout.

Martin was seething. He sent rookie Larry Murray out to center field when the Dodgers came to bat. Rivers returned to the locker room, showered, dressed, and spent most of the sunny afternoon sitting in a golf cart along the right field line, entertaining spectators and exchanging one-liners with teammates as they ran out to the outfield.

Klein was the only member of the Yankees writers corps to make the trip to Vero Beach. He was anxious to see Dodgertown for the first time, while the other veteran writers took the day off. Suddenly Klein had a story—the latest Martin-Rivers flareup. So he joined Rivers in the golf cart for a game-in-progress interview.

"Nothin' wrong with me," Rivers said when Klein asked him if he had a leg injury. "I guess Billy just wanted me along for the ride, just wanted me to bat one time to give the fans a thrill. I was happy to take this ride here and bat one time. Nice day for a ride."

Teammate Jimmy Wynn, a veteran big leaguer but a newcomer to the Yankees, ambled by and listened to Rivers' soliloquy. "Mickey," he said, shaking his head, "you are one crazy individual."

Martin wasn't amused. "Nobody plays like that on my team," he said after the game. "I don't put up with that kind of stuff. I don't care if it's an exhibition or a pee-wee league game. I let Rivers know what I thought of his act. One more time and he gets a long, long rest."

Naturally Rivers would do it again. Then he'd play hard for a while. Then he'd loaf again. And the cycle would repeat itself, over and over—like the time in spring training '78 when Rivers was late two days in a row and was fined $1,000 and told to meet with team president Al Rosen the next day. He was late for the meeting.

In the middle of the Yankees' disastrous 1979 season, however, the cycle ran its course, and Rivers was traded to Texas. As friends pointed out to him, it would probably be the best team for him, because the nearest racetrack to Arlington, Texas, was 250 miles away. And darned if in 1980 Rivers didn't have one of his best seasons. He batted .333, had 210 hits, scored 96 runs—all career highs. Then injuries slowed him, and he gradually faded. But even in his final season, 1984, he batted .300 as a part-timer.

During those last few years with the Rangers, Rivers always waited anxiously for the Yankees to show up for their spring training games against Texas in Pompano Beach. He would regale the writers with his suggestions for the Yankees, always trying to engineer trades that would get him back.

"They need me over there," he said. "They're too serious now. Don't look like nobody's havin' any fun over there. They gotta bring me back for one year. Then I'll take over as manager. I'll let Billy be my top coach. Me, Billy, and George. We're two of a kind, you know."

After the Rangers released him in the spring of 1985, Rivers returned home to Miami and not much was heard about him. One day in the spring of 1988, he slipped into the Yankee camp at Fort Lauderdale, almost unnoticed, to visit Martin. They embraced and talked awhile and then Rivers left. Before going, however, he told Martin he could look him up in the phone book.

"It's under Miguel Rivera," Rivers said.

Asked later why Rivers was using the name Miguel Rivera, Martin said, "I think probably he owes some people some money."

Goose Gossage

Rich Gossage, the formidable Goose, feared no batter, no manager, and no owner.

Goose marched to his own beat, saying what he felt needed to be said, acting on honest instinct. During his six years with the Yankees, from 1978 through 1983, he was intensely focused on winning. If he felt, a teammate or manager or writer or even the owner was interfering with that goal, he would blister that person verbally in the same intimidating fashion with which he confronted opposing batters in the ninth inning of a one-run game.

Gossage could speak his mind without worrying about the consequences because he was the best in his business. He was the king of the bullpen closers, a legend, as they say, in his own time. A big, husky man with a menacing Fu Manchu mustache, he would work his way into a near rage in the bullpen while preparing to go into a game. Once on the mound, he was into his own world, glaring at the batter with a glowering, angry look, then going into his hurly-burly, far-stepping motion that made it seem he was jumping at the cowering hitter. Then he would release the fastest fastball of its time. And sometimes, knowing the hitter was forced to prepare for his "heater," Goose would confound him with his off-speed "slurve," freezing the numbed batter.

With all these histrionics the Goose was almost like a pro wrestler in his approach to the game. He'd lose himself in that world of confrontation and would usually need time in the clubhouse afterward to snap himself out of his rewed-up trance. But then he would return to his real self, a laughing, fun-loving, beer-guzzling country boy from Colorado. He loved the simple life. He didn't go to fancy restaurants on the road, preferring a few burgers or a pizza and hanging out in some bar away from the hotel—preferably one with country and western music. Goose was a flannel-shirt-and-jeans guy who got around the Yankees' stringent jacket-and-tie dress code by wearing a beat-up old sport jacket and one of two ties—a string tie with the head of a bull, or a wild, multicolored tie with pictures of fish. Six years as a Yankee, lots of victories, lots of saves, but only two ties.

He was a prankster in the clubhouse, and the sort of person who would befriend the new players and rookies, trying to make them feel comfortable in the bizarre and crazy world of the Yankees. But during those games when the score was close and it was reaching the seventh inning, the others in the bullpen knew to keep their distance from Goose.

"By then," recalled longtime bullpen coach Jeff Torborg, "his personality would start to change. He'd get himself worked up in case he was needed. He was scary."

And on those infrequent occasions when he failed, he would often be unapproachable in the clubhouse, storming around the room, shouting obscenities, his anger directed at himself.

On one memorable occasion in 1982, Yankee manager Gene Michael stayed with reliever Shane Rawley in the ninth inning of a close game on a night when Gossage was ready and waiting for the call. Rawley blew the game, and afterward in the clubhouse Gossage was breathing fire, making his unhappiness so loud that Michael finally sent for him. The two engaged in a shouting match behind closed doors in the manager's office, and shortly after that episode Michael was fired.

Gossage had wanted to play for the Yankees from his boyhood in Colorado, where, he remembered, "the Yankees were the only team we ever heard about." Gossage was especially close to his father, who died in 1969, the year before Goose signed his first pro contract with the Chicago White Sox. He recalled how his father was largely responsible for the way he approached his pitching.

"The summer after my sophomore year in high school I missed a couple of practices because I was messing around with the guys. That was the only time my dad ever got mad at me. He said, 'Either quit or do it right. If you're not going to make use of your talent, then forget baseball.' I never missed another practice."

The other driving force in Gossage's career was his older brother, Jack, who was likewise a Yankee fan.

"He's fourteen years older than me and had his own place by the time I was nine," said Gossage. "I used to go over there and throw to him. I had always been able to throw harder than other guys my age, but he'd keep saying, 'C'mon, throw harder. You're not even trying.' I'd be getting so upset, firing the ball as fast as I could, and he'd finally say, 'Okay, now you're doing your best.'

"Jack was a catcher and a real good one, too. But one day, when the Yankees had a tryout camp in Denver, he attended it but went out for the outfield. He was embarrassed that he didn't have a catcher's glove. We didn't have much money, and he didn't own a glove. He was one of the last guys cut. I think if he had told them he was a catcher, he might have had a shot."

Gossage spent his first four big-league seasons, 1973 through 1976, with the White Sox, having worked his way up through their minor league system with, among others, shortstop Bucky Dent, who would one day play behind him with the Yankees. When he was traded by the White Sox to the Pittsburgh Pirates in 1977, he was glad. It seemed that Bill Veeck, the flamboyant showman, had regained controlling interest in the White Sox in 1976, and Gossage found little amusement in all his gimmicks and stunts designed to lure fans to the ballpark.

"That '76 season was ridiculous," Gossage said. "Veeck had dancing girls, fire engines, elephants, anything he could think of. Most of the time, the pitchers weren't even allowed to warm up before a game because they'd get in the way. It was a three-ring circus, and the team, the extra act, was definitely the last priority."

After the 1977 season with Pittsburgh, Gossage became a free agent and signed with his boyhood dream team, the Yankees, for a six-year deal worth $2.75 million.

He soon found that the circus atmosphere he experienced with Veeck's White Sox was nothing compared to the circus with Steinbrenner's Yankees. Here a calliope was playing at all times, and the players—not dancing girls or elephants—danced to the music as the featured act.

Typically, the Yankees actually had no need for his services inasmuch as they already had, in Sparky Lyle, the best reliever in the American League. Only the Yankees would pursue a replacement for a pitcher who was only 33 and had just won the Cy Young Award. But Lyle, despite his unhappiness, made the situation easier for Gossage, and they became good friends, probably because they both had that survivor quality about them.

Gossage's first season as a Yankee in 1978—10 wins, 27 saves, a 2.01 ERA, and 122 strikeouts in 134 innings—was nothing short of spectacular and culminated with his retiring future Hall of Famer Carl Yastrzemski for the final out in the Yankee-Red Sox playoff game that decided the American League East pennant. "I figured the worst that could happen is that he'd beat me and I'd be home in Colorado fishing the next day," Gossage said. "That calmed me down."

Gossage had other tense moments as well during that '78 season while trying to adjust to life as a Yankee. If Veeck had been a trip in Chicago, Steinbrenner was something else.

In particular, Gossage never got over the Boss' frequent clubhouse pep talks—probably because he had so much trouble getting through them with a straight face. Steinbrenner would come into the clubhouse and, pacing the room, deliver his speeches, inevitably stopping in front of Gossage's locker. While the Boss looked at Gossage, Thurman Munson, whose locker was directly across the room, made faces, mimicking Steinbrenner in the manner of Chevy Chase, from "Saturday Night Live."

"That Thurman would really get me going. I'd be squeezing my hands, pinching myself, doing whatever I could to keep from laughing in Steinbrenner's face," Gossage said.

But Gossage ran into his first Yankee adversity early in 1979 when, following a 6–3 loss to the Orioles in the 12th game of the season, he and teammate Cliff Johnson engaged in a costly shower-room scuffle. The fight started innocently enough. Johnson, a hulking six-four, 227-pound designated hitter type, was complaining about not having played, as manager Bob Lemon hadn't used him against Orioles' ace right-hander Jim Palmer. Gossage kidded Johnson that he couldn't hit right-handers. Johnson responded by saying, "I sure could hit you." Gossage laughed at that. Johnson, a bruiser who didn't know his own strength and who often, like Lenny in *Of Mice and Men,* hurt people without meaning to, gave Gossage a playful punch. Gossage punched back, and suddenly the situation turned serious.

Johnson, the biggest Yankee on the team, then threw Gossage (the next biggest Yankee at six-three, 215 pounds) against the bathroom wall. When Gossage tried to push him away, his right thumb bent back. Realizing he was injured, Gossage became enraged and started pounding Johnson with punches. Johnson, realizing something serious had happened, backed off.

But the damage was done. Gossage suffered a torn ligament in the thumb, requiring surgery that sidelined him for 12 weeks. The Yankees never recovered from his loss and with the death of Thurman Munson in a plane crash later that year, 1979 turned out to be an absolute disaster of a season. Johnson apologized to Gossage, but as Gossage told Moss Klein a couple of days later, it didn't help. "He does that kind of playing around too much. I'm not the first guy he's been involved with like that."

Johnson, a 31-year-old veteran who had spent 11 seasons in the Houston organization before coming to the Yankees in June of 1977 and participating in two World Series, knew he was in trouble. He tried to downplay the incident by saying it was just a freak accident, that he and Goose were really just playing around. But Steinbrenner wasn't hearing any of it. And as Reggie Jackson explained so eloquently after the incident, "If you mess around with the G-men [Gossage and Ron Guidry], the big guy with the boats [Steinbrenner] is gonna get you."

On June 15, 1979, Steinbrenner got Johnson, exiling him to Cleveland for a pitcher named Don Hood. Upon departing, Johnson said ruefully: "I knew I was gone. After the thing with Goose, I was an outcast."

Gossage's remaining four seasons with the Yankees were highly successful and extremely eventful. The 1980 season was his finest—33 saves, 103 strikeouts in 99 innings—as he helped the team to a 103–59 record and the American League East title. But in the final game of the playoffs that year against Kansas City, he was tagged for a monstrous, tie-breaking three-run homer by George Brett. When Gossage found out after the game that Steinbrenner was second-guessing manager Dick Howser for replacing Tommy John at that point, he was livid. That actually marked the point when Gossage began to sour on life as a Steinbrenner Yankee.

Gossage was overwhelming in the strike-shortened 1981 season, with an 0.77 ERA and 48 strikeouts in 47 innings. And he was even more remarkable in the three postseason series, pitching 14⅓ scoreless innings and striking out 15. But once again there was an unhappy ending for the Yankees, as they lost the World Series to the Dodgers. And when Steinbrenner issued his apology "to the people of New York and to Yankee fans everywhere" during the final game, Gossage was outraged. That was when he started thinking about the two remaining years on his contract, and a possible escape to a better atmosphere.

By 1982, when the Yankees were struggling through a dismal season with players, managers, and coaches being shuttled in and out at a dizzying pace, Gossage reached the boiling point. Typical of that crazy season was his unforgettable explosion after an August 16 doubleheader sweep of the Royals in which he saved both games. When reporters approached him after the game in the clubhouse, he went into a tirade that fortunately was preserved for the ages by the radio reporters who kept their tapes running.

Herewith the unedited transcript of the Gossage tirade with no expletives deleted:

> This cocksucking place is a fucking joke. Everybody...the way they boo fucking Griffey and everybody else. And you motherfuckers [pointing to the reporters] with the fucking pens and fucking tape recorders. You can turn it on and take it upstairs to the *fat man*. Okay?
>
> 'Cause I'm sick of this fucking shit! Negative fucking bullshit! You got it? Everything you guys write these motherfuckers read. These dumb motherfuckers in the seats. Yeah, you turn it on. Turn it on, you

greasy cocksucker. They read everything you fucking write, and we hear the same fucking lines. You know what I mean? Fucking negative motherfuckers! No wonder you carry a pad and fucking pencil! You ain't worth the shit to do anything else.

Now if just about anyone else had called him "the fat man" in anger, Steinbrenner would have swung into immediate retaliatory action. But where Gossage was concerned, Steinbrenner was always uncharacteristically hands-off, as though he knew that Goose was the one player he couldn't replace and shouldn't mess with. When informed of Gossage's insult, Steinbrenner reacted mildly and even with some humor. "Tell Goose," he said, "I've been on a diet and I've lost eleven pounds since June."

Gossage was hardly soothed. He knew Steinbrenner treated him differently than the other players. The fact that the owner criticized others, and kept the team in a constant state of turmoil, was the reason for Gossage's growing unrest.

Still, Goose always managed to have fun. During the 1983 season he and the other relievers pulled a memorable prank on pitching coach Art Fowler. The Yankees were playing in Milwaukee, where the bullpens are behind the center field wall and can't be seen from the dugout. Communication by phone is therefore vital. On this night Gossage and the relief corps removed the hearing equipment from the bullpen phone. In addition, they put lampblack all over the earpiece and mouthpiece.

So each time the phone would ring, Fowler picked it up to get instructions from coach Jeff Torborg in the dugout and couldn't hear anything. All he was getting was black smudges all over his ears and chin—and he wasn't aware of that. After a while one of the relievers put the earpiece back in, and when the phone rang the next time, Fowler really got an earful—from Billy Martin, who wanted to know what the hell was going on out there.

Fowler, in a total state of confusion by now, complained about the phone. When he came into the clubhouse after the game, his ear and chin were all black, prompting more bewilderment on his part and gales of laughter from the players.

If Gossage never lost his sense of humor with the Yankees, he didn't lose his fearsome aura, either. How feared was he? Well, in August of '83 he was tagged for a homer by Tiger outfielder Glenn Wilson. The next day a headline in the *New York Post* screamed: WILSON: GOOSE IS A TURKEY.

When Gossage arrived at the ballpark, there was a two-page note from Wilson lying on his stool. Gossage started reading the note and shook his head. He hadn't seen the *Post* and had no idea what Wilson was apologizing so profusely to him about. In the note Wilson said, "I never said anything of the sort. I never even talked to the New York writers after the game."

Gossage spotted Moss Klein and called him over.

"Do you have any idea what this is all about?" he asked.

Klein told him about the story in the *Post*.

"Well," said Gossage, "either this guy is nuts or the *Post* is up to its usual shit." When Gossage got out onto the field, the frantic Wilson was waiting, having been pacing in front of the Yankee dugout for 20 minutes. He introduced himself to Gossage and reiterated everything he had written in the note.

"Don't worry," said Gossage, "next time I face you, I'll have to throw at your head, but I'll take something off my fastball." Then he laughed, and Wilson nervously joined in.

By the middle of the 1983 season, Gossage had pretty much decided he had reached the end of the road with the Yankees. One day in late July, he told Klein: "They try to brainwash you here, that playing for the Yankees and playing in New York is the only thing to do. But that's not the way it is. There are a lot of other teams with good organizations where the players have fun."

And even though Gossage didn't like Billy Martin, the manager in 1983, he blamed his feelings on one person—George Steinbrenner. "I don't think anybody tries harder or wants to win more than I do," he said. "I'm miserable when we lose, but that doesn't mean I need to hear about it. A year like we had last year [79–83 in 1982] was awful. All the players hated it. But you don't need to hear about it all the time. A lot of the fun is taken out of the game here. There's that constant pressure to win, but no team can win every time. When you don't win here, all you have to do is put up with a lot of bullshit. I'm sick of that."

Sure enough, when the season ended and the Yankees had finished third, Gossage made good on his promise. He filed for free agency. Obviously he still felt some ties with the Yankees and his teammates, and he deliberated as the offers rolled in. Steinbrenner, meanwhile, made it known that resigning Gossage was his top priority. He even re-signed reliever Dale Murray, who had become a close friend of Goose's. Though Murray had gone only 2–4, with a 4.48 ERA in 1983, when Steinbrenner found out he had gone on a week-long hunting trip with Gossage in November, he ordered him re-signed. Even Murray was stunned when the Yankees gave him a guaranteed two-year contract worth $1.2 million. He had earned just $200,000 in '83, and the only other offer he had gotten was for $250,000 from the White Sox.

"After the year I had," he said, "I never thought they'd want me back."

Gossage deliberated until December 20, thinking of all the friends he had with the Yankees and all the good times, even the firing of Billy Martin the previous week. The new manager was Yogi Berra, and Gossage loved Yogi.

But it kept coming back to Steinbrenner. On the night of December 19, Steinbrenner, figuring that the long delay was a good sign, dispatched coaches

Jeff Torborg and Gene Michael to La Jolla, California, and the office of Jerry Kapstein, Gossage's agent. Their assignment was to assure Gossage how much he was needed, how much Yogi wanted him, and how things would be better.

But when they arrived, as Torborg remembered, they faced an ice-cold Gossage. Perhaps their trip made Gossage realize it was time to make his decision, and he had. He told them on December 20 that he wouldn't be returning. When Torborg and Michael tried to say something, he told them not to bother.

"I felt like I'd been punched in the stomach," Torborg said. "We tried to talk him out of it, but he never gave us a chance. His mind was made up."

Gossage issued a brief statement through Kapstein that, as always, made his feelings abundantly clear: "I have today in San Diego personally informed Jeff Torborg and Gene Michael that I will not return to play for George Steinbrenner, and I have advised my close friend and adviser, Jerry Kapstein, that I have no interest in having Jerry receive an offer from George Steinbrenner."

Not once in the statement did Gossage mention the New York Yankees. His only reference was to Steinbrenner.

Steinbrenner, of course, searched for another reason.

"I think Goose was worried about the reaction of the fans, that he would be blamed for the firing of Billy," he said. "He feels responsible for the change of managers because everyone knows how he felt about Billy."

Now how to replace Gossage? The first thought mentioned by the front office officials was John "the Count" Montefusco. The Count, who had been acquired in a trade with San Diego in late August of 1983, was a delightful, engaging character with a reliever's free-spirited makeup. But he had been a starter nearly his whole career and had serious reservations of making the switch to the bullpen now—especially when it meant replacing a Goose Gossage.

"I told them I'd do anything they wanted," said Montefusco, "but I've almost always been a starter. When the Padres tried me as a reliever last year, it didn't work so well. I'm a hyper guy, and when I was a reliever, I'd be nervous every day. I was losing my hair. My arm doesn't mind pitching every day, but my hair needs four days' rest. Maybe if the Yankees give me a hair clause, I can do it."

The Count then proceeded to sum up his brief time as a Yankee.

"You know," he said, "my whole career I had always been the guy who caused all the commotion. But with the Yankees, I'm nothing. *Nothing!* The things that go on here are unbelievable. I love it! It really *is* the zoo—and the animals have the keys."

As Goose Gossage showed, there comes a point when even the animals throw the keys away. But also, as so many Yankees discovered through the years, time heals all wounds—or most of them anyway. So it was that, more than five years after his bitter exit, Gossage returned to Steinbrenner's payroll.

After the San Francisco Giants released him in August 1989, Steinbrenner re-signed him, against the better judgment of manager Dallas Green, who said, "If he was released by a team in the middle of a pennant race, that doesn't speak well for what he can do. My gut feeling is he won't be able to contribute."

Shortly after Gossage's return the Yankees fell hopelessly out of the pennant race. It was ironic, though, that Gossage had supposedly departed the Yankees because he didn't want to become part of a conflict between the manager (in that case, Martin) and the owner. Yet here he was coming back under circumstances that were almost the same. Just a different manager.

Rick Cerone

How many ball players can say they got away with saying "Fuck you, you fat son of a bitch" to George Steinbrenner in front of a roomful of players. Not only got away with it but stayed with the Yankees several more years and were then invited back later when no other teams were interested?

Only one: Rick Cerone.

Cerone wasn't a star, except for that 1980 season when he replaced the late Thurman Munson and exceeded everyone's expectations. But Cerone was a gutsy, street-tough kid from Newark, New Jersey, who knew the whys and ways of New York and the Yankees. And he didn't take any crap from anybody—including Steinbrenner, who obviously respected Cerone's style. Because Cerone was able not only to get away with what he said to the Boss but to actually prosper from it, it's surprising more players didn't try the same approach. But nobody ever did.

Cerone, a Yankee fan as a kid, had become an all-American at Seton Hall, in South Orange, New Jersey, and was the number one pick by the Cleveland Indians in the June 1975 amateur draft. In 1977 Cerone was traded to the expansion Toronto Blue Jays, and by 1979 he had become their regular catcher. That season he also made an impression on Billy Martin, a man whom he would later come to despise. In fact, it was Martin who recommended the trade for Cerone after the 1979 season when the Yankees were desperately seeking a replacement for Munson, who had died in the crash of his private plane on August 2, 1979. (By the time Cerone was acquired by the Yankees, on November 1, Martin had already been fired again as manager for his one-punch fight with a marshmallow salesman in a Bloomington, Minnesota, cocktail lounge.)

Cerone was cocky enough to handle the situation, however.

He demonstrated that the day he was assigned his uniform number, 10, in spring training.

Moss Klein said to him, "You know whose number that is, don't you?" Klein was thinking of Chris Chambliss, the standout, popular first baseman whom the Yankees had traded for Cerone.

"I sure do," said Cerone. "It's Bo Derek's number—and she's perfect, too."

Martin's recommendation proved to be an excellent one. Cerone had a dream season in 1980, batting .277, with 14 home runs and 85 RBIs, while catching 147 games and finishing seventh in the American League Most Valuable Player Award voting. He was exactly what the Yankees needed, a clutch-hitting, take-charge catcher who wasn't afraid to get tough with the veteran pitchers when they weren't following his orders.

The next year was a disappointment, however, as Cerone suffered a broken thumb early in the season and came back just when the seven-week players' strike was about to start. He never was able to get it going again in the second half of the season.

The Yankees, though, by virtue of winning the pre-strike first half, earned their way into the postseason playoffs. Against the Milwaukee Brewers (the second-half winners) in the eastern division playoffs, they won the first two games of the best-of-five series, then lost the next two.

After the fourth game Steinbrenner stormed into the Yankee clubhouse and began chastising the team. Everybody listened in silence, with manager Bob Lemon boiling at this blatant interference. Finally Steinbrenner directed his criticism at Cerone, who had made a baserunning mistake in the 2–1 loss to the Brewers. That's when Cerone lashed back in the best "I'm sick and tired and not gonna take it anymore" style.

"Fuck you, you fat son of a bitch," Cerone said audibly enough for everyone to hear. "You never played the game. You don't know what the fuck you're talking about."

There was stunned silence, with most players (as one said later) trying to refrain from giving Cerone a standing ovation.

Steinbrenner recovered from the momentary shock and said, "And you won't be playing this game as a Yankee next year." Then he told the troops, "We'll find out what you're all made of tomorrow," before stalking out, leaving Cerone to receive excited congratulations from his admiring teammates.

When Cerone arrived at the ballpark the next day, there was an envelope waiting at his locker. In it was a conciliatory note from Steinbrenner. The gist of the message was that Steinbrenner was dismissing the heated exchange between the two the night before as a product of frustration on both their parts. It was all forgotten, the owner said, adding jokingly: "But you better not make any baserunning mistakes tonight."

Actually, Reggie Jackson had played the part of peacemaker between Cerone and Steinbrenner. Reggie visited Steinbrenner's office several hours before that final game with the Brewers and explained to the owner that being too critical of Cerone was unfair. "He's a gamer," Reggie said, "and he's been playing hurt most of the year. We need him."

Whether Steinbrenner's note provided motivation for Cerone isn't known, but in the bottom of the seventh inning of that decisive game, with the Yankees clinging to a 4–3 lead, he blasted a homer to build the lead to 5–3. The Yankees went on to win, 7–3, and moved into the league championship series against Billy Martin's Oakland A's.

"For one second when I got to home plate, I thought about tipping my hat in Steinbrenner's direction," Cerone confessed. "But that would have been showing him up. I don't show up my pitchers, my teammates, or my boss."

That locker-room confrontation was not Cerone's first with Steinbrenner. Back in February he had taken the owner on in public and came out a winner then, too. Cerone had been paid $120,000 in 1980 and was seeking a hefty raise for 1981. He was eligible for salary arbitration for the first time but didn't want to go that route, aware that Steinbrenner took it as an insult. After a series of apparent misunderstandings regarding the Yankees' offer, however, Cerone became the first Yankee since 1974 to go to arbitration. He filed for a $440,000, and arbitrator Jesse Simmons ruled in his favor over the Yankees' offer of $350,000.

Steinbrenner was incensed. "By going to arbitration," he told Klein, "he showed me he's big-headed and greedy, and I don't like that at all."

Klein told Steinbrenner that Cerone had said before the ruling that he would have no hard feelings if he lost. Retorted Steinbrenner, "That's like Brutus telling Julius Caesar that there were no hard feelings after he stabbed him."

As it turned out, there had been a breakdown of communications in the negotiations because Steinbrenner didn't like the loud, rock music on Cerone's answering machine. Steinbrenner told Klein that the Yankees had made a $360,000 offer to Cerone, three times his 1980 salary. When Klein told Cerone that, Cerone said he never received such an offer.

In any event, Steinbrenner said he attempted to call Cerone three times leading up to the arbitration hearing only to get "that damn answering machine every time. And I'll prove that I'm telling the truth because this is the recording...."

With that, the principal Yankee owner, in his best rock music imitation, began humming a tune over the phone that was close enough to the mark to convince Klein, who had heard the same recording several times himself. But why, Klein asked, didn't Steinbrenner just leave a message for Cerone to call him back?

"Because I couldn't stand that goddamn music," Steinbrenner said, "and I don't like talking to recordings."

When spring training began that '81 season, Steinbrenner's quote about "Brutus telling Julius Caesar there were no hard feelings" quickly circulated the clubhouse and the players started referring to Cerone as Brutus. The first time Steinbrenner crossed paths with Cerone in the clubhouse, on February 24, he ignored him. So Cerone, figuring he had nothing to lose—and aware that the "Brutus" name had amused the Boss—stuck out his hand and said, "Howya doin', Julius?"

Steinbrenner laughed. A few days later Cerone arrived at the ballpark for a morning workout and found a package waiting for him. The note taped to the package was inscribed: "From the Boss."

Cerone, holding it up, said jokingly, "Is this from Springsteen?" When he opened it, he found a Yankee uniform jersey. On the back of the jersey were the letters ET and the number 2—Steinbrenner's version of Shakespeare. In *Julius Caesar,* after traitor Brutus joins the conspirators and stabs Caesar, the betrayed ruler says, "Et tu, Brute." ["You, too, Brutus."] Just like that, before Cerone had any reason to beware of the Ideas of March, the feud was settled.

Cerone, who was a prankster in the clubhouse, often tormenting insecure teammates by starting trade rumors, was eventually traded to the Atlanta Braves after the 1984 season. He made a wise and diplomatic exit, thanking "Mr. Steinbrenner for giving me the chance to play for the New York Yankees." Steinbrenner obviously remembered Cerone's gracious departure, and two years later, he gave him a second chance to play for the New York Yankees.

After a year in Atlanta, Cerone was traded to Milwaukee and then released by the Brewers after the 1986 season. He was a free agent with no job offers. Finally, in the first week of February, Cerone called Steinbrenner.

"I told him I could still play, and I was just looking for an invitation to spring training," Cerone recalled. "No contract, just an invitation. I told him even if there was no spot on the Yankees for me, maybe some other team might be interested. I just wanted a chance."

Steinbrenner told Cerone that the Yankees "usually don't do things like that," but added that he appreciated the call and would see what he could do.

An hour later Cerone's phone rang and it was Woody Woodward, the new Yankee general manager. "I don't know what you said to George," said Woodward, "but I've been told to offer you a one-year contract. Is two hundred fifty thousand acceptable?"

Cerone was so stunned he almost blew the deal. "No, Woody," he said, "I think you misunderstood him. I was just looking for an invitation." Now Cerone could have kicked himself because Woodward said he'd have to get back to him. But 20 minutes later the phone rang again and it was Woodward.

"Listen," he said, "we're offering you a one-year contract for two hundred fifty thousand dollars. I just got off the phone with him."

Cerone, who would have gladly accepted less than half that after making the team, made certain not to blow it again. "That's fine," he said. "You've got a deal."

As Cerone said: "I think George likes it when the old guys who've been with him before want to come back. It makes him feel good. Everybody talks about what an evil guy he is, but he really isn't that bad."

Cerone's second coming as a Yankee was far shorter than the first, but it turned out to be well worth Steinbrenner's generosity. With Joel Skinner struggling with the bat, Cerone wound up being the Yankees' number-one catcher in 1987, playing 113 games and batting .243. He was given a raise to $300,000 for 1988 but was released the day before the season opener when Billy Martin and the coaching staff decided to keep Skinner and newcomer Don Slaught as the two catchers.

This time Cerone left with bitterness, all of it directed at Martin, whom he had had differences with in the past over pitch selections. The timing of the release was bad for him, too, since all the clubs had their rosters set. It looked as if his career was over, and he was just about to accept a radio job with WABC in New York when the Red Sox' number-one catcher, Rich Gedman, was injured.

The Red Sox called Cerone, and he launched into a new career, batting in the .340 range for Boston until a late-season slump. He finished at .269 and wound up playing on an American League eastern division champion.

"I have to remember to send roses to Billy Martin," Cerone said late in the season. "He kept my career going by getting rid of me." Cerone kept going with a solid season in 1989, but when the Red Sox didn't ask him back, he became a free agent. And George Steinbrenner was waiting again, with a two-year, $1.4-million contract, the top salary of Cerone's career.

Dave Winfield

In many ways Dave Winfield was the ultimate survivor of the Steinbrenner era—not just because he stayed with the team, prospered financially, and performed at a level that made him a Hall of Fame candidate, but because he almost always managed to get the upper hand in his battles with the principal Yankee owner. With each succeeding year Winfield was in New York, Steinbrenner was more obsessed with bringing the big man down.

Why? It went all the way back to the minute Winfield put his signature on the then-record, 10-year, $23-million contract he signed as a free agent with the Yankees in December of 1980. Steinbrenner, it seemed, didn't realize how lucrative the contract actually was, because he underestimated the compounding value of the cost-of-living clause. When the matter was brought to his attention the day after the announcement of the signing—not by the lawyers but in a *New York Times* article written by Murray Chass—Steinbrenner was in the uncustomary position of having to ask Winfield to agree to a reworking of the wording. Winfield agreed, but right off he had scored a victory on Steinbrenner, and the battle lines between the two were drawn.

Through the years, Steinbrenner went after Winfield in various ways but never came away with any satisfaction. He would leak negative Winfield stats to those members of the media who accepted being leaked to by Steinbrenner. To that, Winfield would merely shrug, point to his numbers, and say: "You see me, fellas. You know nobody plays this game better than me. And you know when the season's over, my numbers will be there."

And inevitably they were—which is why Steinbrenner couldn't beat him from that standpoint. Baseball fans, for the most part, are concerned only with how a player performs on the field. If a ball player isn't performing up to his capabilities or expectations, fans let him know about it. New York fans are as tough as any. Why, back in the fifties and sixties they even used to boo Mickey Mantle. In all his time in New York, Dave Winfield seldom heard boos. His on-the-field effort and the results there have earned him the fans' support.

Still, Steinbrenner would order managers to bench Winfield, platoon him, or keep him out of the cleanup spot, and those efforts, too, backfired. Not only did the team suffer, but the players ultimately supported Winfield, and the manager ultimately defied Steinbrenner. Lou Piniella's 1986 defiance of a Steinbrenner order to platoon Winfield—and his subsequent admission that the benchings were the Boss' doing—caused a huge rift in the Steinbrenner-Piniella relationship.

And then there were all the efforts to trade Winfield, with the outfielder calmly restating his veto power over all trades. Steinbrenner has long contended that a covenant in Winfield's original contract—in which he listed seven teams, the Red Sox, Orioles, Tigers, Blue Jays, Mets, Mariners, and Cubs to which he could be traded without his permission after the fifth year of his contract— gave the Yankees the right to trade him. However, Winfield has maintained that as a 10-and-5 player (10 years in the major leagues, the last 5 with the same club), he has the right to veto any trade.

Nevertheless, Steinbrenner, angered anew in the spring of 1988 over the forthcoming publication of Winfield's relatively innocent and noncontroversial autobiography, moved in earnest to challenge the 10-and-5 rights, ordering his general manager, Piniella, to pursue any and all trade inquiries about Winfield.

Piniella dutifully obliged. The first team to come inquiring was the Toronto Blue Jays. On the afternoon of March 8, Al LaMacchia, one of the Blue Jays' top scouts, ran into Bill Madden in the lobby of the Fort Lauderdale Marriott Hotel, where the Yankees were staying.

"How serious is Steinbrenner about wanting to trade Winfield?" LaMacchia asked.

"As I far as I know, very serious," Madden replied.

"Well, we're *very* interested in trading for him."

A few minutes later Piniella came down to the lobby and talked for about 15 minutes with LaMacchia, who told him the Blue Jays would be willing to trade their right fielder, Jesse Barfield, for Winfield. But while the Yankees considered that proposal—all the while having serious reservations about trading Winfield to a contending team in their own division—Piniella, on Steinbrenner's orders, pursued other clubs, in particular the Houston Astros and California Angels.

It was while he was on the phone to Astros general manager Bill Wood a few days later that Piniella was interrupted by Steinbrenner, who came bursting into his office in the Yankee executive trailer. It was about one o'clock, and the Yankees were playing an exhibition game at home against the Braves that day. Piniella was discussing a possible deal with Wood—Winfield for the Astros' right fielder Kevin Bass—but at Steinbrenner's frantic urgings, he excused himself and told Wood he'd get back to him. Once off the phone, Piniella assumed that Steinbrenner had a different Winfield trade proposal to discuss.

But on this day, Steinbrenner was obsessed by something new, something entirely out of the blue.

"C'mon with me," he ordered Piniella.

Piniella got up from his desk and followed Steinbrenner out of the trailer, through a gate, and along the outside of the stadium.

"Don't let anyone recognize us," Steinbrenner said.

Piniella thought to himself, "Don't let anyone *recognize* us?" There were hundreds of fans milling around outside the stadium and in the walkways above them. How could they *not* recognize the owner of the New York Yankees and his general manager? Piniella began to feel he was on some sort of a secret commando mission.

When they approached the pass gate where all the people with complimentary tickets are admitted, Steinbrenner pulled Piniella behind a giant ficus bush.

"Stay down!" he said. "Don't let anyone see you."

"What the hell are we doing, George?" Piniella asked.

"I'm sick and tired of all these free passes being given out," Steinbrenner said. "There's too many people getting free passes, and I'm going to put a stop to it. Now, I want you to stay here and watch all the people who come through this gate. Count 'em and see who they are."

Piniella couldn't believe it. Here he was, purportedly the general manager of the New York Yankees baseball team, and instead of being on the phone working on trades or, at the very least, watching his own team on the field, he was hiding behind a bush like some 10-year-old playing hide-and-seek, counting heads at the free-pass gate!

It's no wonder that all the Winfield trade talks never came close to fruition. On one hand, Steinbrenner wanted to trade Winfield, just to show he could do it and to let everyone know who was boss. (Remember, he traded both Sparky Lyle and Graig Nettles after *their* books came out.) But on the other hand, he was still fearful of the fan backlash over trading Winfield, and as Piniella kept telling him, it was unlikely they could get equal value in return.

The fallout from the Winfield book dominated the early part of the 1988 season, mostly because Steinbrenner wouldn't let it die. He attempted to use the book to portray Winfield as a selfish player who was incriminating his teammates, and in the case of Willie Randolph, he succeeded. Steinbrenner seized on a passage in the book in which Winfield implies that Randolph felt the Yankees were a racist organization. Steinbrenner urged Randolph to speak out and ordered Billy Martin, who was in his fifth go-round as manager, to denounce the book as well.

Randolph, who had already had a falling out with Winfield that winter after turning down a request to be part of Winfield's wedding party, was both embarrassed and enraged over the quotes attributed to him. He emphatically denied making them and remained decidedly cool to Winfield the rest of the year.

Regarding Steinbrenner, though, Winfield had the last laugh again, because all of the Boss' carrying on about the book and his threats to trade Winfield turned the fans in the big man's favor. When Steinbrenner criticized Winfield in July for "thinking only of himself and not the team"—a reference to Winfield's doing book promotions on all the Yankee road trips—the right fielder retorted: "He must be unhappy. He must be having problems at home."

In the first seven years of his Yankee career, the fans had been respectful of Winfield, but their feelings for him were lukewarm in comparison to their affection for Reggie Jackson or Mattingly. That was never so evident as in 1984 when Winfield and Mattingly engaged in a stirring race for the American League batting title that went right down to the final day of the season (when Mattingly went 4 for 5 to win, .343 to .340). Winfield had been leading

Mattingly most of the year, and with the Yankees out of the pennant race, the baseball focus in New York was entirely on the two of them.

Bill Madden, who did work for the Donruss baseball card company in addition to the *New York Daily News,* was asked by the card company people if he could arrange for Winfield and Mattingly to pose for a special card to be used in the next year's set. Mattingly told Madden he'd be glad to do it, but when Madden went to Winfield, he was put off by the right fielder's response.

"What's in this for you?" Winfield asked.

"Nothing," said Madden. "I don't get a dime more if we do this card or not. I just thought it would be a nice card for the kids next year, you and Donnie facing off with bats or something."

"Well, I don't think I want to do it," said Winfield.

The card thing was no big deal, but Madden was annoyed at Winfield's attitude. So a couple of days later, on a road trip to Detroit, he confronted him about it. It was then, for about the only time Madden could ever remember, that Winfield revealed his true feelings about his relationship with the fans and his teammates.

"Look," he said with a passion, "too much has already been made of this batting race thing, and I don't want to lend any more to it. They're pitting player against player, teammate against teammate. It's becoming a black-white thing, and it's splitting the clubhouse in half."

In Winfield's eyes, Mattingly was the favorite of the fans and a lot of the players because he was white. In fact, he *was* the favorite of most of the players—but not because of anything to do with race. The players perceived Winfield as being too much into himself. He was never one of the guys, usually coming and going from the ballpark alone. The fans, meanwhile, probably favored Mattingly because he was the new kid on the block, the underdog, whereas Winfield could never seem to shake that $23-million-man image.

But beginning with his first at-bat in 1988, the ovations greeted Winfield as if he were just being discovered. Once again Steinbrenner's backlash had worked in Winfield's favor. No longer the high and mighty $23-million man, he was now suddenly looked on as maligned.

It was clear that if Steinbrenner was ever going to succeed at bringing Winfield down after all these misfires, it was going to have be from a different direction. Whatever betrayals of his teammates he might have made in his book, or whatever failings he might have had as a team leader or clutch performer in Steinbrenner's eyes, Winfield had remained virtually impenetrable to the Boss' relentless attacks. A new strategy was obviously in order, and this time Steinbrenner looked to Winfield's foundation as a possible soft spot.

Ironically, on January 6, 1989, Winfield played right into the Boss' hands by filing suit against him for failing to make an annual $300,000 contribution to the foundation. Steinbrenner, who wrote the book on the best defense being a good offense, filed a countersuit four days later, charging the foundation with "fraud, wrongdoing and misappropriations." Among other things Steinbrenner charged that "substantial" funds had been diverted "from the needy children of New York" (which the foundation was said to be serving) and improperly spent on Winfield and his friends. Noted was some $21,000 in "wasteful limousine services." Steinbrenner further demanded that Winfield make restitution and pay $480,000 in donations that Winfield himself was supposed to make to the foundation.

Meanwhile, emerging out of the shadows was one Howard Spira, an admitted gambler and con man who claimed that Winfield had loaned him $15,000—at a usurious 700 percent interest rate—to repay his gambling debts. Spira acknowledged that he was providing Steinbrenner with information in his investigation and lawsuit and claimed to have done public relations work for the foundation.

Actually, Spira had been calling numerous reporters for over a year, attempting to leak dirt on Winfield, who, he said, "destroyed my life." Spira said Winfield had promised him a salary for his public relations services and never delivered on it. When Winfield at first said Spira "was never a part of my life" and denied making any loans to him, Spira made the rounds of all the local TV news shows, brandishing the five-year-old canceled check for $15,000 with Winfield's signature on it.

The double-barreled assault on Winfield and the foundation from Steinbrenner and Spira, along with a subsequent investigation by the Internal Revenue Service, put Winfield's character in serious question for the first time. Heretofore, he had been judged strictly by his all-out style of play on the field and his articulate, polished demeanor off it.

When the Winfield-Steinbrenner dispute over the foundation began to drag on close to spring training, it was proposed by *Daily News* columnist Mike Lupica that the whole thing be settled by binding arbitration. Surprisingly, both sides eventually agreed, but the dispute was almost forgotten when Winfield went down with a season-ending back injury in spring training.

It wasn't until September 6 that the Yankees called a press conference at Yankee Stadium to announce a settlement. In actuality, it was Steinbrenner's ultimate and long-awaited revenge—a public confession of guilt by Winfield. According to the terms of the settlement, Winfield agreed:

1. to make $229,667 in delinquent payments to the foundation.

2. to pay the foundation $30,000 in reimbursement "for certain monies inappropriately expended by the foundation." (No explanation was given.)
3. to admit that "certain allegations made by Steinbrenner and the Yankees were accurate."

Steinbrenner, for his part, agreed to pay the foundation $600,000 in back payments that had been placed in escrow.

For Winfield, it was the culmination of an absolutely awful year. Besides sustaining a career-threatening back injury, he'd been found by a Houston court to have entered into a common-law marriage with a former flight attendant, Sandra Renfro. The result was the possible forfeiture of half his income, dating back to 1982, as alimony/child support payments to Ms. Renfro, who gave birth to Winfield's daughter that same year.

Steinbrenner, meanwhile, had at last beaten Winfield and succeeded in exposing some blemishes in his character.

Those who traveled with Winfield—the players and writers—had previously seen some quirks in Winfield's personality that led them to think he might not be everything his public image made him out to be.

On road trips, beat writers often leave earlier for the ballpark than the team bus. Occasionally players who are going out early will join a couple of writers in a taxi. No big deal. The fares are usually no more than five bucks or so, and the writers, who take the receipts for their expense accounts, usually volunteer to pay. Winfield, however would never wait for the writer to offer. He would open the door and automatically say, "You're paper's getting this, right?" and bolt away. Over the years every beat writer experienced that Winfield line at least once.

Perhaps the best example of Winfield's penny-foolish posture was his go-around with the writers over a limousine in January of 1983. It was ironic that Steinbrenner should cite "wasteful limousine services" in his countersuit against Winfield and the foundation because it was that very thing for which Winfield incurred the writers' wrath.

Moss Klein was chairman of the New York chapter of the Baseball Writers Association and was responsible for running the chapter's annual black-tie dinner at the Sheraton Centre in New York. In attempting to give the dais some added star quality, Klein created a special tribute to Winfield, who was coming off an outstanding 1982 season. Noting that Winfield had been named to all three of *The Sporting News'* postseason all-star teams—All-Star, Silver Slugger, and Gold Glove—Klein arranged for Richard Waters, the publisher of *TSN,* to attend the dinner and present all the awards to Winfield.

A few weeks before the dinner, Klein received a call from a secretary at the Winfield Foundation. She wanted to know the limousine arrangements for Winfield. Klein said he didn't realize a limousine was necessary, since Winfield lived in Fort Lee, New Jersey, right across the George Washington Bridge from Manhattan.

The secretary said she would be in touch in a few days. When she called again, she said the limousine was imperative, that Winfield said he couldn't possibly attend the dinner without limousine service.

The Baseball Writers Association picks up travel expenses for its guests, including airfares, hotel rooms, meals, and any expenses they incur in their two days in New York for the dinner. Despite annual attendances of about 1,500 people, at $60 a person, the dinner is always a money loser.

Klein had never heard of a guest from so close wanting a limo. But after checking with Secretary-Treasurer Jack Lang, Klein informed the secretary that Winfield should make any limo arrangement he wanted and simply submit the bill.

The next day the secretary called again. Winfield would need a room in the hotel as well so he could freshen up after the limo ride and entertain guests. Klein informed her that there was a dais room for guests. That was not sufficient, she said. So Klein informed Lang to make a hotel reservation for Winfield.

Then Klein wondered if maybe he shouldn't expect nearby guests to make their own way to the dinner. So he called Lou Piniella, who was also being honored and who lived in Allendale, New Jersey, about a half hour farther away from the city than Winfield in Fort Lee.

"Lou, are you all set for the dinner?" Klein asked.

Piniella said that he was and that he was looking forward to it.

"Well, do you have any problems getting here?" Klein asked.

Piniella said he didn't understand the question.

"I mean," said Klein, "do you need a limo or anything?"

Piniella laughed. "Of course not," he said.

"How about a room?" Klein asked.

"Look," Piniella said, "I live a half hour, forty-five minutes away. The night of the dinner I'm going to get in my car, drive to the city, park my car, and go to the ballroom. When the dinner's over, I'm going to get back into my car and go home. What else do you need to know?"

Klein didn't tell Piniella about Winfield's requests. But the night of the dinner Klein figured Winfield might have changed his mind about the limo bill. The three *Sporting News* trophies presented to Winfield, after all, dwarfed all the awards that the baseball writers were giving out. Klein, who was the emcee of the affair, was sitting next to the immortal Joe DiMaggio. Throughout the dinner DiMaggio kept looking over at the three huge trophies.

"Who's getting those?" the Yankee Clipper asked.

Klein said he didn't know. He was embarrassed to tell DiMaggio because the trophy the writers were presenting him was about one-fifth the size.

The writers did not hear another thing about Winfield's limo the rest of the month, and when Klein got to spring training, he had all but forgotten it. But on Winfield's first day in camp, he called Klein over.

"Did you take care of the limousine bill?" he asked.

Klein, not sure if he was kidding, shrugged and said no bill had been received.

"I guess it'll be coming soon," said Winfield.

And sure enough, a few days later, the bill surfaced in Klein's mail—$104, broken down into four hours, at $25 per hour, plus $4 in tolls.

Klein phoned Lang and told him he was mailing the bill to him.

"I figured that a guy who makes $2 million a year and who got the three biggest trophies we gave out might at least spring for the $4 in tolls," said Lang.

Then Lang told Klein of the other extreme case at the dinner. The Braves' Dale Murphy, a rising star who wasn't making anywhere near the salary of Winfield, had flown in with his wife from Atlanta. They had spent the weekend in New York, staying at the hotel. When Lang asked for the bills, Murphy refused.

"You guys gave me a great honor," Murphy told Lang. "Why would I want to charge you for it?"

As it turned out, however, the $104 limo bill and the numerous taxi fares Winfield beat the writers out of were peanuts compared to what he made off Steinbrenner in the final two years of his contract. In retrospect, Winfield probably felt Steinbrenner owed him every cent he made as a Yankee and more, considering the constant down-and-dirty infighting that went on between himself and the Boss.

Nevertheless, after the 1988 season, Steinbrenner had to make a decision whether to exercise the option on the final two years of Winfield's contract. As much as he despised Winfield, Steinbrenner would have had to pay half the value of the remaining two years—approximately $2 million—if he didn't want to pick up the option. In effect, that would have meant handing $2 million over to a player who had just come off a .322, 25-homer, 107-RBI season and telling him, "Go out and sign with the team of your choice—on us."

No way Steinbrenner was going to do Winfield a favor like that. That option clause was put in the original contract as a protection/escape for Steinbrenner in the event that Winfield's skills had eroded by the eighth year of his service with the Yankees. But there was no hint of that, just as there was no hint of the herniated disc problem in Winfield's back that subsequently sidelined him for the entire 1989 season.

Dave Righetti

Dave Righetti outlasted everyone. When he walked into the Yankee clubhouse in spring training 1989, there was nobody left from the clubhouse he'd first walked into in spring training 1979, other than Ron Guidry and Tommy John—and neither of them would have been there had manager Dallas Green had his way. Guidry, 38 and coming off a season of rehabilitation from rotator cuff surgery, and John, 45, were non-roster invitees being given one last hurrah by Yankee owner George Steinbrenner. Righetti was 20 years old in 1979, the key player in a 10-player deal the Yankees had made with Texas in November of 1978. In the deal the Yankees sent Sparky Lyle, their Cy Young Award-winning reliever in 1977, to the Rangers. So even on his arrival Righetti was under pressure. At the press conference announcing the trade, Yankee president Al Rosen referred to Righetti as "the next Guidry." Since Ron Guidry had just completed a 25–3 season in 1978, Righetti became a marked man.

And the pressure never lifted. He had always been the man on the spot with the Yankees, but he survived and became a high-paid star—in fact, the highest-paid pitcher in Yankee history. But that first day in spring training, Righetti was a nonroster invitee, the youngest player in the camp of a team that had just won two consecutive world championships.

He was a hard-throwing left-hander, a strikeout pitcher who had fanned 21 batters in a game in 1978, pitching for Tulsa, the Rangers' AA farm team. The rave notices were out for a show that had yet to open. And on that first day in 1979, knowing that everybody was waiting to see what he could do, Righetti threw too hard, hurt his arm, and missed most of spring training.

It was never easy for him. Not because he wasn't talented; his ability and his performance were clearly first-rate. But life as a Steinbrenner Yankee was never simple.

Righetti was first called up by the Yankees on September 16, 1979, and once again the ball club made sure that he didn't have an easy entrance. His debut—as the starting pitcher against Detroit—happened to be "Catfish Hunter Day," in honor of the future Hall of Fame pitcher who was retiring that season. So "the next Guidry" took the mound with more than 40,000 fans on hand.

Righetti wasn't overwhelming, but he did reasonably well, working five innings and allowing three runs and three hits while coming away with a no-decision. He spent the entire 1980 season at Columbus, the Yankees' top farm, and was expected to make the team in 1981. But that spring he had an unnecessary detour.

On the other side of Florida, in St. Petersburg, the big story coming out of the rival Mets' camp was Tim Leary, a young right-hander who was pitching so sensationally there was talk of promoting him all the way from class-A ball to the major leagues. Leary was attracting daily attention from the media, and George Steinbrenner, ever envious of any attention the Mets received (even in those days when the Mets were struggling), decided he had to have his own Leary.

Steinbrenner wanted an unknown, a raw kid who could do what Leary was doing and give the Yankees their own "phenom." Righetti was only 22, but he was already known to Yankee fans and had plenty of AAA experience. He didn't fit the bill, but Gene Nelson did.

Nelson, a 20-year-old right-hander, was an unknown. He'd had a remarkable 20–3 record at Class-A Fort Lauderdale in 1980, and he was pitching impressively in spring training. There wasn't room on the Yankee staff for two rookie pitchers, and Steinbrenner wanted Nelson. Righetti had to go, even though advisers warned Steinbrenner that the demotion could demoralize the kid left-hander. Nelson needs more seasoning, they warned Steinbrenner—to no avail.

On April 5, 1981, four days before the season opener, a stunned Righetti was optioned to Columbus. Moss Klein caught up to him in the parking lot of Fort Lauderdale Stadium.

"I thought I was going to make the team," said Righetti, who seemed near tears. "I guess I should have known better. I know what's going on. I know why certain decisions were made. But there's really no point in saying anything about that now."

Even though the official announcement of Nelson's status was a few days away, Steinbrenner didn't attempt to conceal his intentions. As Righetti was getting into his car in the parking lot, Steinbrenner emerged from his trailer office. The principal owner announced that old reliable Clyde King was being assigned to work with Righetti in Columbus "to correct a minor flaw in his delivery."

Asked about Nelson, Steinbrenner said: "Gene Nelson can be an incredible story if my people think he's ready to make the team. This is a real Frank Merriwell rags-to-riches story. Imagine, a kid coming from class-A ball making the Yankees.

People will come to see him pitch. He'll put fans in the stands."

So Nelson became the first Yankee since Rollie Sheldon in 1960 to make the team out of A ball. But he wasn't ready and wound up going back to Columbus. Leary? He appeared in one game for the Mets and was injured.

Righetti, meanwhile, got off to a 5–0 start at Columbus, was called up to the Yankees in May, and became the American League Rookie of the Year in 1981. But that wasn't easy, either. He had just joined the Yankees on May 21, won his first three decisions, and then the strike started. It lasted seven weeks.

Righetti returned home to San Jose, California, and as always, his father exerted influence on the budding star.

Leo "Pinky" Righetti had spent 14 years in the minor leagues as a shortstop before giving up his dream of making the majors. For seven years he was buried in the Yankee organization, kept down on the farm because of the presence of Phil Rizzuto, the Yankee shortstop. Leo had been signed by the Yankees in 1944. In 1946 he was assigned to Binghamton, where he formed a pretty fair double-play combination with his roommate, future Yankee second baseman Jerry Coleman. Later Leo would have as teammates at Birmingham both Whitey Ford and Gil McDougald, who also went to star with the Yankees. Leo, however, never joined them.

Finally, in 1952, Leo was sold to the Boston Braves, and he stayed in baseball until 1958. When he was 31, he decided it was time to earn a living because, after all, his wife was back home in San Jose and a baby was due in November. So he gave up baseball and went to work in his father's rendering plant, making ingredients for soap, dog food, and other products.

On November 28, 1958, Dave Righetti was born and a little more than 20 years later, Leo Righetti, in a sense, finally made it to the Yankees. He was going to be sure that his son, with whom he had an especially close relationship, was going to stay with the Yankees and prosper for them.

So during the strike, which Leo Righetti cursed nearly every day, he worked diligently with Dave. He'd wake his son early and play catcher for him. "I'm sick about this strike," Leo told Moss Klein, "just sick about it. Dammit, Dave was in that rotation, he was doing his job. Who knows how this layoff is going to affect him? When the strike ends, Guidry and Tommy John can go out there and take a few beatings if they're not sharp and nothing will happen to them. But if Dave gets roughed up, it's back to Columbus. He's had enough of the minors. He's a big leaguer."

And so Righetti stayed sharp. He had no choice about it. Leo set up the pitching schedule that he would have followed during a season, and kept him on it. "I would've worked out regularly anyway," Dave said when the season resumed in August, "but my dad wasn't taking any chances."

When the season started up again, Righetti was ready. He wound up 8–4, with a 2.06 ERA, falling 1⅔ innings shy of qualifying for the ERA title. The combined batting average against him was .196, lowest in the league. And in the playoffs against Milwaukee and then Oakland, he worked 15 innings, allowing one run and striking out 17.

In the final game of the playoffs, the pennant clincher against the A's in the Oakland Coliseum, Leo Righetti saw his son pitch professionally for the first time. He pitched six scoreless innings and was the winner. "He still has a lot to learn," the proud father said. "We don't want him getting a swelled head, you know."

A swelled head? With Steinbrenner around? No way. Righetti lost his only World Series start in 1981, knocked out in the third inning by the Dodgers in the much-ballyhooed matchup of superrookies—Fernando Valenzuela vs. Righetti. By the time 1982 spring camp rolled around, Steinbrenner was still upset at his team's collapse in the World Series, and nobody—not even the 1981 Rookie of the Year—was getting the benefit of the doubt.

So when Righetti had a shaky outing against the Orioles in an exhibition game at Miami Stadium, Steinbrenner bolted from his front-row seats into the Yankee dugout and told his manager, Bob Lemon, he was calling a meeting of the front office staff as soon as everybody got back to Fort Lauderdale that night. The Yankees had played six exhibitions, losing four, and Steinbrenner was already concerned.

"Righetti was bad, terrible, just horrendous," Steinbrenner said. "He couldn't find the plate. Maybe he's been reading his press clippings too much. He'd better not come down with sophomore-itis."

Righetti wasn't concerned and said as much. He also made a remark that came back to haunt him, since Steinbrenner pays close attention to his players' reactions.

"I have to think I have the team made," he said. "They know what I can do."

When Righetti struggled early in the season, guess where he wound up? Back in Columbus, of course. Steinbrenner took pains to say this wasn't punishment, just an effort to get Righetti straightened out. He even telephoned Leo Righetti to tell him he thought the world of his son, but this was a demotion that should help. Leo agreed. Righetti spent three weeks at Columbus, and when he returned, Steinbrenner promoted pitching coach Sammy Ellis as well. Ellis joined the Yankees as "co-pitching coach, in charge of Righetti."

Righetti finished 1982 with an 11–10 record, and any rough edges seemed to have been smoothed. In 1983 he surged into the season by winning 14 of his first 18 decisions, capped by his July 4 no-hitter against the Red Sox. He completed the season 14–8, missing the last couple of weeks with a tired arm.

It seemed apparent he had arrived. He would be the Yankee ace, a projected 20-game winner from here on out. He would be only 25 when the 1984 season started. What a future…and then Goose Gossage took the free-agent route to San Diego, changing Righetti's path.

Shortly after Gossage's defection, Steinbrenner summoned his staff to an emergency meeting. What was to be done about replacing Gossage in the bullpen? Several ideas were tossed around, trade possibilities were discussed. Bruce Sutter was available, and the Cardinals were contacted. But they wanted Righetti in return. Nothing doing.

Clyde King mentioned Righetti as the replacement for Gossage. New manager Yogi Berra liked the idea. So too did Sammy Ellis. The pros and cons were discussed. Righetti had a promising career as a starter. Was it wise to tamper with his career? Could his arm hold up as a reliever?

As Sammy Ellis later revealed to Bill Madden: "I think you know I love this kid like a son. If I thought for a minute we were doing something to hurt him, I'd be dead set against it. But the fact is, and I'd never, ever tell Dave this, every time he pitches, I wince. His pitching style is such that any time his arm could blow out. That's why I think pitching in relief will actually prolong his career, because it'll keep his arm stronger and he won't get tired from pitching all those innings like he did [in 1983]."

Nevertheless, Righetti didn't like the idea. He wanted to remain a starter. One morning that winter, Leo had predicted to him over breakfast that this is what the Yankees would do, and sure enough, Ellis called to talk to him about it, King called, and Jeff Torborg called. In addition, the Yankees signed veteran knuckleballer Phil Niekro two weeks after Gossage left, adding another starter to their rotation.

In fact, the Righetti shift, despite Dave's initial reluctance, was a rousing success—most of the time. There were occasional problems, though.

Toward the end of spring training 1984, Righetti angrily threatened to scrap the plan before it started. That was because Steinbrenner, in his anxiousness to trade Graig Nettles, began leaking stories to the press that Nettles was a bad influence on Righetti. As part of Steinbrenner's propaganda, he said that Nettles was urging Righetti to abandon the bullpen move. There was no truth to it, but the story spread. Righetti was furious when he heard about it. He was close to Nettles, who, at 39, was almost like an older brother to him.

When Nettles was traded to San Diego the night before the Yankees broke camp, Righetti was especially upset. When reporters approached him the next day, his hands were shaking as he began to dispute the "bad influence" claims about Nettles. Finally he asked just to be left alone. When a few reporters started heading back after a while, they were intercepted by the veteran Niekro. "I think you fellas better leave him alone for a while," Niekro said. "He might kill somebody."

Righetti went on to make a smooth adjustment to bullpen closer that '84 season, although the Yankees were out of the race early. In fact, Righetti did more damage to himself than the hitters did. On June 17, 1984, prior to a Sunday afternoon game against the Orioles at Yankee Stadium, Righetti was in the bullpen demonstrating to the other relievers a new hold he had seen on pro wrestling on TV. As he excitedly motioned with his left hand, he caught the jagged edge of the water cooler, suffering a gash on his index finger that required six stitches and landed him on the disabled list.

Steinbrenner was predictably furious. Everything had gone wrong that season, starting with the Tigers' runaway start that made the Yankees also-rans by May. Righetti was one of the team's leading attractions. Now this. Steinbrenner called a meeting after the game. Somebody was going to take the fall for this, it was just a matter of who. The scapegoat turned out to be bullpen coach Jerry McNertney. He was banished to Columbus by Steinbrenner because of "a lack of discipline in the bullpen."

But the firing of McNertney alone didn't appease Steinbrenner. He called all the relievers into the manager's office. "We're going to have a full-scale investigation," he announced. He wanted the truth from them, he said, unsatisfied with the story he'd been told. Obviously suspecting there had been a fight, Steinbrenner said, "We're going to get to the bottom of this even if we have to take lie detector tests."

Happily for all, Steinbrenner did make one rational move that day. He ordered the jagged edge of the water cooler taped up, to avoid future injuries.

By 1986 Righetti was firmly established as one of the premier relievers in the American League. That season he set an all-time saves record with 46 (in 56 chances), but even that didn't make him exempt from Steinbrenner's rages. In fact, he was now under more scrutiny than anyone because of the nature of his job. Every time he came in, the game was on the line and one errant pitch, one blooper, or one bad-hop single could mean an instant loss. And Steinbrenner wanted perfection.

On April 27, 1986, when both Righetti and Brian Fisher failed to hold a big lead against Cleveland, Steinbrenner popped off after the loss. "Righetti and Fisher," he said, "should have gone home with the vendors." The pitchers were annoyed but not surprised, and the "vendors" line became a season-long joke to the bullpen crew.

But in June, when Righetti was still struggling periodically, Steinbrenner became more harsh in his criticism. When the Yankees arrived in Toronto on June 19 to open a four-game series against the Blue Jays, Steinbrenner was quoted in the papers criticizing the team, especially Righetti, who had 16 saves in 22 opportunities to that point. "Righetti has been a big disappointment,"

Steinbrenner was quoted as saying. "I don't know how many games he's blown for us this year."

That night the Yankees lost to the Blue Jays, 10–9, their fifth loss in a row, and Righetti gave up the winning run in the 10th inning. After the game he was pacing around the clubhouse, obviously seething. Reporters were wary about approaching him, but deadlines were nearing and Klein finally asked Righetti about the loss. He stopped pacing.

"We're not panicking like the guy upstairs," Righetti said, spitting out his words. He began pacing again, then broke the silence in the room by slamming a soda machine and hurling a cup, shouting, "Fuck him! He never played a game for this team!"

The next night things got worse. Righetti gave up a two-out, game-tying grand slam homer to Toronto's George Bell in the ninth inning. When manager Lou Piniella headed to the mound, Righetti fired the ball over the right field wall—a mighty heave of nearly 300 feet. That was the ultimate tension breaker, and the Yankees went on to win, 10–8, in 10 innings. But Steinbrenner wasn't amused by Righetti's fit of frustration.

Back at the Sheraton Centre, Steinbrenner was standing in the lobby, anxious to talk about Righetti. "It's incredulous [*sic*] how many games Righetti's blown," Steinbrenner said. "Incredulous!" Steinbrenner also suggested that Righetti be fined for the ball-throwing incident.

And there was another voice to be heard, that of Hank Steinbrenner, the Boss' oldest son, who had been serving as a team official and adviser on the "crack baseball committee" that season. Hank would eventually mellow, and he moved on to the racetrack world later that season, telling other team officials he couldn't stand the way his father ran the team. But in those early days with the club, Hank had a lot of opinions on how things should be run and which players weren't performing, and he expressed his thoughts about Righetti, too.

"I think he should be starting," Hank said. "Alfonso Pulido should be the closer." Pulido, a career minor leaguer, had been with the Yankees one week and had made two impressive outings. He returned to the minors after the season and never surfaced again.

When Righetti heard that one, he was flabbergasted. So was Piniella. But Piniella took a strong hand. "As long as I'm the manager," said Piniella, "Dave Righetti will be my bullpen closer."

And of course, Righetti went on to be the all-time bullpen closer that season.

Following the 1987 season, Righetti had his chance to flee the Yankees and Steinbrenner's constant barbs just as Gossage had four years earlier. He became a free agent and, despite the continuing effects of the baseball owners' collusion, received considerable attention on the market. Both the Giants and Athletics came a-courtin' him, hoping to convince him on the merits of pitching close to home in the San Francisco Bay Area. Then the Dodgers plunged into the bidding and dispatched their manager Tommy Lasorda to do their recruiting. One night Lasorda called Bill Madden at home and asked him to have Righetti call him.

"I love that kid," Lasorda said. "He's Italian, isn't he? How can he not be a star for us? I can see him and Fernando anchoring our starting rotation."

That was the problem. All of the teams pursuing Righetti were envisioning him as a starter. While he may have admitted that he'd never totally cleansed his system of starting, he was a reliever now—a top-drawer reliever—and he took considerable pride in that. Also (and some thought him a masochist for this), despite everything the Yankees and Steinbrenner had done and said to him through the years, he didn't want to leave.

Nevertheless, the Righetti free-agent negotiations turned out to be yet another Yankee circus, only instead of Steinbrenner, the ringmaster was Righetti's agent, William Goodstein. Goodstein would make almost-daily calls to all the beat writers, eagerly updating them on all teams calling with offers for Righetti. Then at the conclusion of each call, Goodstein would always add, "Be sure and get my name in there."

It was never clear who Goodstein was trying to promote more that winter, Righetti or himself. The circuslike proceedings reached center ring at the winter meetings in Dallas when Goodstein made a grandstand entrance and announced to one and all that he had a $10-million offer from an unnamed Japanese team for Righetti. It may well be that a Japanese team had, in fact, inquired about Righetti, but anyone who knew Righetti knew that all the yen in Tokyo couldn't get him to leave the country.

Nevertheless, to Goodstein's credit, Steinbrenner bit—even after Goodstein appeared to have conceded defeat by agreeing to arbitration with the Yankees. In effect, that made Righetti a re-signed player with the Yankees. But instead of waiting for an arbitrator to determine Righetti's salary, Steinbrenner broke ranks with the owners (who had, in concert, been limiting all pitchers to contracts of less than three years) and signed his favorite reliever to a three-year deal worth $4.3 million.

Leo Righetti may never have made the Yankees, but his kid became the highest-paid Yankee pitcher ever. Considering everything it took to get him there, Dave Righetti, using a favorite word of the principal Yankee owner, might only find that "incredulous."

Gene Monahan And Bill "Killer" Kane
(They also served—and survived)

They appear in every official team picture from 1972 through 1987, which in itself tells you everything you need to know about the survival capacities of Gene Monahan and Bill "Killer" Kane, a pair of behind-the-scenes pillars of stability in the eye of the Steinbrenner hurricane. To be sure, Monahan, the team trainer in charge of hamstrings, rib cages, wrists, and calves, and Kane, the traveling secretary whose myriad of responsibilities included all the team travel and hotel accommodations, have been on the receiving end of more profane and scornful rages from the principal Yankee owner over the years than any other organization minions.

There are no documented records as to how many times both Monahan and Kane were fired in fits of Steinbrenner pique, although one suspects that Monahan, who bore the brunt of the blame for every Yankee injury, holds an unbreakable record in that regard. That he lasted so long in his job was a tribute to both his competence (no less than three major league trainers, Hermie Schneider with the White Sox, Barry Weinberg with the Athletics, and Mark Letendre with the Giants, plied their trade as Yankee assistants under Monahan) and his quiet toughness.

Those who were present will never forget a meeting Steinbrenner held in 1986, during a period when the Yankees were beset by injuries. Steinbrenner began the meeting by directing his wrath at Jeff Mangold, the strength coach, and of course, Monahan. "Here," he said, "I've got a strength coach who can't keep my players from getting hurt, and then"—turning to Monahan—"I've got this asshole who can't get 'em healthy again."

After a while the meeting turned into a roundtable discussion of the Yankees' personnel, with Steinbrenner soliciting the opinions of everyone— the manager, coaches, trainers, and other club officials. When he came to Monahan, the trainer stood up and prefaced his remarks by saying, "First of all, I'm not an asshole." Everyone in the room had to suppress a grin, and even Steinbrenner saw the humor in it.

Among Monahan's added duties was the business of keeping Billy Martin at least functional, in Martin's five stormy terms as Yankee manager. More times than Monahan would probably care to remember, Martin would arrive at the ballpark nursing a hangover. A familiar sight to reporters as they sat in the manager's office before a game was Monahan bringing Martin a cup of this thick, pink liquid that looked like a combination of apricot nectar and Pepto Bismol. When asked once what he was bringing Martin every day in the cup, Monahan replied tersely, "Vitamin supplements."

Other times Monahan would dispense with the formalities and simply get right to the point. He would come into Martin's office and administer "old number one," a shot of B_{12} in the rear end.

Monahan's B_{12} shots were not limited to just Martin, however. Members of the Yankee high command tell of the times Steinbrenner would be holding a roundtable meeting in his office, only to be temporarily interrupted by Monahan's appearance. As Steinbrenner continued addressing the manager, coaches, and other high-level team executives, he would get up from his swivel chair, bend down behind it, pull his pants down, and take his shot from Monahan in the behind.

"I often wondered at how many board meetings across the U.S. the board chairman gets up in the middle and moons the other directors?" cracked one member of the Yankee high command.

On one occasion, it was said, Monahan was out of B_{12} when summoned by Steinbrenner to administer his shot in the middle of a meeting. Rather than risk a berating from the Boss in front of everyone, Monahan went through the motions and gave Steinbrenner the shot—with water. Steinbrenner never knew the difference, and the meeting proceeded without further incident.

Similarly, "Killer" Kane had more than his share of volatile and profane go-rounds with Steinbrenner in his nearly 15 years as Yankee traveling secretary. Kane, who joined the Yankees in 1961 as a statistician for Mel Allen in the TV booth, is a hard-drinking Irishman who, despite a pronounced limp from a boyhood bout with polio, has never been afraid of a fight and, in fact, has even been known to instigate a couple. Before taking Kane off the road for good after the 1987 season, Steinbrenner once fired the Killer for half a day and another time for half a season.

Prior to the Yankees' 1978 playoff game with the Red Sox, Steinbrenner was a nervous wreck, nitpicking at everyone from manager Bob Lemon to the batboys. Kane came in for the Boss' wrath for, of all things, having the Yankees' charter plane at the wrong airport. All year long the Yankees had been chartering out of Newark Airport, but Steinbrenner, who was obviously looking for anything to be upset about so as to distract himself from the game at hand, went into a tirade over not having the plane leave from LaGuardia. He demanded that Kane have the place of departure changed. When Kane explained that it was impossible to have the plane moved from Newark to LaGuardia, Steinbrenner replied, "Okay, if you can't get the job done, I'll get somebody else."

With that, Steinbrenner called Jerry Murphy, a young front office intern, and informed him he would be taking over Kane's duties as traveling secretary for the playoff game as well as for any future postseason Yankee travels.

Murphy was understandably terror-stricken over being handed this enormous responsibility with no advance notice or experience. But when he went to find Kane to get fill-in on what had to be done, "Killer" had locked himself in his office. "He thinks anybody can do this job," Kane said, "let him find out."

Needless to say, Steinbrenner relented and restored Kane to his job. The team took off from Newark and went on to beat the Red Sox the next day to win the American League East. That night Steinbrenner bought "Killer" Kane dinner.

Another Kane-Steinbrenner confrontation over the charter flights did not end so amicably. In fact, it is likely to become legend in Yankee annals as it gets repeated (and presumably exaggerated) through the years. Considering that it occurred in 1983, it is amazing that word of it never leaked out to the press before.

It was spring training. The entire Yankee staff was staying at the Royce Hotel in Pompano Beach, Florida. All that spring Steinbrenner had been grousing over his charter contract with United Airlines. He had wanted to shift the team's business to another airline and was constantly haranguing Kane about getting out of the contract. Kane, for his part, wanted nothing to do with it and kept insisting to Steinbrenner that the team couldn't break the contract with United.

Then, on a two-day trip to New Orleans, a lot of the Yankee players came down with food poisoning. Steinbrenner, as was his wont, ordered an investigation as to the origin of the epidemic. After much deliberation it was determined that the players must have been stricken by the airline food.

Well, now Steinbrenner had his ammunition. He called Kane into the executive trailer and demanded once again that the United contract be terminated. When Kane again resisted, the conversation quickly became heated, with Steinbrenner berating the Killer in front of all the secretaries. Kane was both embarrassed and infuriated, but as he left the trailer to return to his office, Steinbrenner followed and continued his profane tirade as Kane was walking across the parking lot.

Kane was shaking by the time he got to his office and threw a few things around to vent his anger. He then proceeded to go out and get drunk.

When he got back to the Royce Hotel late that night, fortified by several martinis, Kane was on a mission. He took the elevator up to the top floor and limped down the hall to Steinbrenner's room, where he commenced pounding on the door.

"C'mon out of their, you fat fucking Fauntleroy!" Kane screamed. "I've had enough of your shit! C'mon out of there, 'cause I'm gonna beat the shit out of you!"

Steinbrenner came to the door dumbfounded.

"What the hell is the matter with you, Killer?" he said. "Get the hell out of here and go to bed. You're disturbing my wife."

"I don't give a shit about your wife," Kane shouted. "You don't give a shit about my wife when you scream at me in front of her, so why should I give a shit about your wife. Now get out here, I'm gonna beat the shit out of you."

"Okay," said Steinbrenner, obviously not wanting this scene to get any more out of hand than it already was. "Go downstairs and wait for me in the lobby. I'll get dressed and be right down."

Kane agreed reluctantly, but as he headed down the hall toward the elevator, he was intercepted by the hotel manager, who had been called by guests on the floor complaining at being awakened by all this commotion.

"What's going on, Mr. Kane?" the manager said.

As Kane slurred about his intentions of beating up on Steinbrenner, the manager explained that he didn't want to have to call the police.

"Ah, go ahead and call 'em," Kane said. "I'm gonna fight this son of a bitch in the lobby."

"Very well," said the manager, seeming almost delighted at the prospect, "he's been breaking our balls all month, too."

A few minutes later, Steinbrenner got down to the lobby, only to find Kane sitting on a chair sound asleep. Approaching the dozing traveling secretary, Steinbrenner began shouting again.

"All right, Killer, wake up. You woke me up, now you wake up. What the hell is all this about?"

Kane slowly began coming to his senses again, rubbing his eyes, only to see Steinbrenner standing in front of him screaming at him. It took him a few more seconds to remember where he was, before he began shouting back. The two went at it verbally for a couple of minutes when suddenly Kane hauled off and slugged Steinbrenner, who retaliated by shoving back. As he did, Kane went toppling over onto the floor.

"I hope you're satisfied now," he screamed at Steinbrenner. "You just punched a cripple!"

Steinbrenner was taken aback. And perhaps fearing a lawsuit—or just realizing how totally foolish and crazy it was to be duking it out with a drunken employee in the lobby of a hotel in the middle of the night—he helped Kane to his feet and had him escorted up to bed.

The next day, and for all the days after that, Steinbrenner never said another word to Kane about the fight. For the record, however, the team did change from United—and from three other airlines as well—before Kane was taken off the job and made an administrative assistant in the front office at the end of

1987. Finally, after a series of problems with Steinbrenner, Kane was taken off the payroll in June 1989.

About the only man who had as many years of continuous service behind the scenes with the Yankees as Kane and Monahan was clubhouse man Nick Priore, who'd served as the venerable Pete Sheehy's assistant for nearly twenty years before assuming the head job in 1985. But shortly after Christmas in 1989, Priore also was fired by Steinbrenner and replaced by Priore's assistant, Bob Fleming.

Fleming, a personable sort, perhaps achieved his greatest bit of Yankee notoriety when he served as Steinbrenner's chauffeur prior to becoming a clubhouse man. One time, he was driving Steinbrenner to LaGuardia Airport for a golfing outing the Boss was attending in Pittsburgh. However, upon arriving at the airport and opening up the trunk, Fleming and Steinbrenner discovered the Boss' golf clubs had all fallen loose from the package they were wrapped in.

"I can't carry these clubs on the plane like this!" Steinbrenner fumed. "What's the matter with you?"

With that, Steinbrenner handed the beleaguered Fleming a $100 bill. "Here," Steinbrenner said, "this ought to be enough to keep you in gas and tolls to Pittsburgh. You get these clubs there. And you better get there before I do. I expect you to be waiting for me in the hotel lobby."

And that was the day Bob Fleming learned what surviving with Steinbrenner was all about—the day he drove the Boss' golf clubs some four hundred miles from New York to Pittsburgh.

CHAPTER 10

Such a Deal!

They were called at various times the Yankee high command, the crack baseball committee, or simply George's baseball people. They were that nebulous, indistinct, ever-changing group of people who were responsible—or rather *held* responsible—for all the New York Yankee trades and signings of recent years.

In the beginning, when there was some sense of order in the Yankee front office, Gabe Paul was *the* baseball person. And not coincidentally, the trades—such as Bobby Bonds for Ed Figueroa and Mickey Rivers, or Doc Medich for Willie Randolph, Dock Ellis, and Ken Brett—turned out to be enormous successes for the Yankees. Back then, Paul didn't have to poll a committee of deposed Yankee managers, front office "advisers," and other assorted George Steinbrenner confidants and flunkies to make a trade. Because of his long career as a front office chief with the Cincinnati Reds and Cleveland Indians before he joined the Yankees, Paul had the credentials to act with autonomy. He was the only genuine baseball man in the Steinbrenner brain trust that took over the team from CBS in 1973.

But after three years Paul departed because Steinbrenner had become more and more of a hands-on owner. (One could not help but recall Steinbrenner's vow at the initial press conference announcing his purchase of the team from CBS that he'd be remaining in the background. "You won't be seeing me again at these things," he said.) In later years Steinbrenner maintained that he—and not Paul—had been the one who made the Randolph and Rivers-Figueroa trades. "Paul was in baseball forty years, twenty-five as a general manager, and did he ever win a pennant before?" Steinbrenner said. "You think he made all those moves with this team himself? You think all of a sudden he got brilliant?"

Once the strong force of Paul was removed from the front office, Steinbrenner began running things by committee—more often than not, a committee of diverse opinions. But that has always seemed to be Steinbrenner's modus operandi in running the Yankees: divide and conquer. He loved watching his minions all fight among themselves over a decision.

That was never more evident than with the group Steinbrenner sent to represent the Yankees at the 1988 winter baseball meetings in Atlanta. There was the new manager, Dallas Green, and his first lieutenant, bench coach Charlie Fox. And there was Clyde King, a former Yankee manager and general manager. And Billy Martin, the five-time former Yankee manager. And Bob Quinn, the new general manager. Quinn had only been general manager for a couple of months, and here he was supposed to preside over this group of antagonists who were poles apart on everything. Martin hated King. King had no use for Martin. Martin hated Fox. King had no use for Fox. Fox had no use for either King or Martin. Martin resented Green and bad-mouthed him to just about everyone he talked to. King had been instrumental in hiring Green but didn't approve of most of the people Green had surrounded himself with.

It was no wonder that the Yankees, though desperately in need of pitching help, instead spent almost the entire four days in Atlanta attempting to trade Dave Winfield, who had veto rights over any deal. While Quinn conducted talks with the Minnesota Twins regarding Winfield, Green and Fox attempted to put together a deal with the Chicago Cubs. At the conclusion of the meetings, even Quinn was forced to concede "there were some things going on that I wasn't aware of." Perhaps the highlight of the four days of Yankee confusion was the Wednesday-afternoon press briefing. Green, who admitted to having had a few drinks with Fox at the Topps baseball card company's hospitality room, launched into a 10-minute dissertation on team discipline and togetherness. But when he mentioned having had a few, King, a teetotaler, wheeled around in his chair in the doorway of the adjoining room with a look of admonishment on his face.

But the winter meetings in Dallas the year before were even more of a Yankee circus. This time the rookie general manager was Lou Piniella who had the unenviable task of trying to put deals together with Steinbrenner looking over his shoulder, and Martin, for his part, offering no support. Piniella and his front office assistant, Quinn, actually did everything possible to keep Martin, the manager, sequestered.

On the first day of those '87 meetings at the Loew's Anatole Hotel, the beat writers were called to the Yankee suite for a late-afternoon briefing. Piniella was in the process of discussing the Yankees' progress on deals when the door opened and Martin, grinning widely, strolled in. Piniella continued talking, only to be interrupted by Martin.

"Want to play golf tomorrow with me and Mickey?" Martin asked Piniella. (Mickey Mantle, who lived in the area, had evidently set up a golf outing.)

"Billy," said Piniella, "I can't play golf. We're supposed to be working here, meeting with teams."

But Martin, who had obviously had a few drinks, seemed oblivious to the business at hand. "Hey," he plugged on, "it's a great course."

The group of reporters began looking at each other, eyes rolling upward, at this ridiculous interruption. But it got even wackier. As Piniella resumed his briefing, he watched aghast as Martin, with a glazed look on his smiling face, got up and began making the rounds of each reporter, reaching out to shake hands and saying, "Merry Christmas!" Piniella merely shook his head and waited for Martin to leave.

Piniella held another briefing in his suite the next day. This time Martin wasn't present—at least not initially. While Piniella was answering questions, there was a sound at the door. Not knocking, exactly, more like scratching, like a dog was trying to get in. Moss Klein, sitting closest to the door, opened it. There was Martin, that same glazed smile on his face. This time, perhaps by prearrangement, publicity man Harvey Greene got up and escorted Martin into the adjoining room of the suite. It was a scene out of a Gothic novel, with the lunatic aunt that the family has hidden away in the attic escaping and wandering into a family party.

Then again, Martin never made any secret of his disinterest in the winter meetings. In the December 1977 meetings in Hawaii, he staged a one-man boycott of the Yankees' business by sitting out at the pool all afternoon, drinking. The Yankees had gone to Hawaii in hopes of swinging a trade for a power-hitting outfielder. Their three primary targets were San Diego's Dave Winfield, Atlanta's Gary Matthews, and Pittsburgh's Dave Parker. Paul had announced before the meetings that he was resigning as club president to return to Cleveland as front office chief of the Indians. At Steinbrenner's request, though, he stayed on through the meetings, working with Al Rosen and Cedric Tallis, who were to share Paul's duties when he left.

"We don't need any deals," Martin said each day when reporters found him at the pool. "I told them if they make any big deal and break up the team, they're crazy. We don't need Parker or Winfield. We have [Roy] White and Lou [Piniella] to play left field."

Inevitably, with a few drinks in him on the first day of the meetings, Martin overstayed in the boiling Hawaii sun. The next day he had a painful sunburn. But that did not deter him in his determination to stay out of reach of the team executives. He simply wrapped himself up in towels and camped out, with a few drinks, on the beach. The mummified Billy was quite a sight. Not surprisingly (and in retrospect probably just as well), the Yankees made no trades at the meetings that year.

Aside from 1975, when they put together the Randolph and Figueroa-Rivers deals under Paul's direction, the only other time the Yankees really seemed organized at the winter meetings was in 1984 at Houston, when King was the general manager. That year it was clear the Yankees had a game plan, and they executed it with precision. Scouts Eddie Robinson and Al Cuccinello each took a team and laid the groundwork for deals, which they brought back to King. At the end of the meetings, the Yankees came home with Rickey Henderson from the A's, Ron Hassey and Rich Bordi from the Cubs, and Brian Fisher from the Braves, all of whom made significant contributions to the Yankees in 1985. Inexplicably, the next year Steinbrenner sent no scouts to the winter meetings.

In 1976, when the Yankees won their first pennant in 12 years, the shortstops were Jim Mason and Fred Stanley. They platooned most of the season until the last two months, when Stanley took over on a semiregular basis.

When the Yankees wound up getting swept four straight by the Cincinnati Reds in the World Series, Steinbrenner realized that, even though his team had come a long way in a short time, improvements were still needed. He went out that winter and signed slugger Reggie Jackson and left-handed pitcher Don Gullett as free agents. But the Yankees still needed a shortstop, since both Stanley and Mason were light hitters who were both considered to be backup players—hardly suitable for the "best team money could buy."

So Steinbrenner ordered Paul to find a good young shortstop who could team with Willie Randolph to form a solid double-play combo up the middle for years to come. Paul knew exactly who was available and who he wanted: Bucky Dent, the 25-year-old shortstop with the Chicago White Sox.

Dent was young but experienced, having played three full seasons for the White Sox. And he was a solid player—sure-handed defensively, with adequate range and a strong arm, and a decent hitter. He was available because the White Sox were operating on a shoestring and didn't want to pay him what he was worth. White Sox owner Bill Veeck saw the opportunity to extract some needed cash and young players from the Yankees for Dent.

In the end, Paul got his man, as he almost always did. And he made a shrewd deal. But dealing with the White Sox was only part of Paul's problems. As the talks dragged on for four months—and they weren't completed until the day before the season opener—Steinbrenner became impatient with Paul. Steinbrenner was ready to get the deal done by throwing in a young pitcher named Ron Guidry, whom he had decided after a few spring training games in 1976 was just "a triple-A pitcher."

Trade talks between the White Sox and Yankees had begun at the winter meetings in Los Angeles in December of '76. White Sox general manager Roland Hemond made it clear he had to get lefty hitter Oscar Gamble back in the deal. That was no problem from the Yankees' standpoint. But the White Sox wanted other players as well, particularly young pitchers.

Hemond wanted Gil Patterson, a 21-year-old right-hander who was the Yankees' prize pitching prospect at the time. Several teams had tried to acquire Patterson, including the Reds, who offered Tony Perez, their perennial 100-RBI-per-year first baseman. Paul refused to consider offers for Patterson, whose career, it turned out, was ruined by arm injuries.

The talks continued with several other players being mentioned, but when spring training began, Dent was still with the White Sox. Then another complication developed. Mickey Klutts, the young infielder who was competing with Stanley for the Yankee shortstop job (pending the trade), suffered a broken middle finger on his left hand as a result of being slid into by the Orioles' Doug DeCinces in the second exhibition game of the spring.

The Yankees attempted to cover up the injury, realizing that the White Sox' asking price for Dent would go up once Hemond realized the Yankees were desperate for a shortstop. So Klutts' injury was announced as a "jammed, sprained finger." Klutts, of course, knew the finger was broken. He was staying at the team's headquarters hotel in Fort Lauderdale, the Galt Ocean Mile, and came out to the pool the day after the injury with his hand in a cast.

Reporter Moss Klein, sitting at the pool, asked how the "sprain" was doing.

"Sprain hell," said Klutts, disgusted at the development that was costing him a chance to win the shortstop job. "It's broken. They know it. They just don't want their trade talks to get screwed up."

Naturally it didn't take long for the White Sox to find out that Klutts' injury was far more serious than the Yankees were admitting. Now Chicago wanted two young pitchers in addition to Gamble. One would be LaMarr Hoyt, a 22-year-old right-hander who had won 15 games on the AA level in '76. The Yankees knew Hoyt had potential but were still willing to include him. The other pitcher the White Sox wanted was Guidry, a hard-throwing lefty who had had brief flings with the Yankees in '75 and '76.

Guidry was already nearing 27 and had been criticized by Steinbrenner after a shaky outing in spring training '76. That was when Steinbrenner said, in earshot of the young pitcher, "He'll never be more than a triple-A pitcher." Guidry proceeded to pack up his car and began driving home to Lafayette, Louisiana, before his wife, Bonnie, convinced him to turn around.

Now, Steinbrenner figured, if the deal for Dent hinges on Guidry, let's get it done. The White Sox' new manager was someone who knew all about Guidry: Bob Lemon. That's why they were demanding him. Lemon had been the Yankees' pitching coach in 1976 and had seen enough of Guidry to recognize his potential.

"I told our guys in Chicago to hold out for him but try not to make it too obvious," Lemon recalled years later. "They were asking for other guys but Guidry was the one we really wanted. I thought we were going to get him, too, but at the last minute they said there could be no deal if he was in it. So we made the other deal."

Why wasn't Guidry included? Because Gabe Paul had told Steinbrenner "over my dead body" when the Boss insisted on Guidry's inclusion to get the deal done.

The deal was completed on April 5, after the final spring training game had ended. Gamble, in fact, had already boarded the team bus for the Fort Lauderdale Airport and the flight home to New York. He was called off the bus and told he was headed for Chicago instead. The trade sent Gamble, Hoyt, and another pitcher, Bob Polinsky, to the White Sox—along with $250,000—for Dent. The Yankees had their shortstop, and even though Hoyt would go on to win the Cy Young Award in 1983 with a 24–10 record for the White Sox, Dent settled in for five-plus seasons as a quality shortstop and a big favorite of the New York fans. His home run to win the historic 1978 playoff game against the Red Sox went down as one of the 10 greatest moments in Yankee history. But if it hadn't been for Paul's refusals, the White Sox could have netted two Cy Young Award winners for Dent.

Gabe Paul deserves much of the credit as the architect of the late 1970s Yankee teams that brought back the winning tradition to Yankee Stadium. In 1973 he became the first president of the Steinbrenner-era Yankees and, in that role, executed a series of trades that turned the Yankees from also-rans into World Champions, including:

- Acquired first baseman Chris Chambliss and reliever Dick Tidrow from Cleveland on April 26, 1974, for pitchers Fritz Peterson, Steve Kline, Fred Beane, and Tom Buskey
- Acquired center fielder Mickey Rivers and pitcher Ed Figueroa from California on December 11, 1975, for outfielder Bobby Bonds
- Also on December 11, 1975, acquired second baseman Willie Randolph and pitchers Dock Ellis and Ken Brett from Pittsburgh for pitcher Doc Medich

Also, in unusual circumstances, Paul made a "bad trade" that turned out to be great for the Yankees. One of his final acts while still in Cleveland (before he joined up with Steinbrenner's group to buy the Yankees) was to trade third baseman Graig Nettles and backup catcher Jerry Moses to the Yankees on November 27, 1972, for catcher John Ellis, infielder Jerry Kenney, and outfielders Charlie Spikes and Rusty Torres.

Five weeks after that deal, Paul joined the Yankees and there were charges that he "rigged" the deal, knowing he was going to New York. In fact, he had dealt honestly, and it was other Indians officials who wanted to make the trade. Nettles was 28 at the time, and Paul had even predicted that he had the type of body that would break down by the time he was 32. Nettles was still playing at 44, after giving the Yankees nearly a decade of All-Star-caliber play at third base.

Paul left the Yankees after the 1977 season to return to the Indians as top executive, with a piece of the club. He had become anxious to escape because of the constant turmoil with the ever-more-active Steinbrenner, especially the battles involving Billy Martin.

Perhaps the last straw as far as Paul was concerned was the hassle Steinbrenner put him through for his 1977 World Series tickets. The late Yankee public relations director, Bob Fishel, recalled having seen Paul at his desk in near tears because he had been unable to secure Series tickets for his brother.

"George had commandeered all the tickets," Paul recalled years later, "including those I'd already paid for. I can tell you this, he didn't get to keep them. My brother went to the games."

Paul remained with the Indians until retiring in 1987. Ironically, he twice attempted to hire Martin as his manager in Cleveland, recognizing that, despite the inevitable commotion and problems, Billy's presence would still serve as a boost to Cleveland's sagging fortunes at the gate and on the field.

Paul was succeeded as George Steinbrenner's chief front office executive by Al Rosen, who learned quickly that there was hell to pay if another team completed a trade for a player the Yankees were seeking. During the 1978 season the Yankees made several attempts to acquire perennial American League batting champion Rod Carew from the Minnesota Twins. Carew was unhappy in Minnesota because of Twins' owner Calvin Griffith's penurious policies when it came to compensating his players. And the Twins, unwilling to meet Carew's salary demands, were making him available.

During the 1978 winter meetings in Orlando, the Carew auction became especially active, with the Yankees, Red Sox, Angels, and Giants all making significant bids for his services. On December 7 the Twins completed a deal with the Giants. It was the 37th anniversary of the Japanese bombing of Pearl Harbor, and it was a day that would live in infamy in the mind—and ears—of Al Rosen.

When the trade was announced, the Giants explained it was pending Carew's approval, which, it turned out, he didn't give. Moss Klein called Rosen in his suite at the headquarters hotel to ask about Carew and other matters. Rosen, always cooperative, told Klein he had to keep the phone lines clear but invited the reporter up for an interview.

A few minutes after Klein arrived in Rosen's suite, the telephone rang. Before answering, Rosen predicted: "George just heard about the Carew trade." Sure enough, Rosen picked up the phone and nodded. The next five minutes, nodding was all he had a chance to do, because the voice at the other end, blaring out of the receiver, was an enraged Steinbrenner, berating Rosen for allowing the Giants to sneak away with Carew.

Rosen tried to interject several times, never getting beyond "But, George…" Klein, meanwhile, sitting directly opposite Rosen, was increasingly uncomfortable about being a witness to this embarrassing scene. A few times Klein motioned to Rosen that he would leave the room, but each time Rosen waved his hand, indicating he should stay. And as the screaming on the other end of the phone went on and Rosen's face reddened in anger, he held the phone at a distance to give his ear a break.

Finally Rosen had enough. "George, there's no sense talking now. I'll get back to you when you've calmed down," he said. He didn't wait for a reply and just hung up.

Klein didn't know what to say. But Rosen, after taking a minute to calm down himself, laughed. "Nothing unusual about that," he said. "Part of life with the Yankees."

The trade with the Giants would have sent first baseman Mike Ivie, outfielder Jim Dwyer, minor league pitcher Phil Nastu, and $400,000 to the Twins for Carew. Steinbrenner had been ranting that the Yankees could have easily made a better offer.

Ultimately, Carew vetoed the deal, despite San Francisco's offer of a $4-million, five-year contract to him. Thus the auction was reopened with the Yankees again actively involved. Finally, on February 3, 1979, after nearly two months of daily talks with the Twins, Steinbrenner announced the Yankees were dropping out of the Carew hunt. The Yankees had emerged as finalists, with the Angels, and had offered first baseman Chris Chambliss, outfielder Juan Beniquez, and two minor league prospects. But Carew had been giving indications he wasn't enthused about playing for the Yankees, referring to them as "the zoo." That's when Steinbrenner decided he didn't want him.

Later that day Carew went to the Angels for outfielder Ken Landreaux, pitchers Paul Hartzell and Brad Havens, and catcher Dave Engle.

In July of 1979, after too many other Carew-type tongue lashings from Steinbrenner, Rosen resigned and went on to a highly successful front office career as general manager of the Houston Astros and San Francisco Giants. His 1½ years with the Yankees were not without considerable success, either, most notably the trade he completed on November 10, 1978, that brought Dave Righetti to the Yankees. In typical Rosen fashion he refused to take credit for the deal, instead citing scout Jerry Walker—and a lost suitcase—as the prime reasons for Righetti's inclusion.

In October of 1978 Rosen took a flight to Kansas City for the start of the American League playoffs between the Yankees and Royals. He was met at the airport by Walker. They waited at the airline carousel for Rosen's suitcase, but it never showed up.

"The luggage was lost, and I needed clothes and other things right away," Rosen recalled. "Jerry had a car, since he had been in Kansas City for about 10 days scouting the Royals. So he said he'd drive me to a shopping center.

"While we were driving, I said to Jerry, 'You saw a lot of minor league games this summer, tell me about some of the kids.'

"And he said, 'Well, there's one guy who really stands out. A left-handed pitcher who is the best prospect I've seen in years.'"

Walker proceeded to tell Rosen about Dave Righetti, the kid he had seen on a scorching July afternoon in Midland, Texas, when the 19-year-old pitcher struck out 21 batters. Of course Walker had filed a report on Righetti, but it hadn't been brought to Rosen's attention.

"I never heard of Dave Righetti before talking to Jerry," Rosen said. "But when a guy like Jerry Walker, who was very knowledgeable about pitching and who never went overboard about anybody, tells you he was this high on a kid, I decided we better go after him."

A few weeks later, after the Yankees completed their World Series triumph over the Dodgers, Rosen was getting involved in trade talks. He made a note: "Righetti, Texas. Walker says he can't miss." Rosen had been talking to Texas about a number of players but didn't want to let on the Yankees thought so highly of Righetti.

The Yankees had players Texas owner Brad Corbett wanted, particularly reliever Sparky Lyle and catcher Mike Heath. Lyle was the 1977 Cy Young Award winner but was available because Goose Gossage had taken over in 1978 as the Yankees' closing reliever.

"We didn't want to trade Heath," said Rosen, "because we saw him as the eventual successor to Thurman Munson. But we weren't entirely sold on his hitting ability, and the Rangers really wanted him."

Rosen and Steinbrenner, though, made it sound like Heath was an untouchable in their talks with Corbett, but maybe...if a couple of top prospects were included...they'd listen. The talks went on for another three weeks with dozens of players mentioned. The Rangers also needed money, which was never a problem in Steinbrenner deals. As long as Righetti was included, the Yankees would be cooperative.

On November 10 the deal was finalized. The Rangers agreed to include Righetti if the Yankees gave them both Lyle and Heath. Seven other players were thrown into the deal from both sides, but for the purposes of history, only Righetti is worth remembering. By 1981 he was the only one of the 10 players who hadn't either been traded again or released.

Jerry Walker, by the way, was dismissed by the Yankees after the 1982 season for no apparent reason. He had no trouble landing another job: Rosen hired him as pitching coach for the Astros.

The Righetti trade was the "up" side of serving as Steinbrenner's front office chief. On that one, Rosen and Steinbrenner worked in tandem toward a common goal and got the job done. Too often, however, Steinbrenner has seemed to work against his own people—with predictable results. The Boss' impetuous nature has led to him become quickly down on players, ordering their banishments and resulting in deals made in haste.

One such deal was consummated on May 23, 1979. A day earlier the Yankees had defeated the Tigers, 12–8, but nearly blew a nine-run lead. They were leading, 12–3, when the Tigers suddenly began battling back against Luis Tiant in the eighth inning. Dick Tidrow, one of the Yankees' most versatile and valuable pitchers on the pennant-winning teams of '76, '77, and '78, came on in relief and proceeded to give up four hits and three runs in 1⅔ innings, including a homer to Rusty Staub.

Minutes after the Yankees had managed to hold on for the win, Rosen got a call from Steinbrenner ordering him to "get rid of Tidrow."

Rather than argue, something he had grown weary of anyway, Rosen agreed to make a deal. He called his longtime friend Bob Kennedy, who was general manager of the Chicago Cubs.

"I felt like I owed Bob one," Rosen explained years later. "A year earlier we had gotten Ron Davis from him for Ken Holtzman. Holtzman was washed up, and Davis wound up winning 14 games in relief for us in 1979. Bob was looking kind of bad on the deal. So I offered him Tidrow, and he gave us Ray Burris."

Burris went 1–3, with a 6.11 ERA, in 15 games for the Yankees in '79 and was subsequently sold on waivers to the Mets. Tidrow, on the other hand, was 11–5, with a 2.71 ERA, in 63 games for the Cubs in '79 and led the National

League in appearances with 84 in 1980. In all, he had four top-quality seasons as a reliever with the Cubs before being traded to the White Sox in 1983.

Steinbrenner did not learn his lesson about making a trade out of spite, however. In 1984 he became disenchanted with left-hander Shane Rawley, who had won 14 and 11 games in his two previous seasons with the Yankees. Rawley was a bit of a flake and would experience periods of inconsistency. But most of the Yankees' pitching people agreed he had the stuff to be a big winner, and as a left-hander, he was even more valuable a commodity.

Nevertheless, when injuries and more inconsistency led to Rawley getting off to a slow start in 1984, Steinbrenner called General Manager Clyde King and said: "Get Rawley out of here. I don't care what you get for him, just get rid of him."

King obliged but knew he was dealing from weakness. He didn't have time to shop Rawley. The Boss wanted the deal done now. So he called the Phillies, who had made several earlier inquiries about Rawley, and agreed to a deal of Rawley for Marty Bystrom, a sore-armed right-hander, and Keith Hughes, a minor league outfielder of some promise. Bystrom was continually beset by injuries and won five games in two seasons for the Yankees, while Rawley won 51 over the next four years for Philadelphia, including a 17–11 season in 1987.

An even worse "spite trade" by the Yankees was Steinbrenner's August 26, 1987, banishment of Dennis Rasmussen, the big, soft-spoken left-hander from Omaha, Nebraska. Steinbrenner never liked Rasmussen, probably because of what Billy Martin always said of the six-foot-seven pitcher with the equally big, sweeping curve: "A guy that big oughta throw harder." Martin let everybody know that Rasmussen would never pitch on one of his staffs.

In the spring of 1986 Rasmussen was vying for a spot in Lou Piniella's starting rotation, having shuttled back and forth between Yankee Stadium and Columbus the previous two seasons. Piniella was determined to keep Rasmussen as one of his starting five but was not helped in that regard by Martin's presence (and constant criticisms of Rasmussen) around the camp that spring. Then one windy afternoon at Pompano Beach, in an exhibition game against the Texas Rangers, Rasmussen gave up three home runs, the last to Curtis Wilkerson, a pint-sized second baseman who had hit only six previous homers in his entire seven-year professional career.

The tiny, ramshackle Pompano ballpark had traditionally been a terrible place to evaluate pitchers, and on this day the wind was blowing out. Unfortunately for Rasmussen, Steinbrenner was at the game, sitting behind home plate. At the sight of the second homer off Rasmussen sailing over the right-center field fence, Steinbrenner turned to *New York Times* reporter Murray Chass (who was interviewing him about another story) and muttered, "Columbus, here I come."

Only a late-spring back injury to veteran Tommy John enabled Piniella to keep Rasmussen—although it proved to be a stroke of good fortune for the Yankees, as Rasmussen wound up leading the staff in victories (18) and innings pitched in '86. So much for small accomplishments, though. In 1987 Rasmussen became another in a long line of young Yankee pitchers to be asked, "What have you done for us lately?"

By late August he was 9–7 and obviously not going to match his 18 wins of the year before. Nevertheless, he was still only 28, and left-handers, as always, were at a premium. None of that mattered to Steinbrenner, though. The Boss wanted a pitcher with more experience and more "mental toughness" and told his general manager, Woody Woodward, to go through with a deal with the Cincinnati Reds, trading Rasmussen for right-hander Bill Gullickson.

In addition to making nearly $700,000 per year more than Rasmussen, Gullickson was also eligible for free agency at the end of the season, which was the primary reason the Reds wanted to move him. They didn't feel they could sign him. As it turned out, the Yankees didn't sign him, either. Amazingly, they went through with the deal without first getting Gullickson's signature on a new contract. Gullickson won four games in a lost cause down the September stretch for the Yankees, and then after taking offense at being initially offered a pay cut as a free agent, he skipped to Japan. The Yankees thus had nothing to show for Rasmussen, a still-promising left-handed pitcher, making barely $200,000. One can only guess what they could have gotten for him had Steinbrenner not acted in such haste and waited until the winter meetings the following December.

In fairness to Steinbrenner, the Reds didn't show much patience with Rasmussen, either. He stayed only a few months with Cincinnati in 1988 before being traded to San Diego for a nonprospect minor league relief pitcher named Candy Sierra. Rasmussen won only two games for the Reds, but with the Padres he went 14–4 the rest of the season.

One lasting memory of Rasmussen with the Yankees was that day in August of '87 when he came into the clubhouse to clean out his locker. As he removed his belongings, he pulled down a baseball card that had been struck in his name-plate above his locker. Turning to a couple of reporters who had come to bid him good-bye, he showed them the card and smiled knowingly. It was a card of Curtis Wilkerson.

There are some days that, looked back upon later, are microcosms of an entire season. Such a day was May 5, 1982, which more than captured all the elements of that zany and chaotic Yankee season. And the Yankees didn't even play a game that day.

Wednesday, May 5, was a scheduled off day for the Yankees, a day on which they were to fly to Seattle for the start of a two-week West Coast road trip. But when the clock struck midnight, signaling the end of May 4 and the dawning of May 5, the Yankees were still on the field in the process of losing a 13-inning game to the Oakland Athletics at Yankee Stadium.

The Yankees were in bad shape. The loss to Oakland, which closed out the home stand, dropped their record to 9–13. The "speed team" that George Steinbrenner had envisioned during the off-season and through spring training had become a colossal blunder. The Yankees clearly weren't running circles around anyone, and they were rarely running circles around the bases, having hit a grand total of 10 homers in 22 games.

Steinbrenner was beside himself with anger. His players were making him look bad again, and so when the game against Oakland ended at 12:08 A.M., with the A's winning, 9–7, he swung into action. He telephoned Gene Michael, who had replaced Bob Lemon as manager 10 days earlier and was already deeply regretting it.

"I want a workout tomorrow," Steinbrenner told Michael.

"But, George, we have a flight to Seattle," Michael protested.

"Then have the workout before the flight," Steinbrenner barked. "These guys have to see there's a penalty for playing the way they've played."

Next, Steinbrenner ordered Vice President Bill Bergesch to finalize a trade that had been discussed with the Toronto Blue Jays for several days. The Yankees would be getting veteran first baseman John Mayberry from Toronto for first baseman Dave Revering and minor league third baseman Jeff Reynolds.

Mayberry was a power hitter with a patented left-handed Yankee Stadium swing. Or at least he had been for many years. With their speed team stuck in the blocks, the Yankees were switching the power back on. In addition to the acquisition of Mayberry, minor league strongman Steve Balboni was to be summoned from Columbus as the right-handed designated hitter.

Most of the Yankees didn't make it home after the Oakland game until two in the morning. Then there was packing to be completed for the long trip. And instead of a leisurely, midafternoon flight to Seattle, there was now a late-morning workout to contend with, which predictably led to a grumbling, discontented state that would characterize the team all season.

"We're being punished, that's all," said Rich Gossage when he arrived at the stadium the next morning. "A slap on the wrist for losing too many games. The workout doesn't accomplish anything, even he [Steinbrenner] must realize that. But we're getting used to this shit."

"We're definitely going to lead the league in one thing—burnout," added Tommy John. "We'll be the first team in the majors to simply wear out."

Oscar Gamble was the angriest of the Yankees. He had seen limited playing time (26 at-bats in those 22 games) because of a Steinbrenner decree. Gamble had exercised his veto power to kill a trade with Texas in late March that would have brought slugger Al Oliver to the Yankees. Steinbrenner even offered Gamble money to waive his veto, but Gamble refused, despite threats by the owner. Now Gamble realized he had blundered, because Steinbrenner ordered Lemon and then Michael to keep him virtually inactive.

"I've had more workouts than at-bats," said Gamble. "It's ridiculous. I'm not trying to be no team spokesman, but all the guys are mad. Working out this morning ain't gonna do nobody no good. I'm ready to waive my trade rights now—for the right amount of cash."

The entire workout lasted 50 minutes, hardly enough time to accomplish anything. It had clearly been a punishment exercise. Then the embittered players dressed again and prepared for the flight to Seattle.

The beat writers who were accompanying the team, however, had been occupied during the workout with the information that Revering was being traded to Toronto for Mayberry. They were given the information by publicity director Irv Kaze but were instructed not to say anything to Revering, since the deal "wasn't completely finalized." It was finalized enough, Kaze explained, that the writers could write and send their stories to their papers so they wouldn't miss their deadlines by waiting until the team got to Seattle.

The writers zipped through their stories, assuming they'd have a chance to talk to Revering after the workout and fill in a few quotes. But when the workout ended, they were told not to say anything to Revering. Revering, still unaware of anything, dressed and got on the bus for the airport with everyone else.

"Doesn't he know he's being traded?" the writers asked Kaze.

"I guess not," Kaze replied, equally puzzled.

To understand why Revering was being made to accompany the team on a six-hour flight to Seattle, when it was known that the trade had been completed, it is necessary to understand that he wasn't a favorite of Steinbrenner's. Revering had fooled the Yankees by being too good in spring training, playing over his head and winning the first base job. He cooled off toward the end of spring training after hurting his leg by tripping on a seam rounding first base in the New Orleans Superdome. He had been told he was the Yankees' everyday first baseman—a status that lasted for the first game of the season. Not even the first day, because snowouts had forced the Yankees to play a rare opening-day doubleheader against the White Sox. Revering went hitless in the opener and was benched for the second game, never to regain his "regular" status.

Revering was indeed a strange character. He was laid-back, seemingly in his own world, and clearly didn't fit in the frenzied Yankee scene. In fact, he would last only three months with Toronto. Later that year, when reporters Klein and Madden asked Toronto manager Bobby Cox about his two designated hitters, Wayne Nordhagen and Revering, he explained why they would have to be replaced. "One guy [Nordhagen] is fucking finished," said Cox, "and the other guy [Revering] is fucking nuts."

Revering finished out the '82 season with the Seattle Mariners and never played again in the majors. At 28, the onetime rising young star with the Oakland A's in the late seventies was through.

But on this day, May 5, 1982, he was merely puzzled. As soon as the team bus arrived at the Seattle hotel, before Revering even picked up his key, he was informed that he had been traded to Toronto. That meant he had to join the Blue Jays in Toronto, flying all the way back across the country. A simple New York-Toronto flight would have taken less than an hour and spared him two cross-country treks in one day.

Revering didn't seem to mind, though. He was just glad to be escaping the Yankees. "I wanted to get out," he said. "Steinbrenner has this team in a state of confusion. Everybody's worried about going 0 for 4 because that means getting benched. So nobody wants to advance the base runners or anything like that. It's a mess here, and this little move isn't going to change anything."

Revering was right. The acquisition of Mayberry was a desperate move to restore power to the Yankee lineup, and it failed miserably. Mayberry was 32, in the second year of a four-year, $3.2-million contract, and the Blue Jays couldn't wait to dump him. Their problem was most scouts had observed Mayberry (who had lost his starting first base job at Toronto to rookie Willie Upshaw) and reported that he had lost it.

Unfortunately, Yankee scout Birdie Tebbetts, who had a long history of making shrewd appraisals of ball players, happened to attend a game three days earlier in which Mayberry hit two homers against the Red Sox—his only two homers of the season to that point. Consequently, Tebbetts turned in a positive report, and the trade went through. Boston manager Ralph Houk, the former Yankee manager and general manager who had no love for Steinbrenner, later said, "If that's why they went ahead and got Mayberry, then I've never been happier to have two homers hit against me."

Mayberry, the former Kansas City star who had hit 247 career homers before coming to the Yankees, had indeed lost it. He hit .209 for the Yankees in 1982, with eight homers and 27 RBIs in 69 games. Just another dud in a season of flops. He was released the following year in spring training with the Yankees owing him nearly $500,000.

The 1982 season was unquestionably the most chaotic of the Steinbrenner era, a dismal failure in almost every respect. In January of 1983, as part of Steinbrenner's general shakeup of the Yankee hierarchy, Murray Cook was hired as director of player development. Cook had previously spent 19 relatively peaceful and productive years in the Pittsburgh Pirates organization, working his way up to director of minor leagues and scouting in 1976 when he was only 35 years old. By June of '83 Cook was named Yankee general manager, a promotion that marked the end of his anonymity and tranquility.

Billy Martin was in his third tour of duty as Yankee manager, and it didn't take long for Cook to run afoul of him on almost every personnel decision. Martin never could get along with any general manager, and in Cook he saw a Steinbrenner-acclaimed "boy wonder" who didn't have one-tenth of the baseball knowledge or experience that he had.

Cook had the further misfortune of being the GM during the pine-tar episode, and he was in charge when Goose Gossage decided to leave as a free agent. But the ultimate misfortune for Murray Cook was being the victim of a questionable loophole in the baseball rules that cost the Yankees a promising young pitching prospect named Tim Belcher.

The Belcher case was the final straw as far as Steinbrenner was concerned. Even though none of the pine-tar, Martin, Gossage, or Belcher problems were Cook's doing, Cook was basically "disappeared" by Steinbrenner in 1984, quarantined to the Yankee offices back in New York while the rest of team and front office officials were in spring training. When he finally did show up in Fort Lauderdale that spring, he was rarely sighted, spending most of his time in the trailer offices. Years later, writers used to joke about spring training colleagues who hadn't gotten much sun as having "Murray Cook tans."

Cook had made a number of trades after taking over in June of '83, following his meteoric and ill-fated rise. Some of them were forced on Martin, who would then refuse to give the new players much of a chance.

On August 10 Cook traded center fielders with the Astros, sending Jerry Mumphrey to Houston for Omar Moreno, a former Pirate whom Cook had known from his days in Pittsburgh.

"It was time to trade Mumphrey," Cook related years later. "He was going downhill. The only team interested was Houston, and Moreno wasn't playing well for them. I knew Moreno could play center field, and that's what we needed at the time. Unfortunately, a week before the trade Mumphrey started to play well, and Billy didn't want to give him up."

Moreno had a quick start as a Yankee and then faded. Martin never liked him. He liked him even less when Klein told him Moreno had a clause in his contract that paid him $214.29 every time he came to bat. Martin pinch-hit for him often, noting with a laugh, "Cost him another two hundred."

Steinbrenner didn't blame Cook directly for the pine-tar episode or the Gossage defection, although both incidents caused plenty of headaches for the front office staff. When Gossage announced he wouldn't return, the addition of another pitcher was imperative, and Steinbrenner ordered Cook to sign veteran knuckleballer Phil Niekro, who had been recommended by the Boss' chief adviser, Clyde King.

"I was at a resort in Poconos with friends on New Year's Day," Cook said, "one of those rare one-day breaks. But George found me. He got hold of me early that morning and told me to get working on the Niekro signing. He didn't want him slipping away. I tracked down Bruce Church, Niekro's agent, and told him there was some urgency. I wound up spending the whole day on the phone while my friends were enjoying the resort. But we got Niekro."

That, it turned out, was the last major accomplishment of the brief Murray Cook regime. Because on February 8, 1984, he was done in by a bizarre set of circumstances that he couldn't possibly have foreseen.

The Oakland Athletics, entitled to a pick in the free-agent compensation pool because they lost free-agent pitcher Tom Underwood to Baltimore, selected Tim Belcher from the Yankees. In those days there was a general pool of available players as compensation for teams that lost free agents to other teams. Each team was allowed to protect 26 players in its organization, and those left unprotected were eligible to be selected from the pool. The system, since abandoned, was the result of the negotiations that settled the 1981 players' strike.

The Yankees had what appeared to be a legitimate protest, however. They had only just signed Belcher on February 2, after having made him the number one pick in the January amateur draft. The protected lists for the free-agent compensation pool had to be submitted on January 16. Therefore the Yankees had no chance to protect Belcher. How could they lose a player they couldn't protect?

The Yankees protested, but as with all their other protests to American League President Lee MacPhail that year, they lost. MacPhail was sympathetic but acknowledged that Oakland had found a loophole and was within its rights to take Belcher under the existing rules.

When the call initially came to Cook's office, informing Cook of Oakland's selection of Belcher, he vented his outrage, vowed to protest, and then took the most advisable measure possible at the time. He summoned team counsel Mel Southard and minor league director Dave Hersh into his office, closed the door, and got out a bottle of scotch.

"We sat around, discussed the news, and talked about what George's reaction would be," Cook said. "Then we had a few drinks as we tried to decide who should break the news to George. Let's say we were confident he wasn't going to take it well."

Steinbrenner was furious. Less than a week earlier he had ordered a press conference at Yankee Stadium for Belcher and the young pitcher's parents. This was a prize prospect, who had been the number one pick of the Minnesota Twins in the previous June's amateur draft but had turned them down when they didn't come up with enough money. The Yankees had dispatched their three top pitching people, Clyde King and coaches Jeff Torborg and Sammy Ellis, to watch Belcher throw at a specially arranged workout at his college, Mt. Vernon Nazarene in Ohio, and they came back with rave reports of his 93-mile-per-hour fastball.

So the Yankees had selected Belcher, signed him, and lost him through that dangling loophole.

Steinbrenner, who accepts no excuses, decided that Cook should have detected that loophole. The Oakland officials had, hadn't they? If the Yankees had held off signing Belcher, Oakland couldn't have selected him, because technically he wasn't a member of the Yankee organization unless he signed a contract. Cook had approved the contract, so Belcher's loss was Cook's fault.

Cook was a marked man. He was soon cut off by Steinbrenner from the team's operations as King moved in. On April 9, 1984, less than 10 months after Cook had been named general manager, the title was bestowed on King. After enduring several months of nonentity status in the Yankee front office, Cook resigned and went on to serve as general manager of both the Montreal Expos and Cincinnati Reds.

Though he had long enjoyed status as George Steinbrenner's most trusted adviser, Clyde King discovered that it is far easier to get the Boss' ear when you're *not* his general manager. As GM from 1984 through 1986, King was successful in bringing in such productive players as Rickey Henderson, Brian Fisher, Ron Hassey, Doug Drabek, and Tim Stoddard via trades, while ridding the Yankees of such high-priced, unwanted disappointments as Ed Whitson, Roy Smalley, and Steve Kemp. But as successful as King might have been in the GM's role, he found himself continually butting heads with Steinbrenner.

It was almost as if the Boss resented King getting credit for the many deals that worked out well for the Yankees. In the end, Steinbrenner was making the deals himself, with King the last to know about them. That was certainly the case on July 30, 1986, when the Yankees sent Hassey, minor league third baseman Carlos Martinez, and a "player to be named later" to the Chicago White Sox for shortstop Wayne Tolleson, catcher Joel Skinner, and designated hitter Ron Kittle. The Yankees were playing in Milwaukee that night, and King was sitting by himself, observing the team from an auxiliary press box behind home plate, when Bill Madden approached him.

"Clyde," said Madden, "there's a rumor running rampant in the press box that you guys have a big trade with the White Sox going."

"If there is," said King, "I don't know anything about it. Then again, George does his own deals with the White Sox. I'm not allowed to talk to them."

As it was, King can probably be thankful he wasn't a party to that particular deal, because the repercussions were quite nasty. It seems that, in exchange for being provided with precisely the players he needed at the time—a catcher, a shortstop, and a right-handed power hitter—Steinbrenner promised the White Sox help for the following year. It was verbally agreed the "player to be named later" whom the White Sox were to get would be promising young pitcher Doug Drabek.

However, because Drabek was already on the Yankees' 25-man roster, it was illegal for him to be a "player to be named later" in a trade—a fact that White Sox' general manager "Hawk" Harrelson was unaware of. Then, in November of that year, Steinbrenner used Drabek in a big trade with Pittsburgh to get pitcher Rick Rhoden. By that time Harrelson was gone as the White Sox general manager. Sox board chairman Jerry Reinsdorf (who was also unaware of the illegality of the arrangement) was understandably upset, especially when the player he wound up getting as a replacement for Drabek turned out to be a journeyman minor league catcher named Bill Lindsey.

Reinsdorf, who had become Steinbrenner's principal ally among the American League owners, was now being roasted in the Chicago press for making such a one-sided deal with the Yankees. But he apparently didn't want to make an issue of it once he learned of the illegality of the arrangement.

Some suspected that Steinbrenner was merely trying to make up for *his* embarrassment over the December 1985 trade between the two clubs in which the White Sox gave the Yankees left-hander Britt Burns, knowing he had a congenital hip condition that could end his career. In that deal Steinbrenner was advised by Yankee team physician, Dr. John Bonamo, not to acquire Burns, but he went ahead with it anyway. Burns subsequently broke down in spring training and never pitched again.

So Bonamo had been right: But when Dr. Bonamo left the room that day after giving his thumbs-down report on Burns, Steinbrenner turned to the others and said, "What does he know about baseball? He's a doctor. We're baseball men."

In March, after Burns faltered and it was announced he'd be sidelined for the season, Steinbrenner still had hopes of salvaging the trade, in unusual style. "Don't worry," he told manager Lou Piniella and the coaches. "They're saying he's never going to pitch again, but I know some experts in the field of hip surgery at the University of Florida. I'm going to send him there. I think they may even be able to fit him with an artificial hip. He could be back this summer."

As one staff member said: "When George started talking about this poor guy pitching with an artificial hip, I figured he had really gone over the edge. He just didn't want to admit that he had screwed up by going ahead with that trade. Can you imagine a guy pitching with an artificial hip?"

In all, over a 23-month period the Yankees and White Sox made six trades with each other, sending 31 players back and forth from December of 1985 to November of '87. Both Hassey and minor league shortstop Mike Soper went back and forth three times, while pitcher Neil Allen was traded from the Yankees to the White Sox, released by the White Sox, and subsequently signed again by the Yankees. Someone quite cleverly dubbed this chummy relationship between the two clubs "The Burns and Allen Show."

One trade Steinbrenner *didn't* make with the White Sox—and probably should have—involved future Hall of Famer Tom Seaver. It was the spring of 1986. Seaver, the onetime "franchise" of the crosstown Mets, was now 40 years old, and although he was still pitching effectively, he was making $1 million a year and really kind of wasting away with the second-division White Sox. He was also urging Harrelson to trade him to a contender closer to his home in Greenwich, Connecticut, and Harrelson was trying earnestly to oblige.

The Yankees were a natural. Steinbrenner had always been infatuated with marquee names, and there was no bigger marquee name in New York than Tom Seaver. The Yankees also needed another starting pitcher to—hopefully—put them over the top in a tight American League East pennant race. And lastly, Seaver desperately wanted to go to the Yankees, so much so that he talked frequently with Bill Madden that spring, asking him to relay his sentiments to Steinbrenner.

Madden did, and Steinbrenner seemed interested but, surprisingly, only mildly. In his initial talks involving Seaver, Steinbrenner said Harrelson was trying to hold him up, asking for, first, starting pitcher Dennis Rasmussen (who was nearly 12 years Seaver's junior) and, later, third baseman Mike Pagliarulo.

"I'd like Tom Seaver," Steinbrenner said. "I think the world of him. But I'm not giving up a front-line player for him."

After weeks of on-again, off-again Seaver talks with the Yankees, Harrelson went to Steinbrenner in late June with a proposal of Seaver and two second-line relief pitchers, Bill Dawley and Bryan Clark, for Brian Fisher (the Yankees' number-two reliever behind Dave Righetti that year) and the aforementioned Carlos Martinez, who was then a highly touted, six-foot-six minor league shortstop. It was the inclusion of Martinez that most troubled Steinbrenner. He was concerned about a fan backlash for trading another of his top minor league prospects for an aging veteran who would give him, at best, two years. It was pointed out to him by Madden that scouts were pretty much agreed Martinez was growing too big to play shortstop and would probably have to be switched to third base or the outfield. Also, as a right-handed hitter, he would have to really hit for power to fill one of those positions at Yankee Stadium.

As Steinbrenner debated with himself, Harrelson started looking elsewhere to trade Seaver and reached a tentative agreement on a deal with the Red Sox. The reason it had to be tentative was because Reinsdorf wanted to give Steinbrenner first refusal on Seaver before sending the star pitcher to the Boss' arch-rivals.

Finally Steinbrenner said he was going to pass on the deal. (He later revealed that he was most concerned about his acquisition of Seaver being perceived as his way of showing up the Mets, who had twice let Seaver go.) The pangs of conscience on Steinbrenner's part came back to haunt him in the months to come, when Seaver (who was traded to Boston for backup third baseman Steve Lyons) pitched well for the Red Sox over the final two months of the season and probably made the difference in their winning the American League East pennant.

Meanwhile, Clyde King was busy on all the other trade fronts, but finding it increasingly difficult to get Steinbrenner's approval on anything. One of King's first deals—or at least what he *thought* was a deal—was a six-player trade with the Red Sox in June of 1984 that would have ridded the Yankees of two of Steinbrenner's most unwanted players, Roy Smalley and Shane Rawley. In return for Smalley and Rawley, the Red Sox agreed to give King pitchers Steve Crawford and Mark Clear, outfielder Reid Nichols, and third baseman Lyons, who was then in the minor leagues. That deal would probably have been made had Smalley not hit a long home run the night before it was to be announced. When that happened, Steinbrenner feared Smalley might come back to haunt the Yankees with a sudden home run spree in Boston, and he nixed the deal.

Later that season King had another deal that would have gone down in history as one of the best the Yankees ever made. The Tigers were looking to make room in their lineup for a young left-handed power hitter named Mike Laga and had decided to dump Darrell Evans, the 37-year-old lefty-hitting first baseman/designated hitter whom they had signed as a free agent the previous winter. Evans had a three-year contract that paid him in excess of $750,000 per, and the Tigers were just looking for anyone who would take that off their hands.

King had managed Evans years earlier with the Atlanta Braves and had always liked his professionalism and his quiet leadership in the clubhouse. He also felt that in Yankee Stadium he could provide the Yankees with some needed long-ball pop from the left side. When the Tigers approached him about Evans, he asked them what they wanted in return. Their answer was Mike Armstrong, a sidearming middle relief pitcher who was one of many to have succumbed to the pressures of pitching for the Yankees.

King was excited. Armstrong was barely the 10th pitcher on the Yankee staff, someone he figured he would probably have to release at season's end, and here were the Tigers offering Darrell Evans for him! He went to Steinbrenner to get quick approval for the deal before the Tigers changed their minds, only to be bitterly disappointed when the Boss said no.

Why? For perhaps the first time in his stewardship of the Yankees, Steinbrenner felt it was not a good idea to take on an aging player with a big contract. The Boss' restraint proved to be a critical mistake. Evans went on to hit 40, 29, and 34 homers in his next three seasons and played a pivotal leadership role on the Tigers' 1984 world championship team. For them it was a classic case of "the best trades are often the ones you don't make."

One other King trade that Steinbrenner undoubtedly regrets vetoing nearly took place in January of 1985. Murray Cook was then in Montreal, running the Expos, and one of his first orders of business was to pare the payroll. In particular, he wanted to unload right-hander Bill Gullickson, who had averaged nearly 15 wins per season over the past four years but who was making nearly $900,000 per.

Cook was also locked in what appeared to be futile contract negotiations with veteran slugger Andre Dawson, who was due to become a free agent after the '86 season. In particular, Cook was concerned about Dawson's knee, which had severely curtailed him in 1984. (Dawson, himself, conceded that the everyday pounding on the artificial turf at Montreal's Olympic Stadium had taken its toll on the knee.)

Anyway, Cook flew into New York one cold January morning and met with King at Yankee Stadium. He had a proposal: Dawson and Gullickson to the Yankees for pitchers Dennis Rasmussen and Rich Bordi and outfielders Dan Pasqua and Henry Cotto.

After mulling it over, Steinbrenner decided the price tag on re-signing Dawson was too high and that his knee problems made him too much of a long-term risk. In addition, he felt that the 23-year-old Pasqua held too much promise as a left-handed power hitter in Yankee Stadium to part with him just yet. Eventually, Dawson wound up walking on the Expos, who failed in their efforts to trade him someplace else. He signed as a free agent with the Cubs, and playing half his games on the grass surface of Wrigley Field, he led the National League in homers (49) and RBIs (137) in 1987 and was named Most Valuable Player. The other cruel irony from the Yankees' standpoint was that in that same 1987 season, they wound up getting Gullickson—in a trade for Rasmussen! Like Dawson with the Expos, Gullickson walked on the Yankees, accepting a lucrative offer from Japan and leaving the Yankees empty-handed.

Lou Piniella knew all about life as a Yankee from the standpoint of player, coach, and manager. And he thought he knew about life as a general manager, too, having dealt closely with several front office execs, especially Woody Woodward. But when Piniella would occasionally seek refuge in Woodward's company, visiting the understanding and sympathetic GM in his office, he learned a valuable lesson.

"Being the general manager is even worse than being the manager," Piniella told reporters Klein and Madden on several occasions in 1987. "At least I get to escape on trips sometimes. That poor guy is stuck in that office and keeps getting hammered day after day. I was up there talking to Woody, and he opened up his top drawer, and I'm telling you it looks like a pharmacy in there. Poor Woody. He's got more pills than the trainer carries around."

By the time the '87 season ended, Piniella knew he wasn't coming back as manager. Even if Steinbrenner wanted him back, which he didn't, Piniella would have refused. They had an amicable meeting on Thursday, October 15, and agreed they would both think about other possibilities for Piniella. Four days later, the same day Billy Martin was announced as returning for the fifth time as manager, there was another announcement. Lou Piniella was being named the Yankees' general manager to replace Woodward, who had resigned.

Why would Piniella take the job he had already labeled as the worst of all Yankee fates? It was an interesting opportunity and a way of remaining in the New York area, which meant he wouldn't have to go elsewhere for a job, uprooting the family and his various business interests. There was also the inducement of more money. And there was one other factor—the timing.

"George called me with the general manager idea early that afternoon," Piniella recalled. "Do you know what day that was?"

Piniella, a heavy investor in the stock market since his playing days, grimly recited that dark date. "October 19, 1987, the day of the crash."

Piniella was at his restaurant, Winners, in Woodbridge, New Jersey, that afternoon. But all Piniella had that day were losers. His stocks were plummeting, collapsing faster than his pitching staff had. Shortly after noon, one of his waitresses approached, knowing this was a bad time. But she had an important message: Mr. Steinbrenner was on the phone.

"He said he wanted me to be the general manager," Piniella related. "Just like that. We had never talked about it before, but I knew Woody was leaving. The thing was, I wasn't even paying attention to George. All I was thinking was IBM was down 43 points. Truthfully, George could have offered me any job at that point—he could have asked me to be the team janitor—and I would have accepted."

So the new GM went to work, only to find the GM seat even hotter than the manager's. Even worse, it seemed as if somebody—usually Steinbrenner—was always pulling the seat out from under you.

In addition to having to deal with Martin, no easy task in itself, Piniella had to cope with players' agents, such as the eccentric William Goodstein, representative for free agent Dave Righetti. Goodstein, a New York lawyer and self-promoter of outrageous extremes, conducted two months of self-serving publicity stunts, including a threat that Righetti was about to be shanghaied to Japan for $10 million. Piniella was forced to endure all the machinations of Goodstein (who made sure to arrange all his announcements around TV appearances), before finally re-signing Righetti.

But in addition to Martin and Goodstein and the other agents and the huge amount of office and telephone work that was so unfamiliar to Piniella, there was also Steinbrenner to contend with.

The Yankees needed a shortstop, a need that became more pressing when it was learned that Wayne Tolleson, the incumbent who had missed half of '87 because of a shoulder injury, would require surgery. Because of the delay, Tolleson probably wouldn't be ready until July at the earliest. There weren't a whole lot of shortstops available. There rarely are. But Piniella knew of one who could help the Yankees: Rafael Santana.

The only problem was that Santana, a onetime Yankee minor league prospect, was now with the Mets, and the Yankees and the Mets rarely did business together. Nevertheless, Piniella was convinced this was a natural, and his general manager counterpart with the Mets, Joe McIlvaine, thought so, too. The Mets were developing a young shortstop in Kevin Elster and were looking to move Santana out to make room for him, but they were especially fond of Santana and appreciative of his contribution to their world championship season of 1986. As such, they wanted to make sure to trade him to a team he'd be happy with. As McIlvaine said: "We're not looking to hold the Yankees up here. We just want to take care of Raffy."

Piniella and McIlvaine quickly struck a deal: the Mets would send Santana to the Yankees for three minor leaguers of only minimum promise, catcher Phil Lombardi, outfielder Darren Reed, and pitcher Steve Frey. The agreement was completed at the winter meetings in Dallas on December 10. Piniella told McIlvaine that only the formality of Steinbrenner's approval was needed.

Steinbrenner, who had been at the meetings, left earlier in the day. When Piniella reached him that night, the initial reaction to the proposed trade was silence. Not a good sign. Then Steinbrenner spoke. He didn't like it. Three for one? Those Mets were trying to put something over on the rookie general manager Piniella. McIlvaine must know something about one of the young players that had escaped all of the Yankee people.

Steinbrenner wanted a player in addition to Santana to even up the trade. And since Steinbrenner had been at the meetings, he had picked up a copy of *Baseball America,* a publication that focuses on minor league players.

"How about that kid on the cover?" Steinbrenner said. "What's his name? Jefferson?"

Piniella winced. The player Steinbrenner was referring to was Gregg Jefferies, the Mets' phenom. He tried to explain to Steinbrenner that the Mets wouldn't trade Jefferies even if the Yankees offered to include Don Mattingly in the deal. But Steinbrenner chided him and told him to ask McIlvaine about Jefferies or else there was no deal.

Piniella was disgusted. He was not going to ask McIlvaine about Jefferies. That would be too embarrassing. But he had to inform McIlvaine that the trade was off. Around lunchtime on December 11, Piniella was about ready to give up.

"I guess we just won't have a shortstop," he told Klein and Madden. "Can you believe this?"

But publicity director Harvey Greene, who was with Piniella, kept imploring that he "get back to George and tell him how important this is."

Piniella agreed. He would make one more effort. This time Steinbrenner listened, but not without making a demand and a warning: "Get one more player anyway," he told Piniella. "And don't forget—this is your trade. If those kids help the Mets or this guy Santana stinks, we'll know whose fault it is."

Piniella hurried up to McIlvaine's suite. The Mets GM was napping, but Piniella pounded on the door until McIlvaine responded. Piniella wanted to get this deal done, right away, before the Boss changed his mind again. McIlvaine agreed to add a minor league pitcher named Victor Garcia. That was good enough. Piniella didn't care if Garcia was the batboy at Tidewater. The two

GMs hurried down to the press room to announce the historic trade between the two New York teams. Santana, who would go on to play 148 games the following season and hit .240, was switching boroughs from Queens to the Bronx, and Jefferies, or whatever his name was, was still property of the Mets.

Not surprisingly, Piniella was able to take the tedium of the general manager's office for barely a half a season. He resigned on May 27, accepting a reduced role as special assignments scout, player evaluator, and consultant. Looking back on it a few months later, Piniella conceded that Steinbrenner had not really bothered him. Dealing with Martin and all *his* foibles—especially his trashing of Santana when the shortstop dropped a double-play ball against the Blue Jays early in the season in Toronto—was far more wearing on Piniella.

He did manage to have some fun in the job because, if there was one thing Piniella always seemed to maintain, it was his sense of humor. One prime example of that was a rainy night in Fort Lauderdale in spring training. The Yankees were playing an exhibition game, which had been delayed by a heavy thunderstorm. In the executive trailer Steinbrenner was raging over a myriad of minor problems that had developed during the day and was now further annoyed by the rain delay.

Piniella, sitting in his adjacent office, listened to Steinbrenner ranting and decided he needed some relief. How to redirect the Boss' fury? Suddenly it hit him: the water hog! The water hog was a new machine the Yankees had bought for the removal of excess water on the field.

"Hey, George," Piniella said, "how come they're not using the water hog out there on the field? Didn't you pay $10,000 for that thing? It's taking forever for them to get that field dried up!"

Steinbrenner momentarily stopped his raging and looked at Piniella.

"Goddamn it," he said, "that's the first brilliant idea you've had since you became general manager!"

With that, Steinbrenner got on the phone and began redirecting his wrath at Mark Zettlemeyer, the president of the Fort Lauderdale ball club, and the groundskeepers. That, in turn, was Piniella's cue to slip out of the office and disappear for the rest of the night. Saved by the water hog.

CHAPTER 11

The PR Men: The Midget, Bottoms Up, and Other Tales of Yankee-Panky

In January of 1984 the New York Chapter of the Baseball Writers Association hosted a dinner at Shea Stadium, honoring eight of the most tireless, tolerant, and maligned individuals in the game—all of them Yankee public relations directors under George Steinbrenner. Steinbrenner was himself invited to attend but declined. Actually, he initially attempted to sabotage the affair by issuing an order that Yankee employees were not to attend. The day of the dinner, however, he relented somewhat, issuing a list of those who would be permitted to attend as Yankee representatives. Yankee president Gene McHale was also told he could attend the dinner "to take attendance." If an employee who wasn't on the list showed up, the inference was that he or she would not remain a Yankee employee.

Steinbrenner missed a great evening of entertainment. He obviously feared the embarrassing nature of the stories that might be told, because, in truth, nobody in baseball has endured more outrageous abuse, worked longer hours, and received less pay for their efforts than the Yankee PR men of the Steinbrenner era.

But while telling the humorous stories of their experiences that night, the PR men came more to praise Steinbrenner than to bury him. Working for the Boss, as demanding and unreasonable as he can be, was viewed by most as an experience they would never forget—and which not only improved their resumes but prepared them for future jobs better than any basic training camp ever prepared soldiers for war.

In truth, being Steinbrenner's PR man is a constant war that, one soon discovers, can never be won. As soon as the first crisis is defused, a second one explodes on another front. Be it Billy Martin, Reggie Jackson, Lou Piniella, Dave Winfield, Lee MacPhail, the American League umpires, the city of New York, or (depending on the week) one or all of the New York newspapers, Steinbrenner is constantly at war with somebody. There is no such thing as peace and tranquility among the Steinbrenner Yankees, and at the pulse center of all this turmoil is the Yankee public relations director.

There were 10 public relations directors in the first 17 years of Steinbrenner's reign of terror, a lineup that is a Murderers' Row in its own right. One of the last and most enduring victims, the indefatigable Harvey Greene, made it to four opening days—a record. Greene had insisted he would never leave the Yankees until he got a World Series ring, and for three-plus years he willingly played the role of punching bag, taking Steinbrenner's best shots and bouncing right back for more abuse. Finally, though, all the banishments to his room on the road, the verbal beratings, and the negative press releases he was ordered to issue on Winfield took their toll. And when an offer from the NFL Miami Dolphins came his way in spring training of 1989, he gave up his dream for a ring and followed the path of his eight predecessors.

Not immediately, however.

Steinbrenner, furious over Greene's desire to leave, at first refused to even consider allowing him to resign. "You're not going anywhere," he told Greene when the diligent and unflappable PR man came in to the Boss' office to give his two weeks' notice.

Instead, Steinbrenner called Dolphins owner Joe Robbie and threatened not to play a scheduled exhibition game at Miami's Joe Robbie Stadium the following spring because Robbie had hired away one of his employees. Robbie, not wishing to lose favor with Steinbrenner, told Greene to try and mollify the Yankee boss and somehow make a clean exit. Suddenly Greene was a captive, not certain if he was going to be able to take the job that had been offered to him and that he'd accepted. In the meantime, he knew if he had to stay with the Yankees, it was only a matter of time until Steinbrenner would fire him for supposedly being disloyal.

It wasn't until May 1 that he finally was able to leave without further repercussions, and Arthur Richman, a longtime friend of Steinbrenner's who had worked for 26 years for the Mets, became the Boss' PR man number 10. Actually, Greene was replaced by a triumvirate of PR men, which surely proved his value to the Yankees. Richman, it seems, was brought in merely to serve as an overseer for a pair of recent PR interns, Jeff Idelson and Jim Dunnigan, who performed all the day-to-day duties of the job.

Richman, who coincidentally had the good sense to have prepared a list of pallbearers (which he carried in his wallet for years, proudly displaying it because of its glamour names such as George Brett and Johnny Bench), got his first taste of what it's like to work for the Boss when, on June 22, he attempted to put together a press conference showcasing the new players obtained from Oakland in the Rickey Henderson trade the previous day. The players had joined the team that morning, and Richman set up the press conference for 12:30, immediately following the pregame warmup.

Even though the Yankee game against the White Sox that day was scheduled to begin at 1:00, Richman had received approval from manager Dallas Green because of the unusual circumstances. Richman was also anxious to have the press write stories on the new players since there had been such a furor over trading Henderson for three relative unknowns.

When Steinbrenner learned that the press conference had been scheduled close to game time, he called and ordered Richman to cancel it, but by that time the media had already assembled in the designated interview room. Idelson was instructed by Richman to inform the writers there would be no press conference, offering no explanation.

In a touch of irony, some of the veteran writers recalled Henderson's first appearance at Yankee Stadium in 1985, when the outfielder brushed off a horde of waiting reporters by saying: "I don't need no press now, man." Said one writer: "Now they got three guys for Rickey, and none of them need no press now, man!"

While all this was going on, Richman was being berated by Steinbrenner over the phone. After hanging up on the Boss, Richman told Senior Vice President Syd Thrift to "tell Steinbrenner I quit."

Steinbrenner eventually relayed word to Richman, asking him to reconsider, and dismissed the whole affair as a misunderstanding.

The saga of the Steinbrenner PR men really began with the venerable Bob Fishel, for whom the Yankee Stadium pressroom is now named. He had joined the team in 1954 after a fabled career as the aide to Bill Veeck, with the old St. Louis Browns. Fishel was the man behind the infamous Eddie Gaedel stunt. Gaedel was a three-foot-seven midget whom Veeck signed to a contract and sent up to bat in a 1951 game for the Browns.

Fishel, the consummate pro, who was universally beloved and respected by people from all walks of baseball, remained with the Yankees year after year. During his tenure the Brooklyn Dodgers and New York Giants moved to California, baseball expanded from 16 to 24 teams, players came up from the minors, played out their careers, and in some cases went on to the Hall of Fame. Free agency, artificial turf, and domed stadiums became part of the game. Everything changed, but Bob Fishel was always there as PR director of the New York Yankees. And then, in 1973, the group headed by Steinbrenner purchased the team. In 1974 Fishel moved on to the American League as public relations director.

Marty Appel, who had been Fishel's assistant, took the job, endured three seasons, and passed the baton to Mickey Morabito, another legendary figure. Morabito was fired numerous times (which Steinbrenner would always forget in the morning) and spent most of his time away from the ballpark in the nearest bar. After setting impossible standards for endurance during his three-year tour of duty, Morabito joined Billy Martin in Oakland in 1980. For New York's bars and nightspots, that dual departure was the worst development since Prohibition.

Larry Wahl, who had been Morabito's assistant, stepped into those huge footsteps and lasted for 15 months before learning that marriage and working for Steinbrenner don't mix. He was replaced by Dave Szen, an irreverent character who served over time as a fill-in for several others—the ultimate interim.

Szen's brief stint ended with the arrival of Irv Kaze. Kaze never met a job he didn't like—at least for two or three months. He was your prototype "bicoastal"—except that he'd never been able to figure out how to live and work on both coasts at the same time. He spent one year with the Yankees, then moved to the West Coast to work for Al Davis' NFL Raiders. George Steinbrenner...Al Davis. Some people are simply gluttons for punishment.

After another off-season appearance by Szen, Ken Nigro assumed the Yankee PR-man incumbency in 1983. Nigro, a maverick who'd spent 15 years as an outstanding reporter and Orioles' beat man for the *Baltimore Sun*, didn't need much time to sum up the situation. Before the '83 season ended, with no other job lined up, Nigro announced his resignation. His parting words, which he released to the two wire services: "After a year like this, I have to check into a rehab center."

Nigro was succeeded by Joe Safety, who managed to hang on for two years before willingly accepting his firing—rejecting an offer to return. Safety was the first of the PR men to be fired, and the first to collect several months of severance (a la Steinbrenner's managers).

Indeed, Safety and his predecessors were grossly underpaid for all their efforts, considering each was on 24-hour call, seven days a week, and most never got a vacation. But they would all have to admit: the job was never dull.

Take Marty Appel for instance. Appel was the only Steinbrenner PR man to twice get called back from West Coast Yankee road trips in the same season. He also had the distinction of issuing a press release announcing the cancellation of a program admitting underprivileged "Con Ed Kids" to Yankee Stadium. This was actually a necessity for which Steinbrenner couldn't be blamed. It seemed that the "Con Ed Kids" were coming into the ballpark unsupervised, and there were reports that some were robbing people in the restrooms and committing other violent crimes in the stands. Steinbrenner had no choice but to cancel the program for the protection of his other—paying—customers. Still, as Appel later related at the PR men's dinner, it was strange "having to announce...to a full house of people that we were banning these underprivileged kids from Yankee Stadium for the rest of the season."

As for his two aborted West Coast road trips in 1976, Appel simply wrote them off to Steinbrenner's whims. On both occasions, Steinbrenner called and ordered Appel to take the all-night "red-eye" flight back to New York for morning meetings. And on both occasions Appel arrived at his office, never to hear from Steinbrenner.

On another occasion Appel was in the middle of a meeting with Steinbrenner in New York and was about to miss a plane for Texas, where the Yankees were playing. When Appel told Steinbrenner he needed to be in Texas in time for the start of the game, the Yankee boss told him to send Morabito for the first few innings. "You can take a later flight and relieve him in the middle of the game," Steinbrenner said.

That road trip became the only one in sports history in which a PR man worked the first four innings of the first game and went home. Morabito, who was relieved by Appel in the fifth inning, spent an hour and a half in Texas and was back at work in New York the next morning.

Life as Steinbrenner's PR man means always walking a tightrope, but Appel remembers only once fearing he might be fired. That was the night he thought he may have personally been responsible for blowing the Reggie Jackson signing. After weeks of recruiting the crowned jewel of the free agent market in the fall of 1976, Steinbrenner reached agreement with Jackson and had him flown into New York for a press conference. It was Appel's assignment to make all the necessary hotel accommodations for Reggie.

At about 3:00 A.M. Appel was awakened at home by a phone call from Steinbrenner. The Boss was furious. It seemed that Reggie's room at the Americana— where the Yankees always booked their people—had twin beds, and Reggie had a lady with him. Steinbrenner informed Appel that Reggie was threatening to fly right back to California and call the whole deal off. "If he does," Steinbrenner told Appel, "you might as well go with him, because you're finished."

Steinbrenner ordered Appel to get in his car and drive from his home in Westchester to the Americana in midtown Manhattan and straighten the problem out. Instead, Appel called the hotel and got the night manager on the phone.

"All our rooms have double beds," the night manager protested. "I told [Reggie] that's the same suite Jimmy Carter and Roslyn stayed in last week."

Apparently that mollified Jackson, and he took the room without further complaint. The next day, the press conference went off without a hitch, and Steinbrenner never mentioned the hotel problem to Appel.

Of all the press releases Appel wrote for Steinbrenner, the most hilarious was the one calling for a lifetime suspension of Bill Lee, the flaky Red Sox pitcher. Lee, who was appropriately called "the Spaceman" because of his far-out philosophies, was the central figure in a Red Sox-Yankee brawl in 1976. After the brawl, in which he suffered a broken arm, Lee denounced Steinbrenner as a "Nazi" and the Yankees as "his brownshirts." American League President Lee MacPhail levied a 15-day suspension on Lee for his intemperate remarks, but Steinbrenner wasn't satisfied. He ordered Appel to issue a release calling for Lee to be given a lifetime suspension "not to run concurrent with his present 15-day suspension."

Looking back, Appel could see the humor of being Steinbrenner's PR man, although none of it seemed quite so funny at the time. Even the most routine meetings often took on the air of burlesque. One time Steinbrenner summoned Appel and Joe Garagiola, Jr., the Yankees' in-house counsel at the time, to a morning meeting at the Boss' East Side town house in Manhattan. When Appel and Garagiola arrived, Steinbrenner asked if they'd like some coffee. He was clearly upended when they both said yes. It soon became clear that Steinbrenner was not in the habit of making his—or anyone else's—coffee. He began fumbling with the coffee package, frantically trying to tear it open from the top. Finally, in exasperation, Steinbrenner grabbed a butcher's knife and speared a gaping hole into the bag as coffee spilled out all over the counter.

After three years on the job, Appel finally reached the point of exasperation himself. When he resigned after the 1976 season, he could hardly believe it. He had grown up a Yankee fan, president of the Bobby Richardson fan club, and this had always been his dream job. No more.

Mickey Morabito, who replaced Appel, had the distinction of being fired by Steinbrenner before he was actually hired. It happened in 1974 when he was attending Hunter College in New York and working part-time for the Yankees. He'd show up at the team's Shea Stadium offices (Yankee Stadium was being refurbished that season) at three o'clock every afternoon to help out in the publicity department. One day Steinbrenner wanted something done, and seeing that Fishel and Appel were occupied with other projects, he told Fishel: "Get that new kid working on it."

Fishel, figuring that Steinbrenner meant Morabito, informed the Boss that "the new kid" wasn't in yet. "The middle of the afternoon and he's not here yet?" Steinbrenner snapped. "Well, when he gets in, tell him he's fired."

Morabito, who had been seeking full-time work, showed up as usual at three. "Fishel called me in, and he was laughing," Morabito recalled. "He told me the good news was I had been hired full-time, but the bad news was that I was fired already."

Morabito was a hustling New Yorker whose love for the Yankees was only surpassed by his infatuation with crowded bars and fast women. He had an amazing capacity for liquor and an equally amazing capacity to do without sleep. Often he would party all night—with anyone he could find—and be fresh (if red-eyed) to deal with Steinbrenner and his high-volume demands in the morning. But Morabito's never-ending pursuit of the good life often got him in hot water—as happened in The Case of the Midget Limo Driver.

Steinbrenner's arrivals—at Yankee Stadium, on road trips, in spring training—were always treated by his employees with utmost care and fear, sort of like the way folks in a midwest town prepare for a tornado. Nobody was expecting Steinbrenner on this day in the early part of spring training 1977. Those early weeks of spring training, before the games begin, were the treasured days for everyone—players, writers, and team employees alike. Workouts were usually over by early afternoon, and then everyone was free to enjoy the city of Fort Lauderdale and its beckoning intoxications.

So when the call came to traveling secretary Bill Kane about four-thirty that afternoon, he was caught off guard. Steinbrenner, who was in New York and wasn't expected in Fort Lauderdale until later in the week, had changed his plans. He would be arriving that night, at about nine o'clock, his secretary told Kane. He would be accompanied by Yankee vice president Cedric Tallis, and Kane was to be at Fort Lauderdale Airport to meet them.

Kane almost always followed orders, but on this night he had made some important plans. If he broke one more dinner arrangement with his wife, there'd be trouble. Maybe even more trouble than with Steinbrenner. And anyway, Kane figured, Morabito could handle the airport duties.

But Morabito had important plans that night, too. He and reporter Klein had met a couple of young ladies in the bar of the Galt Ocean Mile Hotel the previous night, and Morabito had received a message that they were returning that night about eight o'clock.

Morabito had accepted Kane's duties before receiving the message from the ladies. There had to be a way out. Morabito quickly called Gene Michael, who was serving as an administrative aide to Steinbrenner at the time. "I asked Stick if it would be okay if I sent a limo for George," Morabito recalled, "and he said okay, he didn't see any problem with that. So I looked in the phone book and called a limo service that had the biggest ad. I didn't know that George despised limos."

Morabito and Klein, confident that everything was under control, met the two ladies in the bar that night. But by nine o'clock, the women had shifted their allegiances, hooking up with Teeter and McDonald, the comedy duo that provided the lounge entertainment night after night. The two ladies loved them and were the guests of Teeter and McDonald before the second show began.

Morabito and Klein were left at the bar to drink their vodkas and sodas. After too many Teeter and McDonald jokes and too many vodkas, Klein happened to glance out into the lobby, which was clearly visible from the bar. There he spotted Cedric Tallis straggling in, looking as though he had just lost a fight. In fact, he probably had. Klein checked his watch. It was almost eleven. He poked Morabito, who was in the process of telling the woman two stools down from him that he loved her.

"Hey, Mickey," Klein said, "Cedric's out there. It looks like they just got in."

Morabito took a peek into the lobby, just as Steinbrenner came marching in, looking like a raging bull. He was pointing at the sweating, flushed Tallis, obviously issuing orders. Morabito sobered immediately. "Something must have gone wrong," he said.

A few minutes passed and Tallis staggered further into the bar. He had been told by Steinbrenner to find Kane or Morabito, and he knew by instinct that the bar was the best place to start. He spotted Morabito.

"You'd better get out there," Tallis said. "He's going crazy."

"What happened?" Morabito asked.

Tallis related the story. For starters, the plane had been delayed, which Steinbrenner always viewed as a personal insult. He complained throughout the entire flight. Then, when they arrived, he was expecting to see Kane. But Kane wasn't there. When they reached the baggage claim area, a group of people was crowded around, all of them pointing at Steinbrenner. They were gathered around a midget, who was holding up a large cardboard poster with the name STEINBRENNER inscribed across it in huge letters.

The midget, it seems, had been sent by the limo company, and he wanted to make sure Steinbrenner spotted him. Others had seen the sign and figured that the Steinbrenner who was en route must be none other than the Steinbrenner who owned the New York Yankees. So they were all waiting to get his autograph. Steinbrenner usually loved the attention, but this time, Tallis said, he went nuts, embarrassed by the scene.

The ride to the hotel, normally a 20-minute drive, seemed like two hours to Tallis. Steinbrenner sat in total silence, always a bad sign, as Tallis knew. Someone was going to pay dearly for this embarrassing fiasco, and when Morabito confessed to arranging for the limo, Tallis recognized the culprit.

"You'd better get out there, Mickey," he said.

"Please, Cedric," Morabito protested, "don't make me go. Tell him you couldn't find anyone in here. I can go out the back door by the pool."

"I'm sorry, Mickey," Tallis said. "I've taken a shitload all the way from New York, and I'm not taking anymore. This is your mess, you go face the man."

"It's like throwing a lamb to the wolves," Morabito said.

Tallis wasn't sympathetic. Morabito asked Klein to go with him for moral support. "When writers are around, he's never that bad," Morabito said. "He doesn't like writers to see the way he gets with us."

Klein went along with Morabito as requested, but Steinbrenner, in his rage, scarcely noticed his presence. He began berating Morabito, telling him he was through and to be on the first plane back to New York in the morning.

Morabito endured the assault in silence. Making excuses, he knew, would only get Steinbrenner more upset. Besides, Morabito knew a secret. Steinbrenner's "firings" in those situations rarely meant anything. Sure enough, the next morning Morabito reported to work at the spring training complex. Steinbrenner called early, gave him some orders, and never said a word about the limo or the firing.

Morabito's problems in bars weren't always related to Steinbrenner. Usually they were Morabito's fault—like the incident in Peter's Inn, a favorite spot of the Yankees in Seattle. The TV show "20/20" was preparing a segment on Billy Martin in 1979. They had filmed Martin on a fishing boat and at church. Now they wanted the real Billy—in his natural habitat, a bar.

Morabito arranged for the filming to be done at Peter's Inn. Then he spent the next two days in his customary pursuit of women—but with an extra incentive to go along with his usual sales pitch: "I can get you on television."

Much to his delight, a number of women took Morabito up on his offer. But at Peter's Inn, to avoid a crowd scene, the "20/20" directors had roped off the section of the bar where Martin was sitting with some friends and reporters Klein and Madden. Security men and bouncers prevented all the aspiring starlets who had been cultivated by Morabito from making their screen debut. By the end of the night, Morabito discovered that all the sweet-talking young ladies had some foul words stored up for him. One even went to the trouble of purchasing a pitcher of beer and dumping it on his head. "I got my hair done and bought a dress, just for tonight," she cried. "You tricked me."

A girl who loved to take her clothes off—Morabito's favorite kind—almost cost him his job as Yankee PR director. Ironically, Morabito was strictly an innocent bystander that time.

The Yankees were in Chicago for a three-game series against the White Sox beginning July 30. After each of the first two games, a pretty blonde, about 21 years old, waited in front of the team bus after the game. Just as the bus was about the leave, she would pull down her jeans and flash a delightful moon. After the series finale on August 1, the players were rushing to get on the bus to see what she had in store for her farewell undress. They were not disappointed.

Somehow the girl managed to slink past the security guard and boarded the bus. Making her way all the way to the back, she did an up-close mooning for several players, then made a special request. She wanted to collect autographs—on her bare bottom. The players were only too happy to oblige.

Morabito, meanwhile, wasn't on the bus. Neither was Billy Martin, who was managing the Yankees that year. Morabito, at Martin's request, had arranged for a photographer to be ready for the blonde's farewell mooning, but they weren't aware of the unique autograph session being conducted on the bus.

Reporters Klein and t*he Daily News'* Phil Pepe were sitting near the front of the bus, heads craned to the back. When the girl had finished collecting her autographs, she sat in the row next to Klein and Pepe. She was eagerly waiting for Martin and had saved a special area for his autograph.

Pepe could not help notice the girl was wearing an engagement ring. When she confirmed that she was to be married soon, Pepe asked, "Won't your fiancé mind when he finds out what you're doing?"

The girl smiled sweetly. "Oh, no," she said. "He's a *big* Yankee fan. He knows what I was planning. He can't wait to see who I got to sign me."

At that point traveling secretary Bill Kane boarded the bus. When he spotted the girl, he knew her presence would mean big trouble if it ever got back to Steinbrenner. So despite the booing from the players and despite the girl's insistence that she was waiting for Martin, Kane escorted her off the bus and chastised the security guard for letting her aboard. A few minutes later Martin, Morabito, and Martin's son, Billy Joe, boarded the bus, unaware of the activities they had missed. The girl was back in her customary position in front of the bus and, despite repeated warnings from the security man, gave the players one more viewing sample of their penmanship—all over her splendorous behind.

Everyone figured that was the end of the Moon over Chicago incident. The photographer rushed the revealing picture to Morabito, who turned it over to Martin. The manager proudly filed it with all the scouting reports in his desk drawer at Yankee Stadium. The autographs weren't clearly visible, which, it turned out, was fortunate for the signers.

Back in Chicago, an irate woman had telephoned the nationally syndicated *Sun-Times* columnist Mike Royko. Her son, she told Royko, had been waiting for autographs that night, but the Yankee players brushed past him and the other kids, rushing onto the bus to sign their autographs on a girl's bottom. Royko, recognizing a great column, had his fact-checkers call Morabito for a confirmation. The fact-checker, a woman, seemed to be treating the incident lightly, joking about it, and Morabito went along with her approach. "Yeah, when you travel with the Yankees, you get to see everything," Morabito said with a laugh.

Then the column came out. The distraught mother voicing her shock and outrage about the behavior of the Yankees, who were portrayed as leering, lecherous men who knocked starry-eyed kids out of their path to rush into their den of iniquity and assault a bare-bottomed woman. Martin, who wasn't even on the bus, was implicated. And Morabito was quoted, sounding like the ultimate male chauvinist and child hater.

"When that column came out, all hell broke loose," Morabito remembered. "Steinbrenner was livid. He got even worse when he got a directive from Commissioner Bowie Kuhn to look into the situation. The incident was becoming very embarrassing to the Yankee image, George felt."

Steinbrenner ordered one of his famed investigations, and when he found out Martin had a photo of the girl doing her act—incriminating evidence—he had it destroyed. Morabito was summoned to a meeting in Steinbrenner's office, a session that consisted solely of screaming on the part of the owner, with repeated threats of a firing over the Royko column.

Finally Steinbrenner called a meeting in Martin's office, with several of the suspected signers ordered to attend. Steinbrenner lectured them, while several tried to keep from laughing. Not surprisingly, it was Lou Piniella who once again broke the tension and helped put the matter to rest.

"C'mon, George," Piniella said in his inimitable style, "what are you getting so upset about? If you had been on the bus, you would have been the first to sign. You would have signed 'George M. Steinbrenner, the third' and anything else you could have thought of."

For a moment there was silence. Then everyone started to laugh. As Morabito remembered it, "Even George broke a smile." And that was it. Steinbrenner told everyone to avoid talking about it further, and The Girl on the Bus Caper became another infamous chapter in Yankee history.

Oh yes, and once again Morabito kept his job.

A year earlier, in August 1978, Morabito most surely would have been fired had fate not intervened in his behalf. Nearly two weeks had passed since Steinbrenner's famed rehiring of Martin as manager for 1980—that carnival stunt that was announced on July 29, five days after Martin's forced resignation. Several reporters asked Morabito if he could arrange interviews with Martin, who hadn't been around since the stunning Old-timers' Day announcement.

"I mentioned all the requests to [club president] Al Rosen," Morabito recalled, "and I told him I thought we should just have a small press gathering, with just the beat writers."

Rosen agreed, and the session was arranged for August 9, at Alex and Henry's Restaurant in The Bronx. Steinbrenner was out of town for a few days, but Rosen and Morabito saw no harm in the press gathering. They even briefed Martin that morning, in Rosen's office, preparing him for the obvious questions and how he should phrase his answers. But they made one blunder: they underestimated the extent of Martin's potential for controversy—especially when he became lubricated with a little alcoholic refreshment.

When the writers, Martin, and Morabito arrived, a few rounds of drinks were ordered before lunch, during lunch, and after lunch. The session went on for more than two hours, and Martin's responses were getting more and more interesting. Especially regarding Reggie Jackson.

When asked about the famous "One's a born liar and the other one's convicted" remark that had gotten him fired, Martin replied, "I didn't mean what I said about George, but I did mean it about the other guy." So Reggie was still a "born liar" in Martin's opinion. And he wasn't a superstar. "I never looked at Reggie Jackson as a superstar," Martin said. "He never showed me he was a superstar. I never put him over Chris Chambliss or Thurman Munson or Willie Randolph or Mickey Rivers. There were times when I put Chicken Stanley above him."

Morabito was visibly squirming now. This had gotten out of control, and he desperately attempted to bring the luncheon to an end. He realized, however, the damage had been done.

"When I got back to the stadium, it didn't take long for the call from George," Morabito recalled. "The writers had called him right away for reaction to Billy's comments about Reggie. George blew up. He said I had gone against the way he wanted the Billy situation handled. He was mad at Rosen, too. He said to me: 'You think you're so smart. We'll see how this comes out in the papers. If it isn't too negative, fine. But if it's bad, more of that Billy-Reggie stuff, then you're gone.'"

Morabito, of course, knew it would be bad and was just counting the hours as his job ticked away. That night he was waiting for the early editions of the *Daily News* and *Times* to hit the streets, which would signal his unemployment. But a most unexpected development saved him that night—the *News, Times,* and *Post* all suddenly went on strike! There were no August 10 editions of the New York City papers. The suburban papers that traveled with the Yankees—the *Newark Star-Ledger, Newsday,* and the Westchester-Rockland Gannett dailies—usually weren't seen by Steinbrenner until a day later, and it was easy for Morabito to keep those papers away from the Boss if the effort was made.

"I lucked out, plain and simple," Morabito said. "But then I felt bad because the strike lasted as long as it did [two months]. I felt like I was responsible."

When Morabito left the Yankees in March 1980 to join Martin in Oakland for more money and less hours, he was replaced by his assistant, Larry Wahl. But Wahl, a graduate of Penn, was smart enough to have mixed emotions about his promotion. The slight increase in pay really didn't make up for the monumental increase in responsibility and the dangerous assignment of being number one in Steinbrenner's line of fire.

Wahl knew what to expect, though. He had experienced plenty as Morabito's assistant, including a lot of extra packing. Morabito, like Appel before him, was always in danger of being punished—which meant being banned from a road trip at the last minute or called back from one the moment he arrived at his destination.

"When the team was leaving for a trip," Wahl recalled, "we both always came packed. That way, if Mickey got punished, I was ready."

Wahl, a bright young guy, managed to maintain a reasonably good relationship with Steinbrenner, dating back to his first year as an assistant, 1978. That was the year that Steinbrenner summoned the inexperienced Wahl to Tampa when the Old-timers' Day return of Martin was being hatched. Steinbrenner knew if Morabito was missing, the writers would figure out something was going on, but Wahl's absence could be explained away.

Wahl flew to Tampa and awaited his orders. After checking into his room at the Bay Harbor Inn, he was called by Steinbrenner's secretary, who told him to stay in his room and await a call. A short time later Steinbrenner called and told him to be in his office the next morning at 10:00 A.M. But the next morning Steinbrenner's secretary called again, changing the time to noon. And then to 1:00 P.M. Then 2:00 P.M. Finally, she called Wahl and told him to check out of the hotel and meet Steinbrenner at the Tampa airport for a 4:30 flight to New York.

During the flight Steinbrenner dictated the way he wanted the return of Martin handled—the wording of the press release for the PA announcement, the Scoreboard message, and so on. Plans were made to sneak Martin into Yankee Stadium the following morning and to keep him hidden until the announcement was to be made. And the next day, July 29, everything went smoothly. Steinbrenner's P. T. Barnum show was a rousing success, and Wahl was rewarded with a raise—from $10,000 a year to $15,000.

"That was quite a raise for that job," he recalled. But when Wahl got the number-one job, there were lesser raises and greater problems—such as The Great Yearbook Controversy in 1981.

The team was opening the 1981 season at home, a three-game series against Texas, then leaving for a week. An early shipment of 10,000 yearbooks had been rushed in to be available for the opening series. Among the changes in the yearbook was the colorization of a previously black-and-white photo of Steinbrenner. Unfortunately, the process Wahl used proved not to be nearly as skillful as, say, Ted Turner's colorization of all the old Humphrey Bogart flicks, and Steinbrenner's lips were made to appear more red than normal. A friend of Steinbrenner's, seeing the picture, kidded him about it. When Steinbrenner looked at the picture, he went into a rage.

Calling Wahl on the phone, he screamed: "That picture looks ridiculous! It looks like I've got lipstick on! I want all the yearbooks pulled back. Right away, dammit!"

Team officials Gene McHale and Dave Weidler were put on the case, Wahl remembered, and vendors and concession stand operators were ordered to return all copies of the Yankee yearbook. A radio reporter named Keith Olbermann was informed of the situation from a vendor he knew, and the story got out. Wahl, of course, came in for a second blast of Steinbrenner wrath.

Wahl finally resigned in June of 1981. As a newly wed, he found out quickly that working for Steinbrenner and marriage do not go together like a horse and carriage. That's when Dave Szen stepped in as the interim and had the honor of presiding over the most outrageous press conference in Yankee history—The Steinbrenner Elevator Fight Announcement.

The Yankees had won the first two games of the 1981 World Series at Yankee Stadium but went to Los Angeles and lost the next three. Following a 2–1 loss in game five, Steinbrenner bolted from his press-level box and went to the locker room, commandeering the office of manager Bob Lemon and holding mass interviews. It was as if he knew his presence would attract attention and take some of the pressure away from the players. Or perhaps Lemon had it right when, starting into his office and seeing the owner sitting at the desk, he said, "He's just where he's always wanted to be."

That night, back at the Los Angeles Wilshire Hyatt, reporter Klein was watching TV, planning on going to sleep early since he had to make the Yankees' early morning charter flight back to New York. Just then, the phone rang.

"We're going to have a press conference in George's suite at eleven-thirty," Szen said. "Half hour from now. You'll want to be there."

"What's going on?" Klein asked. "Is Lem being fired?"

"Nothing like that," Szen replied, "but I can't tell you what it's all about."

"Dave, it's almost two-thirty in the morning back home," Klein said. "I have early deadlines Sunday night, so I couldn't possibly get a story in now. Just tell me what's going on so I don't have to schlep all the way up there in the middle of the night for another one of George's waste-of-time tirades about umpires or Bowie Kuhn."

"You're not gonna believe this one," Szen said. "George got into a fight on the elevator."

Szen was right. Klein couldn't believe it. When he arrived at Steinbrenner's suite on the 11th floor at 11:30, Steinbrenner answered the door. His left hand was bandaged, his upper lip was bruised and puffy, his right hand was cut, and there was a bump on the right side of his head. Even more noticeable was the fact that instead of wearing his customary blue blazer, he was wearing a plaid shirt—like a nouveau lumberjack. A tough guy, Klein thought.

The scene in the room became riotous. Steinbrenner began telling his story of how he had been involved in a scuffle in the elevator with two men who had been bad-mouthing him and the Yankees.

The six reporters, listening to Steinbrenner's tale about his defense of Yankee honor against these two unknown assailants, were taking down notes when suddenly the venerable Dick Young, then of the *Daily News,* got up and picked up the telephone that was on a table in the middle of the room. Young, a reporter who knew his deadlines, didn't hesitate. "This is Young," he barked into the phone. "Get me Rewrite, right now."

Steinbrenner was taken aback at Young's interruption of his story.

"What are you doing, Dick?" he said. "I told you this is just a briefing. This isn't to be written."

"A thing like this you don't keep out of the paper," Young replied tersely, and went about his business of getting the story to the *News*.

But Young seemed a bit bleary-eyed that night, as though he had been drinking a lot of his favorite red wine or else had just been awakened from a deep sleep by Szen's late call. Or maybe both. At any rate, he began dictating, "George Steinbrenner, president of the Yankees—"

"Wait a minute," Steinbrenner screamed, "I'm not the damn president. I'm the owner!"

Young, annoyed by the interruption, made the correction: "George Steinbrenner, owner of the Yankees, was involved in an altercation early this morning in the hotel where the Dodgers are staying—"

"The *Dodgers?*" Steinbrenner interrupted again. "What's wrong with you? *We're* staying here—the Yankees!"

The rest of the reporters watched this scene in amusement. Here was Steinbrenner, who had at first said his press conference was not to be written, now serving as an editor for Young.

As for Steinbrenner's story, it was a bit hard to believe. He said he had gotten on the elevator to go downstairs to dinner at about eight. A couple of floors down, these two guys had gotten on. "One of them had a bottle of beer in his hand," Steinbrenner said, "and the other one was wearing a Dodger cap. The guy with the beer looked at me and said, 'Steinbrenner, right?' and I said, 'Yeah, that's right.' Then he said, 'Why don't you go back to those fucking animals in New York and take your choke-ass players with you.'"

Steinbrenner continued: "Well, I've had it up to here with that stuff. I'm sick of people in other cities knocking the Yankee fans, and I especially couldn't take it when he said my players were chokes. It's okay for me to criticize them because I pay their checks. But I'm not gonna listen to some drunk fans say that about my players."

So Steinbrenner said he cursed at the guy, and the brawl broke out.

"He hit me on the side of the head with a bottle, and I reacted," Steinbrenner said. "I clocked him, with my left hand. He fell—I think he was drunk to begin with—and the other guy hit me in the mouth. I slugged him, too. The elevator door opened, and I got off. I left them there, one guy on the floor and the other guy kneeling over him. Then I went to the washroom, washed the blood off my mouth, and went to dinner."

When his left hand continued to hurt, Steinbrenner summoned the team physician, Dr. John Bonamo, who wrapped it. Then Steinbrenner decided to call the press conference and reveal the incident.

The next day, on the flight home, Steinbrenner's alleged fight on the elevator was the talk of the team. There was speculation that Steinbrenner had elaborated the incident to provide entertainment and break his slumping team's tension after the three losses. If that was his plan, it appeared to have worked. The players were loose and joking.

"I'd have given half my salary to have seen that fight," said Goose Gossage.

"I wonder what Billy Martin's saying about George, now," said Reggie Jackson.

"You can bet George'll be getting a telegram from Billy," said Lemon.

Adding to the frivolity that day was the 45-minute bus ride to the airport, featuring the most entertaining bus driver since Ralph Kramden. His name was Bob Weddle, and his name tag, hanging at the front of the bus, read: The Singing Bus Driver. Ah, Hollywood. Everyone's a performer.

While he was driving the bus, Weddle grabbed a microphone and began singing. As he warbled "I'm a Yankee-doodle dandy" and "Over there…the Yanks are coming," Graig Nettles yelled from the back of the bus: "Hey, bussie, how about dedicating a song to George? Do you know the words to 'Rocky'?"

By the time the Yankee flight landed at Newark Airport, though, things were back to normal. Dozens of camera crews were waiting for Battling George. And after quickly reviewing his scuffle, he started talking about the World Series. "We'll be an embarrassment if we lose now," he said.

What was becoming increasingly more apparent, however, was that Steinbrenner seemed to be losing it. After the world championship successes of '77 and '78, he seemed unable to deal with adversity. And when the Yankees lost the next game in New York and the Dodgers became world champions, Steinbrenner issued his famous apology "to the people of New York and to Yankee fans everywhere," which, to the players and writers, was an even crazier act than the elevator fight.

And whatever became of those two guys on the elevator? Nobody knows. If he had been as successful as he claimed in defending the honor of the team, wouldn't there have been a chance of a lawsuit by the "victims" against the wealthy owner for clobbering them?

Szen, meanwhile, had handed over the PR reins to Irv Kaze in time to make the apology statement. Unfortunately Szen never became promotions director, which was probably his true calling. He was always coming up with humorous ideas for giveaway promotions. His best, as he told Klein one night, was "George Steinbrenner Mask Day."

"Imagine," he said, "we'd have thousands of George masks made up and all the fans could put them on and start yelling at the manager and at the players and finally at each other. There'd be all kinds of fights in the stands. It would be great. Fifty thousand fans all acting like George!"

Actually, Szen, who became acting PR director when Larry Wahl resigned in June of '81 had reverted to the assistant's role on the arrival of Irv Kaze, the new department head, later in the season. Kaze had been back in New York preparing for the Series to return to Yankee Stadium, when Steinbrenner caused all the commotion over his elevator fight incident. But when the Series ended, it was Kaze's unenviable task of trying to talk the Boss out of issuing the apology.

"In the seventh inning of that last game, George called me into his office," Kaze recalled. "He said he wanted to issue this statement, which was real short. I remember saying to him, 'What are we doing this for?'"

That was only the first of many times Kaze must have wondered what he was doing these things for. The following spring, he came to Fort Lauderdale full of vigor and anticipation. Then, without warning or explanation, he was gone, sent home to New York. The writers asked what had happened to Kaze and were told he was "on business for Mr. Steinbrenner."

When Kaze finally returned with about 10 days to go in spring training, he was noticeably subdued. No more did he invite the writers to dinner or drinks. Instead, he seemed to be preoccupied. Klein and Madden were puzzled. Finally Klein came up with an explanation.

"There's only one answer to what happened to Irv," he said. "Steinbrenner had him sent home to be lobotomized."

Years later, after Kaze had left the Yankees and returned to his normal engaging ways, he insisted he had not undergone a lobotomy that spring.

"Honest," he said. "George simply wanted me to go back to New York to try and get some endorsements for Ron Guidry. He wanted to promote Guidry that year, maybe because he had let Reggie go. But we had no luck in getting anything. There just wasn't much interest in Guidry."

It wasn't long after Kaze returned to Fort Lauderdale from his Guidry assignment that he became involved in one of the crazier nights of his life. The Yankees were playing a night game, and Ken Kaiser, the rotund, often theatrical umpire, tossed one of the Yankee players out of the game for arguing a third strike. Steinbrenner was livid and ordered Kaze to issue a press release ripping the umpires.

While he was typing up the release, however, Kaze received a phone call from New York. There was a report that Lemon was going to be fired as Yankee manager. Kaze was dumbfounded. It was true Lemon hadn't had a good spring and was being hammered nightly by Steinbrenner, but this report was absurd. He'd have to run it by the Boss. As Kaze was about to rush upstairs to Steinbrenner's box above Fort Lauderdale Stadium, he heard a report on the radio of a plane crash in which several kids from a school in Florida had perished. All he could think of was that his son, Benji, who was going to camp in Florida, might have been on the plane.

The whole world seemed to be going crazy around Kaze. His first act was to call Benji and make sure he was all right. Then, a few minutes later when the game ended, Steinbrenner called and began screaming at Kaze not to release the statement about Kaiser.

"Get Kaiser on the phone!" Steinbrenner ordered. "I want to talk to him."

But Kaiser was leaving the ballpark through an exit across the field, where there were no phones. So Kaze, who by now had forgotten all about the Lemon rumor, bolted out of his trailer office and began running frantically across the field in pursuit of Kaiser. The writers, who were finishing up their stories up in the press box, looked down and saw Kaze charging across the empty field and wondered what was wrong with him. Where was he going in such a panic?

Later that year Kaze was simply going, going, gone—like his four predecessors in the Steinbrenner pulse center. He couldn't take any more of the Yankee asylum. He was going someplace more sane. Al Davis' Oakland-Los Angeles-Irwindale NFL Raiders.

In replacing Kaze, Steinbrenner looked beyond the public relations talent pool and hired a former baseball writer from Baltimore, Ken Nigro. In retrospect, Nigro may have been the best-suited of all the Boss' PR men. Why? Because he could be viewed as being just as crazy, in a different way, as Steinbrenner. To be sure, Nigro was an eccentric, never without a stack of newspapers under his arm—all of which inevitably wound up in the backseat of his car.

What Nigro remembered most about his Yankee/Steinbrenner experience were the red phones. On the desk of just about every executive, as well as on the manager's downstairs in the clubhouse, was a red phone in addition to the regular phone. The red phones were a sort of private system installed in the stadium. When they rang, there was no guessing who the caller might be.

"It was unbelievable," remembered Nigro. "Whenever those red phones would ring, people would vault over chairs and desks to answer them! I never saw such panic in the faces of people as when those red phones would ring."

Nigro spent only one season on the job—1983—but from a public relations standpoint it was the most tumultuous of all the Steinbrenner years. Indeed, Nigro probably wrote more releases and spent more time in courtrooms and league-office hearing rooms than all the other Steinbrenner PR men combined. Not only did he have Steinbrenner and his foibles to contend with, but there was also Billy Martin, the umpires, and of course, the pine-tar affair. (For the record, Steinbrenner and Martin received a combined five suspensions/fines that season from the league offices for their run-ins with the umpires.) Steinbrenner actually set the tone for the 1983 season before it began by commissioning an artist to draw a sketch of Martin heaping abuse on an umpire for the cover of the Yankees' press guide.

Right from the start, Nigro got off on the wrong foot with Martin, who viewed him as an outsider, not to be trusted. In one of the first days of spring training, Martin was talking about bringing in 40-year-old Bert Campaneris for a tryout. Nigro, thinking Billy was kidding, made some disparaging remark about Campaneris being washed up years ago.

"Since when does the PR man know more about baseball than the manager?" Martin said, the roomful of reporters suddenly going quiet. "If you don't mind, pal, I'll make the personnel decisions here."

A few days later Campaneris showed up in camp and remained with the team all year, batting .322 in 60 games. From that day on, though, Martin barely communicated with Nigro. Each day, Nigro had to go to the coaches, either Jeff Torborg or Don Zimmer, to find out who the Yankees' probable pitcher was going to be for the next day. One time Nigro was told by General Manager Bill Bergesch that the Yankees were sending pitcher Ray Fontenot to the minors, and he went to the trouble of putting out a press release on it. But when he informed Martin what he had done, the manager said he was keeping Fontenot. Thus Nigro had to go around to all the writers and ask for the press releases back.

That was the spring Steinbrenner drew his first rebuke from Commissioner Bowie Kuhn for questioning the integrity of National League umpire Lee Weyer. Steinbrenner was standing alongside the fence behind first base during an exhibition game between the Yankees and the Expos. When Weyer called a Yankee out at first on a close play, Steinbrenner hollered: "National League homer! That's the way [National League President Chub] Feeney tells them to do it. If it's close, give it to the National League."

Mike McAlary, a reporter for the *New York Post,* was standing behind Steinbrenner and wrote a story the next day recounting the incident, quoting the Boss verbatim. Kuhn's reaction was swift and severe—a $50,000 fine, which, naturally, infuriated Steinbrenner. Nigro caught the brunt of it for having allowed reporters to be standing in the area where the Boss was venting his spleen.

As the season wore on, Steinbrenner and Martin continued their assault on the umpires but also renewed hostilities with each other. As Nigro recalled: "It was really walking a tightrope, being the middleman between these two guys. I mean, I was working for Steinbrenner but trying to serve Martin as well, and as the season wore on, neither of them was talking to the other."

About the only thing Steinbrenner and Martin agreed on was that the umpires were their common enemy. That was never more evident than the night of May 27, which Nigro later referred to as "the night of the dueling press releases."

The Yankees were playing the Oakland A's at Yankee Stadium, and Steinbrenner was in Tampa, watching the game on television. Early in the game Dave Winfield, reacting angrily to a brushback pitch from Oakland right-hander Mike Norris, began to charge the mound. When Oakland catcher Mike Heath attempted to restrain him, Winfield grabbed him around the neck and began choking him. Both benches cleared, and when order was restored, home plate umpire Derryl Cousins ejected only Winfield.

As soon as the ejection of Winfield was announced, the red phone in the press box next to Nigro was ringing. It was Steinbrenner, who was predictably livid. "Start taking down this release," he bellowed at Nigro.

As Nigro remembered it, "George kept dictating and dictating. I was scribbling down everything he said, in the margins, upside down along the side of the page. He just kept going. My wrist was aching. Finally he stopped, and usually he would tell me to go and get it out immediately to the press. But this time he asked me to read it back to him. Well, I couldn't even read it myself. I started stammering and he exploded at me."

Somehow the release got done, the gist of it being a blistering attack by Steinbrenner on the integrity of Cousins and his partner, John Shulock, both of whom, Steinbrenner noted, had been promoted from the minors during the 1979 umpires' strike. Steinbrenner suggested strongly that Shulock and Cousins were scabs and called their work "a disgrace."

As Nigro began distributing the release, Bob Fishel, the former Yankee PR director who was now an assistant to American League President Lee MacPhail, was sitting at the rear of the press box. On reading the release, Fishel rushed to a pay phone and called MacPhail at his apartment. MacPhail was similarly outraged by Steinbrenner's attack on the umpires and instructed Fishel to issue a counterrelease.

There was only one problem, Nigro recalled later. "Fishel couldn't put out a release without using our copy machine. He was laughing when he asked me if he could use it. It *was* funny. I felt like I was consorting with the enemy."

In his release MacPhail said: "Mr. Steinbrenner's intemperate blast is completely unacceptable and will result in disciplinary action [which turned out to be a week's suspension]."

Now it was Nigro's turn to call Steinbrenner and report to him what MacPhail had said in *his* release. After listening to MacPhail's counterattack, Steinbrenner ordered Nigro to issue yet another release, blasting MacPhail.

"We are all free to express our opinion," Steinbrenner said in the new release, "unless Lee MacPhail has authored a new Constitution or Bill of Rights of the United States."

Meanwhile, the writers, who were trying to cover the ball game, were wondering when the press releases were going to stop. "It was wild," Nigro said. "But we outdueled them, 2 to 1."

Of course, nothing was more wild that season than the chaotic and tumultuous pine-tar affair, which, whether they liked it or not, captured the attention of New York baseball fans through most of the dog days of August. It also renewed the war between Steinbrenner and MacPhail, with battles being fought in the courtrooms of The Bronx and Manhattan as well as the American League offices.

It all began on the afternoon of July 24, in the ninth inning of a game between the Yankees and Royals at Yankee Stadium. With two out and Kansas City trailing, 4–3, U. L. Washington singled off Yankee reliever Dale Murray. Martin then summoned Goose Gossage from the bullpen to face George Brett, who proceeded to hit a drive into the right field stands for an apparent go-ahead two-run homer. But after Brett circled the bases, Martin asked the umpires to check Brett's bat.

Plate umpire Tim McClelland, after examining the bat and consulting with his three mates, had crew chief Joe Brinkman measure the pine tar on the bat. Under baseball rule 1.10 b, pine tar cannot extend beyond 18 inches on the handle of the bat, and it was found by the umpires that Brett's bat was in violation. Thus, in a truly unique ruling, the umpires nullified the Brett homer and gave the Yankees an apparent 4–3 victory.

Brett went wild after the ruling and had to be restrained from physically attacking Brinkman. But as it turned out, that was only a prelude to the wild and crazy pine-tar doings that would dominate the rest of the Yankee season—not to mention Ken Nigro's harried life as Steinbrenner's PR man.

The Royals immediately protested the game, and four days later MacPhail upheld their protest, maintaining that it was the intent of the rulemakers to distinguish between a bat carrying excessive pine tar and one that had been "doctored" to "improve the distance factor or cause unusual reaction on the baseball." In citing what he called "the spirit of the rule," MacPhail overturned a decision by the umpires for the first time in the 10 years of his administration as American League president. He further ordered that the game should be replayed from the point of the home run and suggested that the Royals return to Yankee Stadium on August 18, an open date for both clubs, to play the final four outs.

Well, Steinbrenner went absolutely berserk with rage over this latest and most unthinkable setback from MacPhail. Before gearing up his public relations mill for a steady blitzkrieg of "MacPhail is anti-Yankee" propaganda, he ripped the AL prexy, saying, "It sure tests our faith in our leadership. If the Yankees lose the American League pennant by one game, I wouldn't want to be Lee MacPhail living in New York. Maybe he should go house hunting in Kansas City."

That remark would cost Steinbrenner a record $300,000 fine from Commissioner Bowie Kuhn, but not before the Yankee owner had exhausted all avenues of appeal, delay, and distraction over the MacPhail pine-tar ruling.

First, Steinbrenner threatened to forfeit the game, stating that "MacPhail has already made a mess of this thing and I'm not letting him take an off day away from my players." (That certainly must have come as a shocker to Yankee players grown accustomed to Steinbrenner's insistence over the years that his managers use the off days to conduct workouts.) Then, when MacPhail notified the Yankees that the game would be forfeited if they didn't play, a new dispute arose over the starting time of the game.

Steinbrenner, in doing a 360-degree turnaround, announced that the game would begin at 2:00 P.M. so that the day could be a "festive occasion with free gifts and circus acts" and that kids from all the day camps would be bussed in for the gala event. But again he met resistance from MacPhail, who decreed that the game could not begin before 6:00 P.M. because the Royals were playing a night game on August 17.

The Yankees were in Detroit, staying at the Pontchartrain Hotel, when MacPhail made his ruling on the game time. Nigro received a call from Steinbrenner, ordering him to set up an immediate conference call with the beat writers. Upon checking with the hotel switchboard operator, however, Nigro was informed that it would take at least an hour to set up a conference call. Instead, one of the people at the front desk suggested Nigro assemble all the writers in a private room where a special speaker box could be set up for Steinbrenner to call into.

What resulted was one of the more hilarious Steinbrenner press conferences—although the Boss didn't know it. Nigro hastily summoned all the writers to this small meeting room off the lobby of the Pontchartrain. There were a table and chairs in the room, and on the table was a phone equipped with a speaker box.

The phone rang and Nigro said, "Okay, Mr. Steinbrenner, they're all here."

Then, out of the box came Steinbrenner's voice. "What MacPhail is doing," he began, "is depriving children of a pretty darned nice day at the ballpark. Once again Lee MacPhail has favored the culprits. He's accommodating the team that perpetrated the crime. We were planning to bus in thousands of campers, but now he's forcing us to cancel all the plans because the camps have informed us they have to have the kids back by 6:00 p.m."

All the while Steinbrenner was talking, the writers were trying desperately to contain their laughter at this latest, ridiculous episode of Yankee-doodle distraction. Moss Klein didn't help by grabbing a spray bottle that had been left in the room to water the flowers and spraying the speaker box.

Meanwhile, a series of lawsuits had sprung up that had taken the pine-tar game on a wild ride of confusion off the field and into the courtrooms of New York City. A couple of fans, protesting the $2.50 admission that Steinbrenner planned to charge for the game, brought separate lawsuits against the Yankees. Steinbrenner enlisted the services of Roy Cohn, the noted, flamboyant trial lawyer, as well as his in-house team of attorneys, to "defend" the Yankees. (It was, of course, no secret that Steinbrenner would have loved to have the courts delay or even ban the playing of the game, and for that reason, Cohn's presence was viewed cynically by most observers.)

At 10:00 A.M. on August 18, Bronx Supreme Court Judge Orest V. Maresca granted a preliminary injunction barring the game. Maresca said more time was needed to hear the merits of the two lawsuits. It was not until 3:34 P.M.— 2½ hours before the game was scheduled to be resumed—that Justice Joseph Sullivan of the New York Supreme Court in Manhattan stayed the ruling and opened the way for the game to go on.

By then it was clear that everyone—the Yankees, the fans, and all of Steinbrenner's beleaguered front office troops—were spent from the nearly month-long ordeal and just wanted to be done with it. When the Yankees took the field with two out in the ninth inning, now trailing 5–4, Martin had Ron Guidry playing center field and Don Mattingly playing second base.

There was a new crew of umpires for the game, and Martin did exhaust one last Yankee protest, ordering his pitcher, George Frazier, to first throw the ball over to first base and then to third base. But when Martin walked out to home plate, crew chief Dave Phillips produced a notarized letter, signed by the original four umpires, stating that both Brett and Washington had indeed touched all the bases.

The Yankees then went down meekly one-two-three in the ninth, and later, back in the clubhouse, rookie Don Mattingly said to a reporter, "Well, maybe now we can get back to normal around here." As he said that, Goose Gossage walked past Mattingly's locker. Gossage stopped, and with a look of mock terror said, "Normal? Oh, no, not *that.*"

While the game had been in progress, Nigro had attempted to maintain the "festive" atmosphere Steinbrenner supposedly wanted. To the members of the press, he'd distributed cans of pine tar and specially printed T-shirts that read: "I covered the Pine Tar Game 8-18-83." When Yankee president Gene McHale saw that, he was aghast.

"What is this?" he demanded of Nigro. "We didn't authorize this."

"I...well...I...uh, just felt it was a big event that should be promoted," Nigro explained weakly. "It was just something I decided to do. I thought the press would like to have a keepsake of this great event."

"You're making a joke out of this," said McHale, "and it's not funny."

That was not quite the end of the pine-tar affair, though. At the end of the season, Kuhn conducted a hearing on Steinbrenner's behavior throughout the whole process, particularly his remarks about MacPhail. Moss Klein was the only writer called to testify at the hearing. After waiting outside Kuhn's office for nearly two hours, nibbling on Christmas cookies that had been left there by one of the commissioner's secretaries, Klein was called in and asked by one of Steinbrenner's six attorneys in the room if the Boss "was laughing" when he made the remark about MacPhail having to go house hunting in Kansas City.

"Yeah," said Klein, "he did laugh. I think he thought it was funny."

With that, one of the eight attorneys from Kuhn's office countered, "Well, how can you be sure that Steinbrenner was laughing when he said the same thing to all the other reporters?"

"I can't," said Klein.

"So it's possible then, that he said it with malice to them?"

"I guess," said Klein.

"Okay," the lawyer said, "you're dismissed."

And on December 23 Kuhn said "Merry Christmas" early to Steinbrenner by fining him $300,000. There was no official announcement made by the Yankees, and Steinbrenner did not protest, primarily because he was privately relieved that he hadn't been suspended again. Kuhn, it seemed, had enlisted the cooperation of Ken Nigro as an "in-house" material witness to all the Steinbrenner shenanigans in the Pine-Tar Affair. Kuhn was also rumored to have proof that the two fans' lawsuits brought against the Yankees were actually instigated by Steinbrenner to prevent the game from ever being completed. For his part, Nigro had had enough of all the nonsense, cover-ups and nonbaseball distractions that come with being George Steinbrenner's PR man, and he resigned a few days after the season.

Next in the line of succession to the pulse center was Joe Safety. Safety was experienced in the baseball world, having been publicity director for the

Pittsburgh Pirates for several years, including 1979, the year they won the world championship. He had also worked for the noted player agent, Tom Reich, a friend of Steinbrenner's.

"I wasn't exactly some new kid coming in," Safety said, "but working for George was definitely a unique experience."

Among the more "unique" experiences for Safety in his two years as Steinbrenner's PR man was the Canadian national anthem flap, which occurred prior to a crucial game against the first-place Toronto Blue Jays at Yankee Stadium in September 1985. On that night a guest singer named Mary O'Dowd butchered the Canadian anthem and was reduced to tears when the stadium crowd hooted and booed at her incompetence. Not only did she not know the words, she didn't know the tune, either. After a few aborted attempts, she simply walked off the field.

Up in the press box, Safety knew this was going to be big trouble for somebody. "The guy in charge of arranging the anthem singers then was [promotions director] Johnny Fugazy," Safety said. "As she was walking off, before she even made it to the dugout, the phone was ringing. I knew it was George.

"Where's Fugazy?" Steinbrenner barked.

"I don't know," Safety said.

"Find him," Steinbrenner said, and hung up.

Safety had seen Fugazy ducking out of the press box when O'Dowd started screwing up.

"I knew where to find him," Safety said. "He was hiding in the men's room. I told him George was looking for him, and he gave me that look—it's a look that only people who work there can understand. But Johnny stood up to George. He said he couldn't be held responsible for somebody getting mike fright."

As always with Steinbrenner/Yankee fiascos, the incident was not allowed to die quietly. The next day, Steinbrenner ordered Safety to prepare an introduction to be read before the Canadian national anthem that night. "Essentially, he wanted to applaud Canada for helping the United States during the Iran hostage crisis," Safety said. "He wanted a long, drippy statement about Canada. All this because of the anthem screwup."

After several revisions Steinbrenner decided he wanted to coach the Yankees' legendary public address announcer Bob Sheppard on the way to read the statement.

"George had his secretary track down Sheppard in the press room," Safety said. "He was told that Mr. Steinbrenner wanted to see him in his office. You know how prim and proper Sheppard is. He said, 'Fine, I'll be there as soon as I've finished eating, in about 15 minutes.' Well, anyone who works for George knows there's no such thing as 'later' when he wants to see you. But Sheppard had never been involved with him that way.

"So the secretary tells George that Sheppard said he'd be up in 15 minutes. George yells: *What?* Fifteen minutes? You tell him to get up here now or he's fired.'"

It seems, however, that Sheppard, too, had felt that perhaps an apology should be made, and he had taken it upon himself to compose a short statement, which he brought with him to Steinbrenner's office—after he finished his dinner, that is. When he arrived at Steinbrenner's office, the usual group of weary front office officials were sitting around the Boss' big round table.

"There was only one seat available for me," Sheppard recalled. "It was at the right of Steinbrenner."

So Sheppard "sittest at the right hand" of the Boss and showed him his statement.

"This is fine," said Steinbrenner, "but I want to add a few things."

"I don't think that would be good," said Sheppard. "I'll be announcing this, and you don't want to lose the fans' attention. It should be succinct."

Steinbrenner looked curiously at Sheppard and, at first, didn't know what to say.

"I thought I was the owner of this team," he said. "Well, I'll have my people look over this thing, and they'll decide what you'll say."

A while later, Sheppard was handed the statement back from one of Steinbrenner's PR people. It was exactly as Sheppard had written it, with no additions or revisions from the Boss.

So all because of the botched Canadian anthem, the fabled voice of the Yankees, the voice that Reggie Jackson once said sounded "like God was talking to us down on the field" was almost canned.

Fortunately an international crisis was averted, and the Yankees proceeded to do far more for Canada than Steinbrenner's apology could ever have done: having been a mere 1½ games out of first place at the time Sheppard was reading the statement, the Yankees lost the next three, and the Blue Jays went on to win their first AL East title.

Safety eventually got fired—sort of. The 1985 winter baseball meetings were in San Diego, and Safety, having secured written approval from Steinbrenner, had arranged to take a vacation in Los Angeles afterward. This wasn't really a vacation, though. Safety had been having health problems during the season, suffering from a heart condition that, though not brought on by Steinbrenner, certainly wasn't helped by working for him.

Before departing for the winter meeting's, Safety arranged for three days of testing and treatment in Los Angeles. The meetings ended on Friday, December 13. For two weeks Safety's clearance had been all set. Then on December 14, Roger Maris died.

"I was watching a basketball game at a friend's house in L.A.," Safety recalled. "At halftime the announcement about Maris was made. I turned to the people in the room and said, 'This is going to change my life.' Then I called my answering service back in New Jersey and asked if there were any calls from Mr. Steinbrenner. There weren't, but I said there would be, and I gave my numbers."

Within a half hour Safety had a message from the answering service to call Steinbrenner. He was told to return to New York to be involved in arrangements Steinbrenner wanted for a tribute to Maris at St. Patrick's Cathedral.

"I don't think I can be back," said Safety.

End of conversation.

Safety hadn't told Steinbrenner about his health problems. "If I've got a bad heart, it's my business," he said. "That wasn't the issue. I had done things that weren't in my comfort zone thousands of times in the two years I worked there, never saying no. I felt I was entitled to say no one time."

Safety didn't come back. When Steinbrenner called the office at Yankee Stadium on December 16 looking for him, Lou D'Ermilio, Safety's assistant, tried to cover for him by saying he was having trouble with airline reservations. Steinbrenner had his secretary make a reservation, then informed D'Ermilio to contact Safety and tell him he had a reservation. That gave Safety another chance, but he still wasn't coming back.

Two days later, while undergoing tests in Los Angeles, he received a message via team vice president David Weidler that he had been terminated. Safety remained in California and returned as scheduled on December 31. In the interim, several reporters and mutual acquaintances had informed Steinbrenner of Safety's reason for being in California. When Safety got home, he had a message to call Steinbrenner.

"You coming back to work?" Steinbrenner asked.

"I don't think so," Safety said. Safety explained that he had no hard feelings but that he just felt it was time to make a move. Two years in that position, under the usual conditions, were enough.

Steinbrenner listened and then said: "Okay, keep me posted on your progress. We'll pay you until you figure out what you're going to do."

And Safety remained on the payroll until April when he went to work for a public relations firm in Beverly Hills.

Safety's departure opened the way for Harvey Greene, a native New Yorker who coveted the job, despite all the horror stories about Steinbrenner. Greene, in fact, had telephone experience with Steinbrenner, having been Larry Wahl's roommate when Wahl sat in the Yankee PR hot seat. Greene would often answer late-night calls from Steinbrenner when Wahl was either out or hiding out. Steinbrenner once mistook Greene's voice for Wahl's and began berating him, threatening him with being fired.

Finally Greene interrupted: "I'm sorry, Mr. Steinbrenner, but I don't work for you."

Greene, who had been working as the publicity director for the NBA Cleveland Cavaliers when the Yankee PR job opened, quickly established himself as a tireless worker who was able to put up with the periodic punishments, curfews, extra work, and canceled vacations, because he wouldn't give up his dream of wearing a World Series ring. Throughout his three-plus years on the job, Greene turned down numerous offers for more money and shorter hours, much to the wonderment of the writers he so tirelessly served.

The best example of Greene's devotion was a night in Minneapolis in 1986. Greene and some friends wound up at an impromptu party with a group of girls who shared a huge house in Minneapolis. The house had a huge backyard basketball court, a pool table, a stereo system, a refrigerator filled with beer, and the five attractive young women. It was too good to be true. Reporters Moss Klein and *Newsday's* Tom Verducci immediately dubbed the place Club Getaway.

Shortly after arriving at Club Getaway that night, however, Klein noticed Greene getting a little uneasy. The Yankees had a day game the next day, which meant Greene didn't have much time to prepare his famed game notes. (It should be noted that pregame notes, provided by each team's publicity department for the writers and broadcasters, usually consist of one or two typed pages. Greene's, by contrast, customarily were seven or eight pages, prompting other PR directors to refer to them as "Greene's Yankee booklet.")

As such, it usually took Greene a minimum of three hours to prepare them, which is why he was beginning to show worry while everyone else at Club Getaway was just getting into the swing of things.

Finally Greene told Klein he was going to call a taxi and go back to the Yankees' hotel. Klein couldn't believe it.

"Why don't you look at it this way," he said to Greene. "Pretend you're on a quiz show. Behind door number one, you get lucky here, spend the night, and make passionate love with one of our hosts. Behind door number two, you play some pool, relax, drink all the free beer, and maybe get pleasantly smashed in the process. And behind door number three, you get to go back to your room, alone, and do your notes. Which one do you choose?"

Greene hesitated for a moment, sighed and shrugged. "I pick door number three," he said.

And that's why Harvey Greene lasted longer than anyone else as George Steinbrenner's public relations director, until Rick Cerrone came on the scene in 1996 and had the benefit of serving during a time when the Boss' health began to fail and he was no longer the same hands-on tyrant.

CHAPTER 12

George Does Dallas

In just about every way, Dallas Green seemed to epitomize the perfect manager for George Steinbrenner. He had football size and presence—and a bit of a football mentality, believing in frequent pregame pep talks to fire his players up. He was a man of detail who believed in the work ethic. He was strong on discipline, and best of all as far as Steinbrenner was concerned, he was not afraid to rip the players in public when they didn't perform. And Green was a winner, having combined all those Steinbrenner-like characteristics of fire and bluster to whip the perennial bridesmaid Philadelphia Phillies to the world championship of baseball in 1980, two years after the Boss' last Yankee world title.

"I bring some new ideas to the party," Green said on being tapped by Steinbrenner to replace Lou Piniella on October 7, 1988. It was, to be sure, an interesting choice of words. In the decade preceding Green's arrival, the Yankees had seemingly been Steinbrenner's own private party, for which the guest list was revised drastically year after year. And at the end of each season's party, the Boss would play "pin the tail on the donkey" to decide which poor jackass would manage his team the following year. More often than not, as he strode blindfolded across his office clutching his donkey tail, Steinbrenner would stumble on Billy Martin.

But in the fall of 1988 Steinbrenner decided for the first time to take his donkey tail outside his official Yankee family, bypassing all his regular party guests, in his search for a new field leader. Actually, he had already made up his mind to bring in Green the previous June but decided it might be too risky—from a public relations standpoint—to have an outsider replace Martin. So he convinced Lou Piniella to finish up the '88 season, promising him a free hand and "total control" of the ball club before firing him for the second time in a year.

Green was on the job barely a week when he began to realize just why the Yankees were in such decline and disarray. Shortly after the World Series Steinbrenner summoned Green, the new coaches, special adviser Clyde King, the minor league managers, a few scouts, and the team medical staff to Tampa for organization meetings. After one of the meetings, in which player personnel was discussed, Steinbrenner asked everyone to make a list of players from other teams who *(1)* might be available and *(2)* could help the Yankees. As Green and his pitching coach Billy Connors made their lists, they were somewhat astonished to see Dr. Stuart Hershon, the Yankee team physician, making a list, too.

After the meeting, Connors couldn't help but ask Hershon if he routinely was asked to offer his opinion on players. "Why, yes," Hershon said, "but why not? I'm a Yankee fan. I know just as much about this team as anybody."

Later, during the season, Connors discovered that Hershon felt qualified to offer his opinion on how the team should be managed, too. On the night of April 12, John Candelaria, who had been brought along slowly all spring by the Yankees because of off-season knee surgery, pitched eight strong innings in a victory over Toronto. After the game Hershon went up to Connors in the Yankee clubhouse and inquired as to why Candelaria had been allowed to stay in so long.

"Don't you know he's only a seven-inning pitcher?" Hershon said.

"Geez," said Connors, trying not to laugh, "I'm sorry, Doc. Next time we'll be sure to only use him for six."

After that October meeting in Tampa, the next hint Green received as to how Steinbrenner's Yankees operated came at the winter meetings in Atlanta. In his best "divide and conquer" game plan, Steinbrenner sent the diverse group of Green, Quinn, Martin, King, and Charlie Fox, Green's bench coach, to represent the Yankees in trade talks.

After spending the first couple of days spinning their wheels trying to trade Dave Winfield to the Twins (at Steinbrenner's command), Green and Fox resigned themselves to coming home empty-handed. Green remembered leaving the winter meetings saying to himself, "Well, I still have Rick Rhoden to help settle a young pitching staff." But on January 10 Green was vacationing at his island home in the Caribbean, when he was called by Quinn and informed that Rhoden, who had led the Yankee staff in innings pitched in 1988, had been traded to the Houston Astros for three minor league players of little or no potential.

"What's going on here?" Green asked Steinbrenner. "I don't get it. Why did you give him away?"

Steinbrenner replied that Rhoden was on the downside. Furthermore, at $900,000 a year, he was making too much money, and the Yankees were getting pressure from other clubs about their excessive payroll.

"We're going to get this payroll down," Steinbrenner said. "And besides, you have enough pitching."

Green later related another reason Steinbrenner had for trading Rhoden: "He was cutting the ball too much. Everybody knew it and [Commissioner Bart] Giamatti was on his ass."

Steinbrenner told Green an added plus in getting rid of Rhoden's salary was that "it will enable us now to re-sign Claudell Washington [who had become a free agent]."

But a week later Washington signed a three-year deal with the California Angels. So along with the trade of designated hitter Jack Clark to San Diego back on October 24, Green suddenly found himself going to spring training minus his most durable returning starter and a combined 157 RBI from the previous year's lineup.

Remember now, all the while Steinbrenner kept repeating publicly that he was leaving the running of the club up to Green, Quinn, and his baseball people. "This year I'm staying out of it," he said. "I've got too much pressing business with my shipbuilding company."

Ah, but if Green was concerned about how depleted this Yankee team was suddenly starting to look, Steinbrenner had some reinforcements for him: Ron Guidry and Tommy John. The 38-year-old Guidry and the 45-year-old John had been cut loose by the Yankees after the '88 season and Green had made a point of saying he wasn't interested in bringing either of them back. It was time, he said, the Yankees started going in a new direction, building around speed, aggressiveness, and youth.

But when neither Guidry nor John could catch on with another team, Steinbrenner dusted off his "old softie, sugar-daddy image" for the fans and, ignoring Green's wishes, invited both the veteran pitchers to spring training with guaranteed $250,000 contracts.

"After I'd made my statement about T.J. being too old, George called me and told me he felt he had a commitment to John," Green said. "I said, 'Okay, I'll back off and we'll sell it.' It was no big deal, but then a couple of days later he springs Guidry on me."

Still, Green had only gotten relatively subtle hints of the "party" he had chosen to come to. After all, he had not yet put on his Yankee uniform. Over the winter he had embarked on a diet, cutting out hard liquor among other things, in an effort to portray a leaner, svelter image in his new pinstripes. It wasn't long into spring training, however, that he began longing for a few vodkas at night instead of light beer.

Spring training '89 was a camp of injuries and doctors, front office cover-ups and shake-ups, and nonstop talking by Rickey Henderson, who reported late as usual and, in the course of two interviews (one of which he denied), indicted the Yankees as a team of drunks and racists. For Green it was a disaster almost from the start. There were as many surgical procedures as victories, and more controversies than home runs.

Before the Yankees even played their first Grapefruit League game, Green lost Dave Winfield for the season with a herniated disc in his back. Not long after Winfield went down, shortstop Rafael Santana sustained a torn muscle in his elbow and was also lost for the season. Now Green was looking to replace 264 RBIs from the previous year's Yankee lineup, as well as his starting shortstop. And there was still the matter of putting together a pitching staff.

Typically, the MASH operation at Fort Lauderdale reached comical proportions. Santana's injury had occurred just when the Yankees were completing their latest overhaul of the front office. Quinn, who had taken over as general manager from Lou Piniella during the '88 season, obviously hadn't measured up in Steinbrenner's eyes. So on March 20 the Boss finalized a deal with Syd Thrift, the maverick baseball executive who had been fired the previous summer by the Pittsburgh Pirates after rebuilding their team into a contender.

On the day before Thrift was announced as taking over the trade-making duties from Quinn, Bill Madden, through a friend of Steinbrenner's, got wind of the impending move. After checking it out with a few team sources, including Quinn and Clyde King, Madden wrote the story for the *Daily News,* a story he thought was an exclusive. However, when Steinbrenner, through King, found out Madden had the story, he was furious and called PR man Harvey Greene to confirm to the rest of the beat reporters that the Yankees were indeed talking to Syd Thrift. Neither Greene nor any of the other reporters had any idea a change was even in the works.

But Steinbrenner wasn't through. Determined to find out who leaked the story to Madden, he ordered everyone in the organization to take lie detector tests. When, a couple of days later, Madden was sitting watching a game in the stands with Barry Halper, one of Steinbrenner's limited partners, he was taken aback when Halper expressed uneasiness.

"You probably know George has ordered lie detector tests about that Thrift story you wrote," said Halper. "1 don't know if I should be seen sitting here with you. He'll probably think I was the one who told you."

Madden could only laugh to himself at Steinbrenner's paranoia over a news story involving a front office executive—especially when Steinbrenner's ball club was going down in flames even before the season began.

But the one person affected most by Thrift's arrival was Quinn, who had retained his title, but nothing more. Ironically, it was only a few days before that Quinn had taken a stand of sorts by "unfiring" a secretary who had dared to challenge Steinbrenner.

The secretary, who had been hired for spring training to field calls for Quinn and Steinbrenner, wasn't familiar with baseball and club procedures. One day in mid-March Steinbrenner began shouting at the woman in the trailer office when she wasn't completing calls quickly enough. She didn't say anything, but the next day she taped a picture of Ayatollah Khomeini to the wall next to her desk, adding a caption: "Get off the fucking phone!" That had been Steinbrenner's repeated phrase to her the previous day.

When Steinbrenner came into the trailer and spotted the picture, he failed to see the humor in it. He told her to remove it, but she refused, saying: "If you want a secretary, I'm here. If you want slaves to berate, go find someone at Devil's Island."

Steinbrenner fired her, but two days later she was back. Moss Klein, spotting her, was surprised by her return and asked Quinn what happened.

"I needed her," Quinn said, "so I called her and told her to come back. George saw her but didn't say a word."

Before formally tendering the offer of front office chief to Thrift, Steinbrenner asked Green if he would be interested in it. But Green, who had already seen how little input the Yankee general manager really had when it came to making deals, declined the offer.

"I didn't want anything to do with the front office workings, I just wanted to manage," said Green. "So I guess I can't really complain at some of the moves they made. Still, after Washington got away and Winfield went down, I had to really question the haste in trading both Clark and Rhoden."

Steinbrenner's haste in banishing veteran pitcher Luis Sanchez that spring also tried Green's patience. The 35-year-old Sanchez had been invited to spring training as a nonroster player and was about a 100-to-1 shot to make the team anyway. During a March 7 night game against the Dodgers (only the fifth game of the spring for the Yankees), he was bombarded for seven hits, five runs, and a wild pitch in two innings, and sitting next to the Boss while all this was going on was Dallas Green's wife, Sylvia.

Green tells it this way: "Sylvia was sitting up there with George and she told me later he was acting like a maniac, screaming in the phone to Quinn to release the guy on the spot. I told George later that night: 'There's two more days before we make our cuts, I'll take care of it. I just won't pitch him anymore.'

"But that wasn't good enough. George told Quinn to do it right now. I was trying to build a rapport with the players, and this was just the kind of thing that makes a manager look bad in their eyes. There was no way I was going to let them think this was my decision to release the guy just like that. I had [coach Pat] Corrales, who spoke Spanish, talk to Sanchez."

Meanwhile, Green's most pressing need of the spring had become a shortstop to replace Santana. On March 23, following an examination by the Dodgers' renowned elbow and shoulder specialist, Dr. Frank Jobe, it was determined that Santana would need surgery. Naturally, to hold down the price of any shortstop they might be able to acquire in a trade, the Yankees were refusing to discuss the matter, and their spring training physician, the normally cooperative Dr. Dan Kanell, refused comment. So a few of the writers, seeking to find the truth, decided to go to Kanell's office in hopes of talking to Santana himself.

The writers were waiting in a downstairs lobby when Kanell's receptionist, a Nurse Ratched type, came down and informed them if they didn't disperse, she would call the police. Their crime, she said, was trespassing. And besides, she added, Santana wasn't there. He had canceled his appointment.

The writers returned to the Fort Lauderdale ballpark and were working in the press trailer when Santana suddenly pulled into the parking lot. He was quickly surrounded and began informing them of his impending surgery.

Steinbrenner, sitting in his adjacent trailer office, looked out in the parking lot, spotted Santana, and ordered Quinn to "get out there and shut him up." Quinn ran into the lot, grabbed publicity director Greene, and instructed him to break up the interview. Greene obliged and led Santana off to the clubhouse where Quinn was waiting in the trainers' room—an appropriate spot for a meeting if there ever was one.

A few minutes later, Santana stormed out into the lot, got into his car, and told the reporters: "I'm pissed. They don't want me talking at all. I'm leaving."

The message Steinbrenner had instructed Quinn to give Santana was simple: Santana was facing surgery and was in the final year of his contract. According to a source who was in the trailer office, Steinbrenner told Quinn to tell Santana that, if he continued talking, Steinbrenner would do his best to see to it that he never got another chance to play.

The telltale sign of just how bad spring training was going was that the most visible person in camp was Kanell, a Fort Lauderdale physician who normally serves as the Yankees spring team doctor. In the spring of '89 it was as though Kanell was living through the Korean War, with helicopters bringing in casualties on a daily basis. A tall, balding, soft-spoken man, Kanell became the Yankees' answer to Hawkeye Pierce—without the funny lines, of course. His gestures and shrugs to inquiring reporters became hilarious, because he knew that they knew his gag orders were coming from the top.

In Winfield's case the Steinbrenner-ordered cover-ups reached the height of absurdity. His surgery took place in Los Angeles on March 24 and was duly reported in the next day's newspapers with Winfield's attorney, Jeff Klein, issuing a statement from the head surgeon, Dr. Robert Watkins. Two days later the Yankees' official word on the matter was that Winfield was "seeking opinions" and that his playing status was "day-to-day."

By now, no one was getting more uneasy or exasperated by all the lying and cover-ups than Dallas Green, who, inevitably, was left to be the Yankee spokesman to the press on all of them. As Green reflected later: "George simply puts too much pressure on everybody. If the guy needs an operation, you can't change it. But he's there telling the doctors what to do, telling the trainers what to do. It's all part of his game to rule by fear. But all it accomplished was everybody being uptight."

According to Green, Winfield's back injury might have been avoided had the $2-million-per-year outfielder come to spring training in better shape. There had been some suspicion that Winfield knew about his back injury for some time but said nothing—and did nothing about it because he wanted to make sure Steinbrenner picked up the final two option years of his contract. (Steinbrenner did that in October of '88.)

Green, however, discounted that theory, venturing the opinion that the injury was more likely caused by Winfield's reporting to camp "some 10 to 12 pounds overweight" and then trying to do too much too soon in the first couple of sessions. "He wasn't prepared," Green said.

Green was disappointed that, following surgery, Winfield chose to be absent from the team for the entire season. "I wondered: 'Why wouldn't Dave be with the team,'" Green said. "If nothing else, he should have been there to show the guys he cared about them and the team. But there was no rehabilitation program set up with the team. The real reason, I think, he didn't come back was because he didn't give a shit about George."

As if Green didn't already have enough problems, there was Rickey Henderson to contend with. Green knew Henderson's prime asset was running, but he didn't know that included running off at the mouth.

Henderson, as was his spring custom, reported a few days after everyone else and offered one of his usual lame excuses, prompting Green's first public bad-mouthing of one of his players. "Rickey Henderson is not going to run the Yankees in 1989. Dallas Green is," Green said. "We sent letters to everybody about when to report. Maybe Rickey can't read." Then, in a snide reference to Margo Adams, the much-celebrated mistress of Boston Red Sox batting champion Wade Boggs, Green added, "We found out where he is—he's over at Margo's house getting a little bit of luck."

The players, who had learned to accept "Rickey being Rickey," didn't take his tardiness as seriously as Green. As Tommy John confided to Moss Klein sometime later: "Every team had its problems. We had Rickey, the Red Sox had Margo Adams. At least Rickey was a better player."

Not long after Henderson settled into his spring work routine, he found himself the center of controversy once again. It was after a team workout on February 27 that Rickey, in the course of a casual conversation with reporters Tom Pedulla of the Westchester-Rockland newspapers and Steve Serby of the *New York Post,* suddenly blurted out without any provocation that the Yankees had been a team of alcohol abusers in 1988. In particular, Henderson told the astonished reporters that there had been too much drinking going on aboard the team charter flights in 1988 and that it had affected the team's play.

"Alcohol doesn't leave your body overnight," added Dr. Henderson.

Well, what a firestorm *that* stirred up. Lou Piniella quickly reminded the press that, shortly after he replaced Billy Martin as manager, he had removed the hard liquor from the charters. And as one Yankee cracked: "There couldn't have been that severe a problem when the old booze master [Martin] was manager because the booze cart never made it out of the first-class section."

Despite the players' being accustomed to "Rickey being Rickey," this time they felt he had gone too far.

"He drinks along with everyone else," said Dave Righetti. "People in glass houses shouldn't throw rocks. The team will be labeled as alcoholics now, and I don't like to be labeled like that."

Righetti was particularly upset because Henderson had made it clear that he was talking about Righetti's close friends on the team, Bob Shirley, Neil Allen, and Tim Stoddard, all of whom were known to enjoy their spirits while getting airborne—once airborne.

The tension was finally lifted when Gary Ward, Henderson's closest friend on the team, took it upon himself to bring Henderson and Righetti together for a bury-the-hatchet talk on the practice field beyond the left field wall of Fort Lauderdale Stadium.

Later in the spring, however, Henderson contracted "foot-in-mouth disease" once again, reportedly switching his theme from "Bronx Boozers" to "Bronx Bigots." In a *Daily News* story by Michael Kay, Henderson was quoted as charging the Yankee organization with being prejudiced, saying, "If I was white, they'd have built a statue for me already."

Perhaps realizing he had really gone too far this time, Henderson denied ever making those statements to Kay. "I never even talked to Steven Kay," he said, obviously so confused by now that he was unable to keep his reporters straight.

Like all of his predecessors, Green was quickly discovering that once one brushfire is snuffed out, another quickly erupts in a different part of the

Yankee clubhouse. It had been prior to all of Henderson's pronouncements that Green was confronted by the perpetual "Winfield problem." Actually, Green unwittingly brought it on himself when he commented casually to the press one day that "Winfield is really an amazing person to have been able perform so well with all the off-the-field distractions he's had."

The next day, when Steinbrenner (who, remember again, was "staying out of it") saw that quote, he informed Green of one of the cardinal rules of being Yankee manager: never say anything nice about Dave Winfield. In fact, Steinbrenner continued, it was now up to Green to "hammer Winfield." But Green refused, thus laying the seeds for his own inevitable falling-out with the Boss.

Because of Winfield's back injury, Green was spared the headaches his predecessors had encountered regarding Steinbrenner's persistent orders to bench, platoon, or just plain "hammer" Winfield.

That is not to say Green didn't have his share of new and different headaches. The absence of Winfield led to three trades in an effort to fill the void left by his 100-RBI bat. Mel Hall was acquired from Cleveland to help out in right field; Steve Balboni returned from Seattle to bolster the right-handed DH spot; and Jesse Barfield was later obtained from Toronto to take over permanently in right.

The Hall acquisition was particularly interesting, because Green had traded Hall to Cleveland when Green was the Cubs' general manager. The reason, Green later admitted, was the same reason Cleveland couldn't wait to unload him: Hall's talent was too often overshadowed by his off-the-field exploits. In fact, what finally convinced the Indians to trade a productive hitter for Joel Skinner, a backup catcher who never hit, was a series of incidents involving Hall's wife and Hall's girlfriend during spring training in Tucson, Arizona.

According to Cleveland team sources, Hall, who had never been an everyday player, had his own special platoon system. He had both his wife and girlfriend staying at the same hotel, the Viscount Suites in Tucson, presumably counting on the fact that "never the twain shall meet." As fate would have it, they did. While the Indians were playing a game against the Seattle Mariners in Tempe, Hall's wife, Tanya, was sitting at the hotel pool when she was tipped off by one of the other Indians' wives that the woman lounging a few chairs away was Hall's "import" from Minnesota. Tanya Hall immediately confronted the other woman, and the subsequent fistfight between the two became legend, much like a scene out of "Dynasty" between Alexis and Crystal. It took the hotel manager and a few security people to break it up.

Unfortunately for Hall, among the witnesses to the ugly scene was the eight-year-old granddaughter of Indians' general manager Hank Peters. Unaware of what happened, Hall returned to the hotel and headed immediately for his girlfriend's room. Imagine his surprise when he found his bride of five years waiting at the door! Another scene ensued, and Hall wisely decided that his girlfriend had to go. Unwisely, though, he didn't see to it that she went far enough. He got her a room at the nearby Sheraton Pueblo, and sure enough, Tanya Hall found her again. After round three, Peters thrust Hall into the welcoming arms of Steinbrenner's Yankees.

Predictably, Hall wound up getting involved in two clubhouse skirmishes with Henderson, who was his closest friend on the team. The first occurred in the shower room at Yankee Stadium in mid-April when a friendly bout of "slap boxing" got suddenly serious as Hall slapped Henderson in the face. A few weeks later in Chicago, the temperamental friends were trying out wrestling holds when, once again, Hall went too far, prompting a flurry of retaliatory swats from Henderson.

Perhaps fortunately for all concerned, the Henderson-Hall dynamic duo was broken up on June 21 when the Yankees traded Henderson to the Oakland Athletics for pitchers Greg Cadaret and Eric Plunk and outfielder Luis Polonia. Henderson's sluggish start (.247 average, subpar on-base percentage, and generally uninspired play) paralleled the Yankees' rapid descent into mediocrity. At the time of the trade the Yankees were 33–35, after getting off to a 1–7 start. It was decided that Henderson's excessive contract demands (in light of his looming free agency after the season) weren't worth negotiating.

On June 18 Bill Madden reported in the *Daily News* that the Yankees were indeed shopping Henderson, having decided not to sign him. Madden's story stated that the San Francisco Giants were negotiating with the Yankees, but Henderson, who had a no-trade clause in his contract, later informed the Yankees he would approve only a deal to Oakland, his hometown. Three days later Henderson was traded to Oakland, but not before Steinbrenner once again threatened to administer another round of lie detector tests to determine who had been the source of Madden's story.

Shortly after Henderson's departure Green expressed his true feelings about the controversial and moody star. "There's a better feel in the clubhouse now," Green told Moss Klein one night after a rainout in Chicago. "There's more of a sense of camaraderie than there was before. With Rickey, I think everybody was kind of in awe of him, afraid to say anything to him. Everybody suspected Rickey played games at times, and injuries were wondered about. Rickey was more of an 'I' game player than a 'we' game player. The way he played would help the team, but it was more of an individual style."

Henderson had no love for Green, either. In mid-August he so much as confirmed that in an interview with Madden. "I always thought it was better to pat a guy on the back than to tear him down," Henderson said. "But that was never the way in New York. They told me they didn't sign me because they were trying to motivate me. Motivate me? Couldn't they see they were screwing me up? Dallas was no different. He came in and demanded we play better. You can't demand. They won't ever win until they let guys just go out and play.

"When things go wrong, they start changing players all around. They just don't have a game plan."

Two weeks later, in an interview with Lyle Spencer of the *New York Post*, Henderson bashed Green some more and made it clear he never forgave the manager for the spring training comments about Margo Adams and his ability to read. "He never did apologize to me for any of those things he said," said Henderson.

Although Green may have been happy to be rid of the Henderson problem, the overall Yankee situation continued to deteriorate. The team hovered close to .500 through the All-Star break, which was good enough to stay competitive in the weak American League East. But shortly after the break the wheels all fell off; the Yankees went into a disastrous 10–20 tailspin, falling from second place to sixth with a 56–65 record on August 17.

The next day Green was fired in Detroit, but the firing had more to do with his worsening relationship with Steinbrenner than it did with the worsening play of the team.

From the very beginning Dallas Green was an outsider, and in retrospect, that, more than anything else, inhibited his ability to impose his style and philosophies on Steinbrenner's Yankees. He stood out, but he never fit in—not with Steinbrenner, not with the rest of the Yankee front office, and not with the players.

The players, above all, never got used to Green's frequent criticisms of them. If, in the past, they thought that Steinbrenner was excessive in his public blasts, they now felt Green was even worse. In addition, they came to ridicule Green's frequent Steinbrenner-like pep talks.

"I think Dallas probably lost the players in his very first talk to them, down in Florida," said Tommy John. "He got up there and said: 'I'm the toughest SOB you guys will ever play for.' Kind of reminded me of that old flag with the snake on it that said: 'Don't tread on me.' Then he went on about the coaches, who were to be perceived by us as his brute force."

"Even in spring training, it got to be too much," agreed one of the other veteran Yankees. "He kept giving us pep talks every day. Then, when the season started and things weren't going good, we'd have these meetings where he'd be saying, 'C'mon you cocksuckers, start playing or I'm gonna get your ass.' That's not the way to do it. He just lost everybody."

Added another player, who joined the team later in the season: "It had got to the point where guys told me they would just sit there with no emotion, shaking their heads, when he was yelling. They were just waiting for him to shut up. From what I could tell, nobody liked him."

On the Yankees' first trip to the West Coast in mid-May, Green was especially critical of the team's play as they lost three of four to the Angels in Anaheim. After one of the losses, Green told the writers: "So far, I don't like the way we've played. We stink and I told them so. Some of them must have had their heads in Disneyland or somewhere. They didn't play with any life or with any indication that their minds were on the game."

Green went on to say in that session that the performance of pitcher Andy Hawkins "wasn't a professional effort."

That, in turn, brought to a head the players' resentment toward Green, which had started in spring training and been gradually building. Hawkins expressed his displeasure in a meeting with Green the following day. That night, following a 4–3 loss to the Angels in the series finale, a group of players, including Don Mattingly, boarded the team charter for Oakland, armed with funny hats resembling the ears and nose of the Disney character "Goofy." In view and hearing range of Green, the players launched into a parodied rendition of the Mickey Mouse song, spelling out the phrase "We do stink, we do stink" as a substitute for "Mickey Mouse, Mickey Mouse."

Needless to say, Green and his coaches weren't amused. Yet surprisingly, a whole day went by before Green summoned Mattingly to his office in the visitors' clubhouse in Oakland. As Mattingly later explained: "Basically, he wanted to talk about some things that were on my mind and the minds of some of the players. I just voiced some of the opinions of the players. Never in my wildest dreams would I attempt to tell Dallas Green anything in terms of changing his approach. I don't think that would be advisable."

Green, however, in a conversation with Bill Madden, later revealed that Mattingly did, in fact, advise him to tone down his criticisms. According to Green, the Yankee first baseman said: "We get beat around enough by George, and then the fans get on our ass. It's not fair."

Green, in turn, told Mattingly: "You've got to take the heat. I have to answer questions from the reporters for a hundred sixty-two games, but you guys go into the players' room and hide."

Green also insisted to Mattingly that "every time I bang you guys, I try to say something positive as well. But I don't lie, and I expect you guys to stand up."

In his conversation with Madden, though, Green conceded that he was dealing with a team of very sensitive players. "After each mistake, guys were talked to by the coaches," Green said. "I knew the [team] psyche was so fragile."

And as third base coach Lee Elia pointed out: "The problem with this team was that these guys never ragged on each other. It's the only team I'd ever been with that you didn't hear guys getting on each other. It's like they just didn't know each other."

At that point in the season, Steinbrenner was still supporting Green, although an ominous sign for all was the Boss coming out in the open, rising up like the Loch Ness Monster and declaring he was no longer staying out of it.

"The truce is over," Steinbrenner said. "If they're going to attack Dallas, they'll have me to deal with. I'm the one getting gypped here. I ought to get all their agents in a room and tell them they're taking me for a sucker.

"Dallas says we stink? He's right. We stink. Dallas is the only reason we're still in the hunt. He's trying to turn babies into men. They don't like him saying things about them in public? Well, they play in public."

What had particularly upset the players was Green's singling out the play of popular third baseman Mike Pagliarulo. "Nobody tries harder than he does," Green said of Pagliarulo, "but whether his skills have deteriorated to the point where he's not going to get them back, I just don't know."

Pagliarulo responded mildly, saying only that he wasn't accustomed to a manager knocking him and the team in the newspapers. Nevertheless, Steinbrenner, as if on cue, couldn't wait to jump on poor Pagliarulo, too. "It astounds me. He can't catch, throw, or hit," Steinbrenner said of the third baseman who was hitting .154, with 1 homer and 3 RBIs at the time. "He should keep quiet until he can hit his weight, until his RBIs catch up with his age, and until he can play third base like a normal person."

It was not long after that, however, that another insurrection by the players resulted in Steinbrenner second-guessing Green's handling of the team. One can only wonder what Rickey Henderson was thinking on a couple of the team's charter flights when a group of players, after downing too many beers, began tearing apart the seats, throwing food and decks of playing cards, and harassing the flight attendants.

"You walk off the plane and you feel embarrassed," said Tommy John. "There's food all over the floor, pats of butter stuck to the ceiling, seats torn out."

Mattingly called a team meeting to urge a halt to the hijinks, but the damage had been done.

"George got a bill from TWA for something like ten thousand dollars," Green said. "I had to fine five or six guys, and the coaches began sitting in the back. We also took the beer and wine off the planes. I told the players: 'You think I don't fight for you guys, and this is what you do. If you can't go two hours without a drink, you don't need a manager, you need a fucking doctor.'"

At the same time, though, Green got an earful from Steinbrenner. In only the second time the owner called him in for a meeting, Steinbrenner began questioning Green's ability to discipline his troops. Green, now irritated by both his player's embarrassing behavior and Steinbrenner's comments, replied, "I ain't babysitting these guys."

Actually, this was not the first time Steinbrenner had told Green to tighten up the team discipline. On April 14, only the 10th game of the season, the Boss (who wasn't getting involved) became irate over a botched play in which Yankee third baseman Tom Brookens didn't cover third on a double steal against the Twins. The reason Brookens didn't cover third was because, with the runners at first and second, Green called for a play in which Brookens was to charge the plate to protect against a bunt. If the double steal was on, the play was for catcher Don Slaught to throw to second. But Slaught, whose baseball smarts came under frequent question from not only Green and his managerial predecessors but also the players, surprised everybody by throwing to third—which, of course, was uncovered.

Steinbrenner, watching from upstairs, immediately ordered front office chief Syd Thrift to fine Brookens $500. Thrift relayed the order to Green, who explained that Brookens hadn't done anything wrong. Rather than try and explain the play to Steinbrenner—who, they were confident, wouldn't understand what they were talking about—Green and Thrift didn't fine anyone and quietly let the matter drop.

It was also not long before Steinbrenner began questioning Green's handling of the pitchers. On May 30 Seattle's rookie sensation Ken Griffey, Jr., hit a pair of homers off Yankee right-hander Jimmy Jones to give the Mariners a 3–2 win. The next day Green was summoned to Steinbrenner's office. If Green had underestimated the lunacy of the Steinbrenner operation, that meeting must surely have opened his eyes.

When he arrived at Steinbrenner's office, Green was taken aback as the Boss unveiled a series of graphs and charts, outlining the futility of the Yankees in games in which they trailed by six runs after the fifth, sixth, and seventh innings. The point Steinbrenner was apparently trying to make was that Green was leaving his pitchers in too long.

"George," said Green, "I realize that it doesn't look good on paper. But if you do this same project with any other team, Oakland or whatever, you'll get the same results."

Just the same, Steinbrenner wasn't interested in Green's explanation.

"You're leaving them in too long," Steinbrenner insisted, pointing to his graphs.

"He just wanted to bang [pitching coach] Billy [Connors] and me around," Green said later.

It was at that same meeting that Steinbrenner informed Green he was bringing up Deion Sanders, the flamboyant ex-football player from Florida State. Sanders, who had made a surprisingly good impression in spring training, was ultimately headed for the National Football League. But Steinbrenner had another need for him at this point. He was upset that young Griffey had stolen the show at Yankee Stadium the night before and wanted to display his own version of a phenom.

Since Roberto Kelly, the Yankees' regular center fielder, was sidelined by an injury, Green offered no resistance to this latest Steinbrenner gimmick.

"He ain't no Bo [Jackson]" was all Green told Steinbrenner, while hoping privately that the outspoken Sanders, who called himself "Prime Time," would just keep his mouth shut.

The futility of trying to satisfy Steinbrenner and keep the ball club on an even keel was now beginning to set in with both Green and Thrift. Both could see the inevitability of parting company with the Boss. Both were also being treated for high blood pressure by Dr. Hershon. You didn't need to be a doctor to know that blood pressure problems and Steinbrenner were a bad mix.

As Green later related: "Every day, Syd would come down to my office from two-thirty to three-thirty and tell me about George's continual nitpicking. He beat on the coaches, second-guessing Lee [Elia] at third and [Pat] Corrales. He sent a list down about how many guys got picked off first base. He was also always going on about the pitching being .500. I told him: 'That's what you've got here, .500 pitchers.'"

Green said he "tried desperately to stay away from things" in terms of public debates with Steinbrenner. But now the Boss was circling his prey, and it was only a matter of time before he would succeed in provoking Green.

In late June *The Sporting News* had asked *Hartford Courant* reporter Jack O'Connell to do a story for them about the new Yankee camaraderie and how Steinbrenner was relying so much on Green and Thrift to run the show. "I better do this quickly," O'Connell said knowingly, "because we know it's not gonna last."

Sure enough that week, following two consecutive final-at-bat losses to the Detroit Tigers, Steinbrenner told reporters that he thought the team was better than it had been playing and, for the first time, raised questions publicly about Green's managing. "I feel like the principal when he questions the coach in *Hoosiers,* and the coach says, 'Don't worry, I know what I'm doing,'"

Steinbrenner told reporter Tom Pedulla, "I hope this has the same ending as *Hoosiers.*"

Green, sitting in the tiny visiting manager's office at Tiger Stadium, downplayed the Boss' surprise attack. "He has mentioned things about the coaches before," Green said, "when guys are picked off, why guys don't hit, why pitchers aren't pitching good. I've been in this game a long time, and I really haven't seen too many coaches win or lose baseball games. If he feels that what he says is going to be motivation, that ain't gonna work. I don't think we can work any harder than we have.

"But I don't think it's that serious yet. Nobody has been fired."

Six weeks later, when the Yankees returned to Detroit, Green and his four coaches were. Of course, by that time the Yankee season and the Steinbrenner/ Green relationship had, in tandem, almost totally deteriorated. Steinbrenner's continual sniping, capped by a critical attack on Green and his coaches which he leaked to *Daily News* sportswriter Phil Pepe on August 2, finally prompted Green to retaliate. The next day, responding to the Pepe story, Green, who had earlier referred to Steinbrenner as "that guy," gave him a new nickname— "Manager George."

With that said, Green had taken off the gloves. Almost daily thereafter, he taunted Steinbrenner with verbal zingers—knowing full well that he couldn't win on the field as he had hoped, and therefore had nothing to lose but a job he no longer wanted. He twice chided Steinbrenner for taking the Yankees' scouts off the road, and after a game in Toronto in which Mel Hall threw out a runner at home plate from left field, he said: "Hall's play was a result of the work he's done with the coaches. Everybody who's around knows that. Only the ones who aren't around don't realize what the coaches have done."

Hartford Courant baseball columnist Claire Smith, who had covered the Yankees for six years through 1987, had made the trip and couldn't conceal her amusement at this outburst. "It never changes, around here, does it?" Smith said. "Every year, the same plots. Just the characters change."

The day before, Green had been sitting in his office in Toronto's Skydome, celebrating his 55th birthday, when someone asked him if he thought the "Manager George" quote was going to get him fired. "I don't really give a damn," he said. "He should have learned from what happened before. If what you've tried for 10 years hasn't worked, all the changing of managers and coaches and the criticism, you'd think you'd want to try some other way.

"This has happened before to every other manager and the coaches. The only big deal is, I'll stand up and say what I think. I'll do my job and my coaches will do their job as best as we can until the day he calls me up to his office and says that we're no longer wanted."

That day came on August 18 at the Dearborn Hyatt, some 10 miles out of Detroit, the morning after the Yankees had won the opener of a four-game series against the Tigers. Two days earlier, outfielder Luis Polonia had been arrested in Milwaukee for having sex with a 15-year-old girl in his room at the Pfister Hotel, where the Yankees had been staying. If that incident didn't make Green's status more untenable, it surely gave Steinbrenner the impetus to do something drastic to knock it off the front pages of the New York tabloids.

As Green later related, "I couldn't stop Luis from fucking that broad"— nor could he now stop Steinbrenner from firing him. Steinbrenner swooped into Dearborn the night of August 17 and summoned Green to his room the following morning.

"We've reached the point where I've got to make some changes," Steinbrenner told Green. "I've agonized over this and canceled a trip to Morocco to come out here. I'm just gonna make some changes. Every time I mention the coaches, you get protective."

"George," interrupted Green, "you know why I'm that way. These guys busted their ass for me. You don't appreciate that. If you're gonna fire the coaches, fire the head guy. That's the way to do it. You've done this before. It never works. It's disruptive, that's all."

"Okay," said Steinbrenner. "But this is tearing me up. I've talked to my wife about it."

"You know," said Green, now that he was officially terminated, "you've got guys who are stealing from you. You're too good to so many people. But the guys you had here now, you beat the shit out of. They didn't steal from you. They earned every nickel from you."

"Will any of these guys help me?" Steinbrenner asked, almost apologetically.

"They already have," replied Green tersely.

It was then that Steinbrenner, as is his custom in all these unpleasant face-to-face final confrontations with his managers, attempted to keep Green in the organization and thus keep him quiet as well.

"You're the only guy who will tell me the truth," Steinbrenner said. "I need people like you."

"I think part of the reason you pay me is to give you an honest answer," Green agreed. "I don't know how to rose-color anything. Sometimes it hurts."

"Well," said Steinbrenner, "will you stay on? I'll make it worth your while, over and above our present agreement [Green had a two-year contract at $350,000 per]."

"This experience is something I have to get over," said Green.

A few days later Steinbrenner revealed Green's statement to him about "guys stealing from you"—only, according to Steinbrenner, Green mentioned specifically Lou Piniella, Billy Martin, Clyde King, and Gene Michael, all former Yankee managers who were still in the employ of the team. It was a clever ploy by Steinbrenner to rile up Martin and Piniella so they'd return fire on Green, who had himself not relented on his attacks against the Boss. Martin and Piniella both fell for it, too, each issuing statements on Yankee stationery denouncing Green.

But in an interview with Bill Madden, Green angrily denied ever having mentioned any names.

"Above all," he said, "I never would have included Piniella in that group. He was an okay guy who did a lot for Steinbrenner in all his roles there. Martin and Stick, that's something else. And Clyde King. He gets paid a hundred thousand dollars a year for saying 'yes.'"

Green had said all along that when he was fired, he wouldn't go quietly, and he certainly kept his promise. Among his parting shots, in an interview with Bill Conlin of the *Philadelphia Daily News:*

- "For the first time, he [Steinbrenner] didn't have access to the clubhouse as far as spies were concerned, so he gave me a wide berth. He hammered hell out of Syd Thrift about me. Then Syd would come down and moan to me about what an impossible SOB George is to deal with."
- "From all accounts, I was the lucky guy among his managers, not having him breathing down my neck every hour of the day and night."
- "Now George is back with his puppet machine. He doesn't want anybody around he can't command. He couldn't make me change the lineup. He couldn't make me fine people or do anything I didn't want to do."
- "George doesn't know a fucking thing about the game of baseball. That's the bottom line."
- "Let's face it, there is absolutely no hope that their organization will be a winning organization as long as Steinbrenner runs the show.... It's sad. He has no organization there now. He has absolutely no pride. The ballplayers there now have no feeling of being a Yankee."

Suffice it to say, those and other comments ended any chance Green had of staying in the Yankee organization—not that he had any intention of staying anyway. He was perfectly content to sit back and collect Steinbrenner's paychecks for another year.

With Green's departure, along with coaches Charlie Fox, Lee Elia, Pat Corrales, and Frank Howard, Steinbrenner's donkey tail was placed on Bucky Dent, who had been managing at Columbus, the Yankees' AAA farm. Dent, the former Yankee shortstop and '78 playoff and World Series hero, represented the 17th Yankee managerial change in the 17 years of Steinbrenner's ownership.

Before turning to Dent, though, Steinbrenner tried to pin the manager's tail on Lou Piniella for the third time. He called Piniella from Dearborn and asked him if he would take the job again.

"I'm really not interested, George," Piniella said.

"Why not?" Steinbrenner asked.

"We've been through this twice, and I just don't like being fired," Piniella replied.

"Well," said Steinbrenner, "don't give me your answer right away. Talk to your wife. I'll call you back."

Piniella did discuss the offer with his wife, Anita, very briefly, before coming to the same conclusion: there would be no Lou III.

Besides, Piniella had been through a trying enough season in 1989 without managing a game for Steinbrenner. He was on the first year of a three-year $1.2-million manager's contract that became a special services contract because he had been fired before it even began. After turning down offers to manage Seattle and Houston over the winter, Piniella, at Steinbrenner's suggestion, accepted a position as a pre- and postgame analyst for Madison Square Garden Network's Yankee telecasts.

It was not long, however, before Steinbrenner began invoking the "special services" clause in Piniella's contract. Until then, Piniella had gone out of his way to distance himself from Green and the new Yankee staff. He had refused to attend the winter meetings and never set foot in the clubhouse. Steinbrenner's first call on Piniella's services was as part-time hitting coach, an ominous first sign that the Boss was letting Green know he was not happy with the coaching staff.

In late May it looked as if Piniella might finally be able to extract himself from the uncomfortable predicament of being viewed, like Billy Martin, as Steinbrenner's ever-available manager-in-waiting. The Toronto Blue Jays fired their manager, Jimy Williams, and received permission from Steinbrenner to talk to Piniella. But when Toronto general manager Pat Gillick decided Piniella was his man, Steinbrenner sprung a surprise "catch" on him: in order to let Piniella go, Steinbrenner wanted one of four prize pitching prospects from Toronto. While Gillick was considering this, Piniella privately conceded: "If they give him one, he'll want two. He's just not gonna let me go."

Steinbrenner's decision to do everything possible to keep Piniella around proved visionary when, inadvertently, Piniella became involved in a verbal feud with Green. During one of his pregame TV spots, Piniella suggested Roberto Kelly, batting in the .340 range in the ninth spot, might contribute even more hitting higher up in the order. Piniella wasn't the first to suggest it, but because it was the former manager questioning the current manager, the tabloids' TV writers jumped on it. That prompted an angry response from Green, a televised rebuttal from Piniella, and most surely, a great sense of delight on the part of Steinbrenner, who didn't even have to orchestrate this one.

Ironically, after one of his scouting missions at Steinbrenner's behest, Piniella recommended Dent as a possible future manager. So when Steinbrenner fired Green and couldn't talk Piniella into taking the job again, he decided to give Dent the opportunity, rather than recycling Martin for the sixth time.

Initially, it didn't look as if Dent would last very long, either. The Yankees, despite whatever ill feelings they might have had for Green, were again thrown into turmoil and responded to this latest change of command by losing three in a row to the Tigers, the team with the worst record in baseball.

When they returned home, the losing continued and the overall situation worsened. The team lost 11 of its first 13 games under Dent, falling hopelessly out of the race. And now the fans were turning on them, too, viciously voicing their disgust with Steinbrenner and his reckless policies.

On August 27, during a loss to the Baltimore Orioles at Yankee Stadium, a new chant erupted from the fans: "George must go! George must go! George must go!" That became a daily occurrence at the stadium, accompanied by equally expressive banners, most of which were quickly confiscated by Steinbrenner's security people.

But Steinbrenner couldn't silence the growing number of hostile fans. Suddenly numerous groups were being formed, decrying Steinbrenner's systematic destruction of the Yankee franchise and its great tradition and demanding that he sell the team. Among them: FOUL (Fans Opposed to Useless Leadership); SOS (Stamp Out Steinbrenner); Bring Back the Yankees, and even groups from as far away as Phoenix, BOSS (Battered Onlookers Sick of Steinbrenner), and Detroit, GROSS (Get Rid of Steinbrenner Silliness).

Locally, a group called NO BOSS (National Organization to Boycott and Stop Steinbrenner) proposed a boycott of the Yankees' game against the Tigers on September 29.

Still more fans began coming to Yankee Stadium wearing hand-made "George Must Go" T-shirts, some of them with paper bags over their heads. When a lot of these groups began displaying banners in Yankee Stadium, only to have them removed by security patrols, the American Civil Liberties Union got into the act, threatening to sue Steinbrenner for First Amendment violations. This prompted Steinbrenner to hastily arrange a first-ever "Banner Night" at Yankee Stadium, an event that was staged with less than 24 hours' notice for the fans.

Nevertheless, fans produced more than 150 banners on the night of September 15—a huge percentage of which were negative toward Steinbrenner.

One fan, Andy Padian, brought a banner that read: "Pardon US, George, Sell the Yankees," a reference to Steinbrenner's 1989 presidential pardon for illegal contributions to Richard Nixon's 1972 campaign. Padian revealed that Steinbrenner's security people had previously taken that same banner down four different times, once throwing him out of the ballpark and, another time, arresting him for disorderly conduct.

The only fan thrown out of the park on "Banner Night" was Bob DeMartin, founder of the "Bring Back the Yankees" movement, who arrived at the Stadium garbed in a monk's outfit, a huge wooden cross around his neck, and displaying a banner that read: "Forgive Him Lord, He Knows Not What He Does."

Amid all of this fan furor, Steinbrenner was increasingly taking out his frustrations on Thrift, who had come to realize that his position as Yankee front office chief was nothing more than a facade. Not only had Steinbrenner told him that he had no control over the Yankee scouts, but he'd also been informed that he couldn't bring any minor league players to the big leagues without first getting approval from George Bradley, the farm director who was based in Steinbrenner's minor league/scouting "stalag" in Tampa. As Green's bench coach, Charlie Fox (a former general manager of the Montreal Expos), told Thrift: "How can you function as a general manager when you have no control over the scouts or the minor leagues? What good is a general manager like that?"

What good, indeed?

After the Green firing, Steinbrenner publicly ridiculed Thrift for failing to restrain Green from popping off. "It's about time that 'good ole boy' stood up and was counted," Steinbrenner said of the Virginia-born Thrift, adding that he was very disappointed in the performance of his senior vice president.

In his first roundtable meeting with Dent, the coaches, and Thrift, Steinbrenner continued to hammer away at Thrift. Finally Thrift couldn't take it any longer, and on August 29 he resigned. Steinbrenner, however, wasn't through with him. On a local TV show on September 7, Steinbrenner, out of the blue, revealed that the commissioner's office was investigating improprieties on the part of the Yankees regarding information on a scouting computer.

According to Steinbrenner, there had been some evidence that the Yankees had access to the scouting computer of the Pittsburgh Pirates, Thrift's former organization. The investigation later centered on Thrift's assistant, Jim Bowden, who, according to sources, had to be escorted by Yankee security people out of Yankee Stadium the day after Thrift resigned.

"I can't believe Syd Thrift was involved in any wrongdoing," Steinbrenner said in his best sincere manner, while all the time skillfully planting the hint of discredit regarding his former employee.

Steinbrenner had actually intended to go public with his in-house "discovery" over the scouting computer situation on September 1. Earlier that day, he had gone to the trouble of tracking down Commissioner Bart Giamatti at his summer home in Martha's Vineyard to inform him of his "concern" and to solicit the support of the commissioner's office in vigorously pursuing the investigation. Later that day, however, Giamatti dropped dead of a heart attack, and Steinbrenner's calculated leak of the Thrift investigation had to be delayed.

But that didn't prevent Steinbrenner from seizing opportunity. On learning of Giamatti's sudden death, and knowing that he had had a conversation with him earlier in the day (and that he might, in fact, have been the last baseball person to whom the commissioner talked), Steinbrenner had freelance public relations man Howard Rubenstein call the Associated Press in New York to inform them the Yankee Boss would be seen grieving over Giamatti on all three of the national network newscasts that night. And sure enough, there was the Boss on CBS, NBC, and ABC, telling the nation how deeply saddened he was about the loss of Giamatti, who, he said, was the greatest commissioner of them all. And, of course, on all the newscasts he made certain to say that he had "probably" been the last person to talk to Giamatti, although the time of his phone call to the commissioner varied with each telling of the tale.

Said one Giamatti aide, "Bart would have been really sickened over the fact that Steinbrenner wound up being his designated mourner on national TV."

Meanwhile, the day Thrift resigned, the Yankees were humiliated, 19–5, by the Oakland A's. Dent at that time appeared on the way out, with the specter of Billy VI looming ever larger. And Steinbrenner did nothing to discourage that speculation when he said: "We may have rushed Bucky. He might not be ready."

But then a bizarre thing happened. The Yankees, with nothing to lose except another manager, suddenly went on a nine-game winning streak, their longest in more than two years! So excited and impressed was that eternal man of the moment, Steinbrenner, that he announced on the day after the eighth straight win that he was extending Dent's contract through 1990.

Green, who was now a couple of weeks into his paid sabbatical on his farm in West Grove, Pennsylvania, couldn't help but chuckle over Steinbrenner's sudden decision to extend Dent.

"I'm happy for Bucky, he's put in his time," Green said. "But I don't know if he's strong enough to deal with the ups and downs with George."

Actually, Green had been skeptical of Dent long before he was replaced by him. One of the prime concerns of the Yankees leading up to the '89 season was the shortstop position, since the incumbent, Rafael Santana, had sustained an elbow injury late in the '88 season. It turned out that Alvaro Espinoza, a career minor leaguer, more than filled the void in 1989, but as Green said, it was almost by accident.

"I couldn't help but remember those first organizational meetings in Tampa when we were all sitting around going over the player personnel, and the problem at shortstop came up," Green recalled. "We were desperately looking for a shortstop, and Bucky, who had had Espinoza right there at Columbus the year before, never mentioned his name. If it wasn't for [Green's coach] Pat Corrales, who had watched Espinoza as an opposing manager in the minors, we'd have never known about him. Corrales was the one who told me that Espinoza was the answer—even though Steinbrenner wound up trying to take credit for that, too."

The Yankee players, however, clearly had taken a liking to Dent's more mellow approach, which they found to be a refreshing contrast to Green's constant whiplashing.

It was Dave Righetti who probably best summed up their feelings when he said: "Bucky should be judged more by the way he handled the losing. That's the tough part. He didn't panic or scream or yell at us the way we were yelled at all year [by Green]. One way didn't work, and the other way seems to be working."

But with Steinbrenner in control of the Yankee destiny, would things ever *really* work? A few days before the 1989 season ended, Steinbrenner answered the fans' protests with precisely what they didn't want to hear.

"Next year, I'm going to be more involved," the Boss said—a pronouncement that must surely have roused a good laugh from Green and Thrift. Then, Bob Quinn, practically the last bastion of stability and reason in the Yankee front office, informed Steinbrenner that he, too, was resigning.

"I don't understand, Bob," Steinbrenner said. "You have a good situation here. Why do you want to leave?"

"Because," said Quinn, "I've had it. I was the only general manager in baseball who went through spring training with no assistant and no regular secretary, and through it all you blamed me for everything. Then, you brought in Syd Thrift over me, further humiliating me. And to top it all off, I haven't had a vacation in two years."

"Okay," said Steinbrenner, "you can have the month of December."

"That's ridiculous," said Quinn, "the winter meetings are in December and contracts have to be tendered."

"Well, what do you want to stay?" the Boss asked. "I'll increase your salary."

"George," said Quinn, "all I want is the freedom to talk to other clubs. I don't want your money. I've just had enough."

Later, in a parting shot, Quinn joked: "The two biggest expenses for Yankee employees are housing and going-away parties."

Steinbrenner moved quickly to announce that George Bradley, the Yankees' player development and scouting director, would be given increased input in player personnel decisions. During the course of the year, Steinbrenner had frequently cited Bradley's good work in the minor league department, but now, as one Yankee front office mole observed: "It's like an amusement park shooting gallery. Bradley's just become one of those little ducks that's slowly coming into George's range."

Alas, sooner or later they all come into Steinbrenner's line of fire and hear the sound of the gun being cocked. By the time the 1989 season ended, Green, Thrift, Quinn, and Piniella had all been fired or resigned. Quinn and Piniella hooked up as general manager and manager, respectively, of the Reds, and were immediately dubbed "the Cincinnati Quinnella." Ironically, Green was offered the Reds' managing job before Piniella but turned it down. "After going through the year I just had with Steinbrenner," he said, "I didn't want to jump right back into it again. I'm looking forward to sitting home on my farm in 1990 and collecting George's money."

Steinbrenner, meanwhile, was finding it as difficult to recruit good players as it was to hold on to key personnel. Once, as the uncontested champion free agent recruiter, he was able to lure players to New York with such intangibles as Yankee tradition and class—and money, too. Now all he had was money. And that was insufficient to snare superstar free agents such as pitchers Mark Langston and Mark Davis, who made it abundantly clear they wanted no part of the chaos, craziness, and instability that had become Yankee hallmarks.

As Randy Hendricks, the agent for Davis, said when his client rejected a reported five-year, $17 million offer from the Yankees to sign with the Kansas City Royals for $13 million over four years: "Mark Davis' decision portends a trend that players are making their decisions [on where to play] based on things other than money. It is incumbent upon teams to have an enlightened approach to player relations."

Then, on Christmas Day, Billy Martin, the one minion Steinbrenner could always count on for a quick fix to his problems, was killed.

It was as if, in the end, these Yankees were damned to be the Boss alone, presiding over the ruins.

CHAPTER 13

The Final Days

Although no one foresaw it, the death of Billy Martin was actually the prelude to the end of the would-be dynasty of the early-Steinbrenner era. Only a couple of months after Martin was laid to rest, the initial rumblings were heard. Soon, an avalanche of events would leave the Yankees in a state of ruin and effectively drive Steinbrenner into a shamed 30-month exile from his cherished role as Boss.

Ironically, it was Steinbrenner's ten-year blind obsession with bringing down Dave Winfield that led to his own downfall. As the Steinbrenner-Winfield saga reached its denouement, the 1990 Yankee season unraveled in familiar fashion, but only worse. Indeed, all the elements of chaos and craziness that had characterized the previous seventeen years of Steinbrenner's manic reign were there: A hollow preseason guarantee of job security for the manager; a spring training hubbub with the Mets; another free agent fiasco; a further divided front office that defied logic; the continuing futile search for a football player who could play baseball; and the physical breakdown of the last Yankee star.

Steinbrenner's only consolation was that, in the end, he was no longer on the scene to preside over what came full cycle for him. The Yankees he purchased from CBS in 1973 were a sorry lot, but these Yankees, who had plummeted from the heights of 1976–81, were the sorriest Yankees of all. Not only did they finish last for the first time since 1966 (and only the fourth time in the team's eighty-eight-year history), but they had the worst record since 1913, were no-hit for the first time in thirty-two years and even found a way to lose when their own pitcher pitched a no-hitter.

Opening Day 1990, which was delayed nine days due to the spring training lockout and a rainout and snowout in Cleveland, dawned bright and sunny

April 12 at Yankee Stadium. Before the first pitch by Dave LaPoint, a fan in the third base side box seats unleashed several dozen balloons, all imprinted with the message: "George Must Go!"—a carryover from the chant that filled Yankee Stadium in the final days of 1989. The 50,114 fans cheered lustily, not realizing, of course, that the balloons would prove prophetic.

Who, though, would have guessed that it would be Howie Spira, a scared, furtive, small-time gambler, who would be the one to puncture Steinbrenner's balloon? Until 1990, Spira had been only a bit player in the Steinbrenner-Winfield wrangling. An early-on employee of the Winfield Foundation, Spira sometime in the late '80s switched to Steinbrenner's team, offering his services to the Boss as a way of avenging what he felt was shoddy treatment he had received from Winfield.

After literally several years and several hundred phone conversations, Steinbrenner accepted Spira's offer of dirt to help win the September 1989 arbitration case against the Winfield Foundation. But what a price Steinbrenner paid for that small victory—a price that went far beyond the amount he promised (and eventually reneged on) to Spira. Spira, who was unemployed and deeply in debt to gamblers, would maintain the agreed-upon price for his services had been $150,000 plus a job in Tampa at Steinbrenner's Bay Harbor Hotel. Steinbrenner might have escaped the entire Spira deal unscathed if he'd simply ignored Spira's pathetic pleas. But he blundered fatally by agreeing to a $40,000 payoff in January of 1990.

In the months that followed, Steinbrenner would offer a multiple-choice array of explanations for making the payment—none of which satisfied Baseball Commissioner Fay Vincent. Basically, Steinbrenner had hoped Spira would be satisfied with $40,000 and would just go away. But Spira didn't go away and when his demands for more money and the job in Tampa were rejected, he threatened to go public and expose the entire sordid affair. Steinbrenner, for his part, either didn't take Spira seriously or underestimated the seriousness of his own role in paying an admitted gambler a bounty to supply dirt on one of his ballplayers.

"Listen, let me tell you something," Steinbrenner said to Spira in a phone conversation in early March of 1990, "that's extortion in its purest form."

"If that's how it's got to be, then that's how it's got to be," Spira replied.

"All right, fine," said Steinbrenner. "Goodbye, Howard."

Six days after that conversation, four FBI agents, acting on a call from the Yankee owner, raided Spira's apartment in the Riverdale section of the Bronx, seeking tapes, diaries and logs detailing all of Spira's phone conversations with Steinbrenner and Steinbrenner's key aide at the American Shipbuilding Co.

in Tampa, Philip McNiff. McNiff, a former FBI agent himself, served as the middleman in most of the Steinbrenner-Spira dealings.

That's when everything began unraveling for Steinbrenner as Spira told his story to the *New York Daily News*, which broke the details in a front-page exclusive Sunday, March 18. Within a week, Vincent had instructed John Dowd, the same investigator who had brought down Pete Rose the year before, to begin probing the Steinbrenner-Spira relationship.

Dowd's investigation was completed in early June, and Vincent took a month to study it before calling Steinbrenner in for a hearing, July 5. By the time the two-day grilling from Vincent was completed, it was apparent to Steinbrenner that he was in deep trouble. The next three weeks turned into a typical Steinbrenner-orchestrated sideshow of diversions and distractions from the serious business at hand.

Amid threatened lawsuits against Vincent and continuing propaganda releases being churned out by the Boss' public relations firm, there was a hilarious gathering of a handful of his old adversaries from the press in Steinbrenner's suite at the Regency Hotel in Manhattan, July 19. Reminiscent of the Dick Howser firing press conference in Steinbrenner's Yankee Stadium office a decade earlier, the Boss had platters of bite-sized sandwiches and pitchers of drinks for the writers. And, like that Howser press conference, no one among the writers bit for either the sandwiches or Steinbrenner's story. The next day, Mike McAlary's column in the *Daily News* was appropriately headlined: "Iced Tea and Baloney."

If anything, the five writers assembled were both amused and confused by Steinbrenner's behavior during the two-hour session. At one point, the Boss blurted out: "Is the hearing over? When do I get to call my witnesses?"

The writers looked at each other incredulously, wondering how Steinbrenner could be so far out of it.

"George, the hearing was over two weeks ago," Moss Klein reminded him.

"Oh, okay," said Steinbrenner, who seemed satisfied.

Obviously, Steinbrenner was under severe stress, realizing he was facing dire consequences for his dealings with Spira.

On the night of July 30, after day-long haggling and deliberations between Vincent and Steinbrenner and their army of lawyers at Vincent's Park Avenue office, the Commissioner made his way around the corner to the Helmsley Palace to make his historic and, in retrospect, stunning announcement.

Citing that Steinbrenner had accepted that his conduct with Spira was "not in the best interest of baseball," Vincent said: "Mr. Steinbrenner has agreed to resign on or before August 20, 1990, as the general partner of the New York Yankees. From there on, Mr. Steinbrenner will have no further involvement in the management of the New York Yankees or in the day-to-day operations of that club."

While the severity of Steinbrenner's punishment initially shocked everyone who had been following the long-running saga, the manner in which it was agreed upon was even more stunning. It seemed that Vincent had originally decided to impose a two-year suspension and three-year probation on Steinbrenner. But because he was concerned with the stigma of the word *suspension* and because he was confident that his oldest son, Hank, was ready and willing to take the helm of the Yankees, Steinbrenner negotiated what turned out to be a far more absolute punishment for himself.

When Vincent handed Steinbrenner his initial fifty-page decision and told him he was being suspended for two years, he later confirmed: "I thought that would be the end of it."

But Steinbrenner thought that the word *suspension* would hurt his chances of remaining in this role as a vice president on the U. S. Olympic Committee, and so the legal maneuvering began. Finally, Vincent drew up a proposal in which Steinbrenner would resign as general partner, reduce his role to that of a limited partner, remove himself from the day-to-day operations of the Yankees and agree not to sue baseball.

Steinbrenner apparently did not realize that he was negotiating a permanent reduction of his power, because at one point in the proceedings he asked Vincent: "When does it [the penalty] end?"

Vincent replied: "It's permanent."

Steinbrenner and his lawyers were confused and caucused to study the commissioner's revised punishment. By 8 P.M. some eleven hours after Steinbrenner had arrived at the Commissioner's office, Vincent still didn't have the Boss' signature of acceptance. At that point, an exasperated Vincent told Steinbrenner he was going to leave and announce his original two-year suspension penalty. Steinbrenner replied: "Okay, we'll just take our shot in court."

But as Vincent got into the elevator, preparing to go to his press conference around the corner, Stephen Kaufman, Steinbrenner's lead attorney, pushed the elevator door open and announced: "Wait, he'll sign."

The next day, Vincent was still admittedly puzzled by Steinbrenner's decision. "From where I sat," he said, "the second proposal was sterner than the first one I presented. I found some aspects of his decision to be strange."

As one of Steinbrenner's eighteen limited Yankee partners later agreed with a touch of bemusement: "George's worst trade, it turned out, was his last one. He traded himself right out of baseball."

Needless to say, this wasn't quite the end of Steinbrenner. In the three weeks leading up to the deadline for his resignation as general partner, there were a series of typical Steinbrenneresque developments that further complicated the Vincent dictum. Naturally, there were lawsuits and even though Steinbrenner himself was forbidden to sue baseball by terms of the agreement, two of the limited Yankee partners took it upon themselves to sue for him.

Meanwhile, Steinbrenner's son, Hank, whom the Boss had tapped to succeed him as general partner of the Yankees, declined the coronation, choosing to remain in the relative tranquility and anonymity of overseer of the family horse-breeding farm in Ocala, Florida. That, in turn, touched off yet another lawsuit as Lenny Kleinman, the chief operating officer of the Yankees, who was Steinbrenner's next choice, was declared at least temporarily ineligible by Vincent. The Commissioner cited Kleinman's complicated behind-the-scenes role in arranging the $40,000 payment to Spira. Upon learning he was being blocked from becoming general partner, Kleinman launched a $22 million suit against the Commissioner. Both Kleinman's and the limited partners' suits were rejected by the courts.

With Hank out and Kleinman declared out, Steinbrenner had to look beyond both his immediate family and immediate Yankee family for a successor as general partner. His surprise choice was Robert Nederlander, who along with his two theater entrepreneur brothers, owned a limited interest in the Yankees. Nederlander had never previously shown much interest in the Yankee operations according to the other limited partners and, in fact, at one meeting in 1983 he was said to have inquired of Steinbrenner: "By the way, what's become of Reggie Jackson? I haven't seen him in the lineup lately." Steinbrenner had to inform him that Jackson had been let go as a free agent two years earlier.

If nothing else, the meeting of the Yankee partners in Cleveland in which the colorless, low-key Nederlander was selected by Steinbrenner turned out to be another patented cloak and dagger Yankee episode. Originally, Steinbrenner had wanted the meeting to be in his home base of Tampa for his own convenience. But the limited partners, their resolve suddenly buoyed by Steinbrenner's impending departure, insisted the meeting be held in Cleveland, which was home base for many of them.

Subsequently, it was decided the meeting would take place in the Cleveland law office of Daniel McCarthy, one of the limited partners. However, once Steinbrenner realized the press and media hordes would be converging on McCarthy's office, he devised a plan to disperse to another location.

"I have a feeling we're only just going to gather at McCarthy's office," Eddie Rosenthal, one of the limited partners, told some members of the press.

"This could turn out to be a wild, high-speed car chase through the streets of Cleveland."

Sure enough, the partners began leaving McCarthy's office separately through various back door exits, successfully evading the vigilant media corps. Where had they gone? The reporters began scurrying about, discussing all the possibilities. Fortunately, Claire Smith of the *New York Times* had had the foresight to check the airport hotels on arriving in Cleveland the night before.

"There's only one," she said. "Do you think that's where they are?"

At that, Bill Madden placed a call to the hotel in question and identified himself as Lenny Kleinman, president of the New York Yankees. "I'm trying to reach Mr. George Steinbrenner," Madden said, "It's very urgent. Has he arrived there yet? He's supposed to be meeting with some people there."

"Why yes," the clerk replied. "They're here somewhere. I'm just not sure what room. Let me look."

Madden didn't bother to wait for the clerk to get back on the phone. After fulfilling Rosenthal's prophecy with a high-speed ride to the airport, the small group of reporters knew they were in the right hotel when, after getting the runaround from the hotel manager and his two security guards, they saw Jack Satter, one of the limited partners, emerge from one of the meeting rooms.

"You guys are something," Satter said on his way to the men's room. "You're really on the ball."

Alas, that was not something that could be said about the Yankees in 1990.

While every team in baseball was affected by the spring training lockout that delayed the opening of spring training camps for five weeks, the Yankees may have been hindered more than most, if only because they had so many question marks and uncertainties going into the season.

Epitomizing the Yankee troubles was the Pascual Perez situation. Perez, a thirty-two-year-old right-handed pitcher with a history of emotional and drug problems and career record of 64–62, had been signed as a free agent by Steinbrenner in November for a whopping $5.7 million over three years. In his haste to sign Perez, Steinbrenner overlooked the fact that the pitcher had been bothered by a late-season sore arm in 1989. It's customary for clubs to request players to undergo a physical exam before signing them to big money contracts, but, incredibly, the Yankees signed Perez with no questions asked.

Because of the lockout, spring training was reduced to two and a half weeks, but Perez, a native of the Dominican Republic, didn't arrive until the ninth day. Thus, the theme of the 1990 Yankee spring training quickly became "Waiting for Pascual" and Pete Peterson, who over the winter had been the latest in the long line to be given the title of general manager, was in daily contact with Perez' agent, Tom Reich. Not surprisingly, the stories being relayed from Perez to Reich to Peterson to the reporters got increasingly confused and lost in translation. First Perez was said to be having visa problems. Then there was an illness in the family. Then it was said he had been involved in a traffic accident. Finally, the day before he arrived, it emerged that Perez had been detained because of a paternity suit filed against him.

On the night of March 27, the Pascual Perez vigil ended, but the Pascual Perez three-ring circus was just beginning. The Yankees were playing seventy-five miles north at Port St. Lucie against the Mets when Perez drove into the Fort Lauderdale spring training complex in a new Jaguar, driven by one of his agents. In a car behind him was former pitcher Dock Ellis, who had been assigned to him as a drug counselor.

Pitching coach Billy Connors, minor league catcher Jeff Datz and Fort Lauderdale Stadium grounds crew and officials had been ordered to wait for Perez. As soon as he arrived, Perez was hustled into the locker room to don his Yankee pinstripes for a ten-minute "audition." The Yankees had even gone to the trouble of putting on a bank of lights in the empty ballpark to illuminate the side of the field where Perez threw for ten minutes.

Once his bizarre initial Yankee workout was completed, Perez held his first press conference, which quickly left no doubt in the writers' minds that this was a character ripe for the Steinbrenner Yankees mold.

His shoulder-length braided locks flipping as he spoke, Perez immediately addressed the paternity suit issue. Yes, he admitted knowing the woman in question and didn't deny having had relations with her either. But the baby wasn't his. How did he know? He had a foolproof system.

"My two girls and my boy, as soon as you look at my face and theirs, you know they look like me," he said. "This woman doesn't have no proof of anything. The woman says it's mine because I signed the big contract. It's not mine. I can tell. He has green eyes. I don't have no green eyes."

Perez then went on to guarantee his late arrival wouldn't prevent him from assuming his role as the Yankees' new ace.

"I told my wife I'll win eighteen games, that's the number," he said.

Unfortunately, Perez didn't even pitch 18 innings. He made three starts, totaling 14 innings and a 1–2 record, before going down with a shoulder injury in late April. For the rest of the year, Perez provided backpage tabloid fodder with his periodic outbursts regarding the Yankees' ineptitude and his own unhappiness. In addition, he resisted surgery (which had been prescribed in early May) until August.

Although this was to be Peterson's first encounter with Yankee turmoil in his role as the new Yankee front office chief, he was actually no stranger to it. Nine years earlier, he'd been an innocent third party in another Yankee brouhaha with the Commissioner's office, which culminated in a raging Steinbrenner threatening the physical well-being of Bill Murray, Bowie Kuhn's top administrative aide. At the time, Peterson was general manager of the Pittsburgh Pirates. What embroiled him in the Steinbrenner-Murray hostilities was a trade he thought he'd completed with the Yankees—a trade that quickly became unraveled and was eventually aborted by Kuhn.

On, appropriately, April Fool's Day of 1981, Steinbrenner, seeking a left-handed power hitter, turned to the financially strapped Pirates and worked out a complicated three-team trade in which first baseman Jason Thompson was to go from the California Angels to the Yankees via Pittsburgh. The Yankees were to send their own left-handed-hitting first baseman, Jim Spencer, and two minor league pitchers to the Pirates—as well as $850,000 in cash. The Angels and Pirates completed their portion of the trade, but within hours after the Yankees announced having obtained Thompson from Pittsburgh, Kuhn put it on hold because the cash the Yankees were giving the Pirates exceeded the $400,000 limit he'd imposed on all deals five years earlier.

Peterson spent the next two days in what proved to be futile negotiations with the Yankees to restructure the deal to satisfy Kuhn. At one point, it looked as if the teams had reached a satisfactory agreement, with the Pirates sending seven players to the Yankees in exchange for keeping the $450,000 above what they'd gotten for Thompson. But Murray, after consulting several scouts, determined that five of the players (all minor leaguers) were nonprospects and of no value and thus concluded the deal was a sham.

When further efforts failed and the deal was called off on April 3, Steinbrenner inflicted his wrath on Murray, a former comptroller for the cross-town New York Mets.

"I have no argument with Bowie Kuhn, but why is it that Mr. Murray, who was a bookkeeper for the Mets, is made a baseball administrator?" Steinbrenner asked. "Why not make him a comptroller and get a baseball man, someone who knows the game, to be the baseball administrator?"

As it was learned later, though, those comments that Steinbrenner made publicly about Murray were nothing compared to the blistering verbal attack he'd made privately in a phone call to the commissioner's aide. Based on a letter Murray sent to Steinbrenner, dated April 6, in response to that phone call, Kuhn appeared to have sufficient grounds to suspend the Boss—or worse. For reasons known only to himself, Murray chose to let the matter drop.

Saying he was "shocked and disturbed" by Steinbrenner's phone call, Murray wrote: "Your comments and threats that 'I had made an enemy for life'…'keep looking over your shoulder because I'll be after you'…'I'll get you no matter how long it takes'…'I want to hurt you.' etc. were those you might expect from a gangster hit man, rather than from a principal owner of a major league baseball club."

While the Perez distraction only served as a reminder for Peterson of the ever-chaotic Yankee kingdom under Steinbrenner's rule, it was just one of a myriad of spring training problems for Bucky Dent, starting his first full season as Yankee manager. Dent, who'd taken over from Dallas Green the previous August, was already saddled with the curse of another Steinbrenner "full season, win or lose" manager guarantee. Steinbrenner, it was remembered, had issued similar guarantees to Bob Lemon in 1982 and Yogi Berra in 1985, before firing them after fourteen and sixteen games respectively.

Among other things, Dent had to decide in the abbreviated two-and-a-half-week spring training (1) whether Dave Winfield could make a comeback after missing the entire 1989 season with a back injury; (2) whether there were four other competent starting pitchers to join the much-heralded Perez in the rotation and (3) whether there was anyone else who could play third base if struggling rookie Mike Blowers continued to prove he wasn't ready. And, of course, there was the nearly annual spring training Mets hijinks.

As if the Yankee beat reporters hadn't been provided with enough copy for their papers with Perez' arrival, that same night the Mets routed the Yankees 11–0, prompting a predictable Steinbrenner outburst.

"I felt sorry for Bucky," Steinbrenner said. "He looked like General Custer riding into the ambush at Little Big Horn. [Mets manager] Davey Johnson must still be under some pressure over there."

Steinbrenner was particularly upset that Johnson had used both of his Cy Young-Award-winning pitching aces, Dwight Gooden and Frank Viola, in the game, and had played his regulars most of the way. He was also upset over what he perceived as the Mets' attitude, saying that "gloating over an 11–0 score is kind of crummy."

That set the stage for the next Yankees-Mets encounter six days later at Fort Lauderdale. Both teams had split squad games elsewhere that day and the usual practice is to send a representative group of players to each. But while the Mets showed up without Darryl Strawberry, Kevin McReynolds, and many of their other regulars, the Yankees had kept their everyday lineup at home. No one had to guess who had done the selection for the team the Yankees were to field against the Mets. Dent tried in vain to offer other explanations for the "loaded" Yankee team, but finally admitted: "We want to give a good showing after what happened the other night. You get into it a little more against the Mets."

As fate would have it, though, the team the Mets brought to Fort Lauderdale managed to further embarrass Steinbrenner. Not only did they beat the

Yankees again, this time 5–2, but they scored three runs in the ninth inning against Dave Righetti on consecutive two-out hits by three former Yankee farm products, Phil Lombardi, Keith Hughes, and Darren Reed.

It never got any better for Dent, who lasted 49 games into the season before becoming Steinbrenner's eighteenth and last managerial casualty. After getting off to a misleading 4–1 start, the Yankees lost 15 of their next 21 games, leading up to May 11—a day that Steinbrenner had waited and plotted for over the course of nearly eight years. It was on that date that Dave Winfield was finally traded—but not without considerable uproar beforehand.

The first hint that this was not going to be a smoothly executed transaction came when Yankee beat writers were summoned to a hastily arranged press conference in the visiting clubhouse of the Seattle Kingdome. There, Peterson announced that Winfield had been traded to the California Angels for a player to be named later. But Winfield, who had been called into the clubhouse from the field where he was shagging flies, immediately responded: "I'm not going anywhere."

The beat writers all looked at each other in bewilderment. Clearly, this was going to be a classic Yankee press conference.

And that it was. Winfield and Peterson suddenly began arguing with each other in front of the assembled media. What set Peterson off was Winfield's comment that "the one advantage of the trade would be going to a team where I'd be treated like a human being."

"That's not a very nice comment and it's uncalled for," Peterson shot back. "We're supposed to be mature adults here, not twenty-year-old kids."

A few minutes later, Winfield said he planned to talk directly to Steinbrenner because "he's the man who makes the decisions so he's the one to talk to."

"I can't let that go by without answering," Peterson interjected. "We talked to George about this trade, but he wasn't behind it. He said: 'You're the baseball people. If you think this will help the Yankees, then go ahead and do it.'"

Winfield rolled his eyes at that comment.

Dent, who had begun platooning Winfield two weeks prior to the deal, was standing off to the side while Winfield and Peterson sparred. Later, Dent insisted that it had been his decision to platoon Winfield and that it was at his urging the trade was made.

Meanwhile, 1,000 miles to the south in Anaheim, Angel officials were at first insisting they had no knowledge of the trade.

The Angels' reluctance to confirm the deal was understandable. As a player with ten years of experience, the last five with the same team, Winfield had the right to veto a trade, and the Angels didn't want to announce anything until they were certain it was approved by all parties. It had long been

Steinbrenner's contention, however, that Winfield, by inserting a clause in his contract that listed seven teams he would approve being traded to after his fifth year with the Yankees, had in effect waived his veto rights. Winfield said his annual submission of that list was nothing more than a courtesy to give the Yankees an idea which teams he would consider being traded to.

About the only thing that was clear about the whole deal was that it had been badly bungled by the Yankees, who announced it without even first informing Winfield of it. It appeared as if the only resolution to the dispute was to submit it to arbitration.

Three days later, after returning to New York, Winfield, a man without a team, and his agent, Jeff Klein, met with Steinbrenner. Following the meeting, Steinbrenner, sensing the public sentiment about the trade, turned on Peterson and Dent while praising Winfield. He criticized Peterson for the handling of the trade announcement and questioned Dent's decision to platoon Winfield.

The next day, Winfield's Day IV in Limbo, he showed up at Yankee Stadium and announced he was prepared to play. His arrival caught everyone by surprise, especially Peterson and Dent. When Dent saw Winfield in the clubhouse he immediately went upstairs to ask Peterson what was going on. Peterson didn't know either.

Further complicating the situation was the Players Association's contention that Winfield was still a Yankee because the trade was illegal. At the same time Commissioner Fay Vincent was insisting Winfield could not suit up until the issue was resolved. The Players Association was also threatening a grievance seeking damages for "a thirty-eight-year-old player coming off back surgery who needs to be playing."

At last, on May 16, five days after the trade was announced, it became official—but not without another nine hours of legal wrangling. The hearing with arbitrator George Nicolau had been set for 2 P.M., but the involved parties, the Yankees, Angels and Winfield, began negotiating at 11 A.M. and kept going until finally reaching agreement long after sunset. Winfield, who could have been a free agent after 1990, was given a three-year contract extension worth a guaranteed $3.75 million (which could escalate to $9.1 million if he played through 1993), to waive his veto rights. The Yankees got pitcher Mike Witt, who had already reported to them three days earlier. And Steinbrenner got the satisfaction of finally trading the man he had been trying to trade for nearly eight years.

There was, as it turned out, a humorous footnote to all the eleventh-hour negotiating. As a way of settling the threatened grievance by the Players Association, Steinbrenner agreed to contribute $50,000 to the Winfield

Foundation. The last several hours of the talks centered around Steinbrenner's repeated rephrasing of the two-paragraph statement. As all the exasperated and exhausted parties implored Steinbrenner to "word it any way you want," Winfield at one point turned to everyone in the room and smiled broadly. "Now," he said, "do you see what I've been going through all these years?"

Still, after it was all over, Steinbrenner couldn't resist one final parting shot at Winfield.

"[Angels owner] Gene Autry overwhelmed him with that offer," Steinbrenner said. "If I had a horse named Champion and a guitar like the Cowboy, and had made all those old movies, then maybe I could afford that kind of contract for him."

Nevertheless, Steinbrenner was not done paying for Dave Winfield. On July 5, while he was being grilled during the nine-hour hearing with Commissioner Vincent, Steinbrenner was informed that he was being fined a total of $225,000 for tampering with Winfield in the interim period between the trade announcement and its official completion. Vincent cited Steinbrenner's statement that Winfield "would be welcome to return to the Yankees" and "should be a full-time player" as being harmful to the Angels' bargaining position.

Meanwhile, thrust squarely into the middle of this last Winfield-Steinbrenner conflict was Bucky Dent. It was Dent who had decided that the year's layoff had taken too much of a toll on Winfield's skills and had rendered him a part-time performer, and it was Dent who decided that it would thus be in the best interests of everyone to trade the 38-year-old fading superstar.

"I just didn't want him around once I decided he couldn't play every day," Dent told Moss Klein months later. "I was afraid he'd be disruptive because he'd be unhappy about not playing. I didn't need any more problems."

Unfortunately for Dent, Winfield's departure did nothing to solve his problems and, in fact, exactly three weeks later he, too, was history. Steinbrenner, remember, had promised Dent a full year, but, like the Boss' previous "full season, win or lose" promises to Bob Lemon, Yogi Berra and Dallas Green, this one proved just as hollow.

Throughout his 49-game tenure in 1990, Dent was on shaky turf, and the press was not bashful about reporting that on an almost daily basis. It seemed as if not one day went by when Dent didn't have to answer questions about his job status—or about some incident that prompted doubts as to just how much in control he was.

On May 25, the Yankees reached what would actually be their high point of the season—sixth place, 17–22, five games out. They had just defeated the Royals in Kansas in the opener of a three-game series. The next day, though, marked the beginning of the end for Dent. Andy Hawkins, who would become the symbol of the Yankees' futility in 1990, was knocked out in the second inning of a 9–4 loss to the Royals. That dropped the Yankees into last place, from which they never escaped. They lost four more in a row, moving on to Chicago, a city which, it has been well documented, has never been kind to Yankee managers.

It became readily apparent during the three losing games in Chicago that the Yankees were going nowhere and Bucky was going somewhere. Things began to come to a head when Dent for the first time outwardly lost his cool in a confrontation with his center fielder, Roberto Kelly.

Even though Dent and Kelly had had a long relationship, going back to 1985 when Dent was Kelly's Class A manager at Fort Lauderdale, the two were never particularly close. Kelly, a gifted but moody sort, was upset coming into that Chicago series because Dent and the Yankee trainers were minimizing what, he thought, was a potentially serious shoulder injury.

In the ninth inning of what became a 2–1 loss to the White Sox in the opener of the Chicago series, Kelly missed a "take" sign on a 2-0 count and grounded into a double play that effectively killed the Yankees' last-ditch rally. As he came back to the dugout, Kelly was confronted by a visibly angered Dent.

"Didn't you see the sign?" Dent screamed.

But Kelly didn't respond and, instead, just walked away, leaving Dent in a further state of rage. One batter later, Don Mattingly popped up to end the game and Dent returned to the tiny manager's office in the visiting team clubhouse where reporters found him still seething fifteen minutes later.

Up until then, Dent had been able to conceal his inner torment and frustration. In front of the writers, he had always remained stoic and composed despite the mounting losses. But now, it was suddenly becoming obvious to him that this job of Yankee manager, which he'd put in five years in the minors to attain, was slipping away.

Staring straight ahead, clenching and unclenching his fists, Dent blurted out his anger at Kelly's blunder.

"When I'm this mad, I try not to say things in anger," Dent said. "But this bothers me a lot. There's no excuse for missing a sign. I said something to him and I'll deal with him later."

The indication was clear that Dent was planning a fine, a fact that only further alienated Kelly, who told the reporters later: "They can do whatever the hell they want. Nothing here surprises me."

The next day, Dent certainly didn't help to defuse the situation by choosing to confront Kelly at the batting cage before the game in full view of other players and reporters. Dent obviously felt that Kelly, after a night to rethink everything, would be contrite. But he misjudged the temperamental outfielder and after a brief exchange of words, it became an animated scene with Dent pointing his finger at Kelly and Kelly shaking his head.

By night's end, though, Kelly had become a footnote in Dent's trials, since all the elements that would lead to Dent's ultimate demise were gathering around him in Chicago. One element was the Mets firing of Davey Johnson that afternoon. Steinbrenner, who was always sensitive to the contrasts the press made between his impetuous nature and Mets patience and stability, was now off the hook. This would be one year he wouldn't be the first to fire a manager in New York, even though it's worth noting that Johnson's six-plus seasons at the Mets' helm outlasted Yogi Berra, Billy Martin IV and V, Lou Piniella I and II and Dallas Green as Yankee managers over that same span. And Dent seemed to realize that Johnson's firing was more than likely a precursor to his own.

"Do you know how rare it is for the Yankee manager to be senior manager in town?" Moss Klein said to Dent, in an attempt to inject some levity into an otherwise grim atmosphere in the clubhouse before the game.

Dent smiled weakly. "I don't think it'll last too long."

He was right.

As if on cue, Steinbrenner arrived in town that night and, on being confronted by the Yankee beat reporters, refused for the first time to give Dent a vote of confidence. And as the Boss sat upstairs in the owners' box at Comiskey Park, the Yankees proceeded to further embarrass Dent. The 5–4 loss to the White Sox that night was punctuated by (1) a four-run first-inning Chicago uprising against Mike Witt, (2) a crucial base-running gaffe by the flamboyant but flawed Deion Sanders, and, finally, a ninth-inning wild pitch by reliever Lance McCullers. McCullers actually had provided a forewarning of how this game would end when, bringing back fond memories of Steve Trout, he threw three of his warmup pitches to the backstop. McCullers later insisted his errant warmups had not rattled him, but his batterymate, Bob Geren, prepared for the worst.

"I thought a wild pitch was a definite possibility," Geren said.

Sanders' base-running mistake, meanwhile, was just another indication that he was not ready to live up to his "Prime Time" nickname—at least in baseball. A year earlier, he had arrived at Dallas Green's spring training amid considerable hype and hoopla as the Yankees' great two-sport find. Steinbrenner, who could never seem to cut the football roots of his coaching days at Northwestern and Purdue, had long coveted a two-sport athlete. In three of the Yankee's amateur drafts in the '80s, the team selected college football stars—Billy Cannon, Jr., of LSU in 1980, John Elway of Stanford in 1981 and high school phenom Bo

Jackson in 1982. All three picks were wasted, as only Jackson, who spurned the Yankee offer to accept a football scholarship to Auburn, ever committed to a baseball career. And that was to the Royals, who redrafted him in 1986.

Jackson's fast rise as a baseball star undoubtedly whetted Steinbrenner's appetite all the more for a baseball-playing football star. In 1988, he drafted Sanders and a year later ordered his call-up after a brief minor league indoctrination to baseball. Although Sanders seemed lost with the Yankees in '89, he began to get his baseball bearings when sent back to Dent at Columbus later in the season.

So it was that Dent's decision to hand Sanders Winfield's vacated leftfield job initially looked to be a move that could only earn him approval from the Boss. Beginning May 21, Dent, attempting to find some spark for the Yankees' sputtering offense, inserted Sanders into the leadoff spot in the batting order. But by the night of that 5–4 loss in Chicago nine games later, it was apparent that "Neon Deion" was overmatched and the plan to make him the Yankees catalyst was scrapped. (In late September, having earlier changed their minds about signing Sanders to an outrageous $2 million-plus contract, the Yankees released him.)

The day after the Chicago loss, Steinbrenner summoned Dent to his suite at the Hyatt Regency Hotel and while the Boss didn't issue any ultimatums, Dent came away knowing he had no assurances either. To the waiting writers in the clubhouse that day, Dent said: "I told you when I took this job that I could build a shell around myself when it comes to worrying about the job. Now I'm like an armadillo."

A week later, Dent went from shelled to shell-shocked. Two losses in Boston, which gave him 9 losses in the last 10, prompted a phone call in his suite at the Boston-Sheraton at 12:20 P.M.

"He [Steinbrenner] felt the club wasn't turning it around and he wanted to make a change," Dent said. "I had an inkling it was coming."

As usual, life as a Yankee manager was full of cruel twists. It had been nearly twelve years since Dent had provided the Yankees with one of their greatest moments with his 1978 playoff home run against the Red Sox—in Boston.

That Steinbrenner had finally run the full gamut of "glamour" managers was obvious in his choice of Stump Merrill as Dent's successor. Merrill, a career minor leaguer and a "lifer" in the Yankee system who was managing at Columbus, admitted he was surprised to get the job. "I'm a no-name," he said, "and Mr. Steinbrenner has always wanted a marquee name as his manager."

If anything, Steinbrenner didn't want to believe the Yankees were back to what they were—or even worse—than when he purchased them from CBS in 1973. With no Billy Martin anymore to provide a "quick fix" to the Yankees' plight, he saw in Merrill a manager who had at least turned losing Yankee minor league teams around on three previous occasions as a midseason managerial replacement.

What Steinbrenner could not see was that this mess of a Yankee team he had wrought through all the ill-advised trades, free agent signings and management upheavals through the years was beyond fixing. Quite often, a change of managers brings about an initial, if temporary, change in fortunes for a ballclub. But the Yankees of 1990 responded to this last change of managers by Steinbrenner by losing 9 of their first 12 games under Merrill to fall 15 games out of first place by June 18.

By now, the Dowd investigation had been completed and the commissioner was preparing to call Steinbrenner to his hearing. The Boss' empire was collapsing all around him. His Bossness was under attack; his splintered front office of George Bradley, attempting to call most of the player decision-making shots from Tampa, and Pete Peterson, in effect just answering the phones in New York, was in customary chaos; his change of managers had accomplished nothing, and now it was becoming apparent that something was seriously wrong with his last remaining Yankee star.

If there was one thing Steinbrenner thought he could count on to break the fall of his Yankee empire, it was the star quality of Don Mattingly—so much so that, the day before the scheduled season opener, he rewarded him with a record five-year, $19.3 million contract extension. But by season's end, even that seemingly sound investment by Steinbrenner was being questioned, as Mattingly's chronic back condition worsened to the point no one could have envisioned. His production numbers at embarrassingly low levels, Mattingly was finally told by Steinbrenner to take himself out of the lineup July 25 until a determination could be made about his back problem. Mattingly would spend nearly two months on the disabled list before returning for the last three weeks in an effort to get his confidence back and his batting average over the .250 mark.

With Winfield gone and Mattingly severely hindered, the Yankee offense never got untracked and was the worst in the league all season long. That was never more apparent than on the afternoon of July 1 when Andy Hawkins pitched a no-hitter against the White Sox in Chicago—and lost, 4–0, as the Yankees made three eighth-inning errors to account for all the game's runs. Five days later, Hawkins pitched eleven scoreless innings against the Twins, only to lose in the twelfth, 2–0. Then, to complete this unhappy July trifecta for the luckless Hawkins, in his next start the Yankees were victims themselves of a rain-shortened, six-inning no-hitter by the White Sox' Melido Perez.

You would think that at least one Yankee, Melido's brother Pascual, would have found some joy in the no-hitter. Pascual had himself pitched a similar rain-shortened no-hitter two years earlier for Montreal. If only life on the Yankee beat was so predictable. As it turned out, shortly after the reporters talked to Perez about his brother's no-hit feat and were preparing to rush back to the pressroom, they were caught by surprise by a commotion outside Merrill's office. Inexplicably, Perez had launched into a profane tirade at Merrill.

What could have possibly brought *this* on, the reporters wondered. It seems that Perez, who was on the disabled list, had been informed of the latest front-office decree forbidding his presence in the Yankee dugout during games. A week earlier, he'd been reprimanded for cavorting in the dugout during a loss and, as a response to that, he sat through his brother's no-hitter pretending he was asleep.

For their part, the Yankees went through the season without ever getting a wake-up call. Only on occasion did they show any signs of life and, too often, those were negative signs. At various junctures, Mel Hall, Jesse Barfield, Dave LaPoint and other disgruntled and disappointing veterans expressed unhappiness about a lack of playing time and the treatment they were being given, and asked to be traded.

Steinbrenner might have been more outspoken and accommodating to his griping players except that, technically, in the most amazing development of all, he was no longer in charge. Ironically, as his final acts, he sought to restore the stability he had undermined all those years. On August 19, the day before his resignation was due, he rewarded Merrill's efforts with a two-year contract extension and, the following day, he resolved the front office schism by naming his one remaining longtime loyalist, Gene Michael, as general manager. For Michael, it was the second go-round as Yankee GM, only, unlike 1980, this time he seemed clearly in charge of his own and the Yankees' destiny.

September 13, 1990, marked the formal beginning of the new, post-Steinbrenner Yankee era. On that day Robert Nederlander was approved as general partner at the major league owners' meetings in Pittsburgh. Nearly eighteen years earlier, on January 2, 1973, Steinbrenner had stepped on to the podium at a press conference to announce his purchase of the Yankees at New York's swanky 21 Club and proclaimed, "I won't be active in the day-to-day operations of the club at all. I've spread myself so thin. I've got enough headaches with my shipbuilding company."

In *his* inaugural address, Nederlander took the opposite course by announcing that he intended to be active in the day-to-day Yankee operations.

He added, "Whatever Mr. Steinbrenner did, he did. I intend to operate the club the way I think it should be operated."

Nederlander, who'd been not only a limited but a *silent* limited partner in the Yankees all these years, outlined a course that featured continuity rather than chaos. He said he believed in the development of young players and in operating in a fiscally responsible manner, neither of which were hallmarks of the Steinbrenner era. Nederlander also offered hope of a brave new Yankee world in which constant change and frequent firings would no longer be the norm.

"My own philosophy is to give people a chance," he said. "I learned a long time ago that you have to rely on experts. I'm new at the job. I'm going to seek the advice of our baseball people. I believe in letting baseball people take care of baseball matters."

Considering what Nederlander and his Steinbrenner-appointed management team had inherited, that figured to be a lot of caretaking.

"All we need to win the pennant," said Nederlander, "is Ruth, Gehrig and some hot prospects."

There was hope that one of those hot prospects had already arrived in the person of lefty slugger Kevin Maas, who hit a record thirteen home runs in his first 110 at-bats as Mattingly's first base replacement. Otherwise, though, Steinbrenner had left Nederlander without a legacy to stand on.

Steinbrenner's annual forays into the free agent market—too often for expensive busts such as Perez, LaPoint, Hawkins, Ed Whitson, Jose Cruz, John Candelaria, Gary Ward, Al Holland and others—cost the Yankees dearly in amateur draft picks that could have provided a foundation for the '90s. In addition, what quality players the Yankee farm system had managed to produce (despite the handicap of having only one first-round draft pick over an eleven-year period up to 1990). Steinbrenner traded away for more high-priced, often faded veteran players. Scattered throughout baseball in the Yankees' wake of 1990 were such promising young players as pitchers Doug Drabek, Jose Rijo, Tim Burke, Jay Howell, Jim Deshaies, Bob Tewksbury, first basemen Fred McGriff and Hal Morris, shortstop Greg Gagne, and outfielders Dan Pasqua, Jay Buhner and Stan Javier, all of whom had Yankee roots.

Steinbrenner compounded those trades by trading away his established stars and getting little or nothing in return. It seemed hard to believe that in just two short years, only Mattingly remained from an All Star galaxy lineup that had included Winfield, Rickey Henderson, Jack Clark and Willie Randolph. All the Yankees had to show as a return for those players were middle relievers Eric Plunk and Greg Cadaret, pitcher Mike Witt and backup catcher Matt Nokes.

Even with Steinbrenner in exile, though, his legacy of front office mismanagement and confusion lived on. The 1990 season ended with Steinbrenner exiles seemingly everywhere taking bows as examples of how to ruin a franchise. In Cincinnati, Bob Quinn was being acclaimed as executive of the year for putting together the final pieces of the world championship Reds— and Lou Piniella was right by his side as the No. 1 manager in baseball. The Reds' season was topped off by Jose Rijo, yet another ex-Yankee, being hailed as World Series Most Valuable Player for his two wins against the Athletics. And then there was Rickey Henderson winning American League Most Valuable Player honors and Doug Drabek being unanimously voted National League Cy Young Award winner.

Meanwhile, Steinbrenner's legacy of front office confusion reared its ugly head again in the manner in which the Yankees parted ways with Dave Righetti, the last link to their championship past. Throughout their negotiations with Righetti as a free agent after the 1990 season, the Yankees' new front office triumvirate of Nederlander, Michael, and George Bradley held firm to a three-year contract limit. But on the same day Righetti was wooed away by a four-year $10 million offer from Al Rosen and the San Francisco Giants, the Yankee front office showed itself once again to be operating at cross-purposes when it announced the signing of second baseman Steve Sax to a four-year $12.4 million contract. The deal, a record for a second baseman, was made by Bradley and raised the ire of the twenty-five other clubs because Sax was not eligible for free agency for three more years and thus had no bargaining power. Michael, especially, was furious over the Sax deal since it was in clear conflict with the responsible fiscal policy he was attempting to establish with the Yankees.

Going into 1991, it had been nine years since the Yankees played in a World Series, twelve years since they won a Series; and they had reached the Series only four times in twenty-six years after dominating postseason with twenty-nine pennants from 1921 to 1964.

"When I think about the Yankees, I still think about championships," said Al Rosen, who, as a star third baseman with the Indians in the '40s and '50s knew the frustrations of being an opponent of the Yankee dynasty before he came aboard as one of the architects of the early Steinbrenner success years. "I don't think about them having the kind of club they have now. That's not the Yankees.

"I think about the Yankees of my playing days—DiMaggio, Mantle, Berra, Rizzuto, Bauer, Martin, Reynolds, Lopat, Raschi, Ford—and I think about the glorious year of '78—Guidry, Gossage, Munson, Piniella, Dent, Reggie. It's hard to envision what happened. The Yankees I knew never allowed themselves to get in this position, nothing close to this."

With Steinbrenner gone and a new Yankee regime, headed by Nederlander and Michael, a change of philosophy and direction for the better appeared likely. Or did it?

On August 20, at his farewell luncheon at Yankee Stadium (for which the employees each chipped in $20), Steinbrenner made some ominous remarks, captured for posterity by an enterprising employee who had a concealed tape recorder at the affair.

After everyone had finished their meal of Chateaubriand and salmon, Steinbrenner rose from his seat and began to speak. Much to the surprise of the 100 or so employees in the room, this was not a speech of contrition or remorse. Nor was it, they concluded, a farewell address.

"The Steinbrenner family will remain in control of the Yankees," the Boss said in assuring tones. "We will give some stock over to my wife and kids so the family will still be in control of the franchise. Robert Nederlander will be a great replacement. He was picked by me and I think you'll enjoy him. And when the next generation of Steinbrenners gets in, in three or four years, you're going to enjoy that also. Please understand that this will not be the end of the Steinbrenner family with the Yankees."

Nor was it. The Boss returned on March 1, 1993, and the "next generations of Steinbrenners" would not take full control of the Yankees until after his death in 2010.

Appendix: The Early Steinbrenner Era (1973–1990)

All The Man's Presidents
(Yankee presidents/chief executive officers of the Steinbrenner era)
Michael Burke, 1973 *Patrick Cunningham, 1974–75 Gabe Paul, 1973–77 Al Rosen, 1978–79 George M. Steinbrenner, 1979–80 Lou Saban, 1981–82 Gene McHale, 1983–86 Rick Bay, 1988 **Jean LaGotte, 1988 Bill Dowling, 1988 Michael Luczkovich, 1989 Lenny Kleinman, 1990–92

*Served as acting general partner while Steinbrenner was under suspension for making illegal campaign contributions to Richard M. Nixon. Was indicted himself and sentenced to 3½ years in prison for conspiring to obstruct justice, evading federal income taxes, and lying to a grand jury.

**Served less than one week, September 19-22, 1988. Started work on a Monday, was berated by Steinbrenner in a call to his home on a Thursday night, and submitted his resignation on Friday.

All The Man's PR Men
(Yankee public relation directors of the Steinbrenner era)
Bob Fishel, 1973 Marty Appel, 1974–76 Mickey Morabito, 1977–78 Larry Wahl, 1979–80 Irv Kaze, 1981–82 Dave Szen, 1982 Ken Nigro, 1983 Joe Safety, 1984–85 Harvey Greene, 1986–89 Arthur Richman, 1989 Jeff Idelson, 1990

Billy Martin's Ring Record

Date	Opponent	Result
May 1952	Red Sox outfielder Jimmy Piersall	Martin by TKO
July 14, 1952	Brown catcher Clint Courtney	Martin by decision
April 30, 1953	Brown catcher Clint Courtney	Martin by decision
July 1953	Tiger catcher Matt Batts	Draw
May 1956	Athletic pitcher Tommy Lasorda	Martin by decision
May 16, 1957	Copacabana patron punched by unidentified Yankee at Martin's birthday party	Martin traded
August 4, 1960	Cub pitcher Jim Brewer (Martin sued for $10,000 in damages for breaking Brewer's jaw.)	Martin scores TKO
July 12, 1966	Twin traveling secretary Howard Fox (in Statler Hotel lobby in Washington, D.C.)	Martin by decision
August 6, 1969	Twin pitcher Dave Boswell	Martin scores KO
April 20, 1972	Jack Sears, fan, outside Tiger Stadium	Martin by decision
September 26, 1974	Ranger traveling secretary Burt Hawkins (on a team flight)	Martin by decision
June 18, 1977	Yankee outfielder Reggie Jackson	Draw
November 11, 1978	Ray Hagar, sportswriter (in a Reno casino)	Martin scores TKO
October 25, 1979	Joseph Cooper, marshmallow salesman (in a Minneapolis bar)	Martin scores TKO

Date	Opponent	Result
May 25, 1983	Robin Wayne Olson, bar patron (in an Anaheim bar)	Martin by decision
September 21, 1985	Unidentified bar patron (at Cross Keys Inn, Baltimore)	Martin by decision
September 22, 1985	Yankee pitcher Ed Whitson (at Cross Keys Inn, Baltimore)	Whitson scores TKO
May 7, 1988	Bar bouncer and unidentified "aide" (at Lace Topless Bar, in Arlington, Texas)	Bouncer scores TKO

Pitching In
(Yankee pitching coaches of the early Steinbrenner era—1973–1990)
Jim Turner, 1973
Whitey Ford, 1974–75
Cloyd Boyer, 1975, 1977
Bob Lemon, 1976
Art Fowler, 1977–78, 1983, 1988
Clyde King, 1978, 1981, 1982, 1988
Tom Morgan, 1978
Stan Williams, 1980–81, 1982, 1988
Jerry Walker, 1982
Sammy Ellis, 1982, 1983–84, 1986
Jeff Torborg, 1982, 1983–84
Mark Connor, 1984–85, 1986–87
Bill Monboquette, 1985
Billy Connors, 1989–1990

All The Man's Managers
(In order of winning percentage with the Yankees)
Dick Howser (1 term) 103–59, .636 Billy Martin (5 terms) 556–386, .590
Bob Lemon (2 terms) 101–73, .580 Gene Michael (2 terms) 78–64, .549 Lou
Piniella (2 terms) 224–193, .537 Bill Virdon (1 term) 142–124, .534 Yogi Berra
(1 term) 93–85, .522 Ralph Houk (1 term) 80–82, .494 Clyde King (1 term)
29–33, .468 Dallas Green (1 term) 56–65, .463 Stump Merrill (1 term) 49–64,
.434 Bucky Dent (1 term) 36–53, .404

Ron Guidry's Catchers (1975–88)

Scott Bradley
Rick Cerone
Rick Dempsey
Juan Espino
Barry Foote
Bob Geren
Brad Gulden
Ron Hassey
Fran Healy
Mike Heath
Elrod Hendricks
Ed Herrmann
Clifff Johnson
Phil Lombardi
Thurman Munson
Jerry Narron
Johnny Oates
Mike O'Berry
Bobby Ramos
Bruce Robinson
Mark Salas
Joel Skinner
Don Slaught
Dennis Werth
Butch Wynegar

Willie Randolph's Shortstop Partners (1976–88)

Luis Aguayo
Sandy Alomar
Dale Berra
Paul Blair
Ivan DeJesus
Bucky Dent
Brian Doyle
Barry Evans
Mike Fischlin
Tim Foli
Damaso Garcia
Rex Hudler
Mickey Klutts
Jim Mason
Bobby Meacham
Larry Milbourne
Graig Nettles
Mike Pagliarulo
Domingo Ramos
Andre Robertson
Rafael Santana
Rodney Scott
Dennis Sherrill
Roy Smalley
Keith Smith
Fred "Chicken" Stanley
Wayne Tolleson
Randy Velarde
Dennis Werth
George Zeber
Paul Zuvella

Freedom's Just Another Word For Nothing Left To Lose

(The best and worst of the Yankee free agents—1975–1990)

The Best

Catfish Hunter (signed December 1974, 5 years, $3.35 million): 63–53, 3.58 ERA; two-time All-Star. Retired after 1979 season.

Reggie Jackson (signed November 1976, 5 years, $3.3 million): Batted .281, with 144 homers, 461 RBIs; four-time All-Star. Left as a free agent after 1981 and signed with California.

Rich Gossage (signed November 1977, 6 years, $2.75 million): 41–28, 2.10 ERA, 150 saves, 506 strikeouts in 518⅓ innings; four-time All-Star. Left as a free agent after '83 season and signed with San Diego.

Tommy John (signed November 1978, 4 years, $1.42 million): 62–37, 3.21 ERA, two 20-victory seasons; two-time All-Star. Traded to California in August 1982 for pitcher Dennis Rasmussen.

Dave Winfield (signed December 1980, est. $22 million for 10 years): Batted .291, with 203 homers, 812 RBIs over his first eight seasons before a back injury threatened to end his career; eight-time All-Star.

Don Baylor (signed December 1982, 4 years, $3.7 million): Batted .267, with 71 homers, 265 RBIs in 3 seasons. Traded to Boston for DH Mike Easler in March 1986.

Phil Niekro (signed January 1984, 2 years, $1.1 million): 32–20, 3.59 ERA; pitched over 200 innings in each of his two seasons. Released March 1986 at the age of 46.

The Worst

Don Gullett (signed November 1976, 6 years, $2 million): Lasted only parts of two seasons due to rotator cuff injury; 18–6, 3.60 ERA, but only 30 games as a Yankee.

Rawly Eastwick (signed December 1977, 5 years, $1.1 million): Spent less than 3 months as a Yankee; 2–1, 3.28 ERA in eight games. Traded to Philadelphia in June 1978 for Jay Johnstone and Bobby Brown.

Davey Collins (signed December 1981, 3 years, $2.4 million): Never had a position. Lasted only one year, batting .253 in 111 games while in a state of constant confusion. Traded to Toronto with Fred McGriff and Mike Morgan and $400,000 for reliever Dale Murray.

Steve Kemp (signed December 1982,5 years, $5.45 million): Lasted two years as a Yankee, plagued by injuries throughout. Batted .264 with 19 homers and 90 RBI before being traded to Pittsburgh in December 1984 with Tim Foli for Dale Berra and Jay Buhner.

Ed Whitson (signed December 1984, 5 years, $4.5 million): Had misleading 15–10 record, with 5.38 ERA, while teetering on the edge of a nervous breakdown. Mercifully traded back to San Diego for Tim Stoddard in July 1986.

Yankee No Home
(Homegrown Yankees who were traded away during the turbulent and transient Steinbrenner years, only to prosper elsewhere)

LHP Scott McGregor (traded to the Orioles in the infamous 1976 deal in which the Yankees also gave up catcher Rick Dempsey, pitchers Rudy May and Tippy Martinez for Doyle Alexander and Ken Holtzman): Compiled 138–108 career record for the Orioles before his career ended in 1988.

LH reliever Tippy Martinez (traded to the Orioles in the same 1976 deal [above] with McGregor): Had more than 100 saves from 1976 through 1986 with the Orioles.

C Mike Heath (traded to Texas in the Dave Righetti deal in 1978): Became a solid and versatile player, batting .250 over 11 seasons and was still active as of 1989.

2B Damaso Garcia (had to be sacrificed in the Rick Cerone deal with Toronto in 1979 when the Yankees were desperate for a catcher to replace Thurman Munson): Had two All-Star seasons and was still active in 1989, with a lifetime .284 batting average.

DH Pat Tabler (traded to the Cubs as an addendum to the Rick Reuschel trade in 1981): Had a lifetime .291 career average as of 1989. Productive clutch hitter with one of the best all-time averages in bases-loaded situations.

OF Willie McGee (traded to the Cardinals for reliever Bob Sykes in October 1981): National League MVP in 1985, when he led the circuit with a .353 average and 216 hits while scoring 114 runs and stealing 56 bases. A .295 career hitter as of 1989.

RH reliever Gene Nelson (traded to the Mariners for Shane Rawley in 1982): Became a key member of the Oakland A's vaunted bullpen, 1987 through 1989.

SS Greg Gagne (traded to Minnesota for Roy Smalley in 1982): Became Twins' regular shortstop in 1985. Hit in double figure homers in '86, '87, and '88 and was a pivotal part of Twins' 1987 world championship team.

1B Fred McGriff (traded to Toronto in 1982 with Mike Morgan and Davey Collins for Dale Murray): A Tampa product whom Steinbrenner somehow missed. After hitting 34 homers and driving in 82 runs in 1988, he became the American League's top slugger in 1989, leading the circuit with 36 homers.

RHP Jose Rijo (traded to the A's in the 1984 Rickey Henderson deal): Was 13–8, with a 2.39 ERA, for Cincinnati in 1988 and was off to a great start in '89 before a back injury shelved him for the rest of the season.

LHP Jim Deshaies (traded to the Astros for 40-year-old pitcher Joe Niekro in 1985): Quickly emerged as one of the Astros' top pitchers with a 46–34 record over the 1986 through 1989 seasons.

Utility player Scott Bradley (traded to the White Sox in 1986 for catcher Ron Hassey): His best position was really catcher and his best asset really his bat, as evidenced by a lifetime .270 average as of 1989.

3B Carlos Martinez (traded to the White Sox in 1986 in the Ron Kittle, Wayne Tolleson, Joel Skinner deal): Rising young star who was being touted by the White Sox as a Rookie of the Year candidate in 1989.

RHP Doug Drabek (traded to the Pirates in 1986 for Rick Rhoden): Though technically a White Sox product, he was developed in the Yankee farm system and traded away just as he was about to blossom. Was 15–7 in 1988 for the Pirates and had a tough-luck 12–11 year in '89, with one of the lowest ERAs (3.05) in the NL.

OF Dan Pasqua (traded to the White Sox in November of 1987 for pitcher Richard Dotson): Still regarded as a potential slugger of 30-plus homers despite a career short-circuited by injuries in 1989. Had 31 homers over the 1988 and 1989 seasons despite limited playing time with the White Sox.

The One-Liners Of Graig Nettles

On playing for the Yankees: "Some kids want to join the circus when they grow up. Others want to be big league baseball players. I feel lucky. When I came to the Yankees, I got to do both."

Upon being fined $500 for not attending a Yankee luncheon in April 1978: "If they want someone to play third base, they've got me. If they want someone to go to luncheons, they should get Georgie Jessel."

After receiving a telegram from Georgie Jessel thanking him "for getting my name in the papers again" in May 1978: "I was glad to hear from him. After I said what I did, I was worried he might have died, and then I'd have more people mad at me."

In response to a query from the Seattle clubhouse attendant on how his clubhouse compares to others around the league: "If you killed a few of the flies, it would be a big improvement."

While on a bus trip in 1978 when Bob Lemon, whose bulbous nose was renowned, was the manager: "Why are we stopping here? To get batteries for Lem's nose?"

Referring to roly-poly pitcher Luis Tiant when it was learned the Yankees would all have to get inoculations because of Nettles' hepatitis: "To do Tiant's, they'll have to get a harpoon."

In response to Steinbrenner's constant criticisms of his weight: "If George owned the team when Babe Ruth was playing, he'd bat him seventh and tell him he had to lose weight."

Discussing the flap over Dave Winfield's book in 1988 and recalling how both he (Nettles) and Sparky Lyle were traded after writing books of their own: "George isn't big on books, is he? I don't think there's ever going to be a National Library Day at Yankee Stadium."

To a hotel clerk in Baltimore when the players were complaining about the lack of heat in their rooms: "Forget the blankets, how about igloos?"

On the rooms in a Bloomington hotel, which were sweltering and had no air conditioning (on the same road trip): "This is a fancy place. Each room has a 24-hour sauna."

In 1977, after watching Reggie Jackson (who had just had a candy bar named after him) screw up a couple of plays in right field: "What does he need another candy bar for? He's already got one—Butterfingers."

When asked to name the advantages of playing in New York: "Watching Reggie Jackson play."

And the disadvantages: "Watching Reggie Jackson play."

Watching slow-footed catcher Jerry Narron getting thrown out at third base and at home plate in the same game: "For a while there I thought Narron was trying to run for the cycle."

Referring to Cleveland outfielder Wayne Cage, a tough guy who seemed to be looking for a fight in a 1979 game: "He's the only guy in baseball who gets to wear his place of residence on his back."

To Thurman Munson, the spring after Munson had been threatening to retire unless the Yankees traded him to Cleveland: "There he is, the comeback player of the year. Thurman said he wasn't coming back this year unless the Yankees traded him to Cleveland, but here he is."

Read My Lips
(The quotes of George Steinbrenner that somehow just didn't ring true)
On January 3, 1973, at the press conference announcing his syndicate's purchase of the Yankees from CBS: "I won't be active in the day-to-day operations of the club at all. I've spread myself so thin. I've got enough headaches with my shipbuilding company."

Announcing at the winter baseball meetings in December 1981 that Bob Lemon would be returning as Yankee manager: "This time he'll get a full a season, no matter what." (He fired Lemon 14 games into the 1982 season.)

Upon hiring Billy Martin as Yankee manager for the third time, January 11, 1983: "Believe me, this will be different because Billy and I will communicate better with each other." (He fired Martin again 11 months later.)

Announcing on February 20, 1985, that Yogi Berra was secure as Yankee manager: "Yogi will be the manager the entire season, win or lose." (He fired Berra 16 games into the season.)

Announcing his hiring of Billy Martin as Yankee manager for the fourth time in May 1985: "Billy has got his health back and his personal problems resolved. We have never been closer. He is one of the few managerial geniuses in the game." (He fired Martin again the following October.)

On Larry King's TV talk show in July 1989: "Dallas Green and Syd Thrift will be there the whole year. You can mark it down." (On August 18 Green was fired as Yankee manager, and on August 29 Thrift resigned under pressure as Yankee senior vice president.)

In March 1985 after Commissioner Peter Ueberroth reinstated Mickey Mantle and Willie Mays to baseball's good graces: "Peter Ueberroth is the greatest thing since chocolate ice cream. I'm a Ueberroth man."

In June 1989, after Ueberroth had left office as commissioner and been replaced by Bart Giamatti: "Bart Giamatti is a man of substance and integrity—far more substance than Peter Ueberroth. Ueberroth is more show than substance. He's a master opportunist."

Summing It Up
White Sox board chairman Jerry Reinsdorf at the 1983 Chicago All-Star Game party: "How do you know when George Steinbrenner is lying? When his lips are moving."

The Magnificent Nine
The nine dedicated and persevering Yankee employees who made it through the first 17½ years of George Steinbrenner's tyrannical reign as principal Yankee owner:

Phil Rizzuto, Broadcaster
Gene Monahan, Trainer
Bob Sheppard, Public Address Announcer
Kathy Bennett, Accountant
Frankie Albohn, Groundskeeper
Chris Esposito, Groundskeeper
Danny Coletti, Groundskeeper
Alex Karras, Groundskeeper
Armond Uveno, Groundskeeper

* At the time of Steinbrenner's death in July 2010, only Monahan and Bennett remained as the ultimate survivors